The New Medicine
A Modern Approach to Clinical Illness

Written by
Dr. Patrick Kingsley

Foreword by
Mr. Geoffrey Boycott OBE

Distributed by
SureScreen Life Sciences

The explanations given in this book are the result of the experience of the author after many years of practicing medicine. It may surprise you to learn that the methods are practiced by many doctors all over the world, especially in America. In fact many double-blind placebo-controlled studies have been carried out on some of these methods, but they have not become the standard way helping patients at present.

As they have not yet been assessed by the FDA of America and other appropriate authorities, no attempt should be made to use the information in this book to diagnose or treat individual conditions without first consulting a medically qualified doctor

ISBN: 978-0-9557909-1-1

Copyright © Dr. Patrick Kingsley 2013

First published in Great Britain in 2013

Published by SureScreen Life Sciences Ltd

Printed by Berforts Ltd

Dr. Patrick Kingsley asserts the right to be identified as the author of this work.

Contents

Foreword by Geoffrey Boycott OBE

I was diagnosed with cancer of the tongue in September 1992. At first I looked for reasons – tried to work out why me? I had been a professional cricketer for 25 years, never been a smoker or beer drinker and never taken spirits. I only ever had the occasional glass of wine in the evening, kept sensible hours and was 'as fit as a butcher's dog!'

But trying to work out why doesn't solve the problem. Dwelling on the past serves no purpose. Cancer can be a death sentence so time is of the essence. The hardest thing to do is come to terms with this terrible disease. It's emotionally very distressing. My advice is get rid of the tears and the crying – there is no shame in that – then project your mind forward. Sitting in a corner crying and feeling sorry for yourself won't make the cancer go away.

You have to be positive and mentally strong, you have to say to yourself, what am I going to do to give myself the best chance of getting well? It's not easy – I know that, I have been there – because at the back of your mind there will always be the thought that whatever you do it still might not work. That is a terrifying thought but you have to give it your best shot.

There are people out there like Chris Woollams of Canceractive and Patrick Kingsley who can help you if you are prepared to be helped. Listen to them, I did, read and digest what they have to say and follow their advice. But do it with commitment and a belief that you really do have a chance to succeed. There are no guarantees but with the amount of knowledge out there your chances are good.

- Geoffrey Boycott OBE

Introduction

The New Medicine is quite simply a new way of looking at why people have become ill and what to do about it. Yes, drugs can be helpful, but why take drug after drug when there is this new way of dealing with problems. Actually, it is not all that new. It has been practised by countless numbers of doctors all over the world, especially in America, since the middle of the last century. I should know, because I was examined by my peers in The States and made a Fellow of the American Academy of Environmental Medicine in 1986.

Double blind studies are very difficult to carry out on this type of medicine, and, because of the lack, most doctors are not the slightest bit interested in this new way. Besides, it is not that scientific, despite the fact that it works, and works very well.

The trouble is, people have to do something, instead of simply taking the tablets. They have to take control of their lives, stop smoking and drinking alcohol and coffee, change their diet, possibly have their mercury amalgam tooth fillings replaced, or do a bit of exercise you know - simple things. But they have to do it, and most people don't want to have to be bothered. On the other hand, perhaps they are not even aware that doing such things might improve their health. No one has told them about such things. Surely, they say, if there was something in it all, my doctor would have told me about it.

But he doesn't know about it. There are no representatives going round telling doctors all about the latest wonder system, because there is no money in it for anyone. There's no multi-billion pound company backing them up, paying their wages.

For a long time now, I have known that many diseases are at least partly caused by a raised level of homocysteine, a far more dangerous substance to your arteries than a raised cholesterol has ever been. It can be lowered very effectively by a combination of folic acid, vitamins B6 and B12 and betaine, and possibly one or two other nutrients, something that has recently been shown to improve the chances of not getting full-blown Alzheimer's disease by a team at Oxford University in England. For some unknown reason, doctors don't like nutrients. They only like drugs. It has been my opinion that the medical profession will not take the slightest interest in a raised homocysteine, until a drug company comes up with an expensive way of bringing it down. But things could suddenly be different all of a sudden because of this study.

Then there is the statin story. Statin drugs are known to reduce the production not only of cholesterol, but also of Co-Enzyme Q10, which is the heart's most important energy chemical, apart from being possibly the body's most important detoxification chemical. It's also important for the functioning of the brain. There is nothing new about this. Goodness knows what statins are doing to the body. Millions of people are on statins, and no one is suggesting they take Co-Enzyme Q10. Why? It just doesn't make sense to me.

It doesn't matter whether you have cancer, multiple sclerosis, diabetes, arthritis, asthma, or any other sort of medical condition. This new medicine can resolve every problem if you are prepared to take control of your life. That's what this book is all about.

Prologue

What Made Me Think The Way I Do?

Perhaps I was already somewhat different from others around me when I was about sixteen years old. I was at my boarding school and was given responsibility for younger boys when they were doing their prep. In those days, the slightest deviation from the rules meant instant punishment. But, if, say, a boy had lost his ruler and nudged his next-door neighbour asking to borrow his, I saw no reason to punish him, well not the first time anyway. So I did things my way. It would appear there is a far more relaxed way of doing things at that school nowadays, so perhaps I was well ahead of my time. My little bit of responsibility was taken away from me at the end of that one term, and never given back. It's funny how one sometimes remembers little pieces of fact.

When I was studying anatomy and physiology, my fellow students and I found it all vaguely interesting, although we knew it was important to learn it all. What we really wanted to do was get into the wards to start treating patients, really sick people. We felt sure that was where our talents lay.

When we did finally start our clinical work, we were told how to make a diagnosis, first and foremost, and then how to treat that diagnosis. There were only two basic methods of treatment, the prescription of a medicine or an operation. There was no suggestion that one should try to return the patient to normal. It wasn't even considered. Drug trials had shown that such-and-such a medical condition was caused by such-and-such a biochemical abnormality, and here was the drug that could interfere with that situation. The fact that the patient might need to take the drug for the rest of his or her life was completely irrelevant. If it worked, it worked. If it didn't, try a different drug.

Or perhaps the patient needed an operation to remove an offending part. Don't worry; you'll manage without it. Or will you? Still it's gone now, so there's no point in worrying about it. We'll find some way of helping you - try this drug.

When I qualified, I spent the first year as a doctor at the Queen Elizabeth Hospital in Barbados in the West Indies. I had one night's sleep in four for a whole year. Imagine an environment in the UK with 250,000 people somewhere. There would be one hundred General Practitioners and two large District General Hospitals, with a full panoply of Physicians and Surgeons and their teams. In Barbados, there were no GPs, two exhausted Surgeons, one anaesthetist and six junior doctors, of which I was one. I was on duty all day long carrying out my normal surgical responsibilities, and all night long the first night doing emergency surgery and emergency gynaecology.

It was pointless going home to bed, so I grabbed a pillow, told the nurses where I was and rested, possibly for half-an-hour or so. Next day I carried out my normal surgical duties and that night I was on duty for emergency medicine, Paediatrics and Obstetrics. Next day I carried out my normal surgical duties, but that night I was in casualty all night long, and I mean all night long. The fourth night I slept.

I learned a lot of things in that year. I remember when I was on all night long in casualty that first time (remember there were no GPs for them to consult so they consulted us). I saw this little wizened old lady come into Casualty, followed by what I assumed were her daughters, grand-daughters and great-grand-daughters. It was clear the old lady was in pain. I was soon asked to see her.

"Hello, my dear. What's the problem?" Or something like that.
"De belly she ache", came the reply.

"How long has it been hurting you?" I asked.
"De belly she ache."
"Can you put a finger on where the pain is?"
"De belly she ache."

It didn't matter what question I asked her, her answer was always the same. They didn't teach you how to deal with this sort of situation in Medical School, thought I. So I decided I had better examine her. I pulled back the sheet covering her, and there was a head actually being delivered at the time. I gave up guessing women's ages from that day on.

I have lost count of the number of ectopic pregnancies I saw during my year in Barbados. Sometimes they had lost so much blood they were in a really bad way. There was no blood transfusion service at all. For some unknown reason they thought they would catch the disease of the person they gave blood to. To be fair things have changed a lot since those days. The first time it happened, the surgical orderly disappeared, and came back with a coconut, which we carefully prepared and gave the juice intravenously. It worked well the patient survived. We gave intravenous coconut juice on a number of occasions.

Then there was the time when a number of patients went down with Weil's disease, an infection caught from rats, that usually affects the liver, but in fact seemed to affect their kidneys. Some patients needed dialysis, but there was no special Department for that sort of thing. We heard of peritoneal dialysis and sent for some units, read the instructions and simply got on with it. Again, it worked well, as all patients survived.

All the time I was carrying out normal medicine wherever I could, but thinking on my feet at the appropriate times. Back in England I next did an eight months' stint in Anaesthetics, followed by six months in Obstetrics and Gynaecology, gaining appropriate qualification in both. After that I joined Fisons, the Pharmaceutical Company in Loughborough, expecting to stay for six months or so while I decided what I really wanted to do. I stayed for eight years.

While at Fisons, I was allowed to hold a clinical post in the Nottingham City Hospital Allergy Department. I was given all the special cases to deal with, such as a woman who developed a rash when she ate citrus fruit or was sick if she ate fish of any sort. These two were most inconvenient to her way of life, so could we please do anything about it?

At the time I was very much involved in organising clinical trials of Intal, sodium cromoglycate, a drug that was inhaled by asthmatics to prevent attacks, but it only worked if taken before the person was exposed to whatever they were allergic to. It occurred to me that a suitable dose swallowed before eating the allergic food might also block the reaction. It did. I published the results of the trial I did in The Lancet in 1972. I was given £1 for the patent (which basically belonged to the company) the whole thing making a few millions of pounds over the years. That was because I thought about things differently. Eventually I left Fisons, to set up in single-handed, rural dispensing General Practice, because I had been thinking all along about doing things in a different way. I still practised normal medicine, but started to try an alternative approach on a small number of patients, nearly all of who really appreciated what I was trying to do. They all benefited from my attempts, so I persevered and it all became clear to me what I needed to do. In over four years I applied this approach to over two hundred and fifty people.

At that time, Dr. Richard Mackarness had a TV programme about his work, and wrote a book entitled 'Not All in the Mind'©. As an Assistant Psychiatrist in Park Prewett Hospital in Basingstoke, he was saving people from frontal lobotomy, an operation to cut certain nerve tracts in the brain, by simply changing their diet. While working for Fisons, I had started to look for doctors anywhere in the world who had patients suffering from food allergy problems, hoping they would be capable of carrying out proper double-blind placebo-controlled studies. So I sat in with Dr. Mac and listened to his wise ways.

I was one of a small band of young doctors interested in what he was doing and how he was doing it. The only problem was that I was the only doctor north of High Wycombe, so I became increasingly busy seeing not only my usual General Practice patients, but also now a host of other people coming to me from The Midlands, the North of England and Scotland. In the end, I was basically forced to give up GP work to concentrate on what I now wanted to do. Since then I cannot remember prescribing a single drug since setting up in private practice in 1981.

This book is all about a simple approach to ill health. Aspirin may help ease a headache, but the headache is not caused by an aspirin deficiency. It could simply be dehydration. Drinking three glasses of water can sometimes work wonders. There has to be a reason for the pain, or whatever symptoms the patient is showing. Yes, it could be called 'The New Medicine' because it is not the way doctors treat patients in the main. By and large, patients go to their doctor and say "Doctor! I have this problem! Would you please sort it out for me!" All the doctor can do is match the symptoms with the best drug available, or recommend an operation. A visit to a physiotherapist or a psychotherapist are also options, but it is a drug or an operation in the main.

In my opinion, the emergency management of patients in a Casualty Department is brilliant. The immediate handling of an accident victim, a heart attack, a stroke or an acute appendix are brilliant. It is the long-term management of ill health that worries me. Yes, drugs do often help calm symptoms down, but they can have many nasty adverse effects, which tend to be managed by a second drug, then a third drug to calm down the adverse effects of the second drug. I have known some patients on twelve or more drugs, virtually all having been given for an adverse effect of a previously prescribed drug.

What is generally not known is that most adverse effects are caused by a nutritional deficiency. The statin story I described earlier on is a simple example of just that sort of problem. As a result, patients are now suffering from heart failure, surely something the statin was supposed to prevent in the first instance.

Most doctors say we can obtain all the vitamins and minerals we need from our diet. I'm afraid that is simply not true any longer. Farming practices have diminished the amount of nutrients present in our food supply, and even then the choice of what we eat is generally poor. White bread is eaten by the vast majority of people, with all the nutrients missing, although a few are sometimes added in.

So this book is all about the new way. It can be read by doctors or members of the public, as I will describe things in simple terms. It is my hope that many patients will say, "I want to be treated by a doctor in this way", and I hope many doctors will say "I want to learn how to treat people in this way". Perhaps we could start a revolution of a new way of health care. To be fair, many patients will stick to their old ways, mainly because they don't want to help themselves. Far too many foods are addictive in one way or another, so they will continue to eat them. That is their right.

But it is my duty to let people know that there is another way of doing things. I did it for over thirty years, so I know it works. My patients told me so.

Chapter 1

Cancer

I have deliberately started with cancer because it is such an emotive subject. Being given a diagnosis of cancer is so frightening. But why is it so frightening? Is it because you somehow feel there is something uncontrollable growing inside you, or is it because of the stories you have heard of the awful forms of treatment you are likely to have to have? Yet we all have cancer in us. It is absolutely normal, but our immune systems deal with the cancer most of the time. It is only when we let it get out of control that a problem arises. Even then we can easily sort things out ourselves, but we have to change our life styles, and that is something far too many people don't want to have to do.

If you don't want to do anything for yourself, that is fine by me. Go ahead and let the Surgeon or Oncologist treat you. If they eventually give up on you, you are welcome to come back. It need never be too late.

The first thing to point out is that cancer is a whole body condition. Your immune system is involved. Your liver is involved. Your hormones are involved. Your bowels are involved. Your mind is certainly involved. Your whole body is involved. That's why we need to consider the whole of your body.

While your own General Practitioner sees people with any problem, he will often refer you on to a 'Specialist'. In fact people find it perfectly reasonable to be referred to a Dermatologist if they have a skin problem, a GastroEnterologist if they have a bowel problem, or a Chest Physician if they have asthma, etc. So it sometimes comes as a surprise when they meet a doctor who is interested in the whole person, yet is still a Specialist, but in Nutritional and Environmental Medicine, or "Integrated Medicine", as is becoming the modern description.

The current approach followed by the majority of doctors at present concentrates on the organ that seems to be producing the symptoms. Doctors try very hard to make a diagnosis, but, if you listen to the words of that diagnosis, they either have the name of the doctor who first described it such as Von Recklinghausen's Disease or it simply describes the symptoms themselves. A typical diagnosis is irritable bowel syndrome (or IBS for short).   Listen to the words. Any word ending in "itis", such as tonsill-itis, cyst-itis, or appendic-itis, simply means "inflammation of" a particular part of the body.

Once the doctor has made a confident diagnosis, he then has to select the most appropriate treatment for that diagnosis. The choices open to him come from two main areas, namely a surgical operation (and there are thousands of operations being carried out every day) or a prescription item, which includes chemotherapy or radiotherapy for cancer (and again there are literally thousands of prescriptions being written out every day). A small miscellaneous area that is sometimes recommended could involve a dietician, a physiotherapist, or other professionals.

This approach clearly has its uses, especially in acute situations, such as a heart attack, a stroke, acute appendicitis or an accident, for example. But, in long term, chronic conditions, such as migraine, arthritis, multiple sclerosis, cancer, etc., it may be less appropriate. This is where my approach has its merits.

For some doctors, a patient will be considered as "a case of arthritis", rather than "Mrs. Bloggs who has arthritis". In my opinion, everyone is a person who is unique, i.e. different from the last or next person. Therefore I need to know everything about that person. So, if you will let me, I will teach you to understand all about yourself, to understand where things went wrong and therefore what you can do about them.

The Missing Question

Another missing point is "why?" Why has your condition developed? What is the reason, since there must be a reason? Understanding the reason or reasons will help you to do something about them. In addition, there can also be some value in trying to understand when things started to go wrong, because that happened some time before the symptoms of cancer first appeared. Let me explain that further.

Some time ago, it became possible to analyse the presence in the urine of the breakdown products of neurotransmitters, which are chemicals that are produced to instruct the body to think, breathe, digest, work the immune system, etc. They are therefore the basic control chemicals that make the body function on a day-to-day basis, together with a whole host of other chemicals that act as messengers between one cell and another.

As is often the case when something new becomes available, I carried out these analyses on patients with severe cancer or multiple sclerosis, to see if they could be of value to them. Allowing for some variations, they were all grossly abnormal. Out of interest I carried out those same tests on patients who had recently had their first multiple sclerosis symptom or had a lump that had just been diagnosed as cancer. What interested me was that they were just as bad as in the severely affected patients. This gave me scientific evidence that what I had always expected was true, that is that the person's problems began long before the first symptom or sign appeared.

It is interesting to note that people suffering from Alzheimer's Disease may have lost something like 80% of a certain part of their brain before the first features of memory loss begin. This means that the body has an amazing ability to put up with what we do to it, or what we have done to it. Presumably the body finally decides it can no longer tolerate the insults, and starts to produce more obvious evidence of the harm being done to it.

Since it is therefore reasonable to assume that your life's events have somehow been responsible for your current problems, I need to help you to identify what these life events are. We need to discover what went wrong and when, and what you did, or had done to you, that you didn't realise wasn't wise. I need to show you how to uncover these problems as though you are in front of me and we are doing it together. We therefore need to consider your personal history, even going back into childhood. We need to do some simple detective work, which is why I often refer to myself as a "Medical Detective". In fact I wrote a book of my experiences in a narrative form in 2011 entitled "The Medical Detective - Memoirs of a Most Unusual Doctor".♥

As to the reason "why?", there must be a reason or reasons why. To put this into perspective, I use the examples of a blister on your foot or the effect of peeling a pile of onions. Both cause inflammation and pain, but you don't go anywhere near a doctor because you know what the cause is. More to the point, by stopping rubbing the blister or getting away from the onions, the symptoms subside.

But imagine you didn't realise what the cause of all that pain was and you kept rubbing the blister or peeling more onions. What a mess you would be in! These two examples are, of course, of an acute and obvious nature. However, to my way of thinking, it is very likely that you are doing something similarly wrong that is causing your problems, but it is not as obvious as my two examples, so you haven't stopped doing it. Hence you aren't getting better. More to the point, your condition is progressing because you've not stopped doing it.

Cancer is a whole body problem, not merely a simple problem in your breast or prostate, or wherever you have developed cancer. You need to start a process of repair, undo a lot of things you have been doing to yourself over the years. You need to change your life style, make some changes in your life, clean out your body, and improve your immune system. But you need to know where things have gone wrong, because the cancer in you now possibly started to develop five or fifteen years ago. If you had done something at the time, it probably wouldn't have developed in the first place.

So I hope that what I have to say in the following pages will give you ideas about what to do, how to cleanse your body and how to take charge of your life. After all, it is your life, and, as far as I am aware, you have the right to do with it what you want. You can improve things drastically or you can continue doing what you have been doing all along, and let nature and any doctors you chose to see control your life. Or you can take control. The title of the book by Professor Jane Plant 'Your Life In Your Hands'♥ says it all.

Possible Causes

What if, together, we could identify the causes and eliminate them? Wouldn't that give you a chance to start getting better?

Over the more than thirty years that I have been practising this type of medicine, I have found that the causes of someone's problems can be considered among the following: Diet, infections, especially fungi, toxic substances such as heavy metals and chemicals, environmental agents, nutritional, enzymatic and hormonal deficiencies or imbalances, immune deficiencies, other deficiencies, emotional problems and stresses of all kinds, plus there may be something unusual in a new patient that I haven't yet thought of.

Each of these needs to be considered in each person, although it is sometimes obvious where to begin. The person's history (medical jargon for all the details of a person's life) gives the game away. Personal stresses may be hidden or the person may not feel comfortable talking about them until they get to know me better.

Nobody can doubt the wonderful value and principle of the National Health Service in the United Kingdom, that is that treatment is effectively free at the point of need, whatever is needed, as soon as it is needed. Sadly, however, the NHS hasn't adopted the approach that many people are looking for yet, although things are slowly changing. Doctors simply don't have the time to spend on you, but I do.

What Cancer Is

Before we go any further, I want to explain to you what cancer is, how it develops, and what a tumour (a lump) is. As we go through it, you will start to see how such knowledge will help you to understand some of the things that you will need to do to sort it all out.

I think it is generally accepted that chemotherapy can kill cancer cells, mainly because they are rapidly dividing, primitive cells. If you have a tumour the size of the 'lead' sticking out of the end of a pencil (which no scan system in use today can possibly find), there will be about 1 million cancer cells in it. If a tumour is 2 cm in size, there will be approximately 10 billion cancer cells in it. Your Oncologist hopes to kill 100% of all cancer cells, but that is totally unrealistic. If he is lucky he might kill 99.9% of them, but 0.1% of 10 billion is an awful lot of cells that escaped his treatment, and they tend to be the more resistant ones.

Unfortunately the chemicals used in chemotherapy are mostly still related to Mustard Gas that was used in the 1st World War, and, as yet, are not sufficiently targeted not to damage non-cancerous cells. So adverse effects of chemotherapy involve other fairly rapidly dividing cells, namely the bone marrow (so damaging the blood and the immune system), the hair follicles (leading to hair loss) and the lining of the intestines (causing diarrhoea, nausea and loss of appetite). Apart from that there are a lot of dead cells for the body to try to get rid of. Is there any wonder, then, that people often feel really unwell after a dose of chemotherapy? But don't worry. Help is at hand in the form of coffee enemas, which will be explained later.

In fact there is a group of cells that divide even more rapidly than cancer cells, namely the cells that form the basis of the afterbirth. In a newly pregnant woman, the first few cells of her developing foetus divide at an amazing speed, and, of course, have no shape or form to them at this stage. Some of those cells form what is called the trophoblast, which attaches to the inner surface of the womb and starts growing new blood vessels to produce the placenta (afterbirth). Because the foetus needs its nourishment, the afterbirth has to grow quickly; otherwise the foetus might not survive.

If you have ever seen a placenta after a baby has been delivered, you will have noticed the amazing number of very large blood vessels all over it, and they only took nine months to develop to that size! In this way a pregnancy could be likened to cancer, because new blood vessels have been formed to feed the foetus, in a way similar to the new blood vessel growth that cancer tumours sometimes develop. However, this very rapid new blood vessel growth does not go on forever. At day 56 of the pregnancy, the maternal pancreas and the newly developing foetal pancreas combine forces to produce an amazing amount of digestive enzymes, which literally stop this rapid cellular division in its tracks. From then on cell division in the placenta slows down to a normal rate.

The Importance Of Enzymes

One could therefore suggest that digestive enzymes might be a very important factor in controlling the rate of cellular division, and hence might be important as part of the management of a person with cancer.

What is the connection between enzymes, cancer, and life styles? To explain this I need to give you a very simple description of what happens when you eat food. We tend to assume that, when a food is swallowed, the digestive juices are poured onto it and the food is broken down into its constituent parts, which are then absorbed into the blood stream to be used to build up tissue. That is effectively true, but there is a missing statement that needs to be added. The food you swallow should contain all the enzymes and nutrients needed for its own metabolism. Yes, you will borrow them from your body pool of nutrients and enzymes, but they should be returned to that pool when they are released from the food being digested.

Your pool of nutrients should have been provided in the first instance from your mother when she was pregnant with you, and from the food you were given once you were born, from which your pool should have been constantly replenished. However, if you eat a food cooked at over 120°C, that has been pasteurised, micro-waved or is full of pesticides, or was empty of nutrients in the first place (such as refined flour products and probably most 'junk food'), you are not replenishing your stocks of nutrients but are, in fact, stealing from them. In the end there are not enough nutrients for normal bodily metabolism. In particular, a deficiency of enzymes can lead to all sorts of problems, especially inflammatory conditions (as enzymes are anti-inflammatory) and cancer. So cancer may develop in a person because of a chronic deficiency of digestive enzymes, which, remember, have the ability to control the rate of cellular division.

There is another reason for taking digestive enzymes. Many cancer tumours put a mucus/protein coating around themselves to hide from your immune system, so, even if your immune system is good, it won't be effective against the tumour as it can't get at it.

When you were a foetus inside your mother's womb, there was no form or shape to you to begin with. All of those original cells were, in fact, stem cells, a name that is regularly in the news nowadays. Stem cells are truly remarkable in that they can develop into (the technical term is 'differentiate into') a lung cell, a skin cell, or in fact any cell once they have received the appropriate instructions. Throughout life, stem cells are constantly converting into the normal cells they are supposed to develop into. They are the cells that create new tissue as old tissue wears out.

When a new, normal cell is created, it is endowed with a condition called 'apoptosis', which means pre-programmed cellular death. What this means is that every cell 'knows' that, after a certain length of time, it must commit suicide and die. For this to happen, however, there is a 'time-keeper' in the form of the p53 gene. This remarkable gene knows exactly when every cell's time is up, and keeps sending out messages for individual cells to die by apoptosis. Things go wrong when the p53 gene stops working, or is damaged in some way, as it can be damaged by our doing all the things we now know to be wrong.

When cancer develops, mainstream science and medicine believes that three things have basically gone wrong. First, something has stopped stem cells in a particular tissue from developing into normal cells, and, second, something has stopped the p53 gene from sending out a message to certain cells to die by apoptosis. The third thing that may have gone wrong is that something has damaged normal cells so badly that they have reverted to a primitive sort of existence.

The Approach By Dr. Beard

This last attitude is assumed because, when a cancerous tumour is examined under a microscope, a trained eye can still recognise what the original tissue was, even if the majority of cells are cancerous. However, Dr. Beard, an English Embryologist around 1900, believed that cells of the trophoblast spread throughout the developing foetus, leaving nests of primitive cells everywhere. He explained that cancer cells have five main characteristics, namely that they are primitive, undifferentiated, invasive, migratory and angiogenic. A sixth could be added that they divide rapidly. These accurately describe cells of the trophoblast. He believed that inflammation in some way causes these trophoblastic cells to start dividing, but, because they do not have normal influences controlling them, they divide in an uncontrolled fashion and produce a tumour. Inflammation is now recognised to play a part in cancer.

If certain stem cells fail to convert into normal cells in a particular tissue and they remain primitive, they will divide more rapidly than other cells around them. In fact they remain 'undifferentiated', which is the term used by doctors to describe the appearance of cancer cells under the microscope. Similarly, if previously normal cells revert to a primitive state, they will also divide more rapidly than normal cells around them. In addition, such cells are of no value to that tissue because they do not function as normal cells. At the same time, old cells may not be dying by apoptosis, i.e. when they should die, although they will eventually die by other means such as old age or necrosis. So, surprise, surprise, a lump is formed. And that, quite simply, is what a cancer tumour is.

Accepted Causes Of Cancer

So what causes stem cells to fail to convert into normal cells, or to start dividing in an uncontrolled way? What causes normal cells to revert to primitive cells, if that is what sometimes happens? And what damages the p53 gene so that it fails to send out the message for old cells to die because their time is up?

Current mainstream medicine and science accept that a number of environmental factors can cause cancer, so presumably are the causes we are looking for. Known causes are radiation, asbestos, tobacco smoking (and chewing) and probably second-hand smoke, viruses such as the Human Papilloma Virus (HPV) and hepatitis, and a whole load of chemicals such as benzene and acrylamide, to name but a few. They all cause inflammation in tissues.

Other Causes Of Cancer

However, in my experience there are many other things that can either predispose a person to cancer or directly cause it. Stress of any sort is a major cause of cancer. Time and time again, when I go through a person's history, shortly before the cancer was discovered, some form of stress occurred. What is not often realised is what the stress does. In the first place it adversely affects your immune system. Secondly it seems to create a metabolic demand for better and more nutrition. At the same time, because of the stress, people sometimes ignore their diet, snacking on junk food because of its convenience, and drink too much tea and coffee with sugar, more alcohol, and often smoke even more. So, at a time when better attention should be paid to the person's nutritional state, exactly the opposite occurs. This provides an environment more appropriate for cancer to develop in.

The Environment Within The Body

In addition, stress causes the body to become more acidic. It is perfectly normal for the body to produce acid, and it tends to do so all the time. However, the liquid in the blood (the serum) has been designed to be within a narrow range of pH, at around 7.36, i.e. just on the alkaline side of neutral 7.0, and it fights hard to retain that level. If anything happens to disturb this equilibrium, the body has mechanisms to deal with it, namely to excrete a more acid urine, sweat, saliva, breath, and possibly faeces. But this should not continue for too long, otherwise problems can develop in the long run, such as osteoporosis, as calcium is withdrawn from the bones to help neutralise the acid. However, long before that has developed, the too acid status provides a more suitable environment for cancer to develop.

Normal cells thrive in a slightly alkaline environment, while cancer cells thrive in a relatively acid environment. However, it is not just a matter of giving more alkali to reduce the acidic state. Body metabolism is, in fact, quite complicated. For a number of reasons, the area around cells may be too alkaline, even if the cells themselves are too acid. This is part of the body's compensatory mechanisms, which may not be producing the most desirable response.

In addition, a comparatively acidic environment tends to be low in oxygen, and cancer cells thrive in a low oxygen state or one where there is no oxygen, i.e. has a fermentative metabolism. Conversely where there is oxygen, cancer cells cannot survive. So a low oxygen environment goes with an acidic one and a high oxygen environment goes with a comparatively alkaline one.

The Fungal Theory

There is a very interesting, decades old theory that cancer is actually your body trying to protect you from a 'cancer-forming fungus', as various forms of fungus have been identified in, and grown from, the centre of many cancerous tumours. If you examine a fresh sample of blood from a healthy person by dark field microscopy (that is effectively casting shadows instead of shining bright light on the object you are studying), you will see many organisms living in harmony with the body. If you drop a small amount of acid into it, i.e. make that sample slightly acidic, those organisms immediately change their level of activity. They mutate and develop into a harmful form. It is almost as if they have to change to survive in the new (acidic) environment they now find themselves in, and that that form just happens to be harmful. If you reverse that acidity quickly, the organisms lose their harmfulness. However, if the harmful form has become 'established' over a period of time (and I have already said that cancer develops in the body long before the first signs appear), it may not be quite so easy to reverse the situation simply by altering the acidity to a more acceptable level.

This idea that harmless organisms can become harmful under certain circumstances is well understood by nutritionally orientated doctors (even if their mainstream colleagues do not agree) in relation to the 'Candida' story. To be fair it may well be more appropriate to call it 'Fungal-Type Dysbiosis', as suggested by the late Dr Keith Eaton, as the Candida organism may not always be involved, there being many other species of yeast/mould/fungus. However, I doubt the term will catch on, so we may well be stuck for now with a name such as 'candidiasis'.

What this is all about is the fact that a single course of antibiotics taken by mouth can kill off, or at least seriously damage, the 'friendly' organisms within your intestines. This leaves potentially unfriendly ones unopposed to proliferate, as they are not damaged by the antibiotic you are likely to have been given (although there are specific anti-fungal antibiotics). The friendly ones have names such as Lactobacillus acidophilus and Bifido bacteria, which are very easily destroyed by antibiotics.

Throughout your intestines, and on your skin, especially in moist areas such as your groin or under breasts, the single-celled candida organism lives in comparative harmony with the body. But, if you change the environment, such as take oral antibiotics or eat a lot of sugar or refined white flour products, this single-celled, harmless organism sometimes converts to a harmful variety. It does so by developing 'mycelia' (long branching filaments) which can penetrate local tissues, break off and invade other parts of the body. The range of symptoms this can cause is very wide indeed, and I have described this more fully in the book I wrote in 1987, entitled 'Conquering Cystitis'.♥

Perhaps you can see what I am getting at. If your Biological Terrain, i.e. the environment within your body, shows your situation to be considerably out of phase, and likely to be too acidic, and you have had antibiotics in the past and you have eaten considerable amounts of sugar and refined white flour products, you could imagine that that acidity has allowed the 'cancer-forming fungus' to develop, and that your current cancer is trying to protect you from it. This may sound a little far-fetched to some people, but it is quite plausible, and is certainly based on a lot of observations by a lot of open-minded people over the years. It also gives you a mechanism that might be possible to reverse.

Interestingly enough, this whole approach has been brought out into the open by an Italian Oncologist in 2007, Dr. Tullio Simoncini, who feels that nearly all cancers involve a fungus and that that fungus creates so much acidity locally that it is impossible to alkalinise the body sufficiently to neutralise that acidity without doing harm to the rest of the body. He simply injected sodium bicarbonate directly into the tumour with its consequent demise. He has, in fact, taken things further and has written a book entitled 'Cancer Is A Fungus'.♥ Although he may be right, at present I feel he has gone too far, as he believes cancer cells are fungal cells.

If you were to read the book 'Knockout' by Suzanne Somers♥, you would read how she was diagnosed confidently by many doctors as having cancer throughout her body, the most extensive cancer he had ever seen, according to the main Oncologist. It was one of her daughters, a layperson, who suggested that she might be suffering from coccidiomycosis, or Valley Fever, a fungal infection that is prevalent in certain parts of America. In the end, after her diagnosis of cancer was 'reviewed', it was suggested she might have TB, leprosy or coccidiomycosis, and was recommended to start a cocktail of drugs that should never be given together, but which would probably have killed her, having already been offered whole body chemotherapy for her wrongly diagnosed cancer, which she refused.

The point I am making is that Suzanne's cancer was diagnosed on CAT scan, when in fact it was an extensive form of fungus. How many people's cancer the world over is confidently diagnosed as cancer from a scan, when it may not be cancer at all? So Dr Simoncini's approach may not be so bizarre after all. Incidentally, I am fascinated by the possible connection between the increasing use (overuse or abuse some people would say) of antibiotics (including their use in livestock to fatten them) and the rising incidence of cancer generally, associated with all the other ways our world and our environment are being poisoned.

Then there is the work of Dr. Burzynski in America who has shown that cancer patients lack essential cancer protecting peptides (rather like small molecular weight proteins) called 'Antineoplastins', and that, when he replaces these missing chemicals, patients' tumours often disappear.

Professor Jerry Potter, Professor of Pharmacy at Leicester De Montfort University in UK has identified what he has named 'Salvestrols', chemicals that fruits and vegetables naturally produce to protect themselves from fungal invasion. These salvestrols have cancer protective effects, but foods that are sprayed with anti-fungal chemicals don't produce their natural salvestrols. So when we humans eat such sprayed foods, we don't consume the protective salvestrols.

So, what if our poor diet, our stress, our infections, our toxic chemicals, our hormonal imbalances, our nutritional deficiencies, the drugs we take including antibiotics, etc. kill off, or somehow damage, our ability to produce antineoplastins and salvestrols, let alone damage or overwhelm our immune systems?

If any or all of these ideas are relevant, perhaps you can now see why it is so important to go over your history in great detail to try to identify the causes of your cancer. In this way we will have something to start working on. It will help us to start relieving the burden on your body, help you to start healing yourself. I cannot cure anyone, but I believe you can cure yourself, with my help or other peoples'.

Possible Causes

What if, together, we could identify the causes and eliminate them? Wouldn't that give you a chance to start getting better? To repeat, over the more than thirty years that I have been practising this type of medicine, I have found that the causes of someone's problems can be considered among the following: -

Diet, infections, especially fungi, toxic substances such as heavy metals and chemicals, environmental agents, nutritional, enzymatic and hormonal deficiencies or imbalances, other deficiencies, emotional problems and stresses of all kinds, plus there may be something unusual in a new patient that I haven't yet thought of.

Each of these needs to be considered in each person, although it is sometimes obvious where to begin. The person's history (medical jargon for all the details of a person's life) gives the game away. Personal stresses may be hidden or the person may not feel comfortable talking about them until they get to know me better.

Cancer As A Protective Mechanism

I have felt for a long time that cancer is a protective mechanism of sorts, even if the way it has developed is somewhat bizarre, and damaging to your health as well as what it is trying to protect you from. I now feel it is perfectly reasonable to suggest that lung cancer is trying to protect you from cigarette smoke or asbestos, and cervical cancer is trying to protect you from the Human Papilloma Virus. If you accept this hypothesis, you can see that it gives you something to do to try to overcome the cancer that is affecting you at present.

This state of affairs is all the more likely to occur if you have been under a lot of stress, especially shortly before your cancer showed up as a specific symptom or lump. What we also have to explain is why cancer has appeared where it has. This is where your personal history comes in, because it is likely that you have created a target or a weak spot by doing something or by something occurring in your life.

Let me give you an example. Many women suffer from breast swelling, with or without tenderness, for a number of days before the onset of their monthly period, which settles completely as soon as their period starts. Such symptoms can occur for one or up to fourteen days, and may make life really quite miserable. They can't bear to be touched, and the whole time can be made so much worse if they also suffer from mood swings. Naturally this affects their relationships, especially if they also suffer from prolonged, heavy and painful periods. Some women who have consulted me about their pre-menstrual symptoms have told me that they have only one reasonable week out of every four, and that that week may not be very good either.

I will be going into this in more detail later on, but the point I am getting at is that such a history is an immediate give-away to me that such a woman has been demonstrating a serious dominance of oestrogen in relation to progesterone for as long as she has suffered from these problems. As oestrogen's job is to make her a reproductive person, part of its function is to develop the breasts. If it overdoes this for a few days towards the end of each monthly cycle, the breast becomes more sensitive generally to anything. Most patients with breast cancer I have seen have suffered from premenstrual breast swelling and tenderness for a long time, and many of them have had lumpy breasts, becoming more lumpy in the pre-menstrual phase. They may also have had a number of breast cysts removed or aspirated over the years, further evidence of an over-oestrogenic effect. Hence they have created a target for the development of cancer.

If this oestrogen dominance theory is correct, you can see why taking the contraceptive pill or HRT (especially the oestrogen-only form) might make things worse, or at least increase a person's risk factors. This is a common example I regularly come across, so you can see that, if you have cancer somewhere else, taking a personal history will help to reveal why you have cancer where you have it, and what you may need to do to reverse the process.

I gave a lecture to two audiences in 2004, one in Germany and one in Ireland, in which I made the statement that, if you can identify and eliminate the cause of your cancer, you don't need the cancer. However, I also acknowledged that, if cancer had become 'established', it had developed a momentum of its own, and simply removing the cause would not be sufficient. So, to treat cancer, we need to know what the causes are and remove them, as well as interfere with the metabolism of the cancer itself.

Free Radicals And Anti-Oxidants

It is sad to note that many of the early childhood leukaemias, successfully treated with chemotherapy and radiotherapy, are now developing other cancers many years later. Similarly, it is accepted by mainstream medicine that if young women in their late teens or twenties have their upper chest area irradiated because of Hodgkin's Lymphoma, they are at a high risk of developing breast cancer later in life. It is therefore accepted that cancer treatment is itself cancer producing. No one thinks of giving them appropriate anti-oxidants to mop up all the free radicals that the cancer treatment produces.

Virtually all forms of chemotherapy and radiotherapy create an enormous free radical overload in the body, and also make the environment tend towards acidity. They also damage the friendly organisms within the bowel, on which the body depends for so many functions, including maintaining the integrity of the bowel itself. Unfortunately they seem to leave potentially harmful organisms undamaged, so they can proliferate unopposed by the usually outnumbering friendly organisms. This further potentiates the fungal theory.

If there is any truth in the theory I have just described, you can see why mainstream medicine's approach to cancer management (namely remove the cancer by surgery or treat it with radiotherapy or chemotherapy) may not be a sensible one, especially in the long run. However, it is just possible that, when the treatment does work, it has somehow managed to kill the cancer fungus, so the 'protective' cancer cells are no longer needed.

In any case, the 'causes' that have brought your body to its current situation have produced various responses over the years. Your body has tried to compensate, but it hasn't always done the best thing for you, possibly because it was not sure what was coming next. The 'current status' of your body's metabolic profile is, in fact, important to determine, and an analysis of your Biological Terrain, through an examination of samples of your urine and saliva at various times of the day, plus certain physiological measurements, may be of great value. However, we haven't yet found an easy way to recommend you analyse and treat yourself. We are working on that and will update you when we have.

Cancer's Food

Cancer cells feed mainly on sugar (as do fungal cells) and iron, so there is little doubt in my mind that one of the most important dietary changes for a person suffering from any form of cancer to make is to avoid sugar in all its forms. I also advise refined white flour products to be avoided as well, as they are all too easily metabolised and turned into sugar, or, more to the point, can be used as nourishment by fungal-type organisms. Cooking potatoes at a high temperature, such as roasting or in the oven, convert more of the carbohydrate into 'sugar' than if merely boiled or steamed. In addition I nearly always advise cancer patients to avoid foods that contain 'yeast' in any form, such as cheese, mushrooms, vinegar, normal breads and yeast extract preparations, which includes most gravy mixes, as there is something fermentative about their metabolism. I will discuss diet in a later chapter.

The strict 'anti-candida' diet also usually recommends minimal intake of fruit, but I don't always go that far with cancer patients who, in principle, I would normally want to increase their intake of fruits and vegetables, because of their extensive anti-oxidant content. On the other hand, if a very strict anti-candida diet is advisable because the person's history recommends it, capsules containing dehydrated powder of fruits, vegetables and berries can be taken.♥

Iron In Cancer
The second important 'food' for cancer cells is iron, which is also important in the life cycle of parasites and fungi generally. This is why I tend to advise most cancer patients to avoid red meats (which contain a high amount of haem/blood iron), and why they often become anaemic, which does not respond very well to iron supplements or blood transfusions. In fact they may make matters worse. So interrupting the cancer cell's metabolic utilisation of iron is sometimes an essential part of my cancer approach, especially if the patient is short of iron and needs supplementing for clinical reasons.

Iron is, however, an essential element, and is very much needed by the body. Most of it is bound to transferrin or ferritin in the blood stream, where it is carried to tissues mainly to make blood. It is free iron that is harmful, and it causes an inflammatory reaction in any tissue. It also stimulates cancer cells to flourish. Under normal healthy circumstances, there is very little free iron in the circulation, but two things in particular have been shown to free iron from where it is bound. The first is alcohol and the second is oestrogen. It is at least for this reason that anyone with cancer should give up alcohol entirely. Also, as many cases of cancer of the breast, prostate, ovaries and uterus, and possibly other cancers, are caused by too much oestrogen relative to the protective effects of progesterone, the hyper-oestrogenism needs to be dealt with as part of the overall management of a person's cancer.

This whole area of understanding what cancer is all about needs to be considered carefully, because I am constantly asking the question 'why?' Why have you developed cancer in the first place? Yes, it is certainly possible that you have a genetic predisposition, but that predisposition can be turned 'on' or 'off'.

Genetics
A common cause of migraine is eating cheese or chocolate, or drinking red wine. Migraine tends to run in families, so there is no doubt that people who suffer from migraines have a genetic predisposition to it. Yet, if cheese, chocolate and red wine are the only 'triggers' to migraine in a person, avoiding them totally can render the person migraine-free. Continual avoidance will keep their genetic predisposition switched 'off'. However, any time in the future, if that person were to have one of those items, their genetic predisposition could be switched back 'on' again, and a migraine would result. So, despite a genetic predisposition to migraine, a person can

remain symptom free by avoiding any triggers.

A lot of research is currently being carried out into the genetics of cancers, and a specific breast cancer gene has been discovered (the BCR 2 gene). If a woman has the gene, it is considered that she is at a greater risk of developing breast cancer than other people. However, even if she has it, by following the theory I described in the last paragraph, there is no need for her to develop cancer if she does not turn her gene 'on'. All she needs to know is what she must do to keep that gene switched 'off'. This will be described in due course, although there is no way I can tell you all exactly what you should do, because you are all different. However, there are inevitably a lot of basic things everyone can do to give him or herself the best chance. If you already have cancer of any sort, or the treatment you have had from your doctors has put you 'into remission', and you want to stay that way, then avoiding your original 'causes' and following the overall advice I give later on, you should be able to achieve what you want.

To return to the 'acid' story, unfortunately the way humans now live produces more acid than our bodies were originally developed to handle. Foods can basically be divided into two groups, one that leaves an alkaline ash when it has been metabolised, the other leaving an acid ash. The main alkaline foods are vegetables and fruit. The acid-forming foods are all animal produce, including dairy products, all grains, sugar, tea, coffee, and all manufactured beverages. Since many people eat only the acid-forming foods, is there any wonder how unhealthy so many people are?

To be fair to Governments in many countries, they have advised everyone to try to eat at least five portions of fruit and vegetables every day, and you can see how sensible that is. Fortunately there is greater alkalinity in the alkaline foods than acidity in the acid-forming foods. So a little of both in a sensible balance is not necessarily a bad thing in principle.

However, it doesn't stop there, because all the chemicals that now pollute our world, diesel and petrol fumes, the effects of industry, pesticides, food additives, etc., all create additional acidity. Then there are all the extra stresses of modern life, choices to be made, the family to be helped in times of trouble, the emotional problems of birth, moving house, marriage, divorce, death of loved ones, etc. Sometimes it is all too much. The body seems unable to take it all. And sadly, when we should improve our nutritional status, we let it slip.

But don't despair, because once you understand what has allowed cancer to develop in your body, you will be able to see what you need to do to deal with it and help your body to reverse it. Once we have identified all the possible explanations, appropriate tests will be described, some of which may need the co-operation of your doctor. However, I will try to keep it all as simple as possible.

Another area that needs to be considered is the fact that many scientists feel that man's problems are the result of the daily generation of 'free radicals'. The words 'free radicals' have been buzzwords in science and medicine for a number of years now, and are recognised as being a major cause of ill health. In some respects, however, the term may not be the correct one, but it is probably here to stay, for some while at any rate.

A free radical is basically described as an unstable, unpaired oxygen atom, and is simply produced by the normal metabolism and usage of oxygen itself. On this basis every day living produces free radicals. The best example of this is the action of oxygen on metal, turning it to rust, but at the same time, damaging the metal. To be precise, an atom of oxygen is made up of a proton in the centre, with two electrons, exactly opposite each other, spinning round at a phenomenal speed, in perfect balance. When an oxygen atom is used, however, it gives up (loses) one of those electrons and becomes unbalanced.

I like to compare the development of a free radical to the two phases of a spinning top. When it is spinning fast, it is nice and stable, and is similar to an oxygen atom in its natural state, i.e. a proton with two perfectly balanced electrons. But, when it slows down, it becomes unstable and wobbles all over the place, bumping into anything in its way, and is now like the atom when it has lost one of its electrons and has become a free radical. As another example, when your washing machine is on its last spin, if all the clothes inside just happen to have ended up all together at one side, the machine becomes unbalanced, and has a tendency to bounce about.

It is claimed that literally millions of free radicals are produced every second of your life. However, free radicals are desperately trying to find a spare electron to pair up with and put them out of their misery, because, while they remain in this state, they rush around in a blind panic, bumping into normal cell walls, trying to steal an electron from anywhere. They don't care where it comes from, so long as they get what they want, and they will fight tooth and nail to get it, potentially causing havoc in the process.

At the same time as Mother Nature produced this rather strange, damaging metabolic process, she also produced the antidote in anti-oxidants. So, in health, the split second a free radical is formed, it is instantly 'quenched' by the donation of an appropriate electron from an anti-oxidant. Since anti-oxidants come almost exclusively from fruits and vegetables under normal circumstances, you can see why the 'correct' diet is so important.

Trouble begins when your dietary anti-oxidant levels do not equal the amount of free radicals that your life is producing. If your anti-oxidant intake is poor in the first instance because of poor dietary choices, and you then add additional free radical production because of an unwise life style, you can see how things start to go wrong. The chances are that such a process began years ago, long before you first found a lump or whatever it was that was eventually diagnosed as cancer.

Earlier on I mentioned the fact that neurotransmitters were just as abnormal in the urine of patients with established severe disease states as in people whose condition had only just 'appeared'. Perhaps you can now see more clearly why going back into your personal history is so important. While it is possible that you have already made considerable changes to your life style, if you haven't, you can now see why you must.

To put this all into perspective, while increasing your level of anti-oxidants seems a wise thing to do, it is logical to ensure you have adequate ability to neutralise all the acidity you are producing on a daily basis. This is best achieved by drinking water high in redox potential (which means contains adequate free radical quenching power), or doing or taking something to make sure the water you drink has such an effect. However, while some people seem to advise to 'alkalise, alkalise, alkalise', care needs to be taken in this regard, because it may not be as simple as that. In fact understanding your Biological Terrain will help to unravel what can sometimes be quite a complicated situation.

Doing something about all the underlying causes of your cancer is certainly very important, but, unfortunately, this has allowed a 'life force' (your cancer) to develop within your body. Certainly undoing all the wrong will be important as time goes on, but it is not practical to undo it all immediately. A rescue package is needed to get your healing processes kick-started. You need to be shown how to improve the environment within your body, to make it less likely that cancer cells will need to survive, yet more conducive for a healing process to proceed.

Dr. Fryda's Theory

I cannot end this discussion about general, possible causes of cancer without mentioning the theory of a German doctor, the late Dr. Fryda. Dr. Fryda was convinced that all cancers are the result of chronic adrenaline (epinephrine in USA) deficiency. Adrenaline is produced in the adrenal medulla, which is in the centre of the adrenal gland, the adrenal cortex round the outside producing cortico-steroids.

Adrenaline is produced as part of the body's immediate response mechanism to any 'shock'. When someone 'makes you jump' it is the fast production of adrenaline that makes you feel the way you do. The system was developed millions of years ago as the 'fright, fight or flight' response. What it does is to increase the blood flow to those parts of the body that are needed immediately, such as the heart and limb muscles. It also makes the heart pump harder and faster, and dilates your breathing tubes to allow you to take in more oxygen and blow off more carbon dioxide. Adrenaline also causes sugar to be manufactured quickly from stores of glycogen, to be readily available for your muscles to use.

At the same time, the blood flow to your skin and digestion is significantly reduced, which is why you have been told never to go out swimming when you have just had a big meal. There simply isn't enough blood to go round to serve all parts of your body at the same time. You might then develop cramp in your muscles if your digestion blood vessels win the battle for the limited amount of blood in your body.

When this system was originally developed millions of years ago, the result was nearly always a fight, a chase after an animal to kill it, or to run away from a marauding animal. Whatever the reason for the system to be brought into play, the effect was nearly always some form of exercise.

In this modern day and age, there are many times in a day when the system is 'alerted'; someone annoying you while driving; the kids making you late for work in the morning; receiving a bill you can't afford to pay; a letter from a solicitor; an argument with your boss at work. You name it. There are many such little or major episodes in most people's lives nowadays, all stimulating your adrenaline response mechanisms.

But where's the exercise? That game of squash on Friday evening is far too late. So what happens to all that sugar you keep pumping into your blood? Where does it all go, since it won't be used up in any form of exercise, except possibly by storming back to your own office?

Whenever the levels of sugar rise above a certain amount in your blood, insulin is produced to pump it into your muscle cells. Clearly this is important if you need it to fight or run away, when that sugar will be used up. However, even in the dim and distant past, exercise did not always follow the adrenaline response, so insulin would still lower blood sugar back to acceptable resting levels, by pumping it into cells.

Unfortunately in this modern day and age, the insulin mechanism is used far too many times every day when the 'alarm' system is stimulated. In addition, insulin is produced to bring down the levels of raised blood sugar as a result of most people's diet of sugar itself and white refined flour products. What this does is to keep pumping sugar into the body's cells, which gradually poisons them, turning them more and more acidic. As has already been said, an acidic cell favours the development of cancer.

More Specific Causes Of Cancer

If you have a hormonal cancer, such as breast, prostate, cervical, uterine or ovarian cancer, consider seriously if you have a hormonal imbalance, with dominance of oestrogen playing a major part. This is particularly likely in breast cancer. In prostate cancer, I need to raise another important aspect. Mainstream medicine effectively castrates you chemically, by blocking the effect of testosterone in your body, one way or another. However, if testosterone really is the bad guy, why have you developed cancer in your prostate when your levels of testosterone are diminishing as you have got older? Surely, if testosterone were the big bad guy of prostate cancer, wouldn't your randy twenty-year-old young man develop it? In fact testosterone itself kills prostate cancer cells, but it is the first metabolite of testosterone, namely dihydro-testosterone (DHT) that is the real culprit. Then the next question is, what causes us to convert more of our dwindling supplies of testosterone into DHT? Once again, the answer is oestrogen, especially xeno-oestrogens, from pesticides, plasticisers and petrochemicals, etc. Our world is awash with xeno-oestrogens. So in prostate cancer, you need to antagonise oestrogen, namely with bio-identical progesterone, among other things. One other thing. As men get older they tend to put on weight round their middle, and the fat of the body produces oestrogen in men as well as in women.

If you have a lymphoma, i.e. swollen lymph glands anywhere in your body, think of infections. After all, that is what their job is, to deal with any local infection. If you have a tooth abscess, the lymph glands under your chin swell up. It is just that your immune system has not coped with whatever your infection is, so apart from taking a specific anti-infective treatment, you will need to improve your immune system. In my opinion, it's all very basic and simple, but you have to be prepared to do something yourself, that is if you want to.

If you have cancer in your mouth, oesophagus (gullet), stomach or any part of your intestines, think of what you have put into your mouth over the years. In lung cancer, it is nearly always what you have put into it, namely cigarette smoke, allowing for the fact that you have a genetic predisposition to lung cancer. If a person is not exposed to cigarette smoke or asbestos, there is a distinct possibility that over the years they develop a layer of mucus in their lungs caused by an intolerance of milk products. In brain tumours, have you used a mobile phone too much over the years, especially since you were much younger, when your brain was developing? Have you travelled to unusual countries of the world, where you might pick up undesirable infections?

In cervical cancer, have you had any infections in that part of your body? Have you ever had an abnormal smear? Have you ever had thrush?

In kidney cancer, what have you been passing through your kidneys? In pancreatic cancer, have you eaten many foods for a long time with virtually all the enzymes removed from them in their processing? In testicular cancer, did you have mumps some time in the past? In colon cancer, have you been constipated for a long time? I have known patients only open their bowels once every two weeks! How on earth did they manage? Imagine all that mass of partially or wholly digested food putrefying in your bowels for that long. Ugh! The thought appals me. How much inflammation must that cause? All those bugs growing in there, gradually developing in the mess. Also have you eaten a lot of food deficient in selenium, as selenium deficiency is a cause of bowel cancer?

So what I'm looking for is anything that can cause inflammation. Unfortunately, just about everyone starts life with the most inflammatory product - namely milk and milk products - which I will talk about later. Do you see what I'm getting at? These explanations may not be relevant to you, but at least I am giving you some ideas of what could have caused cancer to develop in you, which then gives you something to take control of in your life.

This brings us back to the basic reasons why you have cancer. Yes, it may be as a result of the life style you have led, a poor diet, or the stresses in your life that you couldn't avoid, or the chemical exposures that weren't your fault, or you didn't know at the time were unwise and may have affected your immune system. All of these have led to a number of problems that need to be resolved as soon as possible. You need to start doing something about the state that you find yourself in now.

Your body has probably become too acid and you are most likely producing too many free radicals that are not being adequately quenched and not quickly enough. Your immune system may be overloaded or poorly functioning, which I will describe at a later stage. Your Biological Terrain is probably in a mess. You may be harbouring the cancer-forming fungus. Your diet may be loaded with sugar or contain too much free iron, both of which cancer cells feed on. How much more do you need to begin to realise why you now have cancer?

I have attempted to open your eyes to possible mechanisms for your cancer. Any one, or all, of these may be playing a part. Many of these mechanisms have points in common. There is so much more to teach you, including all the various tests you can have done to clarify your current situation. I need to show you how to identify your 'causes', by having a virtual consultation with you. I need to show you what you can do for yourself, how you can take charge of yourself, take care of yourself, if you want to.

I don't promise that it will be easy, nor can I promise that it will be successful. Also I expect you to search the World Wide Web for as much information as possible to help yourself. After all, this is my approach based on over thirty years of medical practice, and it is always possible there is another approach that I haven't heard of yet.

I hope you now have a greater understanding of yourself and your cancer. I hope you will also have lost some of your understandable fear of cancer, and begin to realise there is a lot you can do for yourself. As far as I am concerned, there is no hurry, so we will take our time.

Start believing in yourself. Start believing that you can make all the difference you want for yourself. Remember, I am the teacher (the word doctor comes from the Latin word docere = to teach) and you are the pupil for now. How much do you want to learn from me? What are you prepared to do to achieve what you want to achieve? It's up to you.

So, enjoy yourself, feel enlightened, smile, be happy and radiate confidence in what you are going to do. Be positive and forget the doom and gloom merchants. If someone has given you a poor prognosis, forget it. You no longer fit into their statistics. You are going to do something for yourself. You are now in charge.

Chapter 2

Various Tests

It is likely that either your own General Practitioner, or, more likely, your hospital doctor, has carried out a number of blood tests. These probably include full haematology and biochemistry as a routine, and sometimes thyroid function tests. There may be others that are considered appropriate for your situation. Some hospitals carry out special blood test markers in cancer patients, but they are not very reliable.

Many patients are told that their tests are all 'normal', whereas they should have been told that they are 'within the laboratory's reference range'. But how are these reference ranges arrived at? Where do they come from? The answer is that they are primarily a statistical analysis of all the samples received by that particular laboratory, those samples coming from people who doctors think might be ill. The results may sometimes be modified by experience plus information from surveys of the general public.

I used to use a number of different laboratories, and they all had their own reference ranges. Not one laboratory agrees with another one, although they are often fairly close to each other. In addition, over the years, the reference range of certain tests has slowly increased, while others have dropped. In the late 1980s, the upper level of uric acid in one laboratory I used regularly was 0.3 units, whereas it is now 0.4, a 33.3% increase over fifteen years or so. In contrast, the upper level of cholesterol has dropped over the years. Whereas most test levels represent what is currently 'found', that upper cholesterol level is what doctors now think it is wise to aim below.

So what really is a normal level? A laboratory reference level is merely a guide, and should not be taken as sacrosanct. Unfortunately it often is. For example, I believe that a normal blood level of vitamin D should be based upon Californian lifeguards, not people living in The British Isles in winter.

Many is the time when I have found a level of something outside the so-called reference range, with the patient feeling really well, only to feel less well when it was brought into the reference range. One possible reason for this is that all cells have a myriad of 'receptors' on their surface for literally thousands of chemicals to latch on to. These receptors may increase or decrease in number and sensitivity under certain circumstances. So a low number of comparatively insensitive receptors might require a higher blood level of a particular substance to achieve the desired effect, and vice versa.

There are two tests I used to try, usually in vain, to persuade many General Practitioners to carry out on the NHS to save my patients any expense I could. One is serum ferritin and the other is a complete set of thyroid function tests. Many laboratory directors understandably try to avoid doing more tests than are necessary, if they can save money. If the standard haemoglobin (which measures whether you are anaemic or not) is at an acceptable level, they often refuse to test serum ferritin, which is an indication of your iron stores. Yet many is the time when a patient's haemoglobin is perfectly acceptable to me, but, when I have measured their serum ferritin, it is disastrously low.

Perhaps the most common symptom patients in general complain of is fatigue. They may describe it in various ways and tell me how it affects them, but, in the end, they are quite simply tired. Yet their doctor has done all the tests he usually does, including haemoglobin, and nothing has been found wrong. To me this is a classic opportunity to reconsider the diagnosis, consider doing other tests or wonder what the explanation might be. Instead, many patients are given a prescription for a tranquilliser, 'as you must be depressed'.

A paper was published in the British Medical Journal in 2003 (F. Verdon et al, BMJ. Volume 326, 24th May 2003, page 1124) which finally put into print what I had been saying for years. That is that a person can have a perfectly respectable haemoglobin level, so is not anaemic, yet they can feel tried all the time. This study measured the serum ferritin in a group of patients, and, if the level was below 50 units, they felt much better when they were given iron supplements. Yet, according to their haemoglobin, they did not need iron.

You see, most laboratories give a serum ferritin level of around 10 at the lower end, give or take a point or two, while the upper level may be around 300 or so. Most doctors are under the misapprehension that everything is all right if a patient's blood level is anywhere above 10, i.e. is within the reference range. The BMJ study shows that assumption to be false.

What tends to be forgotten is that iron is not only needed to make haemoglobin, but is also need for myoglobin (muscle globin), hair follicles, the immune system, and other metabolic functions. For reasons that I don't understand, sometimes nearly all the iron is used to make haemoglobin, and the other needs are effectively starved. Under such circumstances, giving iron supplements can often significantly improve a person's fatigue. I have done it many times.

There is no real substitute for measuring serum ferritin in my opinion. The old-fashioned method of pulling down your lower eyelids and looking to see if you are a little pale may have had its uses, but it is far too inaccurate. Anyway, it was supposed to reflect whether you were anaemic or not, which, as I have already said, may well not reflect your iron stores. So try to have serum ferritin levels measured, but not if you are already anaemic, in which case no one will doubt that you are short of iron.

As I have already said, iron is needed for your immune system. In parts of the world where starvation is rampant, it is accepted that iron deficiency leads to a reduction in the efficiency of people's immune system. If you have cancer, anything we can do to keep your immune system in as good a state as we possibly can, or prevent it from sinking any lower, is surely worthwhile. However, you don't want a level of iron too high, as cancer cells feed on iron as well as sugar. This is one of the reasons why cancer patients become anaemic so often. How to deal with this will be explained in a later section.

The second example I want to discuss is the complete range of thyroid function tests. The ones that I am interested in are FT4 (free thyroxine), FT3 (free tri-iodo-thyronine) and TSH (thyroid stimulating hormone). There is also Reverse T3, but that only applies to a very small number of people, and I think we can ignore it for now, especially in the context of the vast majority of people who are likely to be reading this information.

As with the haemoglobin/ferritin story, most laboratories in the National Health Service do a screening test, this time, of TSH only. If that is within the laboratory's reference range, then the other two (T4 and T3) are seldom measured. It would appear that, if TSH is considered to be 'normal', then it is assumed that the others will be normal. TSH is produced by the pituitary gland, and the thyroid hormones (T4 and T3) are produced by the thyroid gland itself. Although the full mechanism is really quite complex, the principle is that TSH stimulates the thyroid gland to produce its hormones, mainly T4 and T3 (actually there may be as many as fifty-two hormones produced by the thyroid gland). To my mind, it is the levels of thyroid hormones actually circulating in the blood that is important, not the amount of the stimulating hormone.

In perfect health, when the amount of thyroid hormones circulating in the blood stream reaches what nature has decided is a suitable level for normal human functioning, the production of TSH is turned off, or, more likely, turned down. When the level of T4 and T3 fall because of the lack of stimulus from the falling level of TSH, the pituitary gland is stimulated to produce more TSH to once again stimulate the thyroid gland to produce T4 and T3. There is therefore a switch-on/switch-off mechanism going on all day long, in a way just like the thermostat for the water heater in your hot water tank. When the water goes cold, the thermostat switches on automatically to heat up the water, and is then switched off when the water has heated up enough.

Many was the time when the only result of thyroid function tests that the patient had done was the TSH, which was said to be normal. When I was shown it, I accepted that it was within most laboratories' reference ranges, but it was very much at the bottom end. It has been assumed, therefore, that the levels of circulating T4 and T3 were not only acceptable, but probably towards the upper end of the ranges because of the 'thermostatic-like' system of switching on and off.

Because of my extensive experience of the value of the complete set of these tests, when I eventually received what I wanted (patients usually had to pay for them themselves), I found the level of TSH still at the bottom end of the ranges, but T4 and T3 were also at the bottom end, or may even be below an acceptable level. This told me that, not only was the pituitary gland not producing as much TSH as it should have been doing, but also what TSH it was producing was not effectively stimulating the thyroid gland itself. My explanation for this was that both the pituitary and the thyroid glands were not working properly.

While you may not have fully understood my explanation on first reading about it, you can either move on or re-read it until you do understand it if you want to. The point that I am trying to make is that you want to try to obtain the full information on both of these sets of tests if you can, but, if your GP is not able to oblige you, then you can ask him to have these tests done privately. Unfortunately I am not aware of any studies published in acceptable medical journals that support my observations on the thyroid situation, although many of my medical colleagues do. In relation to the serum ferritin situation, you could obtain a copy of the BMJ article from the local library (the full reference to which I gave you when I first mentioned it above) and show it to your doctor. With any luck, it might help you in your request as far as ferritin is concerned.

The reason why these tests are important to have done is because virtually every cancer patient complains of a degree of tiredness that healthy people do not. Yet, as far as your doctor is concerned, your blood tests may not have shown the explanation. I submit that he hasn't done the appropriate blood tests, and these are some simple ones that might explain your fatigue.

Nearly every cancer patient I see has a sub-optimally functioning thyroid system, yet I rarely see an obviously sub-normal set of thyroid function tests in the blood. If it is not working at normal capacity, your overall body metabolism will be sluggish, your body will not function as efficiently as it ought to, and you will have less ability to deal with your cancer yourself. This is exactly the opposite of what you want.   There is a possibility that cancer somehow interferes with your thyroid receptors.   Whatever you decide to do, you need to be able to do it as well as you can, with as much energy as you need for the task ahead.

Vitamin D

There is now a lot of published evidence in the medical literature of the importance of vitamin D, as receptors have been identified in the brain, breast, prostate and lymphocytes circulating in the blood, and many other places in the body. Vitamin D is anti-inflammatory, so if you have inflammation in your body one way of calming it down will be missing. I therefore suggest you try to have a blood test for vitamin D as 25(OH)D, but do not accept your local laboratory's reference levels as they will be based upon local peoples' levels, not on what they should be. Most people are not exposed to enough sunshine, but, if the sun does come out, you are either indoors or fully clothed. I glibly say blood levels should be based on those found in Californian lifeguards, if you see what I mean.

As far as I am concerned, an ideal level to work towards is 65-85 ng/ml (160-210nmol/l). 20-40 (50-100) is insufficient, below 20 ng/ml (50nmol/l) being definitely deficient.

Underarm Temperature Test

As far as your thyroid is concerned, there is a simple test you could do on yourself, which could throw some useful light on the situation. This has been explained in great detail in his book 'Hypothyroidism. The Unsuspected Illness', by Dr. Broda Barnes.♥ Buy an old-fashioned thermometer from the local Chemist of the sort you have to shake down before you pop it under your tongue. Make sure you can read your temperature at a time when it doesn't matter, because it can sometimes be hard to find where the level is. If necessary, ask the Chemist to show you how to read it.

Place it by your bedside, and, as soon as you wake up at roughly your normal time, pop it into your armpit (not your mouth in case you have been sleeping with your mouth open, in which case the temperature there will not reflect your body temperature as accurately as I would like). Snuggle down under the blankets to keep yourself warm, and make sure the thermometer is tucked well into your armpit with full skin contact. Keep it there for at least ten minutes if you can. If you want to, you could check it after about five minutes, but pop it back into your armpit for another five minutes. You want to make sure it is as fully 'cooked' as possible.

Take it out from your armpit and place it carefully by your bedside. It is perfectly safe to leave it there (but don't let a child play with it), and read it later. It won't alter from the level it was when you removed it from your armpit. There is a kink or break in the thermometer that stops the level from dropping as soon as you take it out of your armpit, otherwise you wouldn't be able to obtain an accurate reading. Before you use it again the next morning, you must shake it down with a flicking motion of your wrist (don't bang it on a surface by mistake or you will smash it) to take it down to below where it is likely to register next time you use it. You may have seen 'nurses' doing this in TV hospital plays. Again, your Chemist can explain this to you if you are not sure what to do.

Do your morning armpit temperatures as often as you like, and make a day-to-day record. If you are still having periods, make a note of when they occur. It doesn't matter if you don't do it every morning, so long as you do it often enough to obtain useful information. If your temperature seems to be lower than you think it ought to be, be more deliberate in future to make sure you are getting an accurate reading, and ask someone else to do their temperature to make sure the thermometer is measuring properly.

A normal temperature under the tongue is 98.4°F or 37°C. Your normal armpit temperature is 97.4°F or 36.5°C. Anything less than these last figures suggests the possibility of a thyroid deficiency state, irrespective of your blood levels. Occasionally it can suggest a deficiency of your adrenal glands or a deficiency of both. The lower your morning armpit temperature, the more likely you are to have a problem. What to do about this will be described in another Chapter.

You might find this rather confusing, because what I am suggesting is that a lower than 'normal' underarm temperature first thing in the morning is indicative of either an inefficient thyroid and/or adrenal system, whatever the blood tests show. This is because the blood tests merely show what is circulating in the blood stream. They do not test the efficiency of the receptors at the cellular level. These receptors can be blocked, inactivated, damaged, reduced in numbers or made less sensitive than they should be, so that a 'normal' level of the hormone circulating in the blood stream will not have the clinical effect it should have.

That is why so many of my patients felt so much better when I gave them supplements of whole thyroid, even though their blood levels suggested that supplementation was not needed. I did test their blood levels to make sure they were not becoming abnormal, but I found the supplements didn't seem to alter the blood levels much, if at all. In any case, I felt that giving whole thyroid extract that contains all fifty-two hormones, instead of the single thyroxine, fed the gland.

Candida/Saliva Test

In a later section, I will discuss any dietary changes I suggest you make. There is, unfortunately, no perfect way of telling you what to eat and what not to eat. So I will go over the various options open to you. Earlier on I mentioned 'candida', better known as the organism that causes thrush, which most women understand well enough. If you have a history of taking antibiotics, sometimes only one strong course or, more likely, a number of courses over time, it is likely that the candida organism is playing a part in your cancer.

As dealing with the candida organism involves changes to your diet, it is useful to know whether you are affected by it or not. Many patients, who have a history that strongly suggests the involvement of candida to me, do not suffer the obvious features that thrush would suggest. So a simple test that seems to be remarkably accurate in my experience is worthwhile carrying out, especially as it doesn't cost you a penny.

First thing in the morning, as soon as you get out of bed (after you have done your armpit temperature test if you are going to do it), fill an ordinary glass with water virtually to the top. Gather as much saliva in your mouth as you can and lay it gently on the top of the water. Sorry for the description, but please do not spit it onto the water. Let it float on the surface. Then wait and see what happens.

If the saliva stays on the surface for about half an hour, you do not have a candida problem according to this test. If it all virtually immediately sinks to the bottom, you have a major problem. There are various grades in between, where what is described as 'legs' or 'strings' floating down to the bottom gradually develop. Once you do the test, it becomes fairly obvious what I mean. The test only seems to apply to the saliva you can produce first thing in the morning, before you have had a drink of water or, of course, brushed your teeth. If you do it later in the day, after having consumed something, it can give a false reading. Do this for a few mornings to begin with to establish a pattern, and so that you become comfortable with the procedure.

After that you only need to do it once a week or so, using it as a method to see if your 'candida' problem is diminishing. If you don't have a problem when you first do the test, there is no need to do it on a regular basis, except for under certain circumstances.

In general terms, the medical profession recognises that thrush can occur after a course of antibiotics, and when a person's immune system is compromised. It is a well-known accompaniment of AIDS, where it is accepted that a person's immune system is in a bad state. Muco-cutaneous candidiasis is an accepted medical diagnosis. Yet strangely enough, doctors tend to have a limited understanding of the extent to which 'candida' can be involved. Like-minded doctors and I recognise that its ramifications can be far-reaching indeed, and that it usually needs to be dealt with as part of the overall management before a patient can get better, whether they have cancer or not. There is also the possibility that this test may sometimes identify the involvement of the cancer-forming fungus, but I haven't fully clarified this yet.

There are therefore two situations I need to take into account to consider if your situation may change. If you are currently free of candida according to the candida/saliva test, things can change. The first reason is if you are given a course of antibiotics for any reason. I have already tried to explain more about this earlier on, and I have expanded on this subject in my book 'Conquering Cystitis'.♥

The second situation is if you have a course of chemotherapy and sometimes radiotherapy. Before each course of chemotherapy, a blood sample is taken to check the level of your white blood cells and your haemoglobin. Quite often your blood is said to be 'too low', so the next course of treatment is postponed until your blood levels 'recover' to acceptable levels. Sometimes it needs help with a blood transfusion or an injection of something to boost the production of your white blood cells. When the levels become 'acceptable' again, they will give you the next dose of chemotherapy. This cycle may well be repeated a number of times, most likely with each cycle of chemotherapy. Your blood is seldom checked during a course of radiotherapy, which is usually given on a daily basis Monday to Friday, unless you develop signs of a problem. Even at the end, my experience is that it is not checked as a matter of routine. To be fair, however, radiotherapy is less likely to have immediate adverse effects on your bone marrow than chemotherapy.

The point I am trying to make is that, if you have any of these treatments at any time, there is a strong possibility that your immune system will be adversely affected and that you will develop a 'candida' problem as a result. In the circumstances, you have a test you can carry out any morning you want to, to see if candida is developing. Many doctors like me automatically recommend that a patient have probiotics during a course of chemotherapy in particular, knowing full well that many of the 'friendly' organisms will be killed by the chemotherapy, but in the hope that some of them will survive and keep a degree of control over the unwanted organisms such as candida.

So doing the candida/saliva test periodically can be useful to keep an eye on things in this area. I accept that the candida/saliva test that I have described that you can do first thing in the morning is not guaranteed, but at least it won't cost you anything. But you may prefer to do a scientific test of candida, which means sending a sample of your saliva to a laboratory. There are two laboratories I particularly know of, and I apologise to other excellent laboratories that I do not mention here. One is called Genova Diagnostics in the UK, and the other is Great Smokies Laboratory in USA, which I believe has now been taken over by Genova Diagnostics. There are agents in the UK and other countries that will send samples to USA.♥

When I used to take a history, I discussed the relevance of poorly functioning bowels. If you suffer from any number of bowel symptoms, such as bloating, wind, indigestion, diarrhoea, constipation, itchy rectum or you pass mucus rectally, the chances are that you have some sort of 'infection' in your intestines. You can call them what you like, bacteria, viruses or parasites, but, quite simply, they shouldn't be there if you are in good health. There is now a mass of evidence in the published medical literature that such organisms in the bowel can not only cause inflammation in any organ of the body, so can be responsible for arthritis, as an example, but they may be involved in the development of cancers, especially if you have a genetic predisposition to cancer. Also, it will be difficult for your body to regain its health while they are still present, as they can overwhelm your immune system.

In addition, many people harbour infections in their sinuses and their teeth, especially in root canals, which need the attention of a biological dentist, who is trained in these special situations.

All of these organisms need to be identified and eliminated. If you ask for a Comprehensive Stool Analysis, appropriate tests can be carried out by these laboratories on a sample of your stools. A swab from your nose could be sent to your local laboratory if you have sinusitis. They will identify the relevant organisms and provide a list of antibiotics and herbal preparations that you can take to which the organism(s) are sensitive, although your local laboratory will not test herbal remedies. In many cases, the natural preparations are just as effective as the antibiotics, without any of the potential adverse effects of antibiotics.

Even if you are not aware of specific bowel symptoms that suggest possible unwanted organisms in your bowel, if you have cancer of any sort, I would strongly suggest you seriously consider having these tests done, if for no other reason than to eliminate the possibility that they might be playing a part in your cancer. I have seen many patients over the years whose history was strongly suggestive that they might have fungal infections within their bowel, but who had absolutely no symptoms whatsoever to go with it. Yet, when they had appropriate tests done, they were found to have considerable numbers of different infections. More to the point, when these organisms were eliminated, the symptoms they consulted me about either improved considerably or cleared completely. I know this is the experience of many like-minded medical colleagues.

If you don't want or can't afford these tests, assume you do have problems and treat yourself the way I explain later on.

Geopathic Stress

Before I discuss this subject, I want to make it clear that what I am going to describe is considered very important by many people, but a load of nonsense by others. I tended not to mention it too early in my consultations with new patients, because I preferred to get to know them before I mentioned it, unless their history was so strong in this area I felt obliged to mention it. Having said that, my experience is that it plays a major part in many patients' medical problems, especially if they had cancer. Since I believe in it, and I want to teach you everything I can, I shall now describe what geopathic stress is, how it can affect people, how to identify it and what to do about it.

If you want to read more about geopathic stress, I would like to recommend an excellent book entitled 'Are You Sleeping In A Safe Place?' by Rolf Gordon♥. That title alone almost explains what this is all about.

Many people have heard of the Eastern belief of Feng Shui, where someone skilled in a particular art helps to decide where it is safe to build a house, and which way to have it facing. In other parts of the world most people have heard of Radon Gas, a radioactive gas that permeates through the ground on which certain houses have been built. It seems to occur in particular over granite rock, but is not confined to this. It is recognised as a cause of ill health in those who are exposed to it, and, when it is found, there are ways of protecting the inhabitants of such houses.

The geopathic stress that I am referring to falls into the same category. It is a form of energy that originates deep inside the earth's crust, and comes to the surface, often being magnified by passing through underground water. Most people are unaware that there are many underground streams flowing between layers of rock. Dowsers can identify them and tell engineers exactly where to drill for water. They can also advise oil companies where to start drilling for oil.

If your house just happens, by misfortune, to have been built over one of these stress lines, the effect can be very powerful, and can not only make you feel ill in its own way, it may also be able to affect your immune system. This seems to have happened to many of my patients, as I will explain in a minute. Even if your house were safe when you first moved into it, things can change, especially if you live anywhere near where they are mining, as their frequent explosions can move rock plates sufficiently to channel these energies in a different direction, this time possibly through your house. I can't say that I fully understand what this is all about. On the other hand, I can say that being aware of it and doing something about it can be very valuable at times. Interestingly enough, I am told there are sometimes 'good' geopathic stress lines, even if most are somehow 'bad'. Of course, it is the bad ones that need to be dealt with or avoided.

If you obtain a copy of Rolf Gordon's book, he tells you how to make your own dowsing rods, and dowse for yourself. Not everyone feels comfortable doing this for themselves, whereas others are intrigued enough to have a go and see if they can find anything. Then comes the problem of what to do about it. I could have put the answer later, but I feel it is appropriate to put it here.

Many of my patients have found one or more very bad geopathic stress lines that cross their bed exactly where they lie during the night. They didn't have any idea what was going to happen when they started dowsing, as they had never done it before. Most found the stress lines crossed the bed amazingly close to the part of their body where their cancer was in the middle of the bed of a man with prostate cancer and across the chest area of a woman with breast cancer, as examples.

One tragic case was of a young man in his very early twenties with a form of lung cancer called Hodgkin's Disease. He was very ill when he first came to see me, but his mother found a major stress line right across the bed where his chest would normally be. What caused his mother even more distress was the fact that he had slept there all his life, his original cot being in exactly the same place when he was a baby. When his mother used to tuck him in, he would regularly end up at the far end of the cot, almost as though he was trying to get away from something, which, of course, he was. Not surprisingly she would pick him up and put him back into 'the right place' as she saw it. Night after night she would do the same, not realising that she was placing him in grave danger by doing so.

Babies, and many animals, are particularly sensitive to geopathic stress, many hating it, ants and cats apparently liking it. It is possible that we are all sensitive to it when we are young, but, as we grow older, we lose that sensitivity so are not aware of it at a time and age when we are responsible enough to do something about it. Nevertheless, it can have a very damaging effect upon our metabolism, without our realising it.

In my opinion, it is very important to deal with it or avoid it. It is one of a number of things in your life that may have upset your body's metabolism, but which, more importantly, you can do something about very quickly and cheaply.

So, what can you do about it? First find it yourself if you are happy to do so. If not, you will need to find a dowser who will find it for you, but that may not be easy. Many dowsers are able to 'move' stress lines from within your house to outside round your house where you spend very little time, so it won't affect you. This may seem rather far-fetched, but I can assure you many of my patients have had their own experience of how effectively this can sometimes be done.

Most people's bedrooms are too small to be able to move their bed from a place of danger to a position of safety. If you find a problem and you can move your bed within the room to somewhere safe, then please do so. Alternatively, you might find your spare bedroom is 'safe'. If there is nothing you personally can do about it, then you will need help. What is amazing is that many people say that they sleep much better when they move from a 'harmful' to a 'safe' place. They had no idea why they didn't sleep very well. When a new patient told me they do not sleep well, one of the explanations I sometimes offer was geopathic stress.

For about twenty-five years I helped run a local cancer self-help group. One evening, one of the organisers asked for my help as his grandson, a baby, had suddenly developed a rash covering most of his body. I asked all the usual questions like had his daughter started to use a new washing powder, had they started the baby on any new foods, or had they just brought a new pet into the house. He had already checked on these, as he knew the way my mind worked, and the answer to them all was a clear no.

When I asked if his daughter had recently moved the position of the baby's cot, he left the room and rang her. In a few minutes he came back and asked me how I could possibly know such a thing, because his daughter had moved all the furniture round in the baby's room just before the rash appeared, and, of course, the cot was now in a new position. They moved the cot back into its original position immediately, and he rang me the next day to say the rash had almost gone, clearing within twenty-four hours.

I wouldn't blame you if you said that was pure coincidence, and nothing to do with moving the position of the cot. And, of course, the parents were not prepared to risk putting their baby's cot back there to see if the rash returned. But I have heard far too many stories of this sort that, in the end, you have to believe there may be some truth in it. Far too many ordinary, sensible people have been grateful, over the years, that I mentioned the possibility that geopathic stress might be involved in their cancer.

For years I have worked on the assumption that, if you can discover the causes of your problems, whether you have cancer or not, you have a good chance of becoming well if you undo those problems. Simply put, for example, if cheese, chocolate and red wine are the cause of your migraines, avoiding them will let you become migraine free. If eating potatoes, tomatoes, aubergines and peppers causes your arthritis, you should become totally symptom free if you stop eating them. Often, however, the body needs help to recover from the long time you have been doing the wrong things to it, by giving it extra vitamins and minerals, for example.

This principle has served my patients and me very well for a long time, but it can fail to help some patients if, between us, we are not able to identify what the causes are. The detective work just hasn't been good enough to identify the culprits. There have been plenty of times over the years when I couldn't think of the right question to ask, knowing perfectly well that there was an answer somewhere, but it simply eluded me.

A Story

Many years ago I saw an elderly English man who suffered from Parkinson's disease. He had moved to live in Spain, and came over to see me every so often. I am pleased to say that, over about three years, his Parkinsonism cleared completely. But what would never improve was the skin of his face. I had never seen anything like it, and hadn't a clue what was wrong with it. He had seen two Dermatologists, one in Spain and one in England, and neither could make a diagnosis. Every time he visited me I said to him, "I have not asked you something, and you have not told me something, but I don't know what it is".

One day his wife came with him and said to me, "Do you think it is possible that the problem of the skin on my husband's face could be anything to do with the fact that he was one of the British soldiers who stood on Christmas Island many years ago and watched one of the first atom bombs blow up?" He had a radiation burn, which had caused scaring but had not caused cancer. How do you ever think of asking someone such a question? Yet there was his answer. There always is one, but sometimes we just cannot think what it is. Incidentally, he said, "I'm old and I'm ugly, and I don't mind what I look like, so I'm not coming back just so you can make me look pretty again!"

The point that I am trying to make is that good old-fashioned personalised medical detective work is extremely effective most of the time, and the appropriate advice can help a person regain their health. Irrespective of what your history can tell me, there is great value in knowing exactly what everything has done to your body. How has your body responded to a diet that may have been wrong for you for years? What effect has drinking milk and eating milk products all your life had on your body, if your history suggests to me that you have been intolerant of it virtually from birth? How have alcohol and caffeine damaged your body? In fact, what state is your body really in now?

As a medical student I was taught how to examine a person, and I carried out a standard medical examination on all new patients as a matter of routine. I did, however, look for a number of features that had a particular meaning to me, but, all too often, nothing untoward was found. This tended to suggest to me that such a superficial examination was not nearly deep enough, and that it would have been nice to be able to dig a bit deeper.

Despite the amazing amount of detail available here, it may not be necessary for you to avail yourself of all the advice I am giving you. Some of you may only need to do a minimal amount to help yourself, to see improvements occurring, while others may be in need of a lot more help. When you get to the chapter on Treatment, chapter 4, you will see what I mean. There are many things you can do that don't cost a penny, and I will start with those. Others are more sophisticated and you will need to spend money on them if you want to do them.

Infections
I am convinced that all lymph and blood cancers have some sort of viral cause and probably all cancers if the truth were known. There are various tests that can be done to support such an idea, one of which is Non-Genomic RNA/DNA by Neuro-Lab. The problem is that, although this test can identify a high burden of viral material in your body, it is totally non-specific in that it doesn't identify the name of the organism, so that it is not possible to select a specific treatment.

Various laboratories do a series of screening tests for different organisms, but, as there are so very many possible pathological organisms that could be making you ill, the very one that is causing your problems may not be included in the testing panel, unless you are going to pay for a complete range. Even then, just because an organism is identified in your blood, it doesn't automatically mean it is the one causing your illness.

SureScreen Life Sciences & Neuro-Lab Tests♥
The tests that are available through these laboratories are valuable for a number of reasons. Firstly, they help to identify the status of cancer in the body, so can be useful in assessing progress. They can also tell you the state of your immune system. A major drawback to having these tests done, however, is that the laboratory will only send the results to a doctor, as they can be fairly complicated to interpret. If you don't know a doctor who thinks like I do, you might convince your own GP to at least be prepared to receive a copy of your results, and then hand them over to you. You could print off a copy of the information here and show it to him or her, even if you are going to attempt to use my explanations for yourself.

But, first, let me ask you a question that I think is important for you to ask, and have answered. To do this, I first need to set a scene.

Let us suggest that you were diagnosed, some time in the past, with breast cancer. You had some sort of operation, such as a mastectomy and clearance of lymph glands in your armpit. When you recovered from the operation, you were given a course of radiotherapy and chemotherapy. After a reasonable period of time, you recovered from all your treatment and you are now feeling really quite well. You have been given the all clear at the hospital, where everyone is pleased with how well you have done. Naturally you want to stay that way. You are now looking for advice as to what to do. A friend has suggested you take some vitamins and minerals.

If you were to ask your hospital Specialist, probably your Oncologist, how he will know whether his treatment really has worked forever, do you know what he is likely to say? If you follow any advice from wherever you can find it, how will you know whether it has worked or not? If you follow any advice you take from me, how will you know whether it was good advice or not?

Your Oncologist is likely to say that he will keep an eye on you every so often, to check that everything is all right. He may do a scan every so often, and he is certainly likely to examine you to check everything.

To me, however, his honest answer should be "If you are alive in five years time, you will be categorised as a success. However, apart from that, you won't know if the treatment has worked or not until it comes back again, or doesn't". It doesn't matter how many times you are examined or how many scans are done, they cannot prove a negative. If you are clear at a certain time, they can only say you are clear at that time, but cannot tell what may develop in the future. A doctor's examining hand can only tell you that he can't find a lump at present. A scan can only tell that everything appears to be clear for now. None of these approaches is sophisticated enough to tell if something may be beginning to develop.

This is where the laboratory tests come in. The ones I used to use are listed here, namely Telomerase, Pyruvate kinase, Laevorotatory lactic acid, anti-P53 antibody, P185 Her-2 Protein, Interferon gamma (INT-gamma), Interleukin 12 (Il12), Tumour necrosis factor-beta (TNF-beta), Vascular endothelial growth factor (VEGF), Transforming growth factor-beta (TGFbeta), although some of them have longer names.

The first three, namely telomerase, pyruvate kinase and laevorotatory lactic acid, can tell you if there is any cancer anywhere in your body. These tests are entirely non-specific, in that they don't tell you where the cancer is. If, however, you have, or have had, cancer anywhere in your body, it is logical to assume that, if any of these tests is 'positive', they are reflecting that cancer. If you merely want to know if cancer may, or may not, be developing somewhere in your body, then these tests will go a long way to answering that question. You have to remember, however, that no test is 100% guaranteed to be accurate, but they are state-of-the-art tests as far as I am concerned, and very useful. You also need to remember that the results are simply a snapshot of you at the time the blood is taken, but they can be useful to track your progress.

A simple piece of advice is timely here. If you ever have a test done, for whatever reason, you must be prepared to act on the result. If you are not aware of cancer anywhere in your body, but you simply want to do a screening test, these three are as good as it gets at present. If you receive a positive result, you must be prepared to take some of my advice, or someone else's, or at least do something for yourself, and have the tests repeated at an appropriate interval, to see if there has been an improvement.

The telomerase test is an interesting one. Any word ending in '..ase' indicates an enzyme, and that enzyme is making more of the chemical named in the first part of the word. So the telomerase test measures an enzyme that is making telomeres. Every time your normal DNA divides, you lose part of its tail, called the telomere. Under healthy conditions, so far as I am aware, you cannot manufacture any more telomere than you were born with, so, when it has all been lost, I assume that's it. To be fair, no one has confirmed that to me, so I may be wrong.

Cancer cells produce telomerase so can make telomeres. This effectively makes them immortal. If there is a measurable amount of telomerase is the blood, it merely indicates the presence of that enzyme in the blood stream, and not necessarily cancer cells themselves. When I first did this test on a patient, it was usually comparatively low, perhaps up to a few hundred, which made the patient feel happy, as they assumed it meant their cancer was not spreading much. However, this misses the point. So far as I am aware, raised levels of telomerase in the blood do not reflect the fact that your cancer is spreading. In fact you need a reasonable blood telomerase level, otherwise there is nothing for your immune system to recognise and respond to. When I have other tests done by these laboratories, I usually find the immune system in an appalling state. Under these circumstances, I tend to suggest that your immune system doesn't even know you have cancer. If that is the case, how can you fight back?

When my patients followed some of my advice and they felt better, we usually repeated the important tests. Most commonly, if things were going as well as we suspected, the tests all showed an improvement except telomerase, which usually rose to very high levels. We now interpreted this to mean that cancer cells were being killed and that they were releasing extra enzyme into the blood stream. To the patient's surprise, this was, in fact, a good sign that the immune system was doing its job. It is because of features such as this that it is important not to try to interpret SureScreen or Neuro-Lab test results yourself.

If I described accurately the situation about your cancer about eleven paragraphs ago (which began with 'Let us suggest you were diagnosed'), you can now see the value in having these three tests done. They could clearly also apply to anyone, whatever the state of their cancer. When you first have them done, they merely tell you what the situation is at that time. They don't tell you if things are getting better or worse. Their value is that they can be used to monitor your progress. I have a number of patients who were originally significantly positive at one time and are now, after a period of healing their body, completely clear.

On the other hand, if the tests seem to become worse over a period of time, I encourage the patients not to think of it as all doom and gloom, but to consider it to be an opportunity to do 'more'.

The next test that I usually did was the p-185 Her-2 protein test, which is an indication of the metabolic activity of your cancer. Obviously the lower it is the less active is your cancer, as some people's cancer is very slow growing. Some of the approaches I recommended could clearly slow the rate of cancer cell growth, especially pancreatic enzymes. Yes it is related to herceptin, the so-called latest wonder drug for certain types of breast cancer. The Anti-P53 Antibody test (which I simply call the P53 test) is basically a double negative name, as it is effectively examining the state of the P53 gene, the one that sends out the message for old cells to die by apoptosis. It can either be described as 'wild', which means it is functioning normally, or 'mutated', which means it is damaged in some way, so that the apoptotic message may not be going out correctly.

It can also be described as 'deleted', which is supposed to be bad news, suggesting that it cannot ever come back again. However, I have seen multiple sclerosis patients in wheel chairs get back to normal functioning in due course, something that is not supposed to be possible. So I believe even a deleted P53 gene ought to be able to come back by some means. To be fair, it is not something that I have particularly followed in my cancer patient. There is some evidence that natural progesterone cream can bring it back to normal, and I have had one patient who has done this successfully. Artemisinin is said to be able to get round the chemical cascade to the end point of the apoptotic mechanism, so, in some respects, it may not be necessary to measure it, although I prefer to.

There are eight tests I like to do in general, the last three looking at your immune system. First there is 'Interferon Gamma', which reflects your Natural Killer (NK) cells, a most important aspect of your immune system. Next is Tumour Necrosis Factor Beta (TNF Beta), which reflects your thymus helper cells, similar to CD4 as in AIDS. Finally, there is Interleukin 12 (Il 12), which reflects two important parts of your immune system, namely macrophages and dendritic cells.

I have put the laboratory's reference ranges in the table. Most cancer patients, when I first see them and we do these tests, have levels below 50 for these three tests! Remember, the lower limit of the range is in the thousands. Is there any wonder I say that it would appear that their immune system doesn't even know they have cancer, or that their immune system has been hit really badly by their treatment? Seeing these results is quite an eye-opener, and is usually a spur to get on and do something.

There are so many tests one could do, but each one costs money, so I have to justify whatever I recommend. Two others have a value sometimes and they are Vascular Endothelial Growth Factor (VEGF) and Transforming Growth Factor Beta (TGFBeta). VEGF is raised if new blood vessels are forming, so the timing of such a test needs to be chosen carefully. Yes, a raised VEGF can indicate that a tumour is growing new blood vessels so that it can expand, but it will also be raised after an operation, when new blood vessels form as part of the healing process. So there is no point in doing this test too soon after a mastectomy, for example. For the same reason, the test will also be raised in pregnancy, because of the new blood vessel formation of the afterbirth.

TGF -Beta is an interesting test. Cancer cells sometimes produce large quantities of this chemical to suppress your immune system. This means cancer cells have developed a means of protecting themselves from their natural enemy! It's rather like ballistic and anti-ballistic missiles.

One more of these laboratory tests needs to be considered. Some people think cancer is an inflammatory mechanism, and a chemical produced by the inflammatory cascade is Tumour Necrosis Factor-Alpha (TNF-Alpha, as distinct from TNF-Beta). If this is raised, your cancer is likely to be caused by an NSICI (a Non-Self Inflammatory Cascade Initiator). The most likely origin of an N-SICI is what you are exposed to most frequently in your daily life, namely what you consume as food or drink. Another test of inflammation, and one your own doctor could do on your blood, is called C-Reactive Protein (CRP), which is also a cardio-vascular risk factor, suggesting that heart attacks and strokes may be an inflammatory mechanism as well.

Laboratory Tests Reference Ranges

Telomerase trace or not detectable
Pyruvate Kinase 5.0 15.0 units/ml of plasma
Laevorotatory lactic acid trace or not detectable
Anti-P53 antibody trace 0.85 copies/microlitre of plasma P185 less than 6.8
Interferon-gamma 5,000-10,000 copies/microlitre of plasma
Interleukin 12 3,000-10,000 copies/microlitre of plasma
Tumour Necrosis Factor-beta 2,000-5,000 copies/microlitre of plasma
Vascular Endothelial Growth Factor 3,000-10,000 copies/microlitre of plasma
Transforming Growth Factor-beta 10-1,500 copies/microlitre of plasma

Another set of tests this laboratory can do is Non-Genomic RNA/DNA. This could help to identify if you have a viral, bacterial or fungal infection somewhere in your body. However, there are two drawbacks in that it doesn't tell you where that infection might be, nor does it tell you what the infection is. Genomic RNA/DNA would be yours, so if there is some non-genomic material in your blood, it has to have come from elsewhere, presumably an organism of some sort, which just might be the Human Papilloma virus or any other virus.

The Alcat Test

In the Treatment chapter I go over the different ways I chose from to advise a patient what diet to follow, because there is no doubt in my mind that getting the diet right is important in cancer. One of those methods is to have a blood test, and, while there are many different blood tests on the market, the one I like best in the United Kingdom, and whose mechanisms of action I feel most comfortable with, is the Alcat Test.♥

You will need to book a test on line, where you will be shown how and where to have a blood sample taken. The company is quite happy to have test results sent directly to you, so you don't need a doctor to receive the results for you. You will receive a patient information booklet that will tell you how to follow the test's recommendations, but I would like you to read and follow the instructions I give in the Treatment chapter, chapter 4, where I interpret the test results for you.

So, consider using the Alcat Test for what you can get out of it, but always remember that no testing procedure is perfect. If you live in a country where it is not possible to do the Alcat Test, find a laboratory that does a similar test and talk to them about your needs. Talk to as many as you can find, and select the one you feel is being the most honest with you. One final important fact to have checked in you is your blood level of homocysteine. Homocysteine is a far more important arterial poison than cholesterol has ever been. To obtain the simple facts on homocysteine, buy a copy of the book 'The H Factor'♥ by Patrick Holford and Dr. James Braly. The simple fact is that a raised homocysteine level increases your chances of developing cancer, so, if you already have cancer, it is important that it should be low. As I have already said, laboratory blood levels are considered to be normal by most doctors, but in fact they are only a mathematical result of the samples received in the laboratory. Most laboratories accept as normal a level up to 15 micromoles per litre. That level has been shown to be a significant risk of just about every medical condition, especially cardiovascular ones, such as heart attacks and strokes. The ideal level is below 6. A low level shows that you have the ability to 'methylate', which basically means you can deal with many undesirable chemicals. It also means you have plenty of SAMe and glutathione in your body, two very important detoxification chemicals. Please have yours checked. It is most important. How to deal with it is fully explained in the book, but I give a simple protocol in the treatment chapter.

Chapter 3

Medical History

In this chapter, I will go through your personal history to try to find what allowed cancer to develop in you. All this information is the result of my many years of listening to patients, letting them tell their stories, believing in their observations that have often been ignored, and learning by experience.

So, enjoy yourself, feel enlightened, smile, be happy and radiate confidence in what you are going to do. Be positive and forget the doom and gloom merchants. If someone has given you a poor prognosis, forget it. You no longer fit into their statistics. You are going to do something for yourself. You are now in charge.

The History - What Is A Medical History?

I'm going to repeat this, because I think it is most important. As a medical student, I was taught to take a history for one purpose and one purpose only. That was to make a diagnosis. Once the diagnosis had been made with confidence, then a decision need simply be made on the most appropriate form of treatment for that diagnosis. Effectively that meant a prescription for a medication or a recommendation for some sort of surgical procedure. In fact learning about the treatment options was generally a much later part of the curriculum, as we concentrated on getting the diagnosis right to begin with. A reasonable theory was that the choice of treatment depended on getting the diagnosis right in the first place.

When I was a pre-clinical medical student, I remember being taught all about the anatomy and physiology of the body. While I realised that it was important to know all this, my fellow students and I longed to get into the hospital wards to start treating patients. We were sure that was where our talents lay and what we were learning to become doctors for. In other words we wanted to heal the sick.

I found the pre-clinical studies rather dry and boring at the time, and almost irrelevant. Interestingly enough, it never occurred to me that an ill person is merely someone whose normal anatomy or physiology has simply somehow gone wrong. Nor did our tutors describe this attitude to us. Yet, before I retired, I studied the normal, because that is what I wanted to achieve in my patients. I wanted to understand where and why the abnormal had developed, so that I could help the normal to return, mainly by undoing what caused it to go wrong in the first place.

What I am trying to get across to you is the fact that mainstream medicine as it is practised today attempts to correct the abnormal by treating the abnormal symptoms with unnatural chemicals called pharmaceutical prescription drugs. Studies have been carried out to show the possibility that the symptom has resulted from some chemical abnormality in the body, and that the prescribed drug can correct it. I could waste hours of your time refuting this argument, and will consider doing this at a later stage. Nevertheless, I will repeat that the intention is that the drug is supposed to alter the abnormality that has occurred. No attempt is made to understand why that abnormality occurred in the first place.

While there is a certain value in mainstream medicine's approach, especially for acute situations such as appendicitis, there is the missing question "Why has this occurred?" rather than "Take this medicine" or "I need to operate on you". I was certainly not taught to take a history to find out why the condition had developed. Over the years I have learned that going into a person's history in great depth can help to identify the causes that have led to the eventual presentation of their cancer. I now want to give you all my years of experience so that you can decide for yourself what is relevant to you. I will then show you what to do about them.

Taking a history from you is quite a simple procedure. Since I want to find out as much as possible about you, I have to ask questions. Two questions I try to ask early on are "What do you (the patient) want of me?" and "What do you want to achieve?" Some people with cancer are so worn out, either by the cancer itself or because of the treatment they have been given for it. They often tell me they don't want a cure, or don't expect one. They merely want to feel better and to be allowed to die in peace and with dignity.

What do you want to achieve?

It was fascinating when I asked this question of an older cancer patient. When they said they didn't particularly want to be cured, the look on the face of the loved ones (usually younger relatives) who had brought the patient to me was of genuine amazement. Because they were younger and had a lot of life ahead of them, it never occurred to them that an older person might not have the same outlook on life as they did. Clearly no one had asked them what they wanted. So it is important for me to establish early on what they do want. Others, of course, want to fight in every possible way to stay alive for many more years, or want me to help them conquer their cancer. So, what do you want? What do you hope to achieve by reading this book?

The reason I ask this is because there are various ways you can help yourself. Perhaps all you want to do is as little as possible. Well, that's fine by me, and I will show you some of the simplest things you can do. Maybe, if you keep it simple to start with, you will gradually feel sufficiently improved and encouraged to try a little more. Perhaps you are searching the net for someone else, someone who you desperately want to help, but who you think may be sceptical about, or resistant to, any natural suggestions. Their attitude may be "If it was worth trying, surely my doctor would have told me about it?" Perhaps your response should be something like "He is so busy trying to help so many sick people that he can't possibly have time to learn about everything".

Having asked you what you want, I start with the situation you have come to me about. I naturally ask about your cancer, how it affects you at present, what symptoms you have, especially any pain. What is the most important thing you want dealing with now? Do you, in fact, have any obvious symptoms of your cancer? Interestingly enough, some patients I see have been told they have cancer, possibly because of an X-ray, a scan or a blood test, yet they don't feel at all unwell. They have been told that they need a particular form of treatment, which is likely to make them feel unwell, so they wonder if there is anything else they can do. Each person must be treated as an individual and their own problem resolved.

How It All Started

I then go through how things started. What was the first indication of a problem in you? How did it all begin? How did you first notice something wrong with your breast, or was the first indication as a result of a routine mammogram? Can you remember the time of your monthly cycle, if you are or were still having periods? Or are you postmenopausal? What were you doing at the time? Where were you? Were you under any particular degree of stress at the time, or had you been for some time before it all began? What did you do when you noticed the first problem? Did the lump change in any way, for example with your monthly cycle, if you are a woman?

How soon did you consult a doctor after you first suspected something was wrong? If it was quite some time later, to what extent had the lump altered by then? Had any lump grown?   Had any other changes occurred by then? Were you or was anyone else able to feel any lumps anywhere else?

Tell me about what happened if you went to hospital. I appreciate I occasionally see a person who does not want any operation or chemotherapy, so has not yet consulted anyone else, but the vast number of people I see have already been to see their own General Practitioner and/or someone in the local Breast Care Clinic or prostate centre, usually a Surgeon in the first instance.

Did you have a biopsy, a mammogram or any other test? How did you cope with that? How long ago was all that? Did the biopsy affect the lump? If so, has it settled down? Have you been given a diagnosis? Do you understand what it means? Have you been told what form of treatment your particular diagnosis is likely to be, such as an operation of some sort, followed possibly by chemotherapy and/or radiotherapy?

The above questions apply to you only if you are in the early stages of your cancer, and you want more information about what you should do. You may want help with decisions you have to make, but I cannot tell you what to do. You have to make these decisions yourself. I don't know you. I don't know how you think. I don't know your particular circumstances. In the later section on making decisions, I have provided questions you need answering for you to make the right decisions for yourself.

If you are one of the many people I used to see who had been through the whole range of treatments recommended by a Surgeon and Oncologist, but your cancer has come back, or has possibly spread to another organ, such as your bones, lungs or liver, I need to know what treatment you have been recommended to follow, and what your attitude is to following that advice. You may still have a lot of questions to ask and decisions to make.

If you intend to follow the recommended course of chemotherapy, there are many things you can do to minimise any adverse effects, without stopping the chemotherapy doing its job. You will find details in the Treatment chapter.

If you have decided you don't want any more treatment from orthodox medicine, or you want to know what you can do if you decide not to have any more, again there are many ways of helping yourself. All of this is also discussed in the treatment chapter.

Although I try to remember to ask everyone what the first indication was that something was not quite right, it may not be particularly important, but sometimes it is. For example, some people become aware that something is wrong, or they first feel a lump as a result of a burning sensation or a patch of numbness in that area. This suggests the possibility that the shingles virus may be involved. More about that later. Very often, however, something almost incidental may cause the first symptom or sign to appear. But, if you remember from my overall introduction, things have probably been building up in you for quite a long time, so what the final straw was that started symptoms appearing is often not particularly important. Many specialists believe that cancer probably started to develop in you at least five years before a lump was apparent to an examining finger or some form of scan.

How good is your immune system?   Sometimes the specific problem started after a period of illness, like flu', which may have somehow affected the person's immune system. To be fair, an infection can stimulate the immune system, but sometimes it overwhelms it, depending on the nature and duration of the infection, how often one has occurred, and possibly the state of the immune system at the time. To be honest, there is something about the immune system that I don't understand at present. Most cancer patients say they have been remarkably free of infections for a long time, and often say they cannot remember when they last had one.

If that is the case, why has cancer developed in them? If they have been free of infections, would one not assume that their immune system was in good condition? Apparently not. In the circumstances, you can see why looking at a person's immune system can be a very important aspect of understanding what has gone wrong.

Where you were at the time of onset doesn't often indicate anything in particular, as lumps are often first found in a shower or noticed in a mirror. A patient once told me, however, that she found her breast lump in a shower in a hotel where she had stayed a number of times. The hotel, however, was associated with a number of visits on behalf of her company, the whole situation being particularly stressful. That gave me a clue to looking at levels of stress and their effect upon her body. Perhaps you remember when I discussed the theory put forward by Dr. Fryda in the introduction, and the effect upon the production of adrenaline. While I may have my pet theories about the cause of cancer, I am aware that there may be many causes, and probably more than one in a particular person.

What someone does when they first find a lump varies from person to person. Some go into a state of panic, some go into a state of denial, but the majority consults their General Practitioner as soon as an appointment can be made. Even that can result in an enormous range of what happens next and what the patient's reaction to it was. I liked to write it all down, because sometimes it helped to clarify something about the person's personality. In any case, patients usually like to recount the story of what happened around this time, often because of a particular experience. It also helped me to understand how well they got on with their own doctors, to whom I wished to write about my observations, if I was allowed to.

Pre-Menstrual Symptoms

In a pre-menstrual woman, breast lumps of any sort can change with her menstrual cycle. Non-cancerous (benign) cysts are quite common in the days leading up to a period, and doctors take such cysts seriously, as it is sometimes very difficult to tell merely by the feel which of these lumps are cysts and which cancer. But, to me, pre-menstrual problems of any sort are a strong indicator of a dominance of oestrogen in relation to progesterone.

Let me explain this further. Once again, understanding the normal is most important for realising why things have gone wrong and, just as important, what to do about them.

Although women's menstrual cycles vary somewhat, for the sake of simplicity I will describe a 'classical' twenty-eight day cycle, taking the start of a cycle as the first day of the period. There are two main hormones we talk about, namely oestrogen (estrogen in USA) and progesterone. In fact oestrogen is at least three chemicals, oestriol (E1), oestradiol (E2) and oestrone (E3). Oestradiol is the best known of these three chemicals as a variety of it (such as oestradiol valerate) is present in most forms of the contraceptive pill and HRT. It is also important to be aware that oestradiol and oestrone are proliferative, which means they promote cellular development, while oestriol is anti-proliferative, so calms down cellular growth. Isn't nature clever in providing balancing hormones? But things can go wrong if the balance is lost. Progesterone, on the other hand is one chemical.

For about the first seven days there are low levels of progesterone and oestrogen, but at roughly day 7, Follicle Stimulating Hormone (FSH) is produced in the brain which brings to complete maturity one egg (inside a Graafian follicle), and gradually ripens many others, their turn coming another month. At roughly day14, the time of ovulation, another hormone is released from the brain called Luteinizing Hormone (LH), which instructs the Graafian follicle to release its egg for fertilisation. The Graafian follicle now starts to manufacture progesterone.

Under normal circumstances, the levels of oestrogen may increase, level off or may even decline somewhat, but there is still more circulating oestrogen at this stage than in the first seven days, when levels are quite low. Progesterone's main job is to prepare the lining of the uterus (womb) for pregnancy, and levels of it should gradually rise to balance oestrogen. This balance between oestrogen and progesterone is particularly important. If a pregnancy does not occur, the levels of both oestrogen and progesterone drop towards the resting state at about day 26, a period starting two days later.

If a woman is blessed with such an ideal physiological event, her monthly cycles come and go regularly. She knows exactly when her next period will start, because she has made a note of it in her diary, and all she is aware of before the next onset is the result of minor hormonal changes. None of this causes her any problems or makes her feel ill in any way, and she takes it all in her stride. She is aware of when she ovulates, so could plan a pregnancy any time she wanted to. She may already have done things this way.

Unfortunately, very few women have such a simple cycle nowadays. Far too many women suffer pre-menstrual symptoms, such as breast tenderness or breast swelling, a whole variety of emotional symptoms, such as irritability, depression, bouts of crying, low self-esteem, insomnia and clumsiness, weight gain, sugar and chocolate cravings, bloated abdomen, and sometimes thrush, to name but a few. The length and severity of these symptoms can vary considerably, sometimes lasting up to fourteen days before the onset of the next period. If she also has a bad time with her period itself, she can have three weeks out of every four feeling awful! I have met many such women, and I tell you, it is not difficult to sort out, and without drugs!

So where do things go wrong? It is usually at around the time of ovulation. In fact a woman may not ovulate. If she doesn't ovulate, it means she probably doesn't release an egg or produce much progesterone, if any, from the Graafian follicle. That means that oestrogen is not balanced by progesterone, so she suffers from hyper-oestrogenism. If a woman does not suffer from premenstrual symptoms, she might produce 30 or possibly even 40mg progesterone per day towards the end of her cycle. So progesterone is good for you!

Oestrogen's job is to make you a woman, a natural female capable of reproducing the human species. This means that oestrogen is responsible for developing your breasts, ovaries and womb. As there are oestrogen receptors on all the cells of a woman, including brain cells, oestrogen makes you think and behave like a woman.

The problem is that, whereas a woman needs her oestrogen, too much oestrogen is not good for her, and if it is not balanced by progesterone towards the end of a cycle, the symptoms of hyper-oestrogenism, namely premenstrual symptoms, occur. If one of your female organs is particularly sensitive to the effects of too much oestrogen, then that organ will be stimulated or developed a little bit too much every month. If that organ is your breasts, the stage after pre-menstrual breast tenderness or swellings is breast cysts, and eventually breast cancer.

Time and time again I pick up this story when taking a comprehensive history from a woman with breast cancer. The information is all there, although no one else has thought of considering it. Unfortunately doctors are mostly not interested in why a woman has her problems.

When I took a history from a woman with breast cancer, pre-menstrual breast tenderness, breast swelling or breast cysts was a common finding. Some post-menopausal women do not remember suffering in this way, but when I asked them about any operations, they often said they had a hysterectomy because of fibroids. This means they also had oestrogen dominance, but the effect was mainly on their womb. Others told me of a history of polycystic ovaries, so her ovaries were the main target. Remember too much oestrogen means the balance of the three oestrogens is in favour of oestradiol and oestrone versus oestriol, and out of balance with progesterone.

Consider then what happens to a post-menopausal woman. Her monthly cycles have stopped, so she is not ovulating, she is not releasing an egg because she is not producing a Graafian follicle, so she is not making progesterone. Yet, as her monthly cycles stop, she can still manufacture oestrogen from the fat of her body and her adrenal glands. So, once again, she is potentially in an oestrogen dominant state.

You may think this is the end of the story, but it isn't, because the environment in which we all live is being polluted by xeno-oestrogens, or chemicals that have oestrogen-like activity. These come from plastics and the plasticisers they release, petrochemicals, pesticides and a whole host of chemicals in common use today. Also millions of women are taking pharmaceutical drugs of the contraceptive pill and HRT who urinate every day, which gradually reaches water tables. The water in London is said to be recycled many times, and people drink it!

So, is there any wonder that you and so many other women are exposed to too much oestrogen, some of it false, leading to oestrogen dominant effects on your body? And remember, that oestrogen is proliferative, so is effectively encouraging your breast and uterus cells to divide.

When Do Symptoms Occur?

If you have symptoms that are not normally associated with your specific form of cancer, the question about whether such symptoms are better or worse at any time of day can suggest quite a lot of ideas. If your symptoms are worse in the morning, what makes them better? Do they feel better after a cup of tea or coffee, for example? If they do, it suggests to me that you may be addicted to the tea or the coffee, or possibly the milk or sugar you may add. Over night is the longest time you are without your 'fix', so, by the morning, you may be suffering from withdrawal symptoms, and they can affect you quite badly, and in a way you might not suspect. While this may be adversely affecting your cancer, it may not be as directly involved as you thought. However, the fact that it is having any effect upon you is worth doing something about.

Do some of your symptoms feel better if you have breakfast? If so, you could be suffering from low blood sugar, or something in it is having the same effect I have just described for tea or coffee. If your symptoms feel worse after breakfast, you could be reacting to something you eat then, remembering that, again, you have not had that same food for a number of hours, i.e. over night. Even if you eat that food a number of times during the day, a period of overnight avoidance followed by the first 'challenge' of the day can produce symptoms from that food that might not occur when you eat it later in the day.

Be a detective on yourself. If there is anything slightly unusual about certain symptoms, see if you can analyse when they occur, what makes them better or worse or has any effect upon them in any way. Remember, there has to be a reason, even if it can sometimes be difficult to work it out. If a murder has been committed, the police detective knows someone did it, even if he has difficulty in identifying the culprit. Be aware that I am interested in the whole of you, not just your cancer. As I will be recommending that you change your eating habits if you have not already done so, doing some detective work on yourself may help to identify certain foods that you ought to avoid, which may also be of value in your approach to healing yourself of your cancer.

I remember a man with cancer many years ago telling me that the diet that I recommended to him for his cancer completely cured the migraines he had been suffering from for as long as he could remember. This then had an amazing effect upon his attitude towards his cancer. Without the migraines he felt he had a better chance of sorting the cancer out. He found he had the energy to start to do something for himself. More to the point, since all the GPs in the practice and two Consultants he had seen had not been able to help his migraines, but I had, he felt that my simple approach towards his cancer might not only be worth trying, but might actually work.

Biopsies

Having worked through these starting points, I then find out what happened. Many patients have a biopsy of their lump, especially if it is a breast lump. If the PSA (prostate specific antigen) test is outside the accepted laboratory range of 4.0mcg/litre in a man, a biopsy of the prostate is very commonly done. A biopsy helps your doctor to make, or confirm, a diagnosis of cancer, and also helps him to decide on what he considers from his experience to be the most appropriate treatment. Have you undergone any treatment yet?

If you have had some treatment, how did it affect you? Did you cope with it well, or did it make you feel unwell in any way? Is there more of the same treatment to come, or is a new course of treatment being planned? Do you want some advice on how to minimise possible adverse effects, without stopping it doing what it is supposed to do? I will describe what to do later on.

Decisions To Be Made

If you haven't had a biopsy yet and are trying to decide whether to have one or not, I suggest you also move to the chapter on Decisions, where I will try to help you decide what to do. This applies also to any decisions you have to make about whether to have an operation, or whether to have chemotherapy or radiotherapy. In the later section when decisions are discussed, I will show you the questions you need to ask your specialist about the treatments he has recommended. I will also show you how to make the right decisions for yourself, in relation to your own cancer and its severity. I will also ask you some simple questions about what you want in life and what you expect from your cancer treatment. However, I will not tell you what to do, as it is your cancer, your body and your life. You have to decide for yourself.

My Patient Questionnaire

I am now going to show you what my patient questionnaire used to be like. I wanted every patient to complete it before they came to see me, as this gave them a chance to think about themselves in advance of their first consultation. Clearly the first page was mainly straightforward, but the section at the bottom provided some interesting insights. When most patients indicated what their main symptoms were, they quite understandably tended to confine them to symptoms of their cancer. However, as I have already indicated, I was interested in the whole person, the whole you, and wanted to know about all your symptoms, irrespective of whether they were specific to your cancer or not.

Remember, I was assuming you had now developed cancer because a series of circumstances in your life had gradually overwhelmed your body's ability to cope with them. If between us we can identify them, it is reasonable to try to do something about them and so reverse the effect they may have had on your body's metabolism. In that way, we are doing something about why cancer has developed in you.

Page 1 of Patient Questionnaire
1. Your age
2. Your date of birth
3. Your height
4. Your weight
5. Your occupation
6. How long in this job?
7. Occupation of your spouse
8. Does your condition have an official name? If so, what is it?
9. What are your main symptoms?

Page 2 of Patient Questionnaire
10. Are you taking any medicines from your doctor, anything you buy from the chemist, or any herbals, homoeopathics, vitamins or minerals?
11. If 'yes', please list them, with doses if possible.
12. What do you heat your home or office with?
13. What do you think caused the onset of your symptoms?
14. Is there anything you are reasonably sure makes any of your symptoms better or worse, e.g. hunger, food, heat, cold, damp etc.

The section on what you are taking in the way of drugs prescribed by your doctors and what you have bought from a health food store or your local chemist often reveals features of great importance to me. You may be on eye drops for glaucoma (possibly caused by free radicals), tablets for high blood pressure (possibly caused by food intolerances, stress or a magnesium deficiency, amongst other things), or simple antacids to control what you believe to be excess acid in your stomach. Whatever you are on tells its own story. I always have to check you haven't forgotten something, or I may feel you are overdosing on something or causing an imbalance, often of essential fatty acids or calcium-to-magnesium ratios.

The drugs a person was on may be particularly important by the time I saw a new patient, as most of them have undesirable effects, often called side effects, which usually means someone has prescribed another drug to combat them. There may be a third or a fourth drug, each one having been prescribed to help with the side effects of the previous one.

What is not fully realised, however, is that many of the so-called side effects of a drug are actually nutritional deficiencies caused by the drug. For example, so many people I see for the first time are on statin drugs. The medical profession seems almost determined to put everyone onto them, although I hope some people will say no.

One of the most important nutritional deficiencies the statin drugs cause is of Co-Enzyme Q 10, which is very important for the energy functioning of the heart. The concern is that a long-term deficiency of Co-Enzyme Q 10 will eventually lead to more cardiovascular deaths, the very thing the statin drugs are supposed to prevent.

Anyway, to move on, some people react to the gas they cook with or heat their home with, often not realising this could be causing some of their problems. Yet when asked where they spend much of their day, they often say it is in the kitchen, where they may feel less well than elsewhere in the house. Until the idea is brought to their attention, they naturally never thought it might be part of their 'total load', which has now allowed their body to break down simply because it could not tolerate it all. Could this apply to you?

I always encourage patients to think carefully about any ideas they may have about the cause or causes of their condition. I was the person you could say anything to, however odd it may have seemed to other people. Sometimes patients say they have never felt the same since, for example, they had glandular fever as a teenager, or since a particular child was born, or since they moved to their present house. Patients have considerable insight into their own lives, and have often tried to voice their thoughts to their doctors, only to be put off on the basis that it is not relevant and "Don't worry about that for now. What we have to deal with is your cancer". To me such ideas are most important, and, if I can deal with any underlying problem, it reduces the 'total load' and allows the body to start healing itself. Please give this some thought. Don't ignore your own ideas. They may be of great relevance. The section on what makes you feel better or worse provides some most interesting information. Things that may make you feel worse often include going without food for too long (low blood sugar and a need for chromium supplements), hot damp places (fungal), first thing in the morning (possibly withdrawal from something eaten or drunk the previous night like tea or coffee, or geopathic stress of some sort), or simply doing too much (many possible explanations for this).

What makes people feel better often includes eating regularly, having plenty of rest, and avoiding stress, a holiday in a dry sunny area or simply the summer months. It all tells a story, so think carefully about this one. Feeling better in a dry sunny place can be because of getting away from moulds, which are so prevalent in many people's houses and gardens, or the sun may generate more vitamin D in your skin. Most people spend far too little time in the sun, partially for fear of developing skin cancer. Did you know that exposure to sunlight (and possibly therefore absorbing more vitamin D in your skin) has been shown to be protective of developing cancer.

Page 3 of Patient Questionnaire
15. Do you suffer from headaches?
16. Do you get tired?
17. Do you sleep badly?
18. Do you get thirsty?
19. Do you get dizzy?
20. Is your balance affected?
21. Are there days when you feel generally unwell a little below par?

22. Do you suffer from catarrh?
23. Do your muscles and joints ache?
24. Do you suffer from backache?
25. Do you suffer from pins and needles or numbness?
26. Do you suffer from palpitations, rapid heartbeat or being more aware of your heart than normal?
27. Do you have pains in your chest?
28. Do you suffer from shortness of breath?
29. Do you suffer from tummy pains?
30. Do you suffer from wind or indigestion?
31. Do you suffer from diarrhoea?
32. Do you suffer from constipation?
33. Does your tummy become bloated?
34. Do you have fungal infections such as athletes' foot, a rash between your buttocks or in the groin?
35. Do you have or have you ever had thrush?
36. Do you have, or have you had, any problems with your waterworks, such as cystitis?
37. Does any part of your body swell, such as your eyes, lips, nose, fingers, ankles?
38. Do you suffer from rashes?
39. Do you suffer from eczema or psoriasis?
40. Do you have dry skin or dandruff?
41. Do your eyes trouble you in any way?
42. Do you suffer from sores in or around your mouth, mouth ulcers, cold sores or sore tongue?
43. Do you have a strange or metallic taste?
44. Do you have any metal fillings in your teeth? If so, how many?
45. Do you suffer from mood swings'?

When I first looked at this page of the questionnaire, I was intrigued at how many or how few of these symptoms the patient in front of me suffered from. In principle, the more 'yes' answers, the greater the patient's problems, but sometimes they are not considered important in the overall picture, so are not admitted. For example, you may not acknowledge any particular bowel problems (questions 29-33 inclusive), yet your list of supplements at the top of page 2 may include regular intake of antacids. You might say, when asked, that the antacids keep any bowel symptoms under control. However, the real answer to the question of bowel symptoms is that you do have them, but that the antacids control them. By comparing two separate parts of the questionnaire, I obtain a more complete picture.

Headaches
Headaches are extremely common. Migraines, in particular, can be caused by food intolerances, and, if you suffer from them, I can easily justify a change in the your diet, as any food that causes any symptom may also be more subtly involved in your cancer. At the local Cancer Self Help Group I helped set up well over 25 years ago, I recommended to a man with multiple myeloma that he change his diet in a particular way. That diet totally resolved the migraines he had suffered from for years.

Fatigue

Fatigue is a very common complaint of anyone who is unwell in any way, not only in cancer patients. It is also one of the best indicators that the approach you are following is working or not. If my advice has been correct, your levels of energy are almost always one of the first things to improve. If they don't, I suspect I have yet to put my finger on what is of greater importance for you.

When I was a medical student, I spent some of my time learning at the 'Fatigue Clinic'. It was truly fascinating at the diagnoses that were eventually made in a wide range of people. What I really learned, however, was that fatigue could be a symptom of virtually anything. I have learned a lot more since then, and am aware that I could now teach at that clinic many things that were not even thought of at the time. What is surprising, however, is that some patients who have been given only a few months to live by their hospital doctors, because of the nature of their cancer, do not complain of fatigue at all.

In mainstream medicine, fatigue can be caused by anaemia and/or low thyroid activity, but, when these are not found to be the explanation, because all tests are said to be 'normal', the symptom may be put down to stress. It is seldom considered that some prescribed drug might be the cause. In my experience, however, 'normal' blood tests often miss the point, basically because the important tests have not been done. A measurement of haemoglobin may be perfectly acceptable even to me, indicating no anaemia, but iron stores, as measured by serum ferritin, can show a different picture. Even then, doctors often accept a level of serum ferritin that I do not accept. Fortunately a paper was published in the British Medical Journal (Verdon, F. et al. Iron supplementation for unexplained fatigue in non-anaemic women: double blind randomised placebo-controlled trial. BMJ, Volume 326, 24 May 2003, page 1124) that totally agreed with what I have been saying for years, that is that a level under 50mcg/l is not good enough. Iron supplementation helped improve the fatigue.

It is possible to enumerate all the symptoms that a deficiency of a particular vitamin or mineral might produce, but you will never find all of those features occurring in one person. This certainly applies to iron. Unfortunately most doctors believe that there is no shortage of iron if the haemoglobin is 'normal'. What they have forgotten (or may never have known in the first place), is that iron is not only required to make haemoglobin, but is also required for myoglobin (muscle globin), the immune system, normal hair follicle functioning, and a host of other minor metabolic functions.

The Thyroid

When it comes to the thyroid, most NHS laboratories will only test TSH (Thyroid Stimulating Hormone produced in the brain), assuming that, if the level is within the laboratory's reference range, there is no need to do any more testing. If everything is functioning normally, there is a nice balance between TSH and the production of hormones by the thyroid gland itself. It is rather like the thermostat in your water heater at home. If the water is hot, the thermostat turns off. If the temperature of the water falls, the water heater is turned on by the thermostat. The TSH/thyroid system is similar in this way, there being a constant feedback mechanism between the two.

One problem that this system produces is that laboratories establish their own reference ranges, assuming that the method of analysis they use is comparable to that used in other laboratories. Separate from that, there is a degree of controversy about the ideal level of TSH, and in the opinion of many doctors, most laboratories set it too high. Recently one of the American medical organisations very much involved in thyroid health dropped its upper level of TSH, and I am told this meant that overnight about two million Americans were suddenly accepted as hypothyroid, whereas the day before they were considered as hypochondriacs or merely fussing about nothing.

This, however, all to often totally misses the point as far as I am concerned. It is assumed that the thyroid gland is responding to the TSH, but, in my experience, this is often not the case. In principle, if the thyroid gland is not responding normally, the level of TSH will go up very high to try to force the thyroid to respond, which presumably it cannot do. In addition, when I have done three 'thyroid function tests' I have often found the TSH and Free T4 to be comfortably within an acceptable reference range, but the Free T4 is not being converted into FreeT3, which is probably the active component. So a 'normal' TSH is missing a low FreeT3, which means the patient is effectively hypothyroid.

There is another fact that needs to be considered, which no amount of blood testing can reveal, which can certainly occur with perfectly respectable levels of TSH, FreeT4 and FreeT3 that is cellular receptors. For circulating hormones to work, they have to attach themselves to receptors on the surface of cells. In fact, all cells have countless receptors for countless chemicals, each receptor being totally specific for a certain hormone or other chemical. The 'sensitivity' of these receptors can be increased, decreased, blocked, damaged, deleted or interfered with in all sorts of ways by all sorts of situations, rendering the information purely from standard blood tests to be of little value.

What I'm really saying is that if full blood tests for thyroid function are reported as being ok, it does not necessarily mean that you will not benefit from thyroid support. Indeed, every patient who follows the Gerson Therapy is put onto whole thyroid extract, (which contains the 52 or so hormones your thyroid gland normally produces), on the assumption that you will benefit from it. If nature produces so many different chemicals, I presume there is a purpose to them all, even if we don't yet understand their importance. In addition, I also prefer the whole thyroid extract as I feel it 'feeds' the gland, because, in the end, I will want to get you off it, something that can be difficult to achieve if you are put onto the usual thyroxine that your doctor prescribes if you are found to be genuinely hypothyroid. Again, what I am also trying to say is that nearly all cancer patients, certainly those who complain of a degree of fatigue, are likely to benefit from thyroid support, as the nature of their cancer and any treatment they may have had may have suppressed the thyroid system or blocked or damaged the receptors. This in turn means that they are metabolically underactive, which in turn means that their body's ability to fight the cancer is less efficient than it should be. It is amazing how often I saw a cancer patient for the first time, who had very little energy to fight or follow my recommendations, who became a totally different person with a totally different attitude to their cancer, simply for a small supporting dose of whole thyroid. To me it was important to repeat that I gave patients a supporting thyroid dose.

Applying my 'commonsense' rule, it always amazes me that the activity of the thyroid gland is seldom checked if a patient feels tired after having had radiotherapy applied to his neck because of cancer of his oesophagus (gullet). To me it is obvious and inevitable that the thyroid gland will be damaged by the treatment. It is impossible for it not to be; yet it is seldom considered.

Occasionally when a person is put on whole thyroid, they don't respond very well, or may even feel a little worse. This could be because they don't actually need the supplement, or possibly they are reacting to something in the tablet, such as the lactose filler. However, the most likely reason is because they have an adrenal insufficiency, and, merely supporting the thyroid system, reveals the adrenal problem.

In my experience, when one hormonal system is adversely affected, all hormonal systems are likely to be affected to a degree. After all, many cancers are hormonally driven, usually by a dominance of oestrogen. So, all the hormonal systems need to be considered. When I support the thyroid, I nowadays always support the adrenals. If the cancer is hormonally influenced, I will certainly consider what is the most appropriate approach.

Other Causes Of Fatigue

Low blood sugar can cause fatigue, but that is not difficult to identify, usually because the patient feels less tired after eating. Fatigue generally improves if I am able to identify the correct diet for a patient to follow. Caffeine withdrawal can cause fatigue, so, if a person agrees to stop caffeine all together, I always advise them that they are likely to feel possibly more tired for a few days to begin with, after which they should bounce back up and feel a lot better than they have felt for a long time.

If your adrenal glands have become exhausted by prolonged stress, fatigue can result. Most people are aware of this, and need a period of recuperation after a significantly stressful period. Inflammation and pain can also cause fatigue. Patients suffering from rheumatoid arthritis very commonly complain of fatigue, but they are also often anaemic. The inflammation seems to cause anaemia.

Poor Sleeping Pattern

Not getting a good night's sleep can leave you tired the next day, as mums with young babies are all too well aware. A lot of cancer patients are in pain, so sleeping is very difficult, which is why they are often given something to help them sleep. This is very understandable from their doctor's point of view, but the drugs need to be metabolised by the liver, which may already be under great stress.

Pain and caffeine can switch off your production of melatonin, a chemical that is produced by the pineal gland in your brain. Some doctors prescribe large doses of melatonin to cancer patients, as a good night's sleep induced by melatonin is detoxifying.

But don't forget geopathic stress. When a new patient tells me they don't sleep very well, one possible explanation is geopathic stress. If that is found to be present and is dealt with, it is amazing how much better some people sleep.

Do you remember your dreams? If you don't, or your dream recall is rather poor, you may well have a vitamin B6 deficiency, although some sleeping tablets may produce a false response to this question. I can remember dreams I had a few days ago, and can certainly recall the previous night's dream throughout the next day. Some doctors put their patients on increasing doses of vitamin B6 until their dream recall returns.

Thirst

Thirst is usually a sign of dehydration, but not always. Some people drink a lot of water, yet seem to be permanently thirsty. Certainly too much caffeine as tea, coffee, chocolate and cola drinks, as well as diuretics prescribed by your doctor, can cause dehydration. Every cup of coffee you drink will cause you to eliminate a cup and a bit of fluid. You drink the coffee because you feel thirsty, which it may well help to begin with because of the liquid. But, in the end, you lose more than you gain. I always asked cancer patients to give up all forms of caffeine, as it 'promotes' cancer. At the Brigham Young University in America they have studied the effect of caffeine on the death or survival of cancer cells through the mechanism of apoptosis, or preprogrammed cellular death. Their studies have shown that, while caffeine may not directly cause cancer, it may interfere with the process of apoptosis, thereby interfering with the death of cancer cells.

While I encouraged all cancer patients to make their fluid intake to be from water as much as possible, perhaps around two litres per day, certain herbal teas can be very valuable in cancer, some of which may improve the functioning of the liver or kidneys. Incidentally, I am not happy that you drink water direct from the tap. Water Authorities do a remarkably good job to make tap water suitable for drinking, when most water use is for other purposes such as watering your garden and plants and washing your clothes or car. I would prefer you to at least remove the chlorine, using some sort of water filter, or perhaps reverse osmosis, which is about the only way I know of totally removing fluoride and a host of undesirable chemicals, such as pesticides, hormones and lead, for example. However, it removes the valuable minerals as well.

In the meantime, while it is important to limit your intake of sodium salt, in favour of potassium, make sure you don't let your salt intake fall too low, especially if you sweat a lot for any reason, i.e. if you live in a hot and humid country. Not having enough salt in your body can make you feel tired and lethargic. Your body's salt content is approximately half way between rainwater and seawater, so you need a certain amount of salt, but not too much. As I have already said, some people's problems, especially fatigue, are caused by adrenal exhaustion. Complete destruction of the adrenal glands was more common in the past when they were infected by tuberculosis, leading to a condition called Addison's Disease. The effect was an inability to retain salt in the body because of the lack of a certain adrenal hormone called aldosterone, although all of the adrenal steroids have some salt-retaining function. Anyone who is put onto modern steroids by their doctor because of asthma, rheumatoid arthritis or a brain tumour, knows only too well how they retain salt in many parts of their body, so showing the powerful effect adrenal steroids have on the control of salt balance in the body.

Catarrh

A history of catarrh is classical of a milk intolerance. On page 4 of my Patient Questionnaire, questions 35, 36 and 37, if a significant part of a patient's history, are also a strong indication of a milk intolerance. I know tonsils and adenoids were taken out far more often in the past than they are nowadays, but antibiotics have changed that to a considerable extent. Nevertheless, I think it is unlikely that young patients were operated on for no reason at all. If you have such a history, therefore, I consider it likely you have had a milk intolerance all your life. Your body may have tolerated it to a degree, but adding that to all the other things that your history is identifying, perhaps you can see why eventually your body gave up the unequal fight.

Milk and dairy products are clearly inflammatory as they cause untold inflammation in the throats of ears of young children, who are then given antibiotics much of the time, so their chances of developing another inflammatory problem of a fungus rises considerably. I keep arguing that we are looking for anything that causes inflammation, which is why I try and get cancer patients off animal milks and animal milk products.

General Aches

Aching in muscles and joints is usually caused by a food intolerance, classical rheumatoid arthritis often responding to avoiding foods of the deadly nightshade family, namely potatoes, tomatoes, aubergines (eggplants in USA) and peppers, as well as tobacco. But caffeine and animal milks and animal milk products can also be implicated. Then there can be the odd idiosyncratic reaction to a food or drink you could never suspect, nor could you ever identify it by direct observation of what you eat. It requires either a blood test to suggest the culprit or a process of elimination and challenge, as described in my book 'Conquering Cystitis'.♥   Lower backache, however, is often a sign of a magnesium deficiency. Anything that goes into spasm could be caused by a magnesium deficiency. Calcium is required for muscles to contract, magnesium for them to relax, so there may be an imbalance between the two. A magnesium deficiency can cause other parts of the body to go into spasm, so could be the cause, or one of the causes of, asthma, constipation, cold hands and feet (Raynaud's Syndrome) and migraines.

An imbalance between calcium and magnesium may be caused by consuming too many milk products. I know there are many people who do not agree with me, even if there are many who do. This is one of a number of controversial subjects that I and other like-minded colleagues have discussed over the years from our own and our patients' observations. I recognise that they are controversial issues at present, and therefore I want to make it clear that they are my opinions, but I am perfectly happy for you to disagree with me if you want to. I merely want to open your eyes to a possible alternative explanation for a whole number of things, for you to chose whether to accept them or not.

Sensory Symptoms

I have seen over nine thousand patients suffering from multiple sclerosis, and I am aware that many of them complain of pins and needles and other sensory symptoms in various parts of their body. In my experience, such sensory symptoms can indicate a vitamin B12 deficiency or be an unusual presentation of the chicken pox/shingles virus. Cancer patients don't often complain of sensory symptoms, although I am now of the opinion that the shingles virus somehow plays a part in cancer of the breast in many women, since so many have told me that they were either in contact with someone with shingles, or they themselves had chicken pox or shingles shortly before they first found a breast lump. Cold fingers and toes can sometimes feel like pins and needles and can be a sign of a magnesium deficiency.

Pins and needles or numbness in fingers or toes is often the result of a course of chemotherapy. Usually you are told that it will eventually go away, but it can take a very long time. In my opinion, it is likely to be caused by an effective deficiency of vitamin B12. I say 'effective', because I haven't yet tested vitamin B12 blood levels in cancer patients suffering from pins and needles. Such symptoms are described by doctors as 'peripheral neuropathy', one known cause of which is a deficiency of vitamin B12, and/or folic acid. I found these symptoms cleared rapidly and effectively if I gave the patient decent doses of vitamin B12 intravenously, along with other nutrients.

Palpitations

The heart is particularly sensitive to the effects of caffeine, especially in the presence of a magnesium, vitamin E and/or a Co-Enzyme Q 10 deficiency, so any abnormal heartbeat could be explained in this way. Some dentists believe that mercury from mercury amalgam fillings can cause palpitations and other heart irregularities and abnormalities.

Abdominal Symptoms/Constipation

I could spend hours discussing the significance of abnormal bowel functioning. Many patients tell me they open their bowels once every two weeks! I have heard of even more extreme cases than that. In my opinion, and that of most naturopaths, we should open our bowels at least three times per day, i.e. one meal in and one meal out, provided there is enough fibre overall in the diet, which does not contain items that specifically cause constipation. In my experience, animal milks and milk products are a very common cause of constipation, goat's and sheep's milk sometimes being ok. Patients often have clues from their own experience what causes them to become constipated, but don't take them very seriously.

Naturopaths often say there is no point in doing anything until the bowels are working properly. In many ways I would agree. If you have had stubborn bowels for many years, you probably have a layer of impacted matter/faeces lining your intestines. This matter can harbour toxic chemicals, parasites and heavy metals. It can also prevent nutrients from gaining access to the body via the bowel wall, as well as inflame the bowel wall itself. Sometimes, when someone has a colonic irrigation, the equivalent of a bicycle 'inner tube' is eventually expelled, with all the bowel indentations visible. Can you imagine what that has done over the years?

This questionnaire that patients filled in before they first saw me nearly always indicates some problem or other with their bowels, the most common being constipation. However, many people don't even realise they are constipated, since they have only opened their bowels two or three times a week for as long as they can remember. Even those who open their bowels once a day don't realise that that is not often enough. Can you remember what a baby does? Food going in at the top end leads to an almost immediate reaction at the other end! Unfortunately humans gradually lose this response mechanism over the years of not eating and drinking properly.

Hundreds of people have told me how much easier it has become to open their bowels when they give up such foods as milk and milk products. For some people it can be quite difficult, as foods like cheese have become virtually staple foods, and they can't imagine life without them. Be warned that I am likely to recommend some form of change in your diet when we get round to what I suggest you do to start helping yourself.

The importance of correctly functioning bowels cannot be overstated. There is a mass of scientific evidence that an unhealthy bowel can lead to an amazing variety of health problems. I am sure you have heard it said that "You are what you eat". However, I believe that that statement needs to be modified to "You are the result of what you absorb from what you eat". In terms of your Biological Terrain, this statement could possibly be modified to "You are what you fail to excrete from what you eat". Whichever is true, if you have an unhealthy bowel, you probably have the 'leaky gut syndrome'. You will absorb poorly some of the things that are good for you, and you will absorb other things that your body would prefer not to have to deal with.

As a result of a lifetime of eating the wrong things, which will vary from person to person, it is likely that most people will have developed a layer of impacted faeces in their bowels. This unwanted matter will not only partially block the absorptive layer of the mucous membrane (and damage it at the same time leading to the 'leaky gut syndrome'), but will also harbour parasites and other organisms, unwanted faecal material and a whole host of chemical residues that the body (in particular the liver) thought it had already eliminated. Some of these unwanted substances could sometimes be reabsorbed, so increasing the body's toxic load.

A Story
Many years ago, a patient told me that, before he had first come to see me, he had had a series of colonic irrigations. After the fifth, he passed a pebble that he remembered swallowing about thirty years earlier, when he was a child! Apart from his total amazement at his bowel's ability to hold onto such a thing for so long, it brought back memories of a childhood interest in pebbles, as their variety, colours and different shapes had always fascinated him. If they were dirty, he used to pop them in his mouth to clean them!

Diarrhoea & Bloating
If you suffer from loose stools, it is likely something is irritating your bowels. While this could be a parasite, it is more likely to be a food intolerance. A gluten sensitivity is high on the list of suspects, which means wheat, rye, oats and barley. However, if you have consumed a lot of sugar and white refined flour products over a lifetime, or had a certain amount (sometimes only one strong course) of antibiotics, you might be suffering from a fungal overgrowth within your bowel. While the thrush organism (candida albicans) may be primarily involved, with or without overt symptoms of thrush itself, there are many other fungal organisms that can cause these symptoms.

This whole process can be made worse by courses of steroids (including inhaled ones for asthma) and the contraceptive pill and HRT. Chemotherapy (and possibly radiotherapy) can destroy the friendly organisms within the bowel, allowing 'funguses' to proliferate. This scenario is so common, is there any wonder that the fungal theory of cancer is worth considering? I'm sure it is. This situation is all the more likely if you have other fungal infections anywhere in your body, such as toe nails, athletes' foot, in your groin, between your buttocks or under your breasts, or you have been plagued by thrush, which is the bane of Gynaecologists' lives. Even dandruff can respond to an anti-fungal preparation called Nizoral shampoo, and sometimes psoriasis has a fungal origin. With a history such as this, I was likely to describe you as 'mouldy!'

Dry Skin
Dry skin often improves when patients cut out animal milks and products, but it can also indicate a zinc deficiency (which is important for your immune system, amongst other things) and a deficiency of essential fatty acids, and thyroid deficiency.

Sore Mouth
There is a myriad of symptoms around the mouth that can tell a story. Sore tongue might be simply because of sharp teeth, but can be caused by inflammation from mercury amalgams in your teeth. The herpes virus may be involved, there may

be a deficiency of iron or B vitamins, thrush at the corners of the mouth or a food intolerance, such as a gluten sensitivity. A metallic taste is likely to be caused by metal fillings in your teeth, but can also be a sign of the wrong environment within the bowels, especially if there is halitosis bad breath.

Mercury Amalgam Fillings/Dental Care

This is a controversial issue at present, simply because the majority of dentists and doctors haven't studied the evidence. It must be very hard to admit that how you have been treating patients all your life, i.e. filling their teeth with mercury amalgams, has, in fact, been wrong all along. Nevertheless, many dental colleagues all over the world have done just that. I used to prescribe pharmaceutical drugs when I was first qualified, as I had learned all about their value, tending to assume there was no other way, and that I would deal with any adverse effects when they occurred. I changed my mind and my practice many years ago, although I recognise that drugs have their place and value.

In terms of cancer, my experience is that mercury, which is possibly the most toxic substance known to man after radioactive materials (and about one hundred times more toxic than lead, which no one considers safe), suppresses your immune system. It also seems to make funguses more virulent. It is very difficult to prove this point unequivocally to you as an individual. However, I want all my cancer patients to have their mercury amalgam fillings replaced with a non-metallic alternative material, the work being done by a biologically trained dentist. I then need to chelate mercury from your tissues over a period of weeks or months. If you want to learn more about this, many books have been written on the subject, some being much more forthright than others. The one I like is 'Menace In The Mouth' by the late Dr. Jack Levenson.♥

In the middle of the 20th Century, Dr. Weston Price, an American dentist, travelled the world comparing the state of peoples' teeth in relation to the diet they ate. He made some amazing observations and wrote it all up in a book entitled 'Nutrition and Physical Degeneration', a weighty tome. In some respects the title is the wrong way round, because it seems to suggest that good nutrition leads to physical degeneration, which is exactly the opposite of what he found.

Dr. Price also made some most important additional observations, which were nearly lost to mankind, but which have been bravely resurrected by a colleague. I say bravely because he was a completely orthodox dentist who felt compelled to alert the world to the truth of Dr. Price's observations, especially as they made a mockery of all he had taught and practised for most of his life. What Dr. Price discovered was that root fillings always become infected, because it is impossible to do one in a totally sterile way. He also extracted root filled teeth from ill patients and inserted the tooth under the skin of an unfortunate experimental animal. The result was that the human patient's condition improved, while the poor animal gradually became sick, developing all the problems the human used to have!

Over the years, various open-minded dentists have explained to me that certain teeth are on acupuncture meridians relative to certain organs of the body. Dentists I have referred patients to have found, on a number of occasions, bad teeth, infected cavities or root fillings on acupuncture meridians related to the organ that has cancer in it. Presumably, as acupuncture treatment somehow works through subtle energies, the bad energies from the dental point of view add to the total load causing the cancer.

You can see, therefore, why it is important to find a dentist specially trained in such matters.

Mood Swings

This question is mainly in relation to women's pre-menstrual phase, but sometimes indicates how unwell the patient is. It sometimes opens up a new area for discussion, but otherwise does not necessarily signify anything in particular. When the patient starts to feel better, possibly because of a change in diet, mood swings often settle down.

Page 4 of Patient Questionnaire
46. Do you travel badly?
47. Does your weight fluctuate?
48. Have you suffered from tonsillitis or sore throats in the past?
49. Have you had your tonsils and adenoids out?
50. Have you suffered from earache, especially as a child?
51. Have you had glandular fever?
52. Have you had any operations?
53. Have you had any illnesses?
54. Have you been into hospital for any reason'
55. Do you smoke? If so, how many?
56. Does anyone living with you smoke?
57. Do you have any animals at home?
58. Do you have any classical allergies such as asthma, hay fever, drug allergies such as penicillin, or Elastoplast etc?
59. Do you react adversely to environmental pollutants such as perfume, paint, petrol, car and diesel fumes, gas, etc?

For Women Only
60. Do you have a vaginal discharge?
61. How old were you when your periods began?
62. Have you had any problems with your periods?
63. Do you or did you suffer from premenstrual symptoms of any sort?
64. Have you been through the change of life? If so, did you have any problems?
65. Have you taken the contraceptive pill? If so, for how long? Did the pill upset you in any way, or make you ill?
66. Do you now have or have you ever had a coil?
67. Have you had any miscarriages? If so, how many?
68. Do you have any children? If so, how many?
69. Did you have any difficulties conceiving any of your children?
70. Did you have any problems during your pregnancies?
71. Did you have any complications with any of the births?
72. Did you fail to breast feed, or have any problems with breast-feeding?
73. Did you suffer from postnatal depression?

For Everyone
74. Are there any problems not covered by this questionnaire? If yes, please explain.

The question about travelling badly may not be specific to cancer patients. It is more designed to identify a possible chemical allergy, i.e. car and/or diesel fumes can sometimes make a person feel unwell.

Weight Fluctuations

Many people, whatever their diagnosis, say their weight can fluctuate quite considerably. This is quite common in the pre-menstrual phase, when some women can put on 7 or 8lb (around 3.5kg) in a matter of days, losing it all as soon as the period commences. Other people are aware that their weight can change all too easily, but they don't really know why. In my experience such an observation is most likely to be caused by one or more food intolerances, so that a change in the person's diet can eliminate it. Men, by and large, however, tend to put weight on slowly as they grow older, and tend not to vary much over a short time, like many women can.

Weight fluctuations can involve both weight gain and weight loss. If weight gain is your problem, you are probably retaining fluid as your reaction to specific foods, which need to be identified and eliminated. What I have found over the years is that that fluid can be retained in virtually any organ of the body, thereby producing virtually any symptom you can think of. If it is retained in the brain, it can cause mood swings, depression or headaches. It can cause constipation if retained in the bowel wall, arthritis if in the joints, asthma if in the lungs, etc. Unfortunately there is no one method of identifying these food reactions that is perfect for everyone.

Weight loss, or an inability to put on weight when eating a reasonable diet, usually suggests to me some form of malabsorption syndrome. The foods most likely involved are the gluten grains, namely wheat, rye, oats and barley. Only by avoiding such foods for at least four weeks will you discover whether they are the culprits or not. Many cancer patients, especially if their condition is severe, suffer from a condition called cachexia, when they lose muscle weight and their body clearly shows the effects of the weight loss.

Tonsillitis

One of the commonest childhood conditions that I came across was many episodes of tonsillitis, with or without ear problems. Some children suffer very badly from the whole range of problems, have grommets put in their ears and are plied with antibiotics, while others seem to get away with only minor, but annoying, periodic episodes that keep them off school for a few days. How they were treated usually depended upon the attitude of their parents and their general practitioner. What such a history suggests to me is, once again, a milk intolerance.

Many years ago I was invited to be in the audience of a television programme discussing the work of Dr. Harry Morrow-Brown, the Derby Consultant Physician who started up the Midlands Asthma and Allergy Research Association. There were many general practitioners in the audience and every one of them agreed that, if a child failed to thrive in any way, the first thing to do was take it off animal milks and animal milk products, especially from the cow. Sometimes goats' or sheep's products were subsequently found to be acceptable, but often not. We all agreed that the child was likely to do well from then on, and we had all observed it on many occasions. If you have such a history, what I am really saying is that you have probably had a milk intolerance all your life. Can you imagine what that may have done to your body all these years, and what it may still be doing? Of course, if you have breast or prostate cancer, it will be particularly important to avoid milk and its products. This has been thoroughly researched in the excellent book by Professor Jane Plant in her book

'Your Life In Your Hands'.♥ She explains all about the myriad chemicals and hormones that are present in these products. While organic produce may be better in this respect, I do not recommend them, especially in the first instance.

Childhood Illnesses

Having clarified the various 'other symptoms' (which, later on, may be the first signs that the approach you have decided to follow is actually working), I may go back in time and look at your history in childhood. Which childhood illnesses did you have? Chicken pox, mumps, measles, whooping cough, German measles? You might ask why these could be important, so let me describe.

I think it is generally accepted that, if you suffered from chicken pox as a child, this virus can come out as shingles later on in life, usually when some sort of stress occurs. However, most doctors have what I would call a narrow attitude to shingles, i.e. only accept that a person is suffering from shingles if there is a painful rash that follows the line of a nerve distribution, like over the eye or across a shoulder. In addition the rash should not cross the midline.

My attitude is to consider the possibility that the shingles virus may be presenting in an unusual way. If it is not 'typical' it is not considered to be relevant by most doctors. When I gave a talk about my work to a large group of cancer patients and their companions in London a number of years ago I made the statement that, in my opinion, the shingles virus was somehow involved in patients with breast cancer. During the break I was surrounded by women who asked how I had come to that conclusion. So I asked them what their experience had been, only to be told by just about all of them that they had had either shingles or chicken pox shortly before the first signs of their breast cancer appeared. So I told them that, as so many women with breast cancer I had seen had told me of their experiences (because I had asked them about it), that that was how I had reached such a conclusion. I considered it possible that the virus may somehow have adversely affected the local immunity of their breast tissue.

Once the idea has occurred to me, I consider whether it might be relevant to every cancer patient I see. Just because I don't pick up, in the history, any specific evidence of a viral or other infective involvement, it doesn't mean one isn't relevant. After all, sometimes when a patient with multiple sclerosis has an acute attack of symptoms, he or she is admitted to hospital, where a urinary tract infection is found to have been the cause, yet there were no symptoms of that infection at all. When the patient is given the appropriate antibiotics, the symptoms usually clear.

In my attempts to identify causes of cancer in anyone, I need to consider the unusual or the unexpected. Since it is now accepted that the Human Papilloma Virus is the cause of cancer of the cervix in many women with the condition (and probably all of them if the proof could be obtained) and they probably had had a wart or verruca somewhere on their skin at some time in their life, I see no reason why that virus might not 'surface' later on in life and cause any cancer. Indeed one of my colleagues who studies this sort of thing very carefully is convinced that either the chickenpox/shingles virus or the wart/papilloma virus are very much involved in every patient with cancer, as are other infective agents.

To be fair to my mainstream medical colleagues we haven't proved this connection, but since we can treat any of these 'infections' homoeopathically and with a simple preparation, it is not a problem for us. If the treatment is not needed, it won't matter anyway, or do any harm.

So, taking this whole thinking process forward logically to every patient, if a person has or has had testicular cancer, I am interested in their history of mumps. Is it not reasonable to consider that the mumps virus may be involved in their condition, in a way similar to the chicken pox/shingles story? I think it is worth considering, and, again, the treatment is by homoeopathy and a simple preparation. If you now have lung cancer, did you have whooping cough or possibly tuberculosis, so that your lungs have been 'weakened' and have therefore become a 'target' for something to go wrong?

Are you beginning to see my way of thinking? Did you have warts or verrucas at any time in your life? Even mainstream medicine accepts that the virus involved, the human papilloma virus or HPV, is a cause of cancer of the cervix, so why might it not be coming out now? Also I see no reason why it should be confined to the cervix. Could it not also affect other parts of the reproductive tract, such as the uterus or ovaries, if they have somehow been weakened and become a 'target'?

In terms of 'infections', did you have glandular fever? Many people tell me they have 'not been the same' since that illness affected them. Some of my patients had it twice, sometimes taking six months or more to get back to somewhere near normal. Glandular fever seems to strip people of B vitamins, and, if a person catches it, B vitamins given at the time may well hasten their recovery and stop it being too severe. In any case, glandular fever seems to compromise the functioning of the liver. I will always give such a person a liver tonic at some stage to boost its workings, but, unfortunately, the usual liver function blood tests that your doctor can do rarely show up any abnormality. Far more sophisticated tests need to be done. Glandular fever can also be treated homoeopathically.

Other Infections

I am convinced that all lymph and blood cancers have some sort of viral cause, and probably all cancers if the truth were known. There are various tests that can be done to support such an idea, one of which is Non-Genomic RNA/DNA by Neuro-Lab.♥ The problem is that, although this test can identify a high burden of viral material in your body, it is totally non-specific in that it doesn't identify the name of the organism, so that it is not possible to select a specific treatment.

Various laboratories do a series of screening tests for different organisms, but, as there are so very many possible pathological organisms that could be making you ill, the very one that is causing your problems may not be included in the testing panel, unless you are going to pay for a complete range. Even then, just because an organism is identified in your blood, it doesn't automatically mean it is the one causing your illness.

Anyway, have you ever suffered from any other infections, such as gastroenteritis, infections picked up in other parts of the world, malaria, etc? Might you have parasites or worms in your bowels? You worm your pets once a year (and you touch and stroke them all the time), but you tend not to worm yourself at all! Yet such organisms can affect your bowels' ability to absorb nutrients.

Attending to such infections is not usually the first thing I consider, but I take a note of them when I first take the person's medical history, coming back to them usually at a later stage. However, when I start asking questions from childhood onwards, this is something that is not too difficult for people to remember, and they find quite easy to discuss. It then takes me on to other things. While I am asking about childhood illnesses, it seems logical to ask about any other 'infections' at the same time. I can then go back and ask more questions.

Operations

How many operations have you had? What were they for? How many general anaesthetics have you had? How well did you recover from any of them? Did you take a long time to recover from any of them, and are you taking longer to recover each time? The answers to all these questions tell me about your liver's ability to detoxify the chemicals of the anaesthetics.

Information from any operations you may have had done can be really quite revealing, and can identify something that you had forgotten about, or didn't think could be of interest to me. I have already talked about the significance of having your tonsils and/or adenoids out, but many people think that that used to be such a routine operation that they don't consider it worth mentioning, until I explain my approach to it and what it can signify. It's all about making connections with the information each patient provides. It really is medical detective work.

Having a hysterectomy for fibroids (did you know that the word hysterectomy basically means 'removal of the centre of female hysteria?) suggests oestrogen dominance to me, in relation to progesterone. Did you have your ovaries removed at the same time ("to avoid having to go back in again and to eliminate the risk of your developing cancer in your ovaries")? How old were you at the time? Were you put onto HRT? What form was it? Was it oestrogen only, as was likely since you could no longer have periods? What effect did it have upon you? If you didn't go onto HRT, did you suffer any sort of menopausal symptoms? How did you feel after that operation? Did things seem to go wrong for you from then onwards?

I've never found anything significant about having your appendix removed, although a classical case is clearly an indication of something. When I was a junior doctor we sometimes operated on obvious cases, and sometimes we did not, usually because we were so very tired. We would naturally keep an eye on the patient and be prepared to operate if things became urgent, but often, even though the diagnosis was not in any doubt, we would wait until the morning, only to find that the patient had recovered. I suppose keyhole surgery and having a peep inside through a laparoscope has changed things considerably.

Smoking

Clearly, if you smoke, you are significantly reducing your chances of overcoming your cancer. The toxic chemicals produce free radicals in abundance, which not only damage any tissue in your body, but also squander your meagre nutrients, especially anti-oxidants such as vitamin C.

Interestingly enough, when I ask patients what happens when they smoke a cigarette, they sometimes admit it actually makes them feel unwell in some way. I have an MS patient who recently told me that, having walked to the local pub fairly easily, she found that she couldn't walk home so well if she had a couple of cigarettes while there. From a dietary point of view, that made me suggest that she avoid certain foods that are in the same biological classification with tobacco, namely potatoes, tomatoes, aubergines (eggplant in USA) and peppers.

I have to say I am always amazed when a new cancer patient says he or she is still smoking. In this day and age, everyone knows that is not sensible, yet I acknowledge that, for some people, giving up cigarettes can be harder than giving up crack cocaine. My book 'Stop Smoking' might help you to give up smoking.♥

The rest of the questions in that section tend to be for people who are 'sensitive' or allergic to various features in their environment, but a history of asthma, for example, suggests a milk intolerance to me. What I have found over the years is that classical allergies to things like pollens and animal dander can significantly lessen, or even disappear, if I manage to identify the correct diet. That whole section can provide a lot of ideas for me to work on, and often we digress into other areas of the person's history.

Questions For Women Only

As you will already have realised, this whole series of questions produces some very interesting answers, much of which I have already alluded to. A vaginal discharge, if it is abnormal in any way, may be caused by candida/ thrush or other organisms. Painful periods and pre-menstrual symptoms of any sort indicate to me a dominance of oestrogen relative to progesterone, which I have discussed in great detail already.

How long a woman was on the contraceptive pill for and how she felt on it, are all part of the story. In many women, the pill predisposes her to thrush, plus the long-term risks of cancer that are now being reported, separate from the nutritional deficiencies it causes. What is interesting here is that the studies tend only to look at the effects of the pill in the long run of those women who stayed on it for a fairly long time. In some studies that may have started with, say, one thousand women, as many as half or more may have dropped out because of adverse effects. So many women found they couldn't tolerate the pill that they stopped taking it after only a short time. The studies then reported on only those who stayed the course without any significant adverse symptoms. I wonder what the outcome would have been if all the original women had put up with the side effects for a long time, simply so as not to become pregnant.

Incidentally, I suggested elsewhere that side effects from drugs are often the result of the nutritional deficiencies they cause. The contraceptive pill, and presumably HRT, both of which are not natural substances so should be classified as 'drugs', cause a deficiency of vitamins C, B6 and B12, and zinc and magnesium. So supplementation of these nutrients needs to be considered seriously.

If it hasn't already been discussed, the use of HRT is likely to be considered at this stage. In most female hormonally involved cancers, that is nearly always mentioned early on. Most women I see have already read about the risks they put themselves through, although they didn't know it at the time. Fortunately there is plenty we can do if that is the case. It is not all doom and gloom, but merely part of the person's history and very much part of the cause of their cancer.

Hormones

Because of the importance of hormones in many cancer patients, it is worth considering certain aspects at this stage. There is no doubt that many cancers seem to have a hormonal involvement. Certainly that is likely to be the case in women with breast, ovarian, uterine and cervical cancers, and, of course, in men with prostate cancer. There is increasing evidence that the contraceptive pill and HRT increase a woman's chances of developing cancer of some sort, and, in my opinion and that of many like-minded doctors, too much oestrogen, or oestrogen dominance, predisposes women to cancer, and is probably a significant cause in prostate cancer.

If the contraceptive pill and HRT were made from natural hormones, things might be quite different. Unfortunately, however, the chemicals in them are not exactly the same as a woman produces herself. It is certainly true that some women show evidence of hormonal deficiencies, and supplements may be of value sometimes, but there is a risk in taking unnatural hormones. In addition, too much oestrogen is often a major cause of the hormonal cancers. When a woman takes combined preparations (i.e. an oestrogen with a progestogen), it may only be the latter that she needs. These combined preparations contain what sounds like oestrogen, but is often oestradiol valerate, and it is the valerate that makes it no longer the same chemical that women produce naturally. The progesterone-like chemical in combined preparations is quite a different chemical from progesterone itself. Pharmaceutical Companies describe their preparations as an oestrogen/ progestogen (progestin in USA) preparation. While they are suggesting that the oestrogen is oestrogen, they do at least acknowledge that there is a chemical difference between their progestogen and natural progesterone.

Progestogens may be particularly harmful in the long run, especially as they may eventually become oestrogenic, so adding to oestrogen dominance. Unfortunately natural progesterone is very poorly absorbed from the intestines, so a considerable degree of chemical modification has had to be carried out to produce a form that can be absorbed when it is swallowed. This form may be what the body has difficulty dealing with, as it has never come across it before.

The contraceptive pill is nearly always prescribed for contraceptive purposes, although it is occasionally given for control of irregular periods, or for acne. In terms of contraception, I understand its convenience if it is taken properly (although antibiotics, infections and travelling can make it unreliable). Under normal circumstances, a woman can only become pregnant two or three days out of every month. So to take a foreign chemical twenty-one days per month, with its now recognised risks, may not be very wise.

HRT has been extensively researched for its safety or otherwise, and I think the current publicity has explained it all. There is no longer any doubt that HRT significantly increases a woman's chances of developing a hormonal cancer. I do agree, however, that, when a woman suffers from certain symptoms around the menopause, HRT can make a big difference very quickly. It is the long-term risks that she has to consider. What she is seldom told about is the non-drug approaches that could make the same difference, without any of the risks.

Are you aware that the world's best selling HRT, Premarin, had its name taken from where the hormone is derived, namely PREgnant MAres' urINe! Can you imagine what sort of stress chemicals might also be present in the urine of the pregnant mares?

Your Menstrual Cycle

So, tell me about your menstrual cycle. When did you start your periods, because the earlier you started, the more periods you are likely to have had? This means you will have been exposed to more oestrogen in your lifetime than a woman whose periods started much later. Unfortunately girls are starting their periods so much earlier nowadays than ever before. This has to be the result either of their mothers being on the contraceptive pill and/or possibly eating foods with hormonal contamination. Even if you have eaten organic foods for years, your drinking water may have contained hormone residues in it, especially if you live in London where a lot of water is recycled. All those women taking the pill or HRT must go to the toilet at some time in their lives!

Have you had heavy periods or pre-menstrual problems of any sort, especially tender or swollen breasts, even if only for a few days before each period starts? When I ask about pre-menstrual symptoms, many women say they have not had a problem, assuming I mean the mood swings that can be so annoying. However I always talk about pre-menstrual symptoms rather than pre-menstrual tension, as the non-mood swing problems may be more relevant in hormonally involved cancers. Let me explain.

A Normal Cycle

To put this into perspective, I am going to repeat what I described earlier on, starting with a reminder of what is considered to be a 'classical' menstrual cycle, where one period starts twenty-eight days after the previous one. But first a clarification. Progesterone is only one chemical, whereas there are at least three oestrogens, namely oestriol, oestradiol and oestrone. Oestradiol is the one most commonly referred to when doctors talk about oestrogen.

A cycle is usually described as starting with the day your period begins. On that day, and for the next seven days, your levels of circulating oestrogens and progesterone are low. Around day 7, a part of the brain called the hypothalamic/ pituitary area starts to produce a hormone called follicle-stimulating hormone (FSH for short), which stimulates the ovaries to bring to complete maturity the most mature Graafian follicle. At day 14 another hormone, leuteinising hormone (or LH for short) is released from the hypothalamic/ pituitary area to make the Graafian follicle release its egg for fertilisation. This is called the time of 'ovulation'. The Graafian follicle stays active by starting to produce progesterone, the levels it produces increasing to the end of the cycle.

From mid-cycle onwards, i.e. from ovulation, the levels of oestrogen vary from women to women. In some they continue to rise, in some they remain fairly steady, while in others they may fall. Whatever actually happens, there remains more circulating oestrogen in the second half of the cycle than in the first half. What is important at this time is the relationship between oestrogen and progesterone. In women who suffer from any symptoms of the pre-menstrual syndrome, there is a dominance of oestrogen in relation to progesterone. The actual levels of the hormones are not important, but, if there is too much oestrogen and not enough progesterone relative to each other, premenstrual symptoms will be suffered.

The female of the species is designed to reproduce, and oestrogen's job is, of course, to make you into a reproductive creature. It develops the breasts, the ovaries and the womb (uterus) in the main, although it can also affect many other parts of the body. There are oestrogen receptors in nearly every tissue of the body; so, under the influence of oestrogen you become the female that you are.

Because we are all different, some women have more oestrogen receptors (or possibly more receptive ones) in some parts of their bodies than in others. Hence pre-menstrual hormonal imbalances produce different symptoms in different women. Some suffer horrendous mental symptoms, such as mood swings, depression, anxiety, agitation, sleeplessness, and in fact just about any mental symptom that it is possible to suffer from. Others suffer from tender, swollen breasts, and periodic breast cysts, while many are not aware of any particular pre-menstrual problems, yet they eventually develop polycystic ovaries or fibroids.

All of these medical problems are indications of a dominance of oestrogen in relation to progesterone, and it is now recognised by many doctors that too much oestrogen is not good for you. Unfortunately, it is not only the oestrogen that women produce themselves that is involved. So much of our world is polluted with hormones, mostly of an oestrogenic nature. Plastics, pesticides, petrochemicals all have oestrogenic activity. Such chemicals are called xeno-oestrogens (or false oestrogens). Our world is awash with them. Is there any wonder that hormonal cancers (that should really be excess oestrogen cancers) are becoming so common? But, fear not, all is not lost. There is plenty you can do about it. So read on.

The point I am trying to make is that, with a history of pre-menstrual symptoms of any sort, or polycystic ovaries or fibroids, oestrogen dominance is likely to be a major cause of your cancer. Since too much oestrogen is known to be a cause of a hormonal cancer, to help you we must do something about it. It is your history that suggests you have a hormonally induced cancer, and that oestrogen is probably the culprit.

If you have had pre-menstrual symptoms of any sort, and to a degree that they were at least a bit of a nuisance, rather than merely an awareness that your period was due, you have probably been exposed to a little too much oestrogen every single month, and for as many days as your symptoms lasted. Over-stimulating any organ of your body is a prerequisite to develop cancer in it, although it doesn't do so in everyone.

So, if you have suffered from pre-menstrual breast tenderness, breast cysts, etc., breast cancer is a possible result. Polycystic ovaries are a precursor to ovarian cancer. What to do about it all will come later. But for now, all I am trying to do is build up a picture.

The late Dr John Lee wrote some wonderfully illuminating books on this and related subjects, such as 'Natural Progesterone. The Multiple Roles of a Remarkable Hormone'♥ and 'What Your Doctor May Not Tell You About Breast Cancer'♥. I have repeated some of this because it is such a common problem I see and it is so easy to explain to people.

A Story

I have already explained that my overall approach is to assume that there is always an explanation for a person's problems, and that the most important thing to do is to identify what that problem is or those problems are. I am therefore a medical detective, but my effectiveness in based on my being able to think of what questions to ask and the accuracy and value of the answers I am given.

You would think that all breast cancers are hormonally driven, and may be they all are to a certain extent. However, occasionally I meet a patient, like the one who consulted me for the first time not so long ago, whose history showed absolutely no features of oestrogen dominance that I could find. We had virtually reached the end of my usual question and answer session, when I told her that, so far, I had not found any reason for her cancer at all.

I suggested we complete my questioning and asked her if she had had any operations, to which she replied "Nothing of importance". Her daughter sitting quietly next to her suggested that two hip fractures and two hip replacements were possibly operations of some relevance. In a rather laid back way she explained that she had fallen off a tractor on two separate occasions. When I asked her what that was all about, she told me she had farmed with her husband in the past.

"Did you use any chemicals?" I asked her, to which she replied, "Not really".

That was when her daughter said, "Mum! We all did sheep dipping for ten years!" The chemicals used for such purposes have strong oestrogenic properties, hence identifying a significant cause for her breast cancer.

Reproductive History

The earlier a woman started having periods and the later she went through the menopause, the more cycles she is likely to have had, which means the more oestrogen she may have been exposed to in this way during her lifetime, especially if she had some pre-menstrual symptoms, unless she was 'protected' by a number of pregnancies. I say 'protected' because the placenta (afterbirth) produces a lot of progesterone, which is a protective hormone.

Miscarriages are an unfortunate and unnecessary event, which can seriously upset a woman for a very long time. Some women never quite get over a miscarriage, equating it to the loss of a child. However, miscarriages are nearly always caused by a deficiency of a number of essential nutrients, especially folic acid and zinc.

Difficulties conceiving suggest a number of nutrient deficiencies, and problems during a pregnancy likewise, especially of magnesium, vitamin B6 and zinc. Magnesium supplements, in my opinion, should be given to any woman who starts to develop features of PET (pre-eclamptic toxaemia), especially as magnesium by injection is now one treatment of choice if eclampsia (a fit) occurs.

Post-natal depression can often be helped considerably by the use of natural progesterone cream. After all, the mother had a lot of circulating progesterone while the placenta was still in her womb, and suddenly the levels drop. Vitamin B6, zinc and magnesium, in particular, may also help.

Failure to breast-feed is more complicated, often being influenced by the mother's attitude and desire or lack of interest in breast-feeding. Sometimes, however, it is never properly established despite the mother's and the Health Visitor's best endeavours, which may well be because of a difficult birth, a general anaesthetic, or quite simply a magnesium deficiency caused by the mother becoming stressed if breast-feeding isn't established quickly. Stress itself causes a loss of magnesium from the body, as well as other nutrients such as vitamins C and B5 (pantothenic acid).

Page 5 of Patient Questionnaire

This is where I add my own questions, ones that are not necessarily on my basic patient questionnaire. They are relevant to nearly all cancer patients in one way or another, but I need the information they provide.

Toxic Chemicals From Hobbies

Having clarified your current symptoms and how they affect you, how it all started and what has been done about it so far, I usually ask about any other significant episodes of your medical history that you think might be relevant. Many people have an instinct or a suspicion that something that has happened to them in the past may possibly be relevant to the cancer they are now suffering from. For example, have you been exposed to potentially toxic chemicals at any time in your life? Have you ever bought an old dilapidated house and done it up yourself, using a lot of chemicals on old wood, for example? Did you scrape off a lot of old paint yourself? Did you live in that environment for quite some time? As a further thought on this subject, do you (or does any member of your household) have any particular hobbies, such as model soldiers, which you paint yourself? Are they made of lead? Do you do a lot of painting and lick your paintbrush? Do you make pottery and paint it? Most people have hobbies of some sort, which may possibly involve something potentially toxic. After all, these chemicals have to be detoxified by your liver, and excreted through your kidneys, either or both of which may in any case be under a lot of strain from your condition or any chemical or drug treatment you may have had, either recently or in the past.

When I asked this of a cancer patient a number of years ago, she eventually remembered working in a very cramped kitchen when she was much younger. Someone found some cockroaches in some cupboards, so the management arranged for a pest control company to come in and spray a very smelly and choking chemical every month for the next two years. She had managed to contact five of the six people she had worked with, only to find that two had already died of cancer, two had multiple sclerosis, and the fifth had what would nowadays be diagnosed as chronic fatigue syndrome. She couldn't find the sixth.

So think about what you have done in your life or what you might have had done to you over the years. Consider what it may have done to you in general terms or more specifically to certain organs of your body.

Stress & Problems

If it hasn't already come up, it is at this point that I ask more specifically about stress. It is amazing how often a person with cancer has been under a lot of stress before things came to a head, sometimes for a very long time. Many people have problems that have been with them for a long time and they just don't know how to deal with them. I can see the pain their problems have caused, which I am sure have played a major part in their developing cancer.

I am not a trained Psychologist, but I have been exposed to a lot of people's problems. I have also lived for quite a number of years, which sometimes brings with it a degree of wisdom. I have my own opinions on how to sort problems out and make decisions, and they have worked well over the years. Of course I cannot guarantee success. In any case, although we all say, "I have a problem" from time to time, in my opinion a problem is merely 'a situation that needs a resolution'. So, when you read all the information in the chapter on Problem Solving, you will find ways that will help you to solve your problems in a simple way. No, I won't solve your problems for you, because I cannot possibly feel the situation as you do. Nor can I live your life in your environment.

In the chapter on problem solving, I will explain some simple facts of life, in a way similar to the attitude I describe in the chapter on decisions. I will also describe a number of examples of the advice I have given in the past, and how the person has resolved their situation. Clearly I don't know what your problems might be, but I hope my advice and the examples I give will be of help to you.

One thing I can say at this stage is that, in some people, it is absolutely vital that they resolve their problems. Without such a resolution, recovery may be nigh on impossible, or certainly very difficult. A few years ago, I identified a major stress in a patient's history at her first visit (which is one of the examples I give in the problem solving section) and told her and her husband that that was the first and most important thing she must do. I also suggested a way to deal with it. I don't know whether she is still trying, didn't like my advice, or expected me to resolve her cancer for her. In any case I felt that she would be wasting her and my time and her money if she didn't sort that out first, as it was so severe. Whatever the situation, she hasn't come back to see me. Perhaps she simply couldn't cope with it.

All of this can take quite a long time to talk through as people often have a number of things they want to get off their chest. While telling me some of these details may not be helpful in my quest for useful information about how best to help the patient, I may be the first person who has bothered to listen to them. I therefore have to be understanding, but I also have to be aware that we have a limited amount of time between us. As it is, a first appointment with a cancer patient lasts at least two hours, but rambling anecdotes can use up far too much of that time.

The Dangers Of Antibiotics

I always ask the patient in front of me if he or she has had any antibiotics, how many courses there have been, how long they continued and what they were given for. What's your history of antibiotic usage? The more you have had at any time in your life, the greater the chance of disturbing the balance of your intestinal flora, allowing thrush, other candida organisms or other fungal organisms to gain a foothold, which may suggest to me that the fungal theory of cancer may be relevant. The answer I was often given was "Oh! The usual amount". But I don't know what that is, since I am not aware I have ever had a course of antibiotics in my whole life.

Some people tell me they were on a daily dose for two or three years for acne when they were a teenager! They may have been given periodic courses for sore throats, flu' or cystitis. Asking about antibiotic usage also has the value that it reminds people of treatments and medical conditions they had forgotten to tell me about. Part of this memory game is helped by my asking about any health problems in the years before starting school, at junior school, senior school, late teens and early twenties when possibly at College or University, the rest of the twenties, thirties and forties, etc.

The significance of a history of tonsillitis has an additional meaning, namely the harm that may have been done to you by all the antibiotics you may have been prescribed. While most doctors will happily give anyone a prescription for an antibiotic when they consider it to be appropriate, they often don't recognise the damage such drugs can cause to the bowel flora. In some people, a single course may destroy the friendly bacteria within the bowel, leading to a whole variety of bowel symptoms, from diarrhoea to constipation, pain, wind, indigestion, mucus production and undigested food in your faeces. In other people it may take a number of courses to start a problem, and, of course, thrush is a regular result of a course of antibiotics.

What is usually not recognised is that vaginal thrush is the obvious external indication of a fungal overgrowth of some sort elsewhere in the body. As the antibiotic was taken by mouth, it is logical to suggest that the thrush organism, Candida albicans, is present within the bowel. To be fair, there are many other fungal type organisms that can produce the same effect, but candida albicans is the best known and the most common. There are at least 250 'candida' species, and most don't cause thrush. I have discussed this problem more fully in my book Conquering Cystitis'.♥

While we are on the subject of antibiotics, I have an awful feeling that there may be a connection between the rising incidence of cancers generally and the increasing use (some people would say overuse or abuse) of antibiotics. I can't prove the point, but, if the fungal theory of cancer has any merit, this connection may be genuine.

Leaky Gut Syndrome

An additional harmful effect that antibiotics can have is that they can give rise to a condition called 'the leaky gut syndrome', in which the bowel wall has been damaged and become more 'porous' than it should be. As a result, food particles that have not completed the digestive process gain access to the blood stream in a form that sets up an alarm reaction (called a kinin-inflammatory response). Such a reaction can occur in any organ of the body, possibly where you have set up a 'target', including the organ where your cancer is. This alone may well explain why there is now considerable evidence that cancer involves inflammation.

Where You Live

I always try to ask patients about where they live. There are many aspects that need to be considered here. How happy do you feel in your home? How long after you moved to your present address did your problems begin to reveal themselves? Why did the former owners move away? What is the health like of other people living nearby? Are you aware of any overhead power lines, electricity transformers or mobile phone masts near where you live? Do you feel better when you are away from your home? Do you only feel better away from your home when you travel to a dry country such as the Mediterranean in the summer? Do you tend to feel worse in the dark days of winter?

If the answer to some of these questions is yes, you may have geopathic stress affecting your home, and a book entitled 'Are You Sleeping In A Safe Place?'♥ will help to put this more into perspective. A beneficial effect of a dry country holiday suggests that some or all of your problems are fungal in origin. Feeling worse in the darker months suggests either a condition called Seasonal Affective Disorder or that you are deficient in vitamin D.

Why Has Cancer Developed In You?

As we are coming to the end of your history, I thought it would be reasonable to try to summarise your situation, and see what you have discovered about yourself. Remember, it is my opinion and my way of thinking about all forms of ill health, not only cancer, that you are now ill because you have been exposing your body to things in your environment that might have 'poisoned' you gradually over the years. In addition, you may have been exposed to poisonous substances during your lifetime, unbeknown to you, all of which have gradually overloaded your system, causing it to break down in due course and produce your current condition.

It is vital that you try not to blame yourself for things that you did not know were bad for you, and, likewise, please do not feel guilty about those things that you knew were unwise, like smoking and drinking too much alcohol, because not only should we be able to reverse any harmful effects they may have had upon your body, but also feeling guilty is a total waste of time and energy. You are now going to move forward.

If patients ask their doctors why they have developed cancer, it is unlikely that they will receive a satisfactory answer, because doctors in mainstream medicine are seldom interested in such reasons as 'why?' They are likely to be told something like "It's just one of those things", or "We don't really know", or "It seems to be much more common than ever before". In truth, most doctors are not interested in 'why?' because their whole approach is based upon dealing with the problem the patient is describing. Their job, they feel, is to treat the symptom somehow. To be fair, most patients go to their doctor and effectively say "Doctor. I have a problem. Will you please fix it for me."

So, unfortunately, mainstream medicine, with all its researchers and all its bright-minded doctors, continues to treat patients either by an operation to remove the offending structure or drug it into submission. Yet there must be a reason why cancer has developed in you, and a number of explanations are forth coming. So, if between us we can identify some or all of the reasons, and do something about them, it should be possible to undo your cancer.

It seems logical to me that, if there is something wrong with your bowel, whether or not you have developed cancer, one of the causes to be considered must be what you put into it, i.e. what you consume. Countless thousands of people over the years have lost their symptoms of wind, indigestion, acidity, tummy pain, constipation, diarrhoea, bloating, mucus, etc., all symptoms of so-called irritable bowel syndrome (IBS), by changing their diet. There are many published studies in mainstream medical journals that say that IBS symptoms are caused by inflammation. As cancer is now known to be an inflammatory disease, is it not reasonable to suggest that some of that inflammation may damage the organ that now has cancer in it? And yet, if you ask your doctor about diet, you are likely to be told to eat and drink whatever you want, as diet has nothing to do with cancer.

As far as your body is concerned where your cancer is, there must be something inflaming it, and, if you have some other reason that has made it into a target, I see no reason why what you consume in the form of food and drink may not be involved. I mentioned briefly earlier on about N-SICIs (Non-Self Inflammatory Cascade Initiators), of which foods and drinks are probably the most potent and easily identified.   If a food is unsuitable for you, it will enter the bloodstream and cause a reaction there of a kinin-inflammatory type.   With the release of the inflammatory chemical TNF-alpha.

My patients and I heartily disagree with those people who say diet is irrelevant. We are sure your diet is important, and, if you have not already made some changes, I will be recommending them to you. Professor Jane Plant, in her book 'Your Life In Your Hands'♥ is adamant that diet is relevant to breast and prostate cancer. There is also considerable evidence that the environment within your bowel has something to do with it, and, if over the years you have had drugs that alter that environment, such as steroids and antibiotics, that is a further problem. Certainly chemotherapy is very damaging to your friendly bowel organisms, as is stress.

I am a believer in the 'fungal' theory of cancer, as expanded in 'Cancer Is A Fungus' by Dr. Tullio Simoncini♥, although I don't know how common it is. It may be relevant to nearly everyone, so far as I know. I know of one colleague who is adamant it applies to every cancer patient. I am certainly aware that far too many people have had quite a lot drugs that predispose to it, namely antibiotics and inhaled and oral steroids, and chemotherapy and radiotherapy of course, although those two would have been given after cancer had developed, unless you have had them for earlier cancers. Also a diet high in sugar and refined carbohydrates, yeasty foods and alcohol, provide the ideal environment for fungi to develop and thrive.

There is now considerable evidence that prescription drugs cause an effective loss of certain essential nutrients from the body, and that the so-called adverse effects that many of them often produce may actually be caused by those deficiencies. The mechanism varies from drug to drug, some reducing or blocking their absorption, some interfering with their utilisation and metabolism, while others increase their rate of utilisation or excretion. Whatever the mechanism, your body needs more nutrients to compensate for all this, which is why so many of my cancer patients benefit from having them intravenously.

Then don't forget what I said earlier on about the acidifying nature of stress, and how that causes comparatively harmless organisms to mutate into pathogenic ones. Also that more acid (really a less alkaline) state provides an ideal environment for cancer cells to develop and thrive. A comparatively acid environment is also a poor oxygen environment, and cancer cells thrive in a low oxygen state. So many cancer patients have had more than their fair share of stress before the onset of their cancer, which led many of them to 'abuse' themselves by drinking too many cups of tea or coffee (with milk and sugar) and alcohol and smoking more cigarettes than before, and generally not attending to their diet. All of this will have meant a poor nutrient intake and significant loss of essential nutrients at a time when an improved nutrient status was required.

How much of this applies to you so far? There is considerable evidence that people who develop cancer have lower levels of essential nutrients in their blood. To be fair to you, I do not know whether that applies to you or not, but, in any case, I will certainly want you to have high doses of nutrients as part of your supplementary regime. Apart from that, mercury, especially from mercury amalgam fillings, squanders selenium, and one of the best antidotes to all the chemicals we are exposed to in our daily lives is the powerful antioxidant selenium. Do you have any teeth filled with mercury amalgams, or have they recently been exchanged for a non-metallic alternative material? Were you given any specific chelation treatment? If not, you will need to read the advice I give in that section in the Treatment chapter, chapter 4.

Did you ever have a knock in the area of that part of your body that has now developed cancer in it? Although there are thousands of people who damage a bone and never develop cancer there, such an accident may set up a 'target' for something to go wrong later on. A minority of my breast cancer patients tell me they banged their breast some time earlier where their cancer eventually appeared.

Geopathic stress may well be affecting you. I recognise most people have never heard of it, but if you look for it and find it yourself, the whole process opens your eyes to another possible explanation for your cancer. Remember, there may be five or more possible 'causes' for your cancer. One may be 80%, the rest being 20% between them, or they may each be 20% of your problem. Until you start undoing some of your causes, you won't know. If you did damage the cancerous area of your body in the past, persistent geopathic stress is possibly one of the most potent ways of turning something simple into something quite complicated.

Geopathic stress involves not only harmful rays coming up through the earth's crust, usually magnified by underground water, it also includes electromagnetic waves from electricity pylons, power substations and sometimes electronic and electric devices in your home, including such simple equipment as a radio-alarm clock beside your bed all night long. With brain cancer, mobile phones are thoroughly suspect in my mind, and I am particularly concerned about this risk to young people who use their mobile phones for so long, when their brains have not yet fully developed. These phones use microwaves, the same as in microwave ovens, and you are constantly being advised by the manufacturers to have them checked for leakages because of the known danger from being overexposed to their radiations. To me it is always possible that mobile phone microwaves simply increase the amount of free radicals your body has to deal with.

I have already said that I believe stress to be a major problem in cancer patients. It not only creates a more acidic environment with all that that leads to, it also wears out your adrenal system so that you lack reserves to deal with your cancer. So, if you recognise it in yourself, please do something about it.

In breast cancer, hormones are clearly involved, but to what extent? How did you answer my questions about your menstrual cycle, especially about any pre-menstrual symptoms? This is likely to be of major consequence to you. Even mainstream medicine acknowledges that, so consider it carefully.

What is the state of your immune system? How effective is it for dealing with any cancer cells? Many cancer patients say they have not had a cough, cold, flu' or any sort of infection for years, which one would tend to assume meant they had a good immune system. Unfortunately this does not seem to be the case in my experience, and I'm afraid there is no way of telling that I know of without having some sort of blood test. If that is not possible, a gentle boosting of your immune system is probably worthwhile.

An important possible cause of cancer that is very difficult to identify with any confidence is 'infections', especially viruses such as the chicken pox/ shingles virus, the human papilloma/wart virus and others like chlamydia. The glandular fever virus, usually the Epstein Barr virus, should not be difficult to recognise as a possible cause from your history.

So, in summary, consider the following as possible causes of your cancer; some otherwise innocent damage to the area where you now have cancer; what you consume as foods and drinks and what you miss from the right diet for you; stress in all its forms both recently and possibly hidden deep in your soul; toxic substances such as heavy metals, especially mercury, but also the myriad chemicals we are all exposed to in our daily lives; the more easily identified poisons such as cigarette smoke; root canal fillings on acupuncture meridians of your cancer; infections, especially viruses and fungi; your bowel ecology; hormonal imbalances; nutrient deficiencies including vitamin D if you live in a comparatively poor sun area; your anti-oxidant levels to quench all those free radicals; your pH and biological terrain; an inefficient immune system; the effect of any drugs you have been prescribed either before or for your cancer, especially their nutrient draining effects; and finally geopathic stress.

There may be others I have missed out that you recognise could be important to you. Never assume I know it all. I learn something new every day, often from a patient, so you might be able to teach me something.

I have tried to open your eyes to a whole variety of situations that could so easily apply to you all. Each piece of the jigsaw tells its own story, but remember, we are trying to identify why cancer has developed in you. Armed with that information, there is now something you can do about it. Please read on.

Chapter 4

Treatment

I have heard people say they are fighting their cancer, but when I ask them how they are fighting it, they don't have a very good answer. They may say, "I'm fighting it with all my might. I won't let it beat me". But they still don't tell me what they are doing. If they were to say they had changed their diet, were relaxing, doing chi-gong, and perhaps taking supplements, I would say that was how they were fighting their cancer. They were actually doing something positive; they were in charge. But to say they are fighting it without doing anything in particular makes little sense to me.

So by now I hope you have learned a lot about yourself, about how and why your cancer may have developed and about some of the precipitating factors in your life. You may also have quite a good idea about it all, and are beginning to think about all the things you can do for yourself. So I am now going to explain what you can do. While there are plenty of things that do cost money, there are also many things that will not cost you a penny. So I am going to start with these.

Prayer

It may come as a surprise to you that I should mention prayer as the first recommendation. But you don't need to be a churchgoer of any kind, or even believe in any of the world's faiths, to consider praying. It is up to you what 'praying' means. To some people it means getting down on their knees and talking to whoever they are accustomed to praying to. To others it may mean finding a place of quiet contemplation. Do whatever makes you feel comfortable, but please do something.

By all means go into a place of worship, if you want to. Even if you have never been into one in your life, they can be places of great peace. They often have an aura of extreme calm about them, and seem to have absorbed the feelings and wishes of many people in their walls. If you don't fancy entering such a place, you might at least find peace somewhere else. It can be at home in a room that makes you feel comfortable, or in a peaceful garden. Take a moment for yourself. Make sure the phone can't disturb you for a while. Possibly put on some soothing music. Calm yourself down and try to make peace with yourself.

Many people who will read this book may do so out of curiosity. Others are genuinely looking for ways of helping themselves or someone else. Despite the value of searching the World Wide Web for information, some of you may still be in a state of shock. It may not be long since you were given the shocking news that you have cancer, or that, after having been told you were 'all clear', it has come back again, and they don't have much to give you. Perhaps you have been told to put your things in order, as you only have three months to live. I have heard this story so many times.

By the time you have started reading this chapter, quite a lot of time may have passed, so, having read all you have read so far, you may hopefully be feeling a little more relaxed, more aware there just might be something you can do to help yourself, and confident of trying something.

While there are lots of things you can do for yourself, I would counsel you to have a moment of quiet reflection to begin with. Don't rush into anything. Take a moment for yourself. It won't make the slightest difference to your long-term outcome if you delay doing something for a day or two. Choosing what is right for you will be far more beneficial. So take as much time as you want.

Relaxation, Visualisation & Affirmations

These also don't need to cost you anything, and they are extremely helpful.

When I have explained them to you, you will realise they will help you to take charge of your life. Remember, whatever recommendations you decide to follow, you must be in charge at all times. There may be decisions to make, but you have to make them. You may want someone else to make them for you, but, in the end, you have to make them for yourself, unless you are going to give up completely and let someone else make all the decisions. If that is the case, I doubt if you would have read this far.

Relaxation Exercises

To be able to do relaxation exercises over the next few weeks and months, it would be sensible to try to organise a room in your house where you can be alone if you want to, and where it is peaceful. Interestingly enough, some people like to have someone else in the room with them, usually their spouse or a close member of the family or someone who loves them and who they love. In a later section, I will talk about the 'carers', because they are a vital part of your support network, and I like to look after them as well. They are often neglected, especially in the frenzy to help the patient. They nearly always want to be of use in some way, and always ask what they can do to help.

Relaxation exercises, visualisations and affirmations can be very powerful indeed, and, if there is someone in the room with you who genuinely believes in what you are doing, they can strengthen the effect by doing the same while you are doing it, but directing their efforts towards you. Never ignore the strength and value to you of other people. Let other people help you, especially if they want to. You have no idea what other people can do to help you unless you let them. Perhaps one of your problems is that you have always felt you could cope on your own and that you have never needed anyone to do things for you.

I have heard so many times that it is unkind that so-and-so has now developed cancer. It is usually a woman who is described as always thinking of other people. She never thinks of herself, and is almost spoken of in hushed, saintly whispers. Does this apply to you? Have you tended to shut people out of your inner thoughts? Are you the capable one that everyone turns to in times of need? Has it ever occurred to you that those around you may be just as capable, but perhaps you haven't given them a chance to show what they are capable of?

Whether this describes you or not, now is the time to let other people help you. The power of one person, you, may be considerable, but the power of two of you together can be awesome. You have no idea what you can achieve. Give yourself a chance and have a go.

I accept that some people may not be able to create an oasis in their home. There may simply not be enough room. There may be too many other people about all the time, such as children, who may be young and need what all children need - your attention. But perhaps you have a friend nearby who would love to help in some way. How often do you hear people say, "Let me know if there is anything I can do to help?" Usually they mean it, but are seldom asked for the help they would like to give.

Even if you don't think you know anyone who you could swap kids with, there is almost bound to be someone out there who has a problem in some way similar to yours, and who would love to make contact with someone like you.

So, don't be afraid to ask. Perhaps you could offer to have their children for an hour twice a week in exchange for their having your children for an hour twice a week. That's all you need to start with. In those two separate hours each week you can have your house to yourself. You can create your place of quiet and peace. You can start to heal yourself. It will do you so much good. Remember, from little acorns giant oak trees grow, and how strong they become. I don't believe there is such a thing as a problem. To me it is merely 'a situation that needs a resolution'.

I don't know how you will be able to organise your life, but there is almost always some way it can be done. So I will leave that up to you. Let us therefore discuss what relaxation exercises are all about.

There are many ways to try to achieve a healing relaxation state. You can go to your local library and take out some relaxation tapes, or you could probably buy some from your local Health Food Store. Some of the best are by Matthew Manning,♥ but you don't need to spend money on such tapes if you don't want to, because you can devise your own way of relaxing. Let me describe what you might find suitable.

Once you have created your place of peace, arrange a comfortable fairly upright chair somewhere in the room. Create a gentle light, i.e. don't sit facing the window if it is very bright outside. Don't worry if there are happy sounds outside, such as children playing, but, if you find where you live is too noisy, you may need to buy some headphones, with which to listen to appropriately soothing music. Alternatively, you could put some plugs of cotton wool in your ears to dampen down loud sounds. I find that a very useful thing to do if I am in the presence of very loud music which I can't avoid. It also allows me to hear what people are saying around me more easily.

Make sure your clothes are comfortable. Take off anything even slightly constrictive, such as a tie, a belt, a wristwatch, any bracelets and even your shoes. Sit in the chair with your back fully supported and comfortably upright. Place your feet on the floor in front of you, slightly apart so that they and your legs are not touching each other. Do not cross them. Place your hands somewhere in your lap, again, not touching each other.

When you first do this, you will find that parts of your body suddenly itch, or feel uncomfortable in some way. Okay, scratch them. This is a natural reaction to being suddenly aware of your body. Of course, you may be in pain somewhere, so this might disturb you. But don't worry. I will talk about ways of helping pain in another section. Just do your best and make yourself as comfortable as you can. As time goes on, and you practice relaxation exercises more often, you will find you can do them anywhere and easily. I can do them in a busy airport lounge, with all the noise around me, such as at London's Heathrow Airport!

Once you are as comfortable as you can achieve, close your eyes. Take three fairly deep, but not too deep, controlled breaths. As you gently let your breath out each time, say to yourself 'Relax, relax, relax', i.e. three 'relaxes' with each out breath. Try to breathe through your nose if you can, with your mouth shut.

Then, starting at the top of your head, think about your body, moving down, in your mind, past your face and neck, down your chest and arms, past your tummy and back, through your pelvis, down your thighs and lower legs into your feet. As you sweep slowly from the top of your head down to your feet, tell that part to relax, and think of all parts of your body as being totally normal and completely healthy. Sweep your body clean, and make it relaxed. Conjure up in your mind the idea of complete normality. Remind your body of what it is like to be totally normal. Don't have any negative thoughts in your mind whatsoever. Everything about you from now on must be positive. Negative thoughts should not be allowed to play any sort of part in your psyche from now on at all. I will come back to this again when I discuss affirmations, which should clarify the importance of positivity.

Some people find it difficult to move down their body in the way I have just described. Another way to visualise this process is to imagine your body as a glass structure full of water. As you move down in your mind towards your toes, think of the water level slowly dropping down. Where you imagine the water level to be will concentrate your mind.

Try not to concentrate on the area of your body that you know or suspect has cancer in it. Think only of normality. If you move down from the top of your head to your toes assuming everything is normal, you will be using the power of your mind to induce normality. If necessary, you can sweep past an area a number of times to 'make sure it is normal'. Take as long or as short a time as you feel comfortable with. If you can only manage two minutes a week, that is better than not doing it at all, but do it as often as suits you. If you use tapes to help you, they take up a lot of time, but they take you through various steps, and can be very powerful. It is up to you, but please try to do something. Scientific studies have shown that relaxation is good for your immune system.

Visualisations

I have heard visualisations described as though you should imagine your cancer as a nasty evil blob that you want to get rid of, and that your white blood cells are knights in shining armour attacking it. You are supposed to visualise a fight where your white blood cells slice pieces off your cancer, which fall into the gutter and dissolve. In the cancer self help group that I helped to run locally until more than ten years ago, we had an old man to whom we initially had difficulty teaching visualisations. So we asked him about his background to see if we could find anything in it that might help us to help him.

In due course, he mentioned that he had been in the Special Boat Section of the armed forces in the Second World War, and had regularly gone secretly across to The Continent to place limpet mines on enemy ships, with what he described as devastating effect. That was all he needed to deal with his cancer. He limpet-mined his tumour.

However, despite the value of this method of doing battle with your cancer, I would prefer you to consider a more gentle method that involves a more loving approach.

Love is the most powerful emotion you can imagine, although some people would say survival is. Well, I'm not going to argue. Suffice it to say that, when I have suggested a more gentle approach to visualisations, just about everyone has preferred it to the more fighting approach. I explain it like this. Simply imagine your normal cells as having a happy, normal life, while your cancer cells are bad boys or troublemakers, but who are not very happy with what they do. They are outside the area where your good cells are having fun, playing and laughing together, and they would like to join in. They have been chastised often enough in the past, but that has not changed them. If anything, it has made them worse. Nevertheless, they can still see the fun the normal cells are having, and would like to join them.

So, invite them in. Invite them into normality. Show them how enjoyable it is to be part of the good guys. Invite them in to play football with you and your normal, healthy friends, so that they can become like them. But say to them that, if they will come and join the normal cells, you will do something in return, something that could make a difference to someone else. So, tell them that if they would care to join you, you will endeavour to make one person a day smile who you might otherwise have ignored. Try to make someone else smile and feel happy. That person might then do the same to someone else, who may do the same to another person, and so it might go all the way round the world and come back to you again. Just spreading a little happiness around you can do wonders for you yourself, and make you feel better. That alone can help the process of healing, and it doesn't cost you a penny.

Affirmations

Affirmations involve you making a statement of what you want for yourself, which you claim you already have. You need to work out a series of words that you can repeat to yourself as often as you like, wherever you are. You can write the statement down and learn it by heart, if you want to, but it soon becomes second nature to you.

What you say should all be positive. I hesitate to say you must not have any negatives in it, as that is using a negative phrase, but I need to use a few more negatives, just to get across the importance of the positive side of things.

If you have cancer, part of what you say is 'I am free of cancer', not 'I do not have cancer'. You also say things like 'I am free of pain'. As I say, everything is a positive statement, without any negatives in it at all.

So you might invent for yourself something like this, "I am whole, healthy, happy, loved, loving, lucky, fortunate and worthy. I am free of cancer and free of pain. I can walk, run and go anywhere I want to. I can sing and dance, because I am so happy. I can do anything I want to, because I am in perfect health". There may be other words that you want to use for yourself, because of your personal circumstances. Even if some of what you say is not true at present, you say it as though it were true, in the hope that, by saying it, it will make it come true.

Affirmations are very powerful, and many of my patients have said it was one of the most important lessons they learned from me. I have one myself, to which I keep adding something new whenever the need arises. But let me explain why I believe they are so powerful.

There is now an enormous amount of evidence in the published medical and scientific literature of the influence on the body of a person's attitude to life. It is variously called psycho-neuro-pharmacology or psycho-neuro-immunology. That's a lot of '..ologies', but the point is that scientists are beginning to appreciate the extent that the chemicals we produce in bucket loads every day have on us all. Scientists are also waking up to the fact that all these chemicals can have a dramatic effect upon the body, and that our attitudes can influence the chemicals we produce, creating more bad ones or more good ones according to how we think and act.

Let me put that all a simpler way, by giving you some examples. You and I think it is intelligent to be able to talk to each other. But what is more intelligent than the fact that, if you cut yourself, millions of cells rush to the site of the cut to help heal it. To my way of thinking, that is intelligent, even if we don't think of it as intelligent in the normal way of thinking of things. So, all sorts of events such as that are going on in your body all the time every day, without you even thinking about them. You digest your food, you breathe, your heart pumps blood round your body all day long without you taking any notice of any of it.

You may yourself have feelings that you can't fully explain. You talk of a 'gut feeling' about something. The sight of something or somebody or a place you visit 'rings a bell'. You have all sorts of emotions every day, and these are effected by chemicals that your body keeps producing. A sigh, crying, laughter, a sneeze, a shock all cause your body to produce a variety of neurochemicals, and are caused by a variety of neuro-chemicals, which your body has to metabolise, once it has used them for the appropriate purpose.

So, why not try to make the chemicals that your body does produce predominately good chemicals? Why not try to avoid producing bad chemicals, the ones that do harm to your body? You may say, "How can I keep releasing the good chemicals, and how can you show me that they are good?" Well, there is a very easy demonstration I gave to all my patients to whom I taught affirmations.

I said to the patient, "Please say 'I am happy'. Go on. Say now 'I am happy'". In nearly every case the patient smiled as they said 'I am happy'. Sometimes it was a rather poor smile, or a general relaxation of their facial muscles, but nearly always they smiled, and often it was a very big, happy smile. I always asked anyone they had brought with them to watch them as they said 'I am happy', which somehow reinforced the effect.

I then said to the patient, "Why did you smile when you said 'I am happy'? What made you smile?" The patient nearly always said something like, "I just couldn't help myself. Saying 'I am happy' somehow seemed to make me smile without my even thinking about it". That gave me the perfect opportunity to explain that, by saying 'I am happy', the thought process caused the production of happiness chemicals that, in turn, caused the facial muscles and skin to give the appearance of what we all know is a smile. Ok, so that is a quick response to a thought process, but it perfectly illustrates what I am trying to get at. If, by saying 'I am happy', your body releases chemicals that make you appear happy, why is it not perfectly reasonable to suggest that, if you say 'I am whole, I am healthy and I am free of cancer', healing chemicals will be released to bring about what you have just said? Yes, it may take a longer time than the short while it took for your facial muscles to be affected by saying 'I am happy', but the principle is the same.

At the very beginning, before you decided to read this far, I explained how, when you stop rubbing a blister on your foot, it very rapidly becomes pain free, in contrast to the much longer time it takes for your body to heal when you stop doing things you may have been doing wrong over a lifetime. One is a short, sharp effect, the other a slow, more prolonged response. Despite the difference in the timing, I think the comparison is perfectly reasonable.

I hope you have understood the point of affirmations. Say as often as you can the words you choose to say. Write them down and make sure there are no negatives in them at all. If necessary, ask someone to check your affirmation statement for you. And don't forget, you can add something else any time you want to.

Your relaxation and visualisation exercises need a little time and space to yourself, or need to be organised if someone is going to join you at the time. But your affirmations can be said wherever you are and whenever you want to say them. While washing up, standing in a queue, falling asleep or if you happen to wake up in the middle of the night, are good times to say them. In fact I find that is a good way of helping me to fall asleep, and I have to concentrate to complete what I want to say. I often fail to complete them, falling asleep in the meantime.

91

Happiness & Laughter

Being happy is far better for you than being unhappy. Yes, I know it can sometimes be hard to be happy under certain circumstances with cancer, especially if you are in pain. But, if you can somehow manage to change your attitude, you will be surprised how it will help. In fact, laughter is a very good way of relieving pain, and, for the same reason, if you remain miserable and depressed, the 'bad' chemicals that are produced as a result, make it all worse.

You may think that your problem is worse than that of anyone else. And to you it may well be very serious. But, however serious it is, I can assure you there is someone somewhere who is worse off than you are. Think of all those starving, thirsty people in Africa. Remember the old Chinese saying "The man who has no shoes should weep for the man who has no feet". Yes, I know it is hard to think of other people's hardships when you are suffering yourself, but at least you have food, warmth, a roof over your head and people who care for you and will help you.

So try to minimise your own problems. Try to put them to the back of your mind. Instead of thinking about the bad things in your life, try to concentrate on your good fortune. Be positive rather than negative. Keep your cup half full rather than half empty. Try to smile as much as you can. If necessary, practise smiling in front of a mirror so that you can turn it on if you are feeling down. You never know, just doing that may make you smile or even laugh.

If you understood the point I was trying to make about the 'good' chemicals being produced when you smile affecting your facial muscles, all you need to do is think along the same lines with laughter. In fact, laughter may be even more effective, as the act of laughing involves many more bodily muscles than a simple smile. Out of interest, why not study a few people and see the difference between a smile and a hearty laugh? Laughter in particular releases certain chemicals called 'endorphins' which are natural morphine-like chemicals, and you know how effective at relieving pain morphine is. Also the ones you produce don't have any adverse effects like constipation or becoming addicted to them.

So, think about laughter. Who is your favourite comedian? Is there someone on TV at present whose programmes make you laugh? Would you enjoy watching them again, and would you laugh at the same jokes, if you watched them again? If so, record them so that you can watch them whenever you feel a bit low or in pain. Try to obtain recordings of old laughter makers. Who were your favourites from the past? Old recordings are so much easier to obtain nowadays. Have you seen the film Patch Adams, starring Robin Williams?♥ It is so appropriate to anyone who is ill.

Ignore all the bad news in the world. Avoid watching the main Evening News on TV. It is nearly all bad news. Just don't turn the TV on at that time. For some unknown reason, the people responsible for what is shown seem to think that bad news is what we are all interested in. Perhaps they are right. Someone tried to produce a 'good news' newspaper some time ago, and it failed to sell. Perhaps we prefer to hear of other people's misfortunes than their good fortune. I suppose people are jealous of lottery winners, rather than pleased for them. If someone has had an accident, perhaps we need to hear about it to feel lucky that it didn't happen to us.

Whatever the truth is, you can change the effect it has upon you. There isn't anything you can do about it anyway, so why even be aware of it in the first place? When most people go on holiday, the bad news still happens and they don't know it has happened. When they arrive home, the bad news has passed and they don't even know what they missed.

Are there any beautiful walks or parks near where you live? When did you last visit them? Are there any beautiful buildings anywhere near you? When did you last look at them? Do you live in or near an old city? If you go into the city centre, lift your eyes above the usual shop front at eye level. The buildings above them, usually not seen by most people because they don't look up, are often very beautiful.

When did you last go to the theatre? All of us have a habit of taking for granted all the beautiful things around us. I have a beautiful home at the bottom of a fairly long drive. Every single time I turn into it, I fully appreciate what I have been fortunate to have acquired. It never fails to please me. You may not be as lucky as I am in this respect, but there must be no end to the beauty around you to lift your spirits. You merely have to look for it.

What I am encouraging you to do is to consider all the ways in which you are lucky. Think positively all the time, if you can. Always think of your cup as being half full rather than half empty. Ignore any unhappiness around you, and, if necessary, give up a relationship with someone who depresses you at the present time. Smile as much as you can, and laugh every so often. If you are feeling a bit down, make yourself smile. To repeat what I said earlier, if necessary, look in a mirror and practice smiling, like a model who has to turn on a smile as soon as the photographer tells her to do so. You never know. Doing so may make you laugh.

Concentrating On Yourself

There is a possibility that all you want to do is the things I have described so far. You may have read enough to feel comfortable that that is enough for you. If so, reread what you want and read it again any time you want to. Don't read any further.

If, however, you are hungry for more information, and are going to read about everything you can lay your hands on, I need to give you some special advice. As you read on, you will become aware that there is an enormous amount you can do to help yourself. Some of it may be quite time consuming, or, when you read about it, it may appear that it will take up a lot of your time. If you have cancer now, I strongly advise you to concentrate on yourself for at least the next three months, almost to the exclusion of everything else if at all possible. Once you have decided to take control of your life, you need to be able to do it properly.

To begin with, you need to get properly organised. Give yourself enough time to read all you want, so that you can decide for yourself what you want to do and what not to do. Towards the end of my discussions in this chapter, I will go over a plan with you about how to organise your day. Once you decide what to do, do it as completely as you can to begin with. Remember, it has probably taken many years for your cancer to develop, so you can't expect it to go in a short time. Yes, if you start to do the right things for you, you may well feel a lot better very soon. It always surprises me how quickly most people start to feel better, which immediately gives them confidence that what they are doing is right, and encourages them to do more.

It is important for you to have some idea of any progress you are making, so you will need to have a system of analysis that you can use to assess your status on a regular basis, say once a week. Various outcome studies have tried to identify what are the best factors that give a clue to progress. At the top comes a simple question 'How do you feel?' So use this, and everything you assess, on a simple 0 to 10 scale. Decide where you are now on this scale in relation to how you feel. The bigger the number, the better you are. Grade 10 means you are feeling fabulously well. However, you may have just had a course of chemotherapy and are feeling rather sick, so you may decide you are grade 5 at the present time, but it is only temporary, assuming that you will improve as time goes on. Try to remember how you felt before the chemotherapy made you feel unwell, as a useful form of comparison.

If you have a lump somewhere, give it also a grade. Use the same scale for anything that you feel is relative to your cancer, so that you can watch how it changes as you do things for yourself. If you have a laboratory test, such as a cancer marker, or a series of laboratory tests that are specific to your cancer, give them a grade that you feel they represent to you.

Make a diary, so that, if some aspect of your assessment scale changes at a particular time, you can make a note of it at the time. If you don't, you may forget later on why it changed. You need to know if the approach you are following is making the difference you are looking for. Make a note of when you add or change something. If your assessment of your status changes in relation to something you start or stop, assume there is a connection, even if there is not. Be your own detective.

Geopathic Stress

I first mentioned geopathic stress earlier on, but I want to remind you of it at this stage. So far I have tried to show you how to improve your 'attitude' towards a more happy and contented state. To me it may be just as important to improve the environment in which you spend most of your time, which your home tends to be. Have you checked for possible geopathic stress? If not, please get on and check for its presence and have it dealt with. Also, may I suggest you start making a list of things to do at some stage? All the things I am telling you about, I hope I explain well enough for you to understand their principle. It is up to you which ones you choose to follow. So, start making a list of the things that appeal to you. If you want to read about geopathic stress, the book entitled 'Are You Sleeping In A Safe Place?' explains it all.♥ With the book will come information about a piece of machinery called a Raditech, which Rolf claims can negate the effects of geopathic stress. The experience of my patients is that sometimes it does, and sometimes it doesn't. Some patients want to find someone who can deal with geopathic stress for them in person.

Other Books I Recommend

1. The Journey by Brandon Bays.♥

There is absolutely no doubt in my mind whatsoever that emotions play a part in the development of cancer, sometimes a major part and sometimes a lesser part. Emotions may even be playing a part without your being aware that they might be involved. You may have had an experience in the past that you have totally forgotten about, or that you have somehow suppressed. Yet many of my cancer patients tell me they feel sure that there is something in their past that could be relevant, but that they don't know what it is, or how to get at it. A few years ago, a lady consulted me, accompanied by her husband, because of cancer of her oesophagus (gullet). Her condition was quite bad, and, of course, she had problems with swallowing. Not surprisingly, her dietary intake was getting worse all the time. So her problems were being compromised even further by not being able to take in the nutrients that her body needed to help her overcome her cancer.

One question I like to ask patients early on is whether they have any idea what has caused their problem. It is amazing how often patients do have an idea, but they have either felt unable to voice their opinion to their doctors, or they have done so, only to have it dismissed or ignored. Sometimes the doctor may have said, "Yes, but this is how we are going to treat your cancer". Understanding the cause is not considered to be important all too often.

When I asked this lady that question, her husband immediately said, "Oh! I know what has caused her cancer. For as long as I have known her, she has drunk all her hot drinks unbelievably, scaldingly hot effectively straight out of the kettle. I personally couldn't cope with anything so hot. She must have damaged her throat after all these years". My response was, "While I can understand what you are saying, that such hot liquids might 'burn' her throat, I feel it is more likely to make her throat a 'target' for something to go wrong in due course". I then asked her if there had been any particular problems in her life up to the onset of her cancer.

Her response was a sad eye-opener. "My mother had bad Alzheimer's disease, and it was impossible to find anywhere near us that could take her in and look after her. So we had all that strain because we had to look after her, and, I suppose, I drank even more hot drinks because of the stress. What was particularly distressing for me was that, at a time when she was in a very bad way, because she also had diabetes, I had to sign the paper at the hospital for her to have both legs amputated because of gangrene in both of them."

"How do you feel about that?" I asked her, which was when the tears started to flood.

"I still feel guilty. It was awful. It was terrible for me to have to do that to her." It took some time before she recovered a degree of composure, but I was sure I had uncovered the real underlying cause of her cancer - guilt. Despite my attempting to console her by saying that I was sure she had made the right decision at the time, and that her mother probably wouldn't have been fully aware of what had been done to her, it clearly had had a very bad effect upon her.

Very gently I tried to explain to her that I felt sure that that was the cause of her cancer, and that drinking scalding hot drinks had merely provided the target. I offered to help her in a variety of ways but told her that I felt it was of prime importance to resolve that particular problem first. I suggested that she read The Journey, and, if you read it, you will see how it could have helped her. By going on 'a journey' as is described so well in the book, she would have been able to 'discuss with her mother' her decision to let them amputate her legs. I was sure her mother would have told her that she had made the right decision at the time she was asked to make it, and that there was nothing to forgive her for.

If you have not read The Journey by Brandon Bays, you may find it a little difficult to understand some of this story. But the book explains it all very well, and I would encourage you to get hold of a copy, even if you only borrow it from your local library to begin with. In the long run, however, you will probably want a copy of your own so that you can read it again and again. You might also want to lend it to friends.

For a long time I had felt I ought to be helping patients deal with this side of things, but I didn't know how to help them. Yes, I would talk to them about their problems, but I felt there had to be something somewhere that I could recommend. I had felt that counselling was not what I wanted to recommend, because of what so many patients had previously told me about their experiences of it. They had felt that each session had merely gone over old ground and had not dealt with anything in particular, had not cleared things out, but had merely kept going over things, possibly sometimes stirring things up. This may upset some counsellors, who possibly do a good job for some people. But, somehow I haven't felt it is the right thing to recommend to my patients.

It was a patient who recommended to me that I read the book The Journey, and, when I started reading it, I couldn't put it down. I found it was exactly what I wanted for my patients. To make sure, however, I attended a weekend course run by Brandon Bays herself, which I thoroughly enjoyed. So far as I was aware, everybody was there because they had their own problem to resolve.

Some time during the first morning, Brandon asked us to stand up and gather round in a circle of about six people near each of us. She then asked us to put our hands round the shoulders of the people next to us, and say what we had come to this session to resolve. In my group, I remember there was 'depression', 'guilt', 'anxiety', 'fear of something unknown' and 'lack of confidence'. The others seemed keen to tell us what their problems were, so I was the last to speak. I stunned them by saying 'happiness'.

They were all so sure that everyone had to have a problem they needed to solve. They couldn't imagine anyone declaring that they were happy, yet I consider I am one of the happiest and luckiest people in the world. The two days were a real eye-opener to me about how much sadness there is in the world of ordinary people. To be fair, I attended out of clinical interest, to make sure I fully understood what it was all about, and to be sure that it was something I felt confident to recommend to my patients.

In the afternoon of the first day I was taken through 'a journey' by a trained counsellor, who was also medically qualified. This was the third Journey I had done, as I had been to a one-to-one session with two separate fully trained Journey counsellors prior to then. What really fascinated me was when I paired up on the Sunday afternoon with another attendee, and, watched carefully by a trained Journey counsellor all the time, I took her through 'a Journey'. What I managed to bring out of her was truly fascinating. She had a most cathartic experience, but I felt confident to complete the process, and gradually brought her back to reality, without any interruptions or help from anyone else. Having read the book a number of times, having gone through three 'journeys' myself and having heard Brandon Bays talking for a day and a half, and together with my own experiences of having helped countless thousands of patients over the years, I knew I could help her.

Her story was absolutely amazing, but the important thing here is that she had known there was something that was holding her back in a number of ways, but she had absolutely no idea what it was. The story she told me when she went through her 'Journey' had occurred when she was about eight years old, but she had totally forgotten all about it. It had affected her so badly at the time that she had somehow buried it in her subconscious mind for that long, as she was now probably somewhere in her fifties. I rang her at work the next day and she told me she felt so much better, and thanked me for helping her, even though she had gone through quite an experience the previous day. She also told me that her friends had told her that she somehow looked better and more relaxed.

What I like about The Journey is that it deals with a situation at a time and clears it out, gets rid of it. Yes, some people may have more than one problem, and some may find it hard to go through the process. There is a time in 'a Journey' when you have to 'let go', which some people feel is hard for them to do. My experience nowadays is that, if you combine 'Journey' work with some aspect of healing your physical body in ways that I am discussing here, you will find it easier to 'let go' when you need to. Some people are so screwed up in so many ways when I first see them that I have to work on them gently to begin with. When they start to feel better, we can then move on. Sometimes, however, one particular problem is so important that it must be tackled first, even if it is not fully resolved before moving on to other matters. I never saw the lady with the oesophageal cancer again. Perhaps she wasn't able to face her problems. My hope is that she somehow at least found a degree of peace with herself. If she didn't, but she died, I hope she died with dignity.

2. Love, Medicine and Miracles by Dr Bernie Segal MD.♥

I read this book some time before I first read The Journey. It helps people to understand some aspects of why they have cancer, primarily from the emotional point of view. Bernie Segal was a surgeon in America, where his books are best sellers. Early on in the book, he tells how he became interested in helping patients, whatever their problem, as a result of a particular experience he had with one patient.

He describes how surgeons sometimes do a laparotomy (open up a patient's tummy to have a look inside to see what is wrong), only to find the patient has inoperable cancer. The next day, or shortly after the patient has recovered from the anaesthetic, the surgeon has to tell the patient the bad news. He says that most surgeons, embarrassed to admit there is nothing they can do to help, stand by the door, mumble something and then walk out, leaving the nurses to pick up the pieces.

What changed his whole attitude was a particular patient who watched him enter her room. She clearly realised he was going to give her some bad news and that he didn't really know how to tell her. It was obvious, from his body language, that he felt most uncomfortable about the whole thing, and that he, the surgeon, was in distress about it. So she said to him, "Come here", and she gave him a hug, to put him out of his misery.

That experience apparently totally changed his life, and became a blessing for other patients. It made him reconsider his methods of communicating with patients, because he acknowledges that he was previously one of those high-powered, high profiled, autocratic surgeons he subsequently came to abhor. You could say he had a conversion as on the Road to Damascus.

The whole book is very much on this theme, and is encouraging and uplifting. I have been criticised by other doctors of giving patients 'false hope'. I don't understand what this means, and neither do my patients. I have asked many of them. They want hope. They are appalled when they are told there is no hope, when they are told there is nothing that can be done to help them. I might possibly say there is nothing more I can do to help someone (although I don't ever remember saying that to a person), and some cancer patients who come to see me may still die, but I will always go on trying if the patient wants me to. Bernie Segal's book constantly gives hope, and regularly describes people who have overcome their cancer.

3. Peace, Love and Healing by Dr Bernie Segal MD.♥

I find it is interesting that both books have the word 'love' in the title. This is Bernie Segal's follow-up book after he had so much mail from his first book. He used all the information from these letters to compile this second one. I found it a little disappointing, possibly because I felt the first one, Love Medicine and Miracles, was so inspiring. Maybe, if I were a patient suffering from cancer, my opinion might be quite different. Please don't let that stop you from obtaining a copy. The more you read of value, the greater the chances are that you will find the right approach for yourself.

What You Eat

Before I discuss the relevance of diet to your cancer, there are two important things I want to talk about. The first, which may be one of the most important for your state of health, is the 'condition' of your intestines themselves. It is likely that you are constipated to a degree, even if you are not aware of it. Any Naturopath will tell you that you should open your bowels at least two or three times a day, not merely once, as is considered to be normal by most people. It is therefore likely that you will have accumulated a lot of matter within your bowels over your lifetime. This will harbour not only putrefying material but also many undesirable organisms such as parasites, bacteria and fungi. These in turn will not only damage your bowel wall leading to the leaky gut syndrome, they will also interfere with the correct absorption of nutrients from the food you eat, and allow the absorption into the blood stream of toxic substances that have accumulated within your bowel, which an already overloaded liver will have to try to deal with. Most Naturopaths will tell you not to waste your time with anything else until you have sorted your bowels out.

I would therefore strongly advise you to consider having a series of colonic irrigations to get you started with a clean bowel. Yes, you could take a few 'effective' doses of Epsom Salts or something similar, which may appear to clear out your bowels, but such an approach is not likely to clear out years of accumulated matter. Ask any colonic irrigationist, and you will be told of the most appalling and extraordinary things that are cleared out of people's bowels.

For some unknown reason, our bowel seems to have a habit of sometimes holding onto what it clearly does not need, rather than expelling it. When a patient of mine had his third or fourth colonic enema, he passed a pebble that he remembered having swallowed as a child. He had lived in a house with a pebble drive and had been fascinated by their various shapes. He would pick them up and 'wash' them in his mouth to clean them! He remembered swallowing this one. So, sort out your bowels early on.

There are some contra-indications to having a colonic irrigation, and you will need to check with the person carrying it out. For example, someone with bowel cancer itself might be refused, although, if you have had a bowel resection of some sort and you have completely healed, I can't see that it would be harmful. If, however, you have had most or your entire large bowel removed surgically, then it would be pointless, as it is only this part of your bowel that is washed out. The water should not enter your small bowel. So check before you proceed, and only have it done by an appropriately trained person.

The second idea I want to mention before I start on your diet is the fact that you are extremely likely to be in an acid state. This may well be a result of any stress you have been going through, or any drug treatment you may have received. However, it is also very likely to have resulted from your standard diet.

The items you eat and drink can be divided into acid-forming and alkali-forming ingredients, which basically means the nature of the 'ash', or what is useful to your body, after it has been 'burned' or metabolised. The most common acid-forming foods are all animal produce such as meat, fish, eggs and milk and milk products, plus all the grains, coffee, tea, chocolate and most fizzy drinks, i.e. just about the main items most people consume regularly.

The alkali-forming foods are all vegetables, fruit, salad items, nuts and seeds, i.e. the classical vegan fair. There is a theory that there is only one truly alkali-forming food, namely lemons, but I won't go into the reason for saying that just now.

There is an ages old idea that lemons are especially good for us all, in particular for people suffering from arthritis. If that is the case, there is logic in the idea of starting your whole treatment plan, preferably after you have had your first colonic irrigation, with what I call the 'lemon treatment'. If it works, it should rapidly correct the acid state of your body. While there may well be an ideal order to all the things that you will choose to do, I suggest you simply get on and start doing something.

The 'lemon treatment' is really quite simple. Buy some lemons, preferably organic ones. You will need a total of 42 lemons over 12 days. Take the juice of one lemon on day one, the juice of one lemon twice on day two, and the juice of one lemon three times on day three. Take the juice of four lemons on day four, five on day five and six on day six. On day seven repeat as for day six, so taking the juice of six lemons two days running, then reduce in exactly the same way as you built up, as follows:

Day 1 the juice of 1 lemon
Day 2 the juice of 2 lemons
Day 3 the juice of 3 lemons
Day 4 the juice of 4 lemons
Day 5 the juice of 5 lemons
Day 6 the juice of 6 lemons
Day 7 the juice of 6 lemons again
Day 8 the juice of 5 lemons
Day 9 the juice of 4 lemons
Day 10 the juice of 3 lemons
Day 11 the juice of 2 lemons
Day 12 the juice of 1 lemon, although it may be sensible to take the juice of one lemon twice daily from now on if that is practical.

A word of caution here. As you know, lemons seem to be acidic when taken into the mouth, so please either drink the juice with a straw or swallow the liquid in such a way as to minimise contact with your teeth, otherwise there is a danger of damage to your teeth. Some people will find this whole approach hard to take, so you may 'sweeten' the juice with a little honey. If it appears to irritate your intestines, try to persevere if you can, as the 'reaction' may be doing you good as your pH changes from acid towards alkaline. However, don't persevere if it is obvious it is doing you more harm than good.

How often you repeat the 'lemon treatment' is difficult to state. It really depends upon how acidic you were to begin with, how effective the first treatment is, and how you feel after about a month. If the whole approach you have decided to follow is helping you to feel remarkably well, you may not need to repeat it. If you have not yet improved in any useful way, you could repeat it in one month, but in those circumstances you may need to reconsider whether you are following the right approach or doing enough anyway. So, it may otherwise be reasonable to repeat the 'lemon treatment' in one to three months, and again after that, if necessary.

Alkalinising (De-Acidification) Drops
Under ideal circumstances and when someone is in perfect health, the body is

said to be in perfect balance from an acidity/alkalinity point of view. The pH of your body or any liquid is a scientific measure of the degree of acidity or alkalinity, 7.0 being neutral, down to zero being acid and up to 14 being alkaline. Vinegar is acid and soap is alkaline. Your body tissues want to be very close to a pH of 7.36, so just on the alkaline side of neutral. If there is a change from the ideal level, there may well be a number of consequences, in particular the assimilation of minerals, abnormalities of which will inevitably lead to a degree of ill health.

Your genetic make up identifies what your problems are likely to be, i.e. whether you are likely to develop arthritis, migraines or cancer, for example. What you do in life triggers your genetic predisposition into activity. If you do something wrong for you (which may be fine for someone else) you effectively switch it on. By not doing it you can switch it off. When you are unwell it is important to identify what the switches are so they can be avoided or eliminated.

Almost everything in life, breathing, eating, digesting, moving, working, thinking, talking, laughing, etc., create acid as a normal process, but the body has mechanisms to deal with this. Firstly, the body is capable of excreting acid in urine, faeces, sweat, saliva, tears and breath. In addition it can neutralise the acid by the presence of what are called 'buffers'. These are proteins circulating in the blood stream, plus the elements calcium, magnesium, sodium and potassium. Such substances are manufactured or obtained from your diet in the main, so you can see why the correct diet is so important. However, if a so-called 'good' food happens not to suit you (i.e. you react to it in some way) it tends to produce an inflammatory reaction somewhere in your body, producing more acid as a by-product.

A lot of your buffering capacity is by calcium, so, if your life style is unreasonably acidic, calcium will be drawn from your bones, so leading in the long run to osteoporosis.

The development of an acidic state is a basic trigger that is likely to affect just about everyone, certainly anyone who is unwell. While most things in life tend to make the body acidic, if you then add the effects of stress, pollution, street drugs, tobacco, medicines, toxic substances like mercury, lead, aluminium and pesticides, etc., many 'normal' everyday occurrences for many people, you can see why the development of an acidic state is the more likely, and why the body is sometimes overwhelmed. To be perfectly accurate, one should really talk about 'a less alkaline state', because you would not survive if you actually became acidic. Nevertheless, even the perfect alkaline diet may not be able to achieve catch-up, if years of producing too much acid has left its effects.

There are two main points of interest here. First, an acidic state means that nutrients will be absorbed, assimilated and used less efficiently. Secondly, many 'organisms' become more virulent, in that they seem to adapt to the new environment in which they now find themselves. Unfortunately that adaptation makes them all the more harmful. There is a school of thought that cancer is actually the body trying to protect you from a 'cancer-forming fungus' that has become active in the acidic conditions. If this is so, you can see why alkalinising the tissues should help to reverse the process, as, presumably, the organism will then lose its harmfulness.

This approach has been tried by Dr. Tulio Simoncini, an Italian Oncologist, as described in his book 'Cancer Is A Fungus'.♥ He injected sodium bicarbonate directly into cancerous tumours, leading to their destruction. However, such treatment is not available generally, but using preparations to improve the alkalinity of the body should help to change the pH at the site of the cancer, making the local environment less conducive to the progression of the cancer. As it is likely that the site of the cancer is where the greatest amount of acid is being produced, it is reasonable to assume that the alkali will try to neutralise it first.

By all means start with a change to as alkaline a diet as possible, and see what happens. But, because whatever has caused your cancer to develop over the years has produced a significant change in your metabolism, it may not be possible for merely changing your diet to undo everything. You probably need help. This is where AlkaLiza comes in.

AlkaLiza is a very alkaline preparation of water-soluble silicon, having a pH of 14 in the concentrated form, so it MUST be diluted and the dose built up slowly according to your response. A simple way is to measure the pH of your urine. Yes, you could measure it many times a day, but, if you do so, you will soon discover that the pH of your urine varies too much to give you useful information on how to respond. So I suggest you follow these comparatively simple instructions.

A supply of pH measuring sticks will come with supplies of AlkaLiza. When you get up in the morning, pass urine as normal and discard it. Have a full glass of quality water and set about washing and dressing before you do anything else. Do not have any food or other drink at this stage such as a cup of tea. The urine you pass as soon as you get up in the morning will contain all the results of the night's detoxifying metabolism, so is likely to be acidic anyway, even if you are in good health.

By the time you have washed and dressed, a number of minutes are likely to have passed and your bladder will start to fill up from the water you drank earlier on. This is the sample, i.e. the second urine sample of the day (discard any urine you pass if you need to get up in the middle of the night), which you want to test on a regular basis. Pass some of the urine into a clean dry glass. When you have finished, dip one of the pH paper dipsticks into the urine and read the result after about 15 seconds. Record the pH.

Assuming you are ill in some way and you are acidic, start by putting one drop of AlkaLiza in each of 6 glasses of water you drink throughout the day, i.e. don't take AlkaLiza all in one go but spread it out. Do this for a few days and measure the pH of your second urine sample of the morning as explained above. This may be all you need to do, but the chances are that you will need to increase the dose, so simply put 2 drops of AlkaLiza in each of your 6 glasses of water. Keep testing the pH of your urine and increase the dose of AlkaLiza slowly, until your second morning urine sample measures a pH of somewhere around 6.5 to 6.8. Yes it is perfectly normal for it to be slightly acid. 40 drops of AlkaLiza in 24 hours should be an absolute maximum.

As time goes on and you are hopefully bringing your condition under control, you will presumably have neutralised the acidity in your body to a greater or less extent so you may find your second morning urine sample starts to achieve a pH reading nearer 7.0 or above, in which case it shows that the dose of AlkaLiza you have been taking has done its job. Reduce the dose appropriately until the pH reading reduces to the ideal 6.5 to 6.8. Thereafter take a dose of AlkaLiza every so often according to the result of testing your second morning urine sample.

Some women who know their breast cancer is bad, and whose second morning urine is clearly too acidic, have taken 40 drops (yes forty drops) of AlkaLiza spread throughout the day for seven days. If you do this, it will make your second morning urine sample very alkaline, at least 8.0. Pushing your body to this degree of alkalinity has a good chance of killing pockets of fungus, that is assuming the cause of your cancer is a fungus. DO NOT take such a high dose of AlkaLiza for more than seven days, and, when you have completed the seven days, if you do this, leave off the AlkaLiza until your second morning urine returns to between 6.5 and 6.8. After that you can take sufficient AlkaLiza to keep your second morning urine between 6.5 and 6.8.

It is always important to know whether anything you do is having the desired effect. As I have already said you need to have something by which you can measure your progress, whatever form of approach you choose. This could be how you feel in general terms, whether a lump gets bigger or smaller or any blood test you have regularly to monitor your progress.

It may be possible to repeat the forty drops of AlkaLiza approach after a gap of four weeks, if for no other reason than it might take that long to see if the AlkaLiza treatment protocol you have just done has had any effect. DO NOT repeat it too soon, and be aware that making your body too alkaline for too long can damage your health in various ways.

More About What You Eat

There is now an increasing amount of information that suggests that your diet is an important factor in the development of cancer. It is generally accepted that, all the time, we are all producing 'rogue' cells that are effectively cancer cells, but that our immune systems destroy them as soon as they develop. You could liken this to a factory producing nuts and bolts. With the best will in the world, an oddly shaped one will be produced every so often, but mechanisms should have been installed to pick them out and eliminate them. Even then, the odd one still gets through. There is, unfortunately, no one diet that is right for everyone. Nor is there one way of telling you what is the ideal diet for you. Every time I discussed diet with a new patient, I went through all the different methods that were available for the patient to choose from, we came to an agreement between us, and we saw what happened. I never asked a patient to follow any approach if it either didn't seem to be making them feel better after about four weeks, or if it somehow seemed to be making them worse. I acknowledged that occasionally the advice I gave a person was wrong. If that happened, I apologised and we saw what lessons could be learned from it. Nothing is guaranteed to be right, and I am certainly aware that I am not infallible. Fortunately, however, the wrong advice never caused any actual harm, although it may occasionally have made the patient feel less well, which soon changed when they rang me and I made appropriate changes.

The World Health Organisation and other august bodies are constantly encouraging people to eat more fruit and vegetables, presumably because of the large range of anti-oxidants they contain. I assume they are also aware of their value for quenching all those free radicals that life causes us to produce. Nearly everyone has heard of vitamins A, C and E, beta-carotene and selenium as major anti-oxidants, but the same people are often unaware that every fruit and vegetable has a myriad of chemicals that are also anti-oxidants. The ideal thing to do is to share out the free radical quenching responsibility between as many different anti-oxidants as possible. That way, no individual one is overused or used up.

So, all things being equal, eating as much in the way of fruits and vegetables, ideally uncooked as nature originally provided them, and in an organic state, should be very much a part of your diet. This would constitute a fully vegan diet, if other items of non-animal source were added, such as grains, nuts, seeds, pulses and herbs. There is certainly a great many people who firmly believe that a vegan diet is a must for anyone with cancer. If you have become too acidic and that is part of why you now have cancer, a vegan diet will be mainly alkaline, except for the grains, which, strangely enough, are acidic. In the early 1900s a dentist by the name of Dr Kelly, who lived in The Bahamas, discovered that he could 'type' people. I have studied what he found, but I feel it has become rather complicated, and not easy to put into a book such as this. However, Dr Nicholas Gonzales♥ in New York has continued Dr. Kelly's work, and, to put it simply, states that people who have what are called 'solid tumours', such as breast, lung, prostate, kidney and bowel cancer, should follow as close to a vegan diet as they can. Patients with multiple myeloma, lymphomas or any of the leukaemias should definitely have animal produce, he says, but this may be because of their greater need of vitamin B12, in my experience, which basically only comes from animal produce.

Basically, however, I prefer to work with the patient and recommend some sort of dietary change that I think they will be willing to follow. For many patients, too great a change too quickly will inevitably result in failure. I always ask the patient how far they are prepared to go. Often, for example, patients will say that they just couldn't give up all alcohol straightaway, so there is no point in my pushing too hard. I am aware that there are some doctors who tell patients what to do, and also tell them not to come back if they are not prepared to follow their advice to the letter. They say such patients are wasting their time.

I am not so dogmatic as that, because I like to advise my patients what to do, in the hope and expectation that it will be the best for them. Since people are so complicated, and their reasons for having cancer are so variable and often multi-factorial, I cannot be absolutely sure that concentrating on one aspect alone is the right way to go. I therefore advise and teach, and hope my patients will see the common sense in the whole of my approach and will follow it. At all times I monitor their progress to make sure my advice is appropriate, and change it if it is not. I am firmly of the opinion that advice is to be listened to but not necessarily followed. I like to give my patients credit for having the same intelligence as I possess, and that they can decide for themselves what advice to follow.

If a patient wants to follow a strictly vegan diet, I will always support their decision. In many ways, there is some justification for cancer patients to become vegan for a while, but it may not suit everyone. However, I am aware that there is some evidence to suggest people often feel better soon after they start a strict vegan diet, but that, after a time, possibly years to be fair, they start to lack zest and become rather pale. It may be that they have somehow failed to absorb all the nutrients they need, and I am aware that vegans in general run the risk of suffering from a deficiency of vitamin B12, iron and zinc, as humans obtain most of these nutrients from animal produce. I would therefore supplement anyone who wanted to be vegan with these nutrients.

My Anti-Cancer Diet

Because of the extensive experience I have had with patients suffering from various forms of cancer, and because I have found that making some sort of change to most people's diet can considerably improve how they feel in general, I have identified what I could call a middle-of-the-road diet. This may, of course, need to be modified significantly if you have any problems with eating, swallowing, your appetite in general, or any physical effects of your cancer, which I discuss later on.

Your own dietary observations may suggest that you have an idiosyncratic reaction to an item you sometimes consume, without it necessarily causing you too much harm. Please stop that food immediately. It may be causing some sort of inflammatory reaction in your body, possibly causing the 'leaky gut syndrome' with its consequent results. In addition there is now considerable evidence that inflammation plays a significant part in cancer.

Introduction

Certain foods need to be avoided because they are positively harmful to the body. Some foods are neutral, but it is best to take into the body as much of foods that are positively beneficial. Colourful foods from fruits and vegetables contain flavanoids, which are not only protective against cancer, but also can help heal cancer. They are strong anti-oxidants and have anti-inflammatory effects.

The principle behind my anti-cancer diet is to try to work towards making 75% of your food intake from foods that can be (but don't need to be) eaten in a raw, organic and whole food state. Such foods are vegetables, salad items, pulses, fruit and seeds. If these can make up the bulk of your diet, it is so much more healthy in the circumstances. To this may be added nuts. A third group is whole grains, in particular rice. You may make up the rest of your intake from eggs, deep-sea fish and wild or white meat such as chicken and turkey, if you wish. If you prefer to be strictly vegan, that is all right by me, but you may need to take specific supplements.

So this is a copy of what I give to all my cancer patients, as a starting point: -

Please try to avoid the following: -
- All animal milks and animal milk products (oat, rice and cashew nut milks are excellent alternatives).
- All forms of added sugar, but natural sugar in fruit is ok. Sugar is the perfect food for cancer cells!
- Red meats, refined carbohydrates, tea and coffee and their decaffeinated forms, all food additives, anything in a packet (with a list of ingredients on it) or a tin. The only 'packets' should be, for example, the skin of a banana.
- All 'yeasty' foods, such as bought bread, mushrooms and vinegars, etc. The reason for this is that the metabolism of cancer cells is often fermentative, so it is wise to avoid foods of a similar nature.
- Salt, unless you live in a hot country and run the risk of becoming salt deficient through sweating. Otherwise, do not add salt at all, nor consume foods that have had salt added to them. Salt tends to unbalance your potassium levels, which we need to boost instead of salt. You will obtain a lot of potassium from fruits and vegetables. However, if you become lethargic in any way that you cannot explain, take a little salt and see if you improve. If you do, only take as little salt as makes you feel better.
- Alcohol in all forms. Alcohol has to be metabolised by the liver, which needs to be relieved of as much work as possible, so it can do its job.
- At present there is considerable controversy over soya. I am beginning to feel a little suspicious at the hype around the benefits of soya. In the circumstance, it may be sensible to avoid it for now, or not take too much.
- Oils. Use olive or coconut oils, but try not to heat them to too high a temperature. Adding turmeric to olive oil can help prevent it from oxidising

when heated.
- It is very important for you to try to introduce such a diet at your own speed. If trying to get onto this 'ideal' anti-cancer diet becomes stressful for you, then it could become counter-productive and do more harm than good. So take your time.
- An example of what you may eat is as follows, recognising that some of these foods may not suit you or you may not like them. This is general advice, not necessarily specific for you.

Breakfast
- Porridge plus milk substitute.
- Puffed or Shredded Wheat plus milk substitute.
- Home-made muesli. Buy a selection of organic flakes of wheat, rye, oats, barley, maize (corn), rice, millet and coconut from your local health food store, and add fresh fruit of your choice, nuts and seeds. If you add any dried fruit, wash it thoroughly in warm water to eliminate as much sugar as possible. Moisten with naturally prepared fruit juice, quality water or milk substitute.
- Fish, especially deep-sea fish, but not in batter.
- Rice cakes, Ryvita or yeast-free wholemeal bread.

Lunch or Supper
- Salad items with or without slices of cold meat or fish.
- Salad dressings should be made from olive oil, lemon juice, garlic, pepper and mustard, or any combinations of these, but no vinegar.
- Meat or fish and two or three vegetables, but no commercial gravy mixes.
- Stir-fry vegetables or kedgeree.
- Wholemeal spaghetti, pasta, vermicelli, etc.
- Whole grain rice.
- Homemade soups.
- Vegetables and fruit mixed in any proportions in a liquidiser or juicer.

Snacks
- Raw vegetables.
- Fruit, nuts and seeds.
- Ryvita, rice cakes and yeast-free bread.
- Homemade soups. Soups can be used as gravy.

Drinks
- Quality water, by which I mean filtered or bottled in glass bottles, herbal teas (check what they are made of), especially decaffeinated green tea.
- Fresh fruit juices.
- You could use a little Stevia if you need to 'sweeten' something.
- Herbs. Most herbs are ok, but try to use turmeric as often as you can. There is considerable evidence that turmeric is cancer healing and cancer preventing.

Professor Jane Plant has written extensively on the diet she insists breast and prostate cancer patients follow, in her book 'Your Life In Your Hands'.♥ She gives a lot of really useful recipes, but unfortunately does suggest the use of sugar which I would not include.

Diet For Patients With Special Eating Problems

The particular problems with your digestive system that I was thinking of a few paragraphs ago include if you have cancer in your mouth or you have had part of your jaw removed surgically, so that you cannot chew. You may not be able to swallow certain types of food, or may not be able to swallow normally because you have cancer in your oesophagus (gullet) and therefore a restricted passageway. You may have cancer of your stomach, with all the problems that entails. You may have an obstructed bowel because your cancer is causing a blockage. You may have an ileostomy or an upper colostomy, in which case food passes through like diarrhoea. And, finally, you may have a very poor appetite because of your cancer or the treatment you have had, which may have caused a sore mouth, and nothing appeals to you anyway, so you don't feel like eating anyway.

Under these circumstances it is tempting to eat what you fancy and what is easy. That tends to be food such as ice cream, tea, coffee and food of very little nutritional value. Because of such nutritional paucity, they should be avoided like the plague, and replaced with food of nutritional value. There is no way you can heal your body if you don't feed it useful healing food.

My experience is that many of you cannot manage solid food at all, although some of you find very liquid liquids cause you to choke. I have found that the best approach is to liquidise, using a liquidiser, or preferably juice, fruit and vegetables, in any combination you care for, using a proper Juicer. Liquidised or juiced fruit and vegetables can play a significant part in your diet, especially juiced vegetables. I am told that about 40% of a day's regular energy expenditure goes on digesting food, juicing considerably reducing what your body has to do. Liquidising helps but is not so effective.

I am aware that some of you may have a 'candida' problem, in which case it may be sensible to limit your fruit intake, but, with all your other problems, that approach may need to be shelved for the time being. If you have rip-roaring thrush, because your immune system is in a terrible state, then you may have to limit your fruit intake, or even avoid it totally to begin with. Taking special capsules of dehydrated fruits, vegetables and berries could be a useful way of 'consuming' fruit in the circumstances.♥

Patients are often told that there is no evidence that diet makes any difference to their cancer. This is basically because no one has seen any point in spending money on such a study. I can assure you that the advice I have given above has been very helpful to many cancer patients. Foods of poor nutritional quality should be replaced by foods with clear nutritional value. Professor Jane Plant's book 'Your Life In Your Hands'♥ can be very helpful as she gives excellent recipes. I repeat there is no way you can heal your body if you don't feed it useful, healing foods.

I am also aware that some people think it is a good idea to separate fruits from vegetables. I'm not sure where that piece of advice came from, or whether it is a good approach or not. For now I am happy for you to mix fruits and vegetables, if that means that you find certain combinations make a more palatable mixture for you.

So obtain any organic fruit and vegetables you can lay your hands on, and mix them together in your liquidiser or juicer. As so much energy is spent on the process of digestion, you want to avoid using up energy in any way you can. Digesting food may therefore be a waste of energy if you have cancer of any sort, although the worse your condition, the more you need to think about such things. If you have a tendency towards diarrhoea, and you have found that virtually any form of fibre makes it worse, then juicing may be an answer.

I have found vegetable soups to be of real value to many patients, not only those with cancer, but anyone who has special digestive problems. Naturally there are certain vegetables, such as potatoes, that need to be cooked, but the amount of potato you put in will help to control how thick the soup is. Incidentally, do not consume potatoes that have been cooked in an oven. This means avoiding 'jacket' or roast potatoes. The reason for this is that cooking potatoes at high temperature converts more of the starch into sugar than if it were cooked at a lower temperature. So steam or boil your potatoes. Thin soup is easy for some patients, while thicker soup suits others. You can prepare a day's soup in the morning and only have half a cupful every hour or so, if having too much at any one time is difficult for you.

I have also found over the years that, if a person for whatever reason needs to put on weight, protein is really quite effective. For many people I prescribe capsules of amino acids, but for the patients I am considering in this special section, I find G and G Good Morning Protein Plus♥ is really helpful, which can be mixed into absolutely anything, including fruit juice or soup, in any amount you want. However, don't add it to very hot soup as it may congeal and spoil the enjoyment of your soup. If necessary add a small amount frequently, or, alternatively, stir it up in anything you find acceptable, and take it before your pleasant-tasting soup. I also recommend that such patients in particular add the contents of the special capsules of dehydrated fruits, berries and vegetables to whatever they are taking.

While there is little doubt about the general advice that everyone should eat more fruits and vegetables, a study was recently published that showed an alarming reduction in the content of certain essential nutrients in these foods over the years. Therefore, to obtain a sufficient amount of nutrients from these foods, the amount of the foods you may need to consume is not likely to be practical, especially if you have specific digestive problems.

A Very Difficult Situation

Because of the extensive experience I have had with cancer patients, I was inevitably being asked to see some patients who were in a very bad way, in the hope that I may have been able to do something. I sadly have to accept that sometimes the person was so ill it was very difficult to know what to do. I sometimes felt that the person should never have been brought to me in the first place, and that it simply wasn't reasonable for me to recommend anything because it was sadly too late.

I also recognise I am not a miracle maker and that I did not have a hospital facility to admit patients and look after them twenty-four hours a day. I often took a telephone call from a loving relative who wanted me to make recommendations, as the person they were ringing about was too ill to come to see me. It would be all too easy to ignore them and say there was nothing I could do to help, but that would be unfair.

A particular problem I have to face often enough is someone whose tumour is pressing on their intestines, causing all sorts of problems. Sometimes only liquid faeces can get past the obstruction, so they complain of diarrhoea, and inevitably they feel constantly full, because they are. They can't take any tablets because they make them feel sick, and in any case they seem to fill them up even more. Apart from that they can't reach the part where the ingredients can be absorbed into the blood stream as the contents in the bowel are obstructed and can't move on. What to feed such people is a real nightmare for the carers.

This is therefore an approach I suggest you consider, if the person you are looking after is seriously ill, and especially if he or she hardly wants to do anything and is not interested in eating. Do those parts that you find to be practical in the circumstances. Please also be aware that these are just suggestions and that I don't know they are right for you or your loved one, or that they are even practical. I just hope they help. I will describe them as though you, a carer, are looking after someone, and will be applying my ideas. Presumably, if someone were so ill, they would not be searching the World Wide Web themselves.

So, from a 'dietary' point of view, only give liquid products with all the fibre taken out, as often as you like. You will need to obtain a juicer, as any fibre will merely add to the bulk the bowel is unable to clear. It is reasonable to assume that, unless there is total bowel obstruction (in which case the patient will have to be admitted to hospital for emergency treatment), some of the 'solid' material is very slowly managing to pass the obstruction with the diarrhoea, so you don't want to add to it. Giving liquidised ingredients will at least mash up the fibre, but that will add to the problem. So Juice.

If there is no particular bowel obstruction such as I have described above, juicing will still be appropriate since about 40% of one's daily energy expenditure goes on the process of digestion. Although the process of digestion involves the breaking down of complex food substances into smaller more readily absorbed molecules, a big part is the separation of what the body wants to absorb from the waste, mainly the fibre. Juicing virtually gets round that problem for you.

So please use juiced fruits and vegetables not liquidised ones, and try to give freshly made juices to the patient. Try to obtain organic foods, but don't be too fussy about organic produce at this stage. If you can find a mixture of vegetables that make an acceptable taste, it is all right to warm it up like soup. You could steam or boil potatoes, but they don't juice very well whether cooked or uncooked.

Most patients find they like a dominant taste of fruit, so it may be sensible to start there and try to add juiced vegetables in small quantities as time goes by. Carrots and watermelon make a very useful and tasty base. Pull open the special capsules of dehydrated fruits, berries and vegetables♥ and add some of the powder to whatever juiced liquid you have prepared.

There are two supplements that I would like you to consider adding to the juiced items, or giving separately, all of which are, or can be, liquid and do not contain any fibre. One is vitamin C, ideally as powder in the form of the product Bio En'R-Gy C♥. Most other formulations of vitamin C that my patients and I have tried can upset the bowels, sometimes at too low a dose to be of value. At least 10g of vitamin C in this form should be trouble free for nearly everyone, which is the dose I would like you to try to reach. Go even higher if you can. Start by adding 'a pinch' of the powder to every drink, and gradually increase the amount, but take your time.

The second preparation is Essiac tea♥, which I have mentioned under the section on 'supplements', so you can look up the details there. I suggest 2.5ml of the Harmonik Ojibwa Indian Herbal Tincture three times a day ideally as a separate drink. I find it quite a pleasant taste, especially if it is well diluted. This can form part of the day's total fluid intake, which should otherwise be of quality water, by which I mean any form of filtered tap water, or glass bottled water. Preferably don't use plastic bottled water as the plasticisers can sometimes be tasted, but again, this is not something to worry about in the present circumstances. Also, try to put a few drops of the neat tonic under the person's tongue as soon as he or she has drunk the tonic. There are three more preparations that you could consider once you and the patient are coping with all the others. One is selenium. If you read the article from Nexus Magazine in the appendix, you will see why I recommend it, although it doesn't talk about all types of cancer. The preparation of selenium I recommend is said to be non-toxic, and the dose is a 5-ml teaspoonful twice a day in water with food.

One theory of cancer says that it develops in a mineral deficient body. You may be able to obtain sufficient vitamins from your food, or even manufacture them within your body, but you cannot conjure up minerals unless it is from your diet. Unfortunately the mineral content of the food available to us is lower than it used to be because of modern high intensity farming methods that do not involve putting minerals back into the over-farmed soil. I therefore recommend a particular form of multiminerals in the same form as the selenium. As with the selenium, the dose is a 5-ml teaspoonful twice a day in water with food.

The last preparation is AlkaLiza. Because of the nature of the patient's condition and its causes, its seriousness and the likelihood of having had many drug treatments, he or she is virtually bound to be in an acidic state, which promotes the growth of cancer cells. I suggest you put two drops into five liquids per day, so a total of ten drops in a day, to try to return the body towards the correct pH of about 7.36, but reread the detail above where AlkaLiza is discussed in greater detail.

The ABO Blood Group Diet

The principles of the blood group diet are well explained in the book 'Eat Right 4 Your Type', by Dr Peter d'Adamo.♥ He explains that, over thousands of years, as the human race spread all over the world, people's blood group gradually changed according to where they settled and the type of life they led. When people changed from a hunter-gatherer existence (blood group O), when they ate what animal flesh they could kill and what they could literally pluck from trees and find around their world, to a largely agrarian life style, when they cultivated their own grains and ate domesticated animal flesh, their blood group gradually changed to either blood group A or B, with some inevitable mixing. So, if you know what your blood group is, Dr. d'Adamo suggests that you ought to eat mainly the food that that blood group suggests from a historical point of view.

I have had a number of patients who have done quite well by following that approach, but I can't remember anyone with cancer following it. However, some of my medical colleagues find it excellent for cancer patients. If you would like to try the blood group diet, because the principle upon which it is based appeals to you, his book makes excellent reading.

The Alcat Test

Any one of the above methods of identifying a diet for you may be very effective, and, if you want to start by following one of the basic approaches, such as the vegan diet or my anti-cancer diet, which basically won't cost you anything more than the cost of the food itself, then that is fine by me. Many of my cancer patients have started that way and we have made the occasional adjustment as we have seen fit. However, some people like a more scientific, individually tailored approach, and would like a blood test that tells them what to eat and what not to eat. This is where the Alcat Test comes in.♥ It is a state-of-the-art blood test that incubates a tiny amount of your blood with a tiny amount of about one hundred and ten named foods. After an appropriate length of time, the blood and food mixture are examined by an automatic haematology (blood) analyser to see what changes have occurred. Specific changes indicate that particular foods need to be avoided. You are given a red, orange and yellow list (to be avoided, the red list presumably being the worst offenders, according to the test), and a green list (assumed to be safe for you to consume). There is effectively a third list of foods, i.e. the ones that have not been tested, and they need to be avoided in the first instance, as you would not know if they would have been put in the red or the green list had they been tested. They tend to be foods that are generally not consumed very often anyway.

You are sent an information pack containing your results, which shows you how to start to make the recommended changes to your eating habits. In my experience, the best way is to be aware of the foods in the red list, but to concentrate on the green list. You are likely to have been given seventy or eighty different foods from which to construct your diet, and, for the first four weeks at least, you should confine your diet to the foods in the green list and not eat any other foods. If a food is not in the green list, it should be strictly avoided for the first four weeks in the first instance.

However, because the method of identifying food 'intolerances' does not necessarily cover absolutely every mechanism by which a food could be identified as being unsuitable for a cancer patient, if you have the Alcat Test carried out on your blood, please make your diet in the first instance from only foods that are in the 'green' list, but, at the same time, please do not consume any of the foods I recommend you avoid in my 'ideal anti-cancer diet' above that might appear to be safe for you because they are in the Alcat Test green list.

When you have eaten from the green list (minus my other recommendations) for at least four weeks, there are two choices open to you. If you have clearly felt better, even though that may be because of some of the other things you have done at the same time, you would be well advised to continue on the same diet for a while longer. The longer you stay on a diet that seems to be helping to make you feel healthier, the longer you will benefit from it. Put another way, the longer you stay off foods that may possibly have contributed to your cancer, the more likely it is that your body will start to heal itself.

The alternative is that you start to reintroduce any of the foods that you have avoided for the past four weeks that were not on the red, orange or yellow lists. For the time being, you must assume that any food on the red list (plus the ones I have asked you to avoid) should be avoided for some time to come, possibly until your cancer has gone into remission. So start with the foods that were not listed at all, i.e. foods not tested by the Alcat Test. Make a separate list for yourself of any foods you would like, or would be happy, to eat that you have not consumed for the past four weeks. Then see how you could add each food into your diet, i.e., which other foods it would fit with. Add one food every third day and no sooner nor any faster. Eat a sensible portion of that food, so not too much of it, and make a note of how you feel on the next two or three days.

If you do not notice any adverse effects from introducing that food on one single occasion, do not assume that you are safe to eat it as often as you want to, or in large quantities. Merely be thankful that it might be safe to eat that food no more often than once in four days. Just because that food eaten once did not make you feel ill in any obvious way, do not assume that it was not a previous cause of your cancer. Remember that the foods in your red list did not make you feel clearly ill when you ate them; otherwise I assume you would have avoided them. You were presumably unaware that they were causing an underlying inflammatory reaction, which gradually poisoned certain cells in your body and turned them cancerous.

If the first food you test appears to be safe, leave it out for now, while you test other foods. Apply the same sensible approach to each food you test, eating it in moderation and only once. If it clearly makes you feel ill in any way, or you feel ill in the next two or three days and you assume that food was responsible, leave it out for now, but be prepared to test it again at a later stage. If, however, it is a food you are quite happy to stay off for the rest of your life, don't bother to retest it. If it is a food that you might possibly come across were you to eat away from your home, for example, it might be sensible to test it later on just to make sure whether it was that food or not.

Even if it does cause an untoward reaction, leaving it out of your diet for a further three months may cause your sensitivity to it to become so reduced that next time you eat it, you may not react to it at all. However, some people do seem to develop permanent reactions to odd foods, once they have identified them.

There is now considerable evidence, but which the majority of doctors are not aware of, that cancer is another chronic inflammatory disease, like arthritis, etc. While that may not be the cause in your case, or possibly not the major cause, it may be playing a part. Since food is what we are exposed to more than anything else, it is not unreasonable to try to identify what may be, and may not be, causing any degree of inflammation in you. If you were to read the book 'Your Life In Your Hands' by Professor Jane Plant, you would be told how she identified that milk and milk products were the cause of her breast cancer, and how she effectively cured herself by cutting them totally out of her diet. She was lucky that it seemed she had only one cause of her breast cancer, but she explains that it is the carcinogenic chemicals present in cow's milk that were the real culprits. For a very long time, I have recommended that all cancer patients, especially those with hormonal cancers, such as breast, uterine, ovarian and prostate cancers, avoid all animal milks and their products. Sometimes you have to accept the fact that it is wise to remain off a particular food for the rest of your life, if you are fortunate enough to be able to identify what is causing you harm.

I have described the Alcat Test for people living in many European countries, the North American continent and the Caribbean, but if you live where the Alcat Test is not available, and you still want a 'scientific' way of advising you what diet to follow, you will need to search locally for an alternative blood test. Please, however, speak to someone in the company and ask whether they think their test would be suitable for your condition. Make sure, however, that, whatever dietary approach you follow, you don't find it to be more of a stress than not changing your diet. Also, please make sure that you benefit in some measurable way.

I cannot leave this section on what to eat and what not to eat without describing possibly the harshest approach to cancer, especially if you have brain cancer, as there is effectively no hope for such patients from mainstream medicine. The brain uses up so much sugar that it is possible to manage without sugar getting to the brain if you have any carbohydrate in your diet. A ketogenic diet solves that problem. That simply means cutting out all forms of carbohydrate entirely from the diet.

Normal brain cells can use ketone bodies for their metabolism and ketone bodies are formed on the ketogenic diet, instead of sugar but cancer cells cannot.

The cancer cells will simply die. This work has been suggested by Professor Thomas Seyfried PhD whose work can be found on the web.

Oxygen Treatment

Cancer thrives in a low oxygen environment and even more so if there is no oxygen at all. Such an environment tends to be acidic. As an acidic environment is, in turn, low in oxygen, if anything in your life creates either of these environments, it is likely that the other will also occur. Thus these two situations are mutually effective in a harmful way. If cancer has developed in you, it is most likely that both are present to a degree, and the more they are present, the more it will encourage cancer to grow.

At every stage I have been trying to explain to you that, if you can find the causes of your cancer and do something about them, you are starting a process or ridding cancer from your body. I gave a lecture about my work with cancer patients in Germany and Ireland not so long ago, and made a statement that had the audience audibly gasping. I said that, if you can find the cause of cancer and eliminate it, you don't need cancer any longer. I firmly believe that cancer is protecting you from something. I believe lung cancer is trying to protect you from the toxic effects of asbestos or smoking, or whatever the cause is in your particular cancer, even though it is a rather bizarre system, because it does not switch itself off when you eliminate the cause. Once cancer has become established in your body, it has developed a lifecycle of its own, with your body as the host.

So once again, we are back to the question of why cancer has developed in you in the first place, and what effect the causes have had on your body, because, if you can alter these, you are altering the environment that is allowing cancer to flourish.

Because of the world we live in and the lifestyles we have adopted, the environment within our bodies has almost inevitably become more acidic than is good for us and has a lower content of oxygen than it should. In intensive care units, the oxygen content of patients' blood is measured regularly, and there is an acceptable level that has become established by experience. However, I have a suspicion that it would be better for the patients if a higher level were achieved. You see, the level of blood oxygen is measured in the person at rest. If you are at rest, and you are being given oxygen to breathe, your tissues are not particularly active, so they won't take in oxygen actively, but passively. Hence you won't take in as much oxygen as you could were you to exercise.

It is generally recognised that the most important oxygen-carrying component of your blood is your red blood cells. If they are in good numbers and in good condition, then you should have plenty of oxygen being carried in your blood stream to be passed on to your tissues. Unfortunately, many cancer patients have somewhat reduced numbers of circulating red blood cells, and those cells are often in a fairly poor condition. Cancer patients often have iron-deficiency anaemia (in which there is less total haemoglobin in the blood, and also the cells themselves tend to be smaller than they should be called microcytic anaemia), so the oxygen-carrying capacity of their red blood cells is less than ideal (remember cancer cells feed on iron, as well as sugar).

In these circumstances, it surprises me that cancer patients are not given oxygen to inhale on a regular basis, remembering that, whatever the nature of their red blood cells, if they only breathe 'normal' air, it merely contains around 21% oxygen, the rest being mainly nitrogen (plus pollutants, of course). When you are given oxygen to inhale, it is 100% oxygen that is piped to you, even if it is mixed with ordinary air containing oxygen at around 21% through the holes in the sides of the mask.

However, it is sometimes forgotten that the liquid in your blood, the serum, is also capable of absorbing oxygen and carrying it round in your blood stream. Thus the total oxygen-carrying capacity of your blood involves the whole lot, the red cells and the serum. Saturating your serum with oxygen could make a very significant difference. However, just giving you oxygen to breathe at rest may not achieve anything like the beneficial effect that inhaling oxygen with exercise may achieve.

So, by doing some form of exercise and breathing in oxygen at the same time, you will take in a lot more oxygen into your tissues than you would without the exercise. And remember, when you do any form of exercise in the usual way, while your heart and lungs become more active, you only inhale the air around you, still only containing oxygen at around 21% if you are lucky.

Part of what I consider to be an important aspect of your whole healing programme is exercising with oxygen, as described in the book 'Stop Ageing or Slow the Process. Exercise with Oxygen Therapy (EWOT) Can Help' by William Campbell Douglass II MD.♥ What I don't know about you is how much exercise you are capable of, so you will have to come up with a plan that suits you. If you are still a marathon runner, I doubt you will be able to run with an oxygen cylinder on your back!

Just about everyone can do a bit of exercise, although for some, the amount may be tiny. If that is the case, then start off with a tiny amount of work. If you become short of breath merely taking a step or two, make sure you always take those steps breathing oxygen. If you already do that, it may be that you are one of those for whom this idea may not work, and I am sorry about that.

What you need to do is some sort of exercise that makes you breathe a bit deeper, and makes your heart pump a little harder than at rest, at least to begin with. As you need a supply of oxygen for this, you clearly need to think of something you can do at home. If you have an exercise bike, or something similar, that is perfect, but, as an idea for those that do not, consider starting at the bottom of the stairs (with your oxygen cylinder on the second or third step up from the bottom, if your doctor will prescribe a large cylinder). You could begin by stepping up and down the bottom step a number of times, according to what is practical. Be sensible and cautious to begin with, and gradually build up the amount of exercise you do. Try to achieve fifteen minutes a day in due course, even if you only start with half a minute or less of exercise.

Another form of exercise is to buy or make some simple hand weights, you know, the sort used in gymnasia, but light ones to start with, or simply fill some water bottles with varying amounts of water according to the weight you want to use. These will exercise your arms as an alternative to your legs. If you can't use either, buy a Rebounder (which some people describe as a mini-trampoline, although it should NEVER be used like one), and read the book 'Rebounding For Health' by Margaret Hawkins.♥ Have someone sit you on it, put on your oxygen mask, turn on the oxygen, and have your companion put their hands on your shoulders and gently bounce you up and down, increasing the 'bounce' as time goes on. Even this bouncing can make some people become short of breath.

The oxygen apparatus that I use has only two speeds of oxygen flow, namely 2 litres and 4 litres flow per minute. If at rest, it is sufficient to keep it at 2 litres per minute flow rate, but use the 4 litres per minute flow rate with exercise.

These are ideas for the most severely disabled cancer sufferers, but I would imagine that the vast majority of you should be able to carry out some simple form of exercise while breathing in oxygen. In principle, it should be possible for you to obtain a prescription from your doctor for a cylinder of oxygen with all the necessary attachments, as though you are suffering from severe respiratory problems, like emphysema. Explain to him or her why you want it, and hope that you will be lucky. Unfortunately, however, it is distinctly possible that your doctor may not see the need for it, so may feel that it could not be justified on a state health system like the National Health System in the UK. You should then offer to pay for it on a private prescription. SureScreen Diagnostics♥ has a suitable piece of equipment called the Oxygen Concentrator that people may either buy or rent at a reasonable cost.

There is a possibility that a simple preparation may solve your problem, but it has not been shown categorically to improve your oxygen levels. It is a preparation called Oxyboost Pro♥, that you simply inhale into your lungs either while exercising or immediately after you have finished exercising.

Essiac Tea

Sometimes one comes across a simple preparation that it is probably sensible for everyone to take, let alone if you have cancer. Such a preparation is Essiac Tea. The story goes back to the early part of the 1900s involving a nurse in Canada called Rene Caisse (Essiac spelled backwards), who treated cancer patients with various herbs with remarkable success. Not surprisingly she got into trouble with the medical authorities. Her story is told in an article by James Percival, which you can read in the Appendix.

The name Essiac Tea is a trademark name, and there are various preparations now available on the market. Over the years expert herbalists have 'improved' on the original formula, but it would appear that Rene Caisse injected one of the ingredients into her patients to improve the effect. Clearly that is not going to be practical for you. However, were you to use the preparation I used in my clinic (called Harmonic Ojibwa Indian Herbal Tonic♥ - it was an Ojibwa Indian who gave her the formula), which is a liquid mixture of the herbs, you could put a few drops of the prepared solution under your tongue for more rapid and effective absorption of the ingredients.

The reason I am suggesting anyone could take it is because it is a general immune system stimulant, a cleanser and a gentle detoxifier. It has many other attributes to its name, two others being of value to you if you have cancer. It appears to raise the level of oxygen in cells, which, as I have already suggested, cancer cells do not thrive in. Just achieving that will help to diminish acidity at the site of cancer. This in turn will help pain, which is what Essiac Tea is said to be capable of. It is possible that pain relief is achieved by improving the oxygen levels of cells and reducing the degree of acidity.

Detoxification

In the minds of many doctors, the idea of 'detoxification' conjures up a picture of rich people, mainly women, lazing around an expensive resort, being pampered, massaged and fussed over, eating nothing but salads and drinking freshly squeezed fruit juices, all at great expense. For those that can afford it, it can be a most relaxing and pleasant experience, but, while it might be nice for you to do this, it usually lasts only one or two weeks. Most people then go back to their old habits.

114

Many doctors don't really understand why anyone should even need to undergo a process of detoxification, because, when you attend them for a particular medical problem, they feel their job is to 'fix' it. To be fair to most doctors, patients attend their doctor with a problem that they want their doctor to fix. The methods available to doctors are principally an operation or a prescription for a medicine, as I described right at the beginning.

Sadly our medical training does not include much, if any, discussion about what has caused us to be ill. If it did, doctors might be more open to the idea that our environment has a lot to do with it. Many of us are being 'poisoned' by the world we live in, by the food we eat or some aspect of it, the fluids we drink and the air we breathe in, let alone anything nasty that lands on our skin or the effects of machinery such as computers and mobile phones. Many people are simply suffering from 'toxic overload', or the 'total load syndrome' as Dr. Theron G Randolph started calling it in the early part of the 1900s. If a person is sick as a result of all this, is it surprising that so many of the medicines we are given for our medical problems make us even sicker? Our bodies just can't take anything more that it has to detoxify in the liver. The liver has just too much to do. It is overloaded, even if the standard blood tests for liver function appear to be normal, or, more to the point, are within the local laboratory's reference ranges.

So, may be the idea of doing something to try to clear out all those toxins is not such a bad idea after all. If some, or all of them, are playing a major part in why you are ill, it seems logical to me to start getting rid of some of them. That is what I mean when I use the word 'detoxification'.

The process of detoxification will start when you tidy up your diet, when you cut out all the items you know are bad for you and everyone else, such as caffeine, alcohol, sugar and chemical additives, and, of course, smoking. If you have the Alcat blood test, you might also discover that you have been eating on a regular basis certain foods that may have initiated an inflammatory cascade mechanism, which may be partially or wholly responsible for your cancer. Many people with cancer acknowledge, when questioned, that they also suffer from other non-cancerous symptoms that could all too easily be described as 'inflammatory' in nature, such as joint problems, migraines or other headaches, asthma or bronchitis, and inflammatory bowel disease.

There are many additional methods you can apply to detoxify your body, and I will describe as many as I can think of, starting with something that can be a pleasure, at least in winter, and, at the same time, is inexpensive.

1 - Salt & Peroxide Baths

A hot bath with Epsom Salts or hydrogen peroxide, both of which you should be able to buy from your local chemist. Any time you want to, take a nice long leisurely bath, into which you have put either Epsom Salts or hydrogen peroxide. To begin with put a tablespoonful of Epsom Salts into the water and stir it round to make sure the granules dissolve fully. At your second and subsequent baths, gradually increase the amount of salts you put in, to check the effect on your skin. There is probably no point in putting more than six tablespoonful in a full bath. Likewise with the hydrogen peroxide, if you can find some in a chemist's shop, start low, but don't go higher than six tablespoonsful of 6 volume $H2O2$ in a full bath. Don't put Epsom Salts and hydrogen peroxide in at the same time, but see if you can tell whether you feel better after one rather than the other. If so, concentrate on that preparation.

Before you fill the bath, turn on the heaters to warm up your bathroom first. Soak in the bath as long as you want to, keeping the water as hot as you can tolerate. When you have finished, get out and wrap yourself in two or three big towels and sit on the floor and sweat a little, just like a sauna but at home. You can then open the window to let out the steam, shower to clean off any residue you have sweated out and dress in something comfortable. Plan to do very little for the next two hours, so do something relaxing. This is best done towards bedtime.

Be aware that you will have sweated out a number of electrolytes, which it would be sensible to replace. The important and relevant ones are potassium, magnesium and sodium, so you will need an electrolyte replacement preparation, such as E-Lyte♥.

2 - Foot Baths

Find or buy a bowl large enough to put both your feet in. Alternatively you could use two separate bowls, one for each foot. Fill them with comfortably hot water and put in a tablespoonful of Epsom Salts, a tablespoonful of Sea Salt and a tablespoonful of olive oil. Put your feet in the bowls and leave them there as long as you want to, perhaps while you watch TV or listen to some soothing music. If you are really comfortable, perhaps you could use some of the time to do some relaxation exercises. Top up the water with extra hot water every so often to keep the temperature at a comfortable level. If you add hot or boiling water, please take your feet out so as not to burn them.

You can do this as often as you like and as is convenient for you and those around you. Anyone can do it, but it can be particularly helpful to, and pleasant for, people with cancer or any chronic debilitating illness. You may even have the odd bowl lying around that you didn't know what to do with anyway, but couldn't bear to throw away!

3 - Saunas

Saunas, especially Far Infra-Red Saunas♥, are an excellent way of clearing toxins out of your body, but they must be used with care. For a start, do not use a sauna used by the public. You are likely to inhale or absorb toxins that other users have excreted, even if the system is carefully cleaned out and monitored after being used. Just don't take the risk. Buy one for yourself if you want to, but they can be expensive, and it is worth trying out the effect upon you before buying one, as you may not find a sauna to your liking. While I know many people thoroughly enjoy them, ordinary saunas make me feel washed out and lethargic, so I don't ever go into one nowadays. However, I have a Far Infra-red personal blanket-type sauna♥ that does not need to become too hot to work properly which I enjoy.

4 - LL's Magnetic Clay

LL's Magnetic Clay♥ is a special bentonite, volcanic clay that, when used as a bath, draws toxic metals and chemicals out through the skin. It contains calcium, magnesium, potassium and sodium in their natural state. Packets of this clay also contain herbs and spices that you mix with the clay to enhance its effectiveness. As a caution, do not use more than once a week in a bath. However, for those who are too ill to get into a bath, the mixture can be used perhaps every three days in a footbath system.

The company that has produced this clay has a variety of different clays for different purposes, but, in general terms, it is probably best for most cancer patients to use the Environmental Detox Bath Kit and the Clear Out Detox Bath Kit.

5 - Coffee Enemas

Most young doctors have never heard of coffee enemas. They were probably first used on a regular basis by Florence Nightingale, even if she didn't exactly invent them. They were also still described in the doctors' 'bible', the Merck Manual, until 1977, being replaced by a description of some of the modern drugs coming into usage at the time. Also, doctors probably stopped recommending them.

If you were to take yourself off to the clinic in Mexico started by Dr. Max Gerson, you would have five coffee enemas a day, amongst other things, because they believe they are so valuable in patients with cancer and other chronic diseases. I try to encourage everyone suffering from cancer to carry out coffee enemas on themselves.   They are particularly beneficial the evening of a dose of chemotherapy or radiotherapy.

'The Little Enema Booklet'♥ describes the whole procedure, which is not as complicated as you might think, but the procedure is fully described below by a patient. The idea of doing a coffee enema fills some people with horror when I first mention them, but, once I have explained them, they usually try them and find that they are not only easy to carry out, but are most beneficial. They often clear the pain of cancer, and nearly always make a person feel far less ill after a dose of chemotherapy or radiotherapy, without diminishing the effects of either of those two treatments.

The Little Enema Booklet seems to suggest that you should not do a coffee enema while having chemotherapy or radiotherapy, but it is actually referring to a castor oil enema, and I would agree with that.

While a coffee enema may help to clear the bowels of some people, it often doesn't have any effect upon a person's bowel habits. In any case, its aim is quite different. The principle behind coffee enemas is that, whereas drinking coffee, or taking in any form of caffeine, should be avoided by someone with cancer, it is an effective method of increasing the body's ability to detoxify when given rectally. There is a specific large bowel/liver circulation so that coffee reaching the liver from this area helps the liver to eliminate more rapidly what it has already metabolised, by opening up the channels that collect into the bile duct to be emptied into the bowel and excreted at the next bowel movement.

You might think that coffee enemas should not be done when a person is jaundiced, because it would be reasonable to assume that the liver cannot pass its metabolised chemicals into the bowel when there is a blockage to the flow of bile out of the liver. When a person is jaundiced, the only other way out is back into the blood stream, hence the appearance of the yellow colour of the eyes and skin, as that is the colour of bile, which you will have noticed if you have ever been sick and brought up 'bile'.

However, it is not only safe, especially if you halve the dose of coffee you might use were you not jaundiced, it is also effective and can help to clear the jaundice, as some of my patients have found to their delight. I recently saw a young man who was becoming more jaundiced when I first saw him late one evening, when it was too late to give him a vitamin and mineral infusion that takes about 1½ hours to run in. I advised him to start coffee enemas straight away, and he did his first one the very next morning. When I saw him the day after that for his first infusion, his yellow skin colour was nearly back to normal, and his eyes were far less yellow. He was also feeling a lot better.

An additional, important feature of a coffee enema is that it stimulates the liver to produce more of an enzyme called glutathione-S-transferase, the enzyme that helps to manufacture glutathione, which is the body's most important detoxification chemical. If your cancer has been partially the result of a lifetime's accumulation of toxic chemicals, it is likely that you will long ago have used up all your supplies of glutathione. Hence, making fresh supplies can only be a good thing for you. This function of coffee enemas is certainly important if you are jaundiced.

How often you do a coffee enema depends upon how bad your condition is and how much better you feel when you start doing them. You should start with a small amount of coffee, in any case, perhaps half a teaspoonful, and gradually work up the dose to, say, a maximum of three teaspoonsful in one litre of body warm water. It would be best if you did not do one too close to bedtime, in case it disturbs your sleep, so the earlier in the day the better. In the end, do coffee enemas as often as your lifestyle allows, and, if your condition is serious, work up to doing as many as you can manage in a day, certainly to begin with when you are trying to get your cancer under control, although it may be sensible to do only one on the first day.

Some people report that they develop a caffeine 'high' when they have a coffee enema. This is because they do not insert the catheter far enough in. You must try to insert it at least six inches into your rectum, so that the coffee enters that part of your lower large bowel that connects into the liver via the portal blood vessel system. For that reason, you should apply the lubricant to at least six inches of the catheter. If you want to do a coffee enema late at night, for example, if you arrive home after a course of chemotherapy shortly before you would normally go to bed, put a bag of camomile tea in the hot water and make it strong before you add the coffee. This will help you to have a relaxed night's sleep, something that is important for all cancer patients.

You could obtain a copy of 'The Little Enema Booklet' if you want to, but the following is a personal case history a patient kindly prepared for me: I'd read 'The Little Enema' book and all the horror stories it contained of needing to redecorate the bathroom, and approached my first coffee enema with great trepidation. The good news is that I have now successfully completed dozens of them and find them relaxing and very pleasant (ok, the bathroom does need re-decorating, but that has nothing to do with the coffee enemas!) I was asked to share my experiences, in the hope they might be of use to someone else (maybe she thinks that, if I can do it, anyone can), so here goes:

Preparing the coffee

Call me stupid, but many times I boiled the coffee in the full litre of water, and then had to wait ages for it to cool. I even destroyed a glass jug by plunging it into cold water in a desperate attempt to hurry the cooling procedure. I've now developed a brain and use only half a litre of water to boil the coffee, then add cold water to bring it to body temperature (this is when it just feels warm when you put your finger in). I started with a teaspoon of coffee, and have now graduated to two teaspoons and a teaspoon of organic molasses (best to add the molasses to the hot coffee so they dissolve more easily)

Preparing the bathroom

I always have the enema in the bathroom so that the toilet is comfortingly close by, even though our bathroom is not very large. I cut up a bin liner, which covers a lot of the carpet, then lay an old towel on top. I also have a pillow to rest my head on for added comfort. I take in a book, a clock and some organic Aloe Vera to lubricate the tube (or olive oil is good). Most important is a few sheets of kitchen roll, which help mop up stray dribbles of coffee. I've found that a slightly bent wire coat hanger fits easily over the sink top and the hooked end makes a safe place to hang the enema bucket.

The enema

Next I attach the plastic tube to the bucket as firmly as possible, to avoid any leakages and then close the valve. After that I pour the full litre of coffee into the bucket. Holding the end of the tube over the toilet, I open the valve and let the coffee run through, closing the valve quickly as soon as the coffee has reached the end of the tube. Then I lubricate the end of the tube, lie down on my left side, and insert the tube. I've always found this easy and not painful, and I can only hope you do too.

Next I open the valve and let half the coffee flow in, which usually takes about a minute. At that stage I shut the valve and withdraw the enema tube and place it on the kitchen roll to catch the drips. I find that this makes it more comfortable to turn over, and, if I am desperate to use the toilet after the ten minutes is up, then I don't have to bother about withdrawing the tube at that delicate stage when muscle control is at its full limits anyway!

When I have expelled the first enema, I re-lubricate the tube and insert it again, open the valve and let in the remaining half litre. When the bucket is empty, I repeat the same procedure of shutting the valve and withdrawing the tube. (Don't forget this, as there is plenty of coffee in the tube to make a mess everywhere if you withdraw the tube without shutting the valve!) After a further ten minutes, I get rid of the second enema. Keeping the tube clean is not very easy, but I wash it every time with Ecover washing up liquid in hot water as soon as possible after the enema.

Occasionally I run boiling water through it and always hang it over a door so that it can dry out as much as possible.

And finally...
The first few times I did the enema, my stomach felt slightly odd all day, like a mild stomach bug, but this soon calmed down and now I have no after-effects at all. However, bearing this in mind, it may be a good idea not to plan any outings for the first couple of days after you start enemas.
- Anon (I mean, would you put your name to a document like this?)

6 - Colonic Irrigations

Many Naturopaths I have spoken to are very much of the opinion that we are wasting our time if we don't first sort out our bowels. I would agree with that. Very many people are thoroughly constipated when they first consult me. They may be opening their bowels once every 14 days, and have done so for as long as they can remember, yet the normal is 2 or 3 bowel movements a day, i.e. one meal in and one meal out, so long as there is enough fibre in the diet overall. Most people think once a day is good.

If there is any reason to think you might be constipated, a series of colonic irrigations is a good way of starting. It is distinctly possible that you have laid down a layer of undigested and unwanted matter in your bowels, which may well be harbouring undesirable germs, as well as blocking efficient nutrient absorption through the bowel wall. It is astonishing what some people can hold on to in their bowels. One of my patients passed a pebble that he remembered having swallowed as a child, 30 years earlier!

7 - Liver Herbs

There are various herbs that have been found to cleanse and stimulate the liver. Perhaps the best known is silymarin. Many companies provide their own mix, but the one I tend to use is a liquid, Harmonik Liver Cleans and Tonic♥, which my patients can prepare like an herbal tea. As all liquid herbal remedies are preserved in alcohol, I suggest you put half or one teaspoonful into a cup, add boiling water, leave it to stand for a few minutes for the alcohol to evaporate, add suitably cool water and drink it, preferably 10 to 30 minutes before meals three times daily, certainly to begin with.

8 - Foot Patches

The final suggestion under the heading of 'detoxification' is that you consider putting some specially designed patches on the soles of your feet at night. The best-known ones are called Segiun Patches♥, which are the ones I use and recommend. They are only available through a multilevel marketing scheme. They are the easiest to use as they have been produced like an ordinary plaster. You simply peel off the backing and apply them to the soles of your feet, keeping them on for eight hours over night if you can.

If you don't spend eight hours in bed, you simply put them on eight hours before you expect to get up in the morning. In the meantime, you can wander around the house in slippers until you are ready to go to bed. Having said that, I recommend that all cancer patients try to spend at least eight hours in bed at night because of the beneficial effects of a good night's detoxifying sleep. In addition, the more hours you can be in bed before midnight, the greater the value of that sleep.

There are cheaper versions of Segiun Patches that I have used (although I have just been informed that the price has come down), but I will leave you to find them for yourselves if you want to. Although I don't wish to be unduly critical, they are not the same, so I don't feel I can recommend them. From the labels, some of them appear to contain exactly the same ingredients, but, when you place them on the soles of your feet over night, there is a considerable difference in the colour of the matter that has been absorbed onto the patches by the morning. The matter on the Segiun Patches looks plausible to me, but it is almost as though some of the others contain a dye to make them look as though they have absorbed more from your feet. They also feel stiffer when taken off in the mornings.

Supplements

As it is likely that you are nutritionally deficient, it would be sensible for you to take a multivitamin/multimineral supplement every day, which you will benefit from far more effectively if your bowels have been cleaned out first. There are some excellent companies around and you may want to choose one for yourself. I tend to recommend products by Biocare. However, you may want to think about the origin of any supplements you take. Most are chemically made and are apparently identical to the vitamins and minerals we all need, to all intents and purposes.

But there is a company that believes that you will benefit far more if you take supplements whose origin is from foods that you would normally consume. The assumption is that your body has become accustomed to recognising nutrients in food, and knows how to extract them. So, if supplements originate from foods, the whole process should be that much more easy for you.

For example, most forms of pycnogenol, a powerful anti-oxidant, are extracted from pine bark, which you don't eat. A source from foods you do eat might be more effective. To be fair, however, I have not researched this process enough yet to know whether it is better or not.

Essential Fatty Acids (EFAs)

There is a lot of evidence that EFAs are important to people in general, and especially in patients with cancer. The omega-3 EFAs are likely to be deficient rather than omega-6, as vegetable oils tend to give the omega-6, while oily fish and flaxseed oil provide omega-3 oils. If you take significantly more omega-6 in your diet than omega-3, the result may be the promotion of inflammation through an omega-6 breakdown product called arachidonic acid. You can prevent this, and therefore have an anti-inflammatory effect, if you take more omega-3 than omega-6. There is increasing evidence in the scientific literature that chronic diseases of any sort, including cancer, are promoted by inflammation. Therefore you need to improve your anti-inflammatory side of things.

If you are a vegan, or don't like or can't take fish, hemp seeds or flax seeds (far better than the oil) would be for you. Otherwise I would suggest Eskimo-3 oil♥, a 5ml teaspoonful twice daily with food.

Pancreatic Enzymes

There is a considerable amount of scientific evidence that pancreatic enzymes are also anti-inflammatory. If the theory that cancer is just another way the body sometimes expresses an inflammatory cascade mechanism, it seems perfectly reasonable to me that, if you have cancer, you should take pancreatic enzymes.

Can you remember where I discussed in the introduction that one of the causes of cancer could be a deficiency of pancreatic enzymes? I explained that most of us eat a lot of food over a lifetime that contains very little enzymes, either because the food didn't have much in it in the first place or because we destroyed much of it by the way we cooked it. If cancer is an inflammatory response to something in our environment, you can see why the lack of sufficient enzymes over a lifetime could make cancer all the more likely to develop, especially if we have a genetic predisposition to cancer.

There are many stories of the importance of pancreatic enzymes in cancer, but, to be fair, no double-blind studies have been carried out on this so far as I am aware. Having said that, there is a wealth of studies carried out in Germany on a particularly useful pancreatic enzyme formula that I use in my cancer patients, called Wobenzym, although I only use a special reformulated preparation that I obtain from America called Wobenzym N. The German variety is covered in a sugar coating and a bright red dye! The American version is not.

If the same enzymes present in the pancreas are formulated from a vegetarian source, they don't seem to have the same anti-cancer effect or potency. I therefore only use a pancreatic source. It is as though there is another chemical present in the pancreas that we are not aware of at present, which has additional anti-cancer activity. For anyone who is interested, this might be a subject for a Nobel Prize!

If Wobenzym N♥, or any other pancreatic enzyme preparation, is taken for cancer, it should not be taken around meals to help digest food as you might expect, but should be taken well away from food. It should ideally be taken in the gap at least two hours after one meal and one hour before the next, three times a day, although there is no need to have food one hour after taking a dose, such as in the gap after your evening meal and before going to bed.

So, ideal times to take some are in the gap between two hours after breakfast and one hour before lunch. That means that, if you finish breakfast at 8 am and start lunch around 1 pm, you can take some anywhere between 10 am and midday. The same applies for the afternoon between lunch and your evening meal. Another ideal time to take more is two hours after supper and anywhere before going to bed. So, if you finish your evening meal at 8 pm, you can take some any time after 10 pm. You don't have to eat one hour later, and, in fact, if you take some around the time you go to bed, or in the middle of the night, it may be even more effective. I often take a handful just before going to bed.

How many you should take is a difficult question to answer, but basically the answer is the worse your condition the more you should take. The maximum I recommend to any of my patients is 12 Wobenzym N tablets three times a day between meals, but, when you start taking them, start with one three times a day, and add an extra one three times a day each day, so that, if everything works well, by day 6 you will be on six tablets three times a day, and so on. Some people find that a certain dose seems to suit them, but more does not. When taking any tablets or capsules by mouth, always take them with a full glass of water, otherwise they can sit on your stomach lining and irritate it.

Vitamin D♥

Most doctors seem to be afraid of vitamin D, which can be obtained from your diet, although the best source is from the sun. However, most skin Specialists seem now to be advising you to avoid sun exposure virtually completely, because of what they consider to be a risk of developing skin cancer, yet a study has suggested that 'sun exposure is associated with *increased* survival from melanoma'. This is therefore a controversial issue, but I like many of my cancer patients to take at least 5000iu vitamin D orally per day, especially in the winter months. Oily fish provide not only omega-3 EFAs, but also vitamins A and D, so there may well be a connection between all of the fat-soluble vitamins.

If you have a blood test done on your vitamin D levels, as far as other specialists and I are concerned, an ideal level to work towards is 65-85ng/ml (160-210nmol/l). 20-40 (50-100) is insufficient, below 20ng/ml (50nmol/l) being definitely deficient.

Vitamin C

I like all my cancer patients to take as much vitamin C as they can. Obviously this will be taken by mouth by the vast majority of people, although some patients are fortunate enough to be able to have high doses administered intravenously. I encourage all my patients to try to reach at least 10g per day, preferably in at least four divided doses. I use a particular preparation called Bio En'R-Gy C, by Longevity Plus♥. It is very well tolerated by the bowel, and I recommend that patients start low, and gradually work up to their bowel tolerance.

For a long time now I personally have been using 10g Bio En'R-Gy C powder by Longevity Plus per day, which does not upset my bowels, having previously never really found a formulation that I could tolerate at the doses I wanted to take.

If too much vitamin C is taken orally, it can upset your bowels, in the form of wind, indigestion, diarrhoea or sometimes pain. If any of these occur, simply reduce the dose for a few days to eliminate the symptoms, and then try to increase the dose back up again.

It will be best if you could have vitamin C intravenously, but that is not likely to happen. A new form of vitamin C has recently been produced that suggests that 1g of liposomed vitamin C might be equivalent to 10,000mg intravenously♥. That means you could take 3 or 4 sachets a day.

Other Anti-Oxidants

Mainstream medicine uses drugs that are single chemicals that are so powerful they can work alone. They have been designed to interfere, or block, a particular chemical abnormality that is assumed from research to be why the particular symptom or disease has occurred. Unfortunately they often interfere with other chemical reactions that remain desirable, so producing adverse reactions of one sort or another. Basically such drugs are not sufficiently targeted.

Complimentary or Integrated medicine uses a variety of preparations, which compliment each other. So you derive the benefits of each, hopefully without developing adverse reactions. They can occur but rarely do any significant harm. The first additional anti-oxidant I would recommend is Alphalipoic acid♥, at 100mg with each dose of vitamin C, as it helps to regenerate vitamin C, and is therefore likely to keep the levels of vitamin C as high as possible.

I would also recommend you take a certain dose of other anti-oxidants, such as 800IU vitamin E, 4,500IU vitamin A, and at least 400mcg selenium, if you want to take them separately, although you may need more selenium during replacement of your mercury amalgam fillings (see that section). Various companies do an A C E and selenium combination product, and you can take more than one capsule a day if you want to, or you could add individual items to reach a particular level. I have already said that bowel cancers tend to occur in areas where the soil is low in selenium, and people eat produce grown in that soil, so make sure you are taking it, preferably in two or three divided doses, and about half-an-hour before food.

Artemisinin♥ & Iron

Earlier on I mentioned the fact that cancer cells feed on iron, amongst other things. If your iron levels are low, it is important to bring them up to an adequate level, but I am concerned that you might take iron supplements, many of which cause constipation. There are some forms that you can usually buy from your local health food store that should not do this, but I don't want you to take any iron supplements unless there is clear evidence that you need it, i.e. from a blood test. You need to be aware that most multivitamin/multimineral preparations tend to contain some iron, so please check and only take one that does not if you don't need it. If you have evidence that you are anaemic around 10g/litre, you probably should take a non-constipating form of iron, one to three capsules last thing at night, always starting with just one to make sure they suit you. You improve your absorption of iron if you take vitamin C with it, which you are likely to do at that time anyway. Do not take any other minerals with iron as they compete for absorption sites. If you are around 8g/

litre or lower, you will probably need a blood transfusion, although I would be intrigued to know what might happen were you to take Quinton Marine Plasma (see below).

If you need to improve your iron status, but it is not too bad, or you can't find a form that suits you, or you are not prepared to have a blood transfusion, you would be wise to try Spirulina. This preparation is full of chlorophyll, and, if you know anything about chemistry, chlorophyll is structurally remarkably similar to haemoglobin. This will make it easier for your body to make haemoglobin from it and any available iron.

If you have a normal compliment of iron, there is a possibility that your cancer cells may try to feed on it, so this is where artemisinin comes in. It is apparently able to block the absorption and utilisation of iron by cancer cells. In addition, it is also able to stop parasites using iron, so is considered by some doctors to be the nutritional choice for treating malaria.

Quinton Marine Plasma♥

Quinton Marine Plasma is a very exciting preparation that has, in fact, been around for many decades, especially in Europe. The reason why I have chosen to describe it here in relation to iron status is because of an animal experiment that produced a totally remarkable result, and it is reasonable to consider that if your levels of iron are very low, such as would normally require a blood transfusion, taking Quinton Marine Plasma by mouth may help avoid the need of a transfusion, with all its risks.

A dog was effectively exanguinated, i.e. all its blood was completely removed, in which case it should have died. However, as its blood was removed, it was given an infusion of Quinton Marine plasma at the same time, and, in three days it was up and about and running round in apparently better health than before. No one has had the guts to do the same to a human, although I would have thought that if some patients, possibly a scientist interested in the whole area, were so moribund after numerous blood transfusions that hadn't really worked that they would have tried it by now.

I can't say that it would do this, but taking it by mouth has been remarkably effective in thousands of people for all sorts of reasons, if the anecdotal reports are anything to go by.

Anti-Oestrogen Preparations

It is almost inevitable that your breast cancer is at least partially caused by a dominance of oestrogen relative to progesterone. Mainstream medicine uses a number of drugs that have anti-oestrogenic activity, the best known of which is probably tamoxifen, although newer drugs are regularly in the news these days. A natural form is a chemical called Indole-3-carbinol, which is extracted from broccoli and other vegetables. There are other forms that are often combined, and I currently use a preparation called Dim Vitex♥, one capsule three times daily, preferably half-an-hour before meals.

By improving the functioning of the liver, either using Essiac Tea as Harmonik Ojibwa Indian Herbal Tonic or more specific herbs, such as silymarin, your ability to break down oestrogen in the liver will be enhanced. However, I often add a preparation called Calcium-D-glucarate♥, 500mg, also best taken three times a day half-an-hour before meals, which helps prevent oestrogen from being reformed in the intestines, which clearly you don't want.

A third effectively anti-oestrogen preparation is bio-identical or 'natural' progesterone cream♥, about 20mg rubbed onto any soft skin once a day for 3 weeks out of 4 if you are post-menopausal. It is simpler to remember if you stop for the first three to five days in each calendar month, restarting applying it on about day 4 or 6. You could possibly halve the dose and take homoeopathic progesterone 200C♥ at least once a day while applying the cream. If you are still having a menstrual cycle (which is unlikely if you have been treated with anti-oestrogen drugs or chemotherapy, etc.), start applying progesterone cream from about day 14, if your cycle is a regular 28 days. Likewise you could take the homoeopathic drops at the same time. If you lose all pre-menstrual symptoms by these methods, if you previously had them, you could then leave off the cream, which is the more expensive of the two, and see if those symptoms stay away using the homoeopathic drops on their own. Remember, you are trying to have a hormonal balancing effect and eliminate all oestrogen dominant effects. Doctors' drugs tend to chemically castrate you, which cause you the discomfort of menopausal symptoms. My intention is to rid you of the excess, which is doing you so much harm, but leave you still feeling like a normal woman.

Co-Enzyme Q10

There are many studies that have shown the value of Co-enzyme Q 10 in breast cancer.

They used 390mg in the main, so 400mg would be the appropriate dose per day. It is an excellent anti-oxidant, among other things, so helps to share the anti-oxidant responsibilities.

Two Exciting New Approaches

There are two exciting new simple approaches to managing breast cancer that were described to us at a recent conference in America. One was the application of Co-enzyme Q 10 to the cancerous breast. I wish to give full credit to Dr. Alan Lieberman and his team for this discovery. Patients had undergone a thermogram before and a while after applying the cream daily, and the results were clear for all to see. I am in the process of recommending some of my breast cancer patients apply it to any glands they can feel in their armpit as well, to see whether this can be effective or not.

As it is sensible for you to take Co Enzyme Q10 400mg per day, as I have already suggested above, it is logical to also apply it topically to the breast itself, to concentrate the effect, and I suggest you apply it to the unaffected breast as well. I don't know why I didn't think of it myself. This is the value of my attending meetings of like-minded doctors.

The second new approach is the use of iodine, and I give full credit to Dr. Sherri Tenpenny for the information. The explanation for its use is somewhat complex, and is not entirely to do with your thyroid gland as you might have expected. Iodine is known for its anti-infective effects, being particularly effective against fungi. It is also anti-oestrogenic, although I didn't know that until very recently. Apply it at least to your affected breast twice a day, so perhaps iodine first thing in the morning and mid-afternoon, and Co Enzyme Q 10 late morning and last thing at night.

Using Magnascent Iodine♥, put three drops in a glass of water and take it twice a day, the second dose mid afternoon. Although iodine is thought of as being only important for your thyroid gland, it is in fact important for all hormonal functions, with the thyroid being the most greedy. If you are deficient in iodine, your thyroid gland will take as much as it can get hold of, so leaving your other hormonal suppliers a bit short. I have always felt there is a significant connection between all our glands. If you apply iodine directly to your breast twice a day, there is no need to take it by mouth.

Perhaps you can remember when I explained earlier that the absorption of iodine needs as close to perfect a pH as possible. If you are too acidic, as you are likely to be if you have cancer, your absorption of iodine will be incomplete, which is why so many people are deficient in iodine. Anyone with cancer is likely to benefit from iodine.

To compliment the whole process you are advised to take magnesium (I suggest Transdermal Magnesium Lotion♥), selenium (at least 100mcg daily half an hour before breakfast and your evening meal) and tyrosine (500mg three times daily at the same time as the selenium). As thyroxine is effectively a molecule of tyrosine containing four iodine atoms, this will make sure that thyroid hormone is not only adequately manufactured but is converted effectively into T3 called tri-iodo thyronine.

Immune Enhancing Preparations

If you have one of the tests done that shows your immune system to be in a poor state, such as by SureScreen Life Sciences or Neuro-Lab, then there will be other supplements that can help to boost this aspect of your metabolism. If your Natural Killer cells are poorly functioning, I like the preparation Biobran, but a 1g sachet costs just over £3.00 each. I would advise you to take one three times a day for the first four weeks, then leave off for one week, restarting at once a day, pulsing the treatment 3 weeks on and 1 week off, to maintain a stimulus to these essential cells of your immune response to cancer. If two other aspects of your immune system are poor, i.e. Interleukin 12 (IL12) and/or Tumour Necrosis Factor Beta (TNF-Beta), I recommend ImmKine, at one capsule three times a day, until a subsequent blood test, possibly in three months time, shows an adequate, or preferably higher than normal, level.

TNF-Beta is a chemical that reflects the functioning of your thymus, a gland that lies behind your sternum (breastbone), so, whether or not a blood test shows poor functioning of it, it is certainly worth trying to stimulate it in a simple, cheap way. Three times a day, tap your breastbone sixty times with all four fingers of your dominant hand. You don't need to bang hard, merely tap sufficiently hard to cause a gentle vibration of the bone itself.

Managing Infections

I have given you a lot of advice as to how to eliminate certain infections from your body, especially from your bowels, but there are other 'infections' that are more difficult to identify and therefore to know what to do about them. I am referring in particular to the chickenpox/shingles and the human papilloma/wart viruses. In the History chapter I mentioned the fact that some like-minded doctors believe that one or both of these viruses are involved in all forms of cancer. Unless there is a very strong history of shingles, this virus seems somehow to be involved with breast cancer, and I would certainly agree that I have become very suspicious of it.

The human papilloma/wart virus is certainly accepted by mainstream medicine as being involved in cancer of the cervix, but I am sure it is involved in all cancers of the reproductive tract, so also uterine, ovarian, vaginal and prostate cancers, as well as cancer of the bladder (what a surgeon sees when he looks into the bladder he often describes as looking wart-like) and skin cancers. It is a little difficult to explain why the papilloma virus is probably involved in other cancers such as of the lung or brain, but colleagues who study this area in great detail are convinced that it is.

My problem is what to advise you to do, how to identify if these viruses are involved, and, if so, how to treat them. You could have the Neuro-Lab Non-genomic DNA/RNA test, or something similar, but, as I have already explained, this can merely tell you that you have a viral or bacterial load, but not identify the organism involved. If this test is raised, you could assume what it is telling you and have a course of homoeopathic treatment for either or both of these organisms. I would suggest Malandrinum 200C a dose twice daily for 14 days, wait one week then a combination of Rhus tox 12C and Box jellyfish 12C also a dose twice daily for 14 days, for the chickenpox/ shingles virus. For the papilloma/wart virus, you could take a dose of papilloma 200C twice daily for 14 days♥. These doses and potencies should ideally be worked out for each individual, but clearly I cannot do that for you all.

You could then repeat the Non-genomic DNA/RNA test approximately two weeks after finishing the course, and, if the level has come down but not reduced to normal, it would be a reasonable assumption that you were on the right track, so repeat the treatment. If the test has become normal, you have done the trick. If there were no improvement in the level, it would be reasonable to assume that you either took the wrong treatment, or there is another virus that needs to be eliminated.

All viruses and organisms have their own frequency, which it may be possible to identify using a Vega Testing machine or equivalent. Unfortunately I have not had much experience of using these machines, so, if you are interested in this idea, you will have to find your own practitioner.

However, various 'zappers' have been produced that are said to be able to clear any undesirable organisms from the body. Dr Hulda Clarke has written extensively on this subject in her book 'A Cure For All Cancers',♥ and she explains how to make a Zapper, although I believe she has now organised for them to be made commercially. In some respects I think she goes over the top in her descriptions, but I'm sure they are appropriate for some people.

I was recently shown a rather expensive piece of equipment that the manufacturer said was capable of being programmed for virtually any medical condition, including cancer. I haven't had a chance to test it yet, but you are welcome to contact the manufacturer and see if it could be of value to you♥.

Colloidal Silver♥

There is now increasing evidence that using colloidal silver in an ionised form can help to eliminate many infections from the body, if not all of them in due course. Using a form that can be sprayed into the mouth is probably the best and easiest way of delivering it, especially as the mouth, and the teeth in particular, harbour a lot of organisms, as TV commercials keep reminding us. However, I understand the EU in its eternal wisdom has recently banned its use for humans and animals. A sceptic might say this is because it is effective, safe, cheap and without any adverse effects!

Chlorine Dioxide

Chlorine dioxide is rather like hydrogen peroxide. There are many websites that explain what it is all about and I have prepared one that is available if you are interested. As it may be very difficult for many of you to find someone to hold your hand through all this information and do some of the tests I have suggested, it may be more logical to assume that a number of infections are playing a part in your cancer, and simply take a certain amount of iodine, colloidal silver and/or chlorine dioxide♥, taking them at different times of the day.

I have already suggested that you will need to plan your day as carefully as possible, so you will need to work out when to take all the supplements you plan to take. Iodine should perhaps be taken in any liquid twice a day perhaps with breakfast and mid-afternoon snack or drink, silver can be sprayed into your mouth possibly every two hours in between doing all the other things, while it is probably best to take your first dose of chlorine dioxide some time after your evening meal and repeat the same dose between one and two hours later. However, a new formulation of chlorine dioxide has become available, and it may be better to follow its instructions.

Unfortunately the FDA in America and the European Authorities have recently come out against chlorine dioxide for their own reasons, basically saying it is a concentrated bleach and there are no studies to say it works in human beings. However the United States Department of Health, an organisation over the FDA, says they have tested it and it is safe for humans to take by mouth. It was basically tested because various people wished to use it in swimming pools, and it was essential to identify whether it was safe if swallowed. They found it was, so it is up to you.

How long you should go on taking all these depends on how things progress. At all stages you must regularly assess how you are doing. If you are sure you are doing well, continue doing the same until you are confident you have eliminated your cancer. The best form of assessment is how you feel.

An Important Piece of Advice

If you seem to benefit from a particular approach, but then start to feel something is not quite right, such as you suddenly develop more pain or feel a lot more tired, don't assume that everything has gone wrong, as would be quite logical, but consider the possibility that what you are doing is killing off a lot of cancer cells, and your body is struggling to eliminate all that debris. In the circumstances I suggest you give your body a rest by stopping taking all supplements for a few days and do some coffee enemas (if you are not doing them, but, if you are, even consider stop doing them as well). Drink a lot of quality water and eat less food than usual possibly confining your intake to organic soups sipped throughout the day. Even a fast for a couple of days on water only might be worth considering. If this works, restart your supplementary regime after a few days off them all. You may need to repeat this process every so often. If, however, you don't feel well when you restart all the supplements, you will need to stop them all again, let the adverse symptoms settle down again, then reintroduce them one by one to identify which one or ones do not suit you.

What To Do About Stress

In your history, it is extremely likely that you admitted to a significant degree of stress, which may have been going on for years. In that case you have two areas that you need to do something about, one being the stress itself, the other being the physiological effect that stress has had, and is now having, upon your body. The effect upon your physiology is many-fold, especially the wearing out of your adrenal glands (remember the approach by Dr. Fryda?) and the overall acidity the whole process has caused. The additional problem is whether the acidity in particular has created harmful organisms from ones that your body was living in perfect harmony with.

There are various glandular preparations that some of my colleagues use, but I have found a preparation that contains specific nutrients and herbs to support and feed your adrenal glands. It is Biocare's AD206.♥ The worse and longer-standing your stress the more you may need to take, so you can decide for yourself.

Stress strips magnesium from your body as well as other nutrients. So many people are under stress and many studies have shown just how many people are deficient in magnesium. The problem is that trying to improve your magnesium status by taking supplements by mouth often fails. I suspect that magnesium absorption is partially under the influence of an enzyme that is itself magnesium dependent. So, if your magnesium levels are low, your magnesium absorption mechanisms become inefficient. Also calcium, which most doctors insist we should all be taking in large amounts to prevent osteoporosis, especially post-menopausal women, competes with magnesium for absorption. This means that the more calcium we take in our diet (including in the form of dairy products) the less magnesium we might absorb. The Kelly approach basically suggests that breast cancers do well on magnesium, but badly on calcium, assuming that you have a sympathetic nervous system dominant personality, i.e. you are generally a positive, extroverted type who likes to take charge, rather than an introverted quiet parasympathetic nervous system type.

I found that giving patient's magnesium by intravenous injection to be very effective, together with other nutrients, and, once their magnesium levels had improved, giving magnesium by mouth then worked well enough. However, it is unlikely that you will be able to find someone who will give you injections of magnesium.

In the circumstances Transdermal Magnesium Lotion♥ has been found to work well, and I know of many people who have found it to be the answer to their magnesium problems. All you have to do is apply it to any part of your body as often as is practical. Also it saves you having to swallow yet another tablet.

In the chapter on Problem Solving, I hope you will find some really useful ways of doing something about any current problems you may be having. It is equally important that you follow some of the advice to wash your soul clear of any deep-seated problems, because they are slowly poisoning you, especially undermining the functioning of your immune system.

I have also already mentioned that stress causes you to become more acidic, so consider what I said in the section on 'Alkalising (de-acidification) Drops' earlier on with AlkaLiza.

It is likely also that your thyroid may not be as efficient as it ought to be, as it seems also to be adversely affected by stress, although routine blood tests for thyroid function may not show this up. I have explained why this is elsewhere. As it is unlikely that you will be able to obtain whole thyroid, and certainly not thyroxine, from your doctor without blood test evidence of your needing it, taking Biocare's TH207 one capsule three times a day with meals, may suffice.

Herpes Virus

At a conference in London recently, a colleague confirmed that she also had found that the herpes/chicken pox/shingles virus is somehow involved in many cancers, especially breast cancer. Neither of us knows why, but, again, it may be something to do with the immune system. Its treatment is by homoeopathy, using Malandrinum followed by a combination of Rhus Tox and Box jellyfish, as described earlier twice daily for at least fourteen days, although, if your situation is very serious, it may need to continue for fifty days (so the worse your condition, the longer it would be sensible for you to take it).

If, however, you start to develop odd nerve symptoms, or chicken pox/ shingles-like symptoms, stop the treatment. If you know anything about homoeopathy, that will be suggesting you have had enough and you are now 'proving' the treatment, which effectively means you are bringing the symptoms back.

However long you take the Malandrinum for, wait one week and then take a combination of Rhus tox and Box jellyfish, twice daily, for the same length as you took the Malandrinum. This is a little tricky and ideally needs to be adjusted individually, but this is the best advice I can give you in this web site.

One more thing. Ideally you should try to do things in the reverse order in which they occurred in your life. As you probably had chicken pox before you had any mercury amalgams put into your teeth, it would be best if you did the dental work before you took the homoeopathic treatments. I always prefer people to order drops of any treatments, rather than sugar or lactose pills, for the obvious reasons.

If all of this seems a bit too complicated for you, it might be simpler to take iodine, colloidal silver (possibly now banned in the EU) and chlorine dioxide for a while in the hope of eliminating all infections from your body.

Additional Aspects To Treatment

Although the heading of this section is 'supplements', it is important to make sure you will benefit from any supplements you take by mouth. When I saw a patient for the first time, I seldom recommended they took any nutritional supplements at that stage, advising them that they would absorb nutrients from their diet far more efficiently if their intestines were working properly. It was at the second visit that I was likely to recommend appropriate nutrients, although I had the luxury of being able to administer vitamins and minerals intravenously in the meantime, which naturally bypasses any intestinal malabsorption problems. In the past I have carried out tests of nutrient status in new patients, to find that they have improved on retesting within one month of the patient following my recommended diet. There is absolutely no doubt in my mind that the 'wrong' diet for a person causes nutritional deficiencies, many of which can be improved by following the 'right' diet.

Over the years, however, my patients have had even better results by clearing out undesirable infections, and, now that laboratory tests are available that really do identify what organisms are involved and what natural preparations those organisms are sensitive to, it has been much easier to help many patients. What fascinates me is the range of symptoms that respond to this approach, which certainly includes many patients with cancer.

What I am really saying is that, although you understandably want to 'get on with things', unless your condition is very urgent, identifying what organisms you may be harbouring and starting the process of eliminating them is very important right from the beginning, and could be considered one of the more important approaches to apply early on.

In the circumstances, I suggest you contact one of the laboratories, ask them to send the relevant kit for whichever samples you or they think are appropriate (a sample of saliva for the candida test or samples of faeces for the Comprehensive

Stool Analysis by Genova Diagnostics), and start taking Diatomaceous Earth♥ and a herbal mixture called Paracleanse♥, while waiting for the results of your tests to be sent to you. You should also start the anticancer diet I have already described, of course. If you suffer from sinusitis, I find chlorine dioxide to be best.

This doesn't mean to say that it is a waste of time and money taking nutritional supplements by mouth immediately. They are likely to be better than not taking any, but, if time is on your side, it may be all right to wait while you sort out your bowels. Having a colonic irrigation very early on is an excellent way to start your whole programme, and you would be surprised what you may pass at that time.

Heavy Metal Toxicity

I have already discussed how important I think this may be if you have breast cancer, and such dental work is not likely to be started very early on, possibly because it takes time to find a properly trained dentist and even get an appointment with him. In the first instance there are not many or them around, and in the second instance they tend to be booked up some way ahead. In the meantime, you can start on some of my other recommendations.

The important toxic heavy metals that you need to be aware of are mercury, lead, cadmium, arsenic and aluminium. Most of us of a certain age played with balls of mercury when we were young. It was called 'quick silver' in those days, and it was fascinating to watch it rolling around our hands and sometimes all over the floor if we dropped some of it. Whether that was dangerous or not, I couldn't tell you, but it was soon recognised to be the toxic substance it is now known to be. It is considered to be one of the most toxic substances known to man after radioactive materials.

Incidentally, are you aware of the origin of the word 'quack', which is sometimes applied to doctors who practice the sort of drug-free medicine that I prefer? It comes from the German word 'quecksilber', which means 'mercury', although there is a German word 'quacksalver' which means 'quack'. So maybe the dentists who first started using mercury are the real quacks!

There are many ways you can be exposed to mercury in life, including through eating large fish, such as tuna, which are on the end of the life chain. Various vaccinations contain mercury as a preservative, which some people think is very dangerous, even if the authorities don't agree. It is also sometimes used as a preservative in contact lens solutions. There are various books that can frighten people about the dangers of mercury, but I think some of them go over the top. The one I recommend is 'Menace In The Mouth' by the late Dr. Jack Levenson.♥ While it is now very difficult to obtain an oldfashioned mercury thermometer in the UK, we are being encouraged to use long-life electric bulbs, which contain mercury, producing is a disposal problem. If you ask your dentist if you can keep an amalgam filling if he extracts or replaces one, he will tell you he has to dispose of it as toxic waste. It is all very silly, yet mercury is clearly dangerous.

Most people have a number of teeth with mercury amalgam fillings in them. Some people have a 'mouthful'. If they are examined carefully, it can often be noticed that some of them appear to be leaking or are corroded, or pieces have broken off exposing an extra surface of amalgam. A dental amalgam is a mixture of metals, which is what the word 'amalgam' means. The mixture contains 50% mercury, the remaining 50% being a mixture of more then one other metal. The final mixture is made up in the dentist's surgery just before being inserted into a hole prepared in your tooth. To be fair, it is a very easy material to handle, and the job can be completed competently and quickly. Some people think the public has been conned by calling them 'silver amalgams' not mercury amalgams.

The fact that there is more than one metal in your mouth, surrounded by an electrolyte-containing liquid, your saliva, turns that filling into a mini battery. Any physics teacher will tell you that electrons will move from one metal to another in the circumstances. This mixture tends to make the mercury in the amalgam move more than the others. Therefore mercury vaporizes constantly from your teeth, the whole process being promoted by eating hot food, drinking acidic liquids such as orange juice, and by the simple act of brushing your teeth. Yes, it is a gradual process, but it is going on slowly all the time.

When I was a kid at school, somewhere between the ages of seven and thirteen, we were taught art by a wonderful, but strict, artist, whose dwelling was typical of the rose-covered cottages that Rupert Bear used to find, when he and his friends went on their adventures in the woods. This man's cottage was at the bottom of the football pitch.

He came in to teach us art once a week, but he also had a fund of knowledge about so many other things. One of those was how to make a crystal set, to listen to the BBC, using hairs from our heads, although exactly how he did it I have forgotten. What I do remember very clearly was that, if a wire was somehow attached to the amalgam fillings that some of us had in our teeth, the battery-like effect could be used to provide amplification of the sound his simple contraption produced!

Despite the fact that Dr. Mats Hansen has identified around thirteen thousand articles published in scientific journals that describe the dangers of mercury and how some of that mercury gradually leaks out (some of which Dr. Levenson discusses in his book), the idea that the mercury amalgams in your teeth are a danger to your health has not yet become the prevailing opinion of the medical and dental professions. There are, however, many dentists, scientists and doctors who honestly believe that anyone who has a significant illness should have their mercury amalgams assessed by a properly trained biological dentist, with a view to having them replaced by an appropriate alternative non-metallic material. I happen to be one of those doctors who believe it is a danger to your health, and, if you have cancer, you should seriously consider having them sorted out.

In my opinion, there are many reasons why a person with cancer should have their mercury amalgam fillings replaced. In the first place mercury is an established toxic substance. Secondly, mercury has no place in your body, and the simple act of eating, especially hot or acidic foods, grinding or brushing your teeth, and drinking anything even slightly acidic, will cause mercury to vaporize from your amalgam fillings. While some of that mercury will be exhaled, most of it will either be inhaled or swallowed, or will enter your tissues through the mucous membranes in your mouth. Some will also gradually migrate through the nerve roots in your teeth and enter your brain. It may take years, but, if you have had yours for years, it will already have entered your tissues.

Mercury disturbs many metabolic functions in your body. Dr. Levenson's book makes that perfectly clear. So, if you want the scientific facts, read his book. This toxic metal also wastes important nutrients, such as selenium and zinc, both of which are deficient in most people's body anyway, especially if they have cancer, and both of which are important for your immune system, and your fight against cancer.

If you do decide to have your mercury amalgam fillings replaced, it is essential that you take chelating minerals, starting shortly before the first dental session, and continuing throughout the time that the work is done, i.e. continue between visits to the dentist. I try to establish what is appropriate for each individual patient, but clearly I cannot tell you exactly what dose to use, although I can give you some guidelines. In principle, the more fillings you have to be replaced, the more chelating nutrients you might need to take on a daily basis and for that much longer.

As a rough guide, I suggest you take a total of 300 to 900 micrograms of elemental selenium, 3 to 6 grammes of vitamin C (you may have already reached at least 10g by the time you start any dental work, possibly using Bio En'R-Gy C) and 90 to 150 milligrammes of elemental zinc per day. Ideally you should take selenium ½ hour before meals, vitamin C with meals and zinc 1 hour after meals, preferably taking each substance three times a day (possibly more often for vitamin C). So, try to take 100-300 micrograms of selenium ½ hour before breakfast, lunch and your evening meal, 1 or 2 grammes of vitamin C with those meals, and take 30-50 mg of zinc about 1 hour after breakfast, lunch and your evening meal. If you are rather a forgetful type, it is better to divide them into two separate doses than not to take them at all.

How long should you take such doses, when 900 micrograms could mean eighteen tablets a day, 6 grammes of vitamin C means six tablets and 150 milligrammes of zinc could mean ten capsules, making a possible thirty-four tablets a day? In theory, the best answer I could give is for as long as you need to clear mercury (and any other heavy metals) completely from your body. However, that is not a very practical answer.

So my recommendation is that you take whatever dose you decide to take, up to the maximum I suggest, starting at least one or two weeks before the amalgam replacements start, ideally reaching your target dose by the time the dental work begins. This is to make sure that you can tolerate such high doses. Please make sure you take all tablets and capsules with a full glass of water, especially if away from food, so that they don't sit dry on your stomach, in which case they might irritate it. In any case, you need to make sure that they suit you. There is a small possibility that one or more of them just might not agree with you, and you need to know this before the dental work commences.

I can well understand if someone tells you such high doses are, or might be, dangerous, or cause imbalances of other nutrients, i.e. copper, for example. However, many thousands of my patients have followed this approach successfully, although, to be fair, not 100% of them. So you need to know they suit you, and you will only find out by starting them and taking a few days to reach your target doses.

What I have found from experience is that, in general but not always, the more teeth you have filled with amalgam, the larger the fillings with a big total surface area (so the greater the amount of amalgam in your mouth) plus the longer they or some of them have been there, the bigger the doses of selenium, vitamin C and zinc you need, and the longer after the dental replacements have been completed you will need to be on such high doses, possibly for up to nine months or longer. Studies of body content of mercury support these observations.

What I also discovered very early on when I recognised the importance of dealing with mercury amalgam fillings was that the best way of telling a patient when they had been on those chelating agents for long enough, was that new symptoms coming out of the blue would occur. Such symptoms could be unusual or new headaches, spots anywhere on the body, boils, dry corners of the mouth, pain or aching in joints not previously a problem, or just suddenly not feeling so well as before in a variety of ways. These I surmised could be adverse effects of too much selenium in particular, i.e. selenium toxicity. I assumed that when these selenium toxic symptoms occurred, mercury had essentially been cleared from the body, so large doses of selenium were no longer required.

This seemed logical to me and justified their not taking, or needing, any more selenium. When they stopped the selenium (and the vitamin C and zinc, of course) these new symptoms cleared, but it took as long for them to clear as they had been present. Many patients restarted selenium, only to find the same symptoms returned very quickly. Over the years, hundreds of patients have told me of their experiences, so I have been able to warn the next ones what might happen. In every case I have been right.

When, many years ago, I learned how important it was to deal with mercury amalgam fillings in my patients, there were very few of us who were doing anything about it. I had been aware that selenium was the specific antidote to mercury, but it took me some time to identify a total programme for chelating mercury from the body that seemed to work.

Over the years, more and more doctors and scientists have become involved, and various other regimes have been recommended, some of which I have also tried. However, my patients and I did not find them any more effective than my original approach, allowing for the fact that I have increased the doses over the years. But to continue taking such large doses for many months is probably not practical, which is why I changed the programme about two weeks after the amalgam filling replacements had been completed, assuming that was roughly the time I next saw a patient for consultation. To be fair I don't know how long you need to continue on a chelation programme after the dental work has been completed, although you could follow the advice I have given above about selenium toxic symptoms developing. You can understand why I am unhappy about that, as I cannot keep an eye on you myself.

More and more people are aware of the dangers of mercury, because they have read about it, so it rarely came as a surprise to a patient when I brought up the subject, and were quite willing to proceed to have their amalgam fillings replaced when I recommended it. Some, however, wanted to have scientific evidence that they may have a raised body burden of mercury or a reaction to it. I therefore offered to do two tests, one the Kelmer Test for levels of body mercury, the other a Lymphocyte Transformation Test that assesses your white blood cell 'response' to the presence of mercury in a laboratory setting.♥

These tests are done by Biolab in London, but I am sure there are labs in other countries that can do similar tests. However, Biolab requires a request to come from an appropriate practitioner, so that the results can be sent to a responsible person for correct interpretation in relation to your medical condition.

The Kelmer test can also be used to assess your body burden of other heavy metals, such as aluminium, arsenic, cadmium and lead, which you need to be aware may have accumulated in your body over the years, which may now be affecting your health. One toxic metal in your body is bad enough, but the affect of two is not additive but multiplied. If there are three, well, who knows what the effect might be?

After Amalgam Replacements

You will have noticed that I am recommending a considerable number of tablets to be taken around the actual dental work to replace mercury amalgam fillings.

Recently I have changed my protocol to a far more convenient programme, using Segiun Patches♥ at night and Bio-Chelat drops just before meals, starting with five drops three times a day for the first week, ten drops three times a day for the next week, then up to twenty drops three times daily for then on.

Exactly how long you should remain on the dose of twenty drops three times a day will vary from person to person, but, by and large, the more fillings you had, the larger they were, and the longer they have been in your mouth, the longer it is likely to take to chelate all mercury (and other heavy metals) from your body. Even then, we are all being exposed to toxic heavy metals that we can't avoid, so taking a few doses every so often will probably be valuable.

Perhaps the best way of answering the question 'How long should I take the Bio-Chelat?' is to say continue for about three months on the full dose (it doesn't matter if you forget or leave it off every now and then) and then take it occasionally. If you feel you have benefited from it, but you deteriorate in any way when you stop it, restart it for about a month and see what happens. So far as I am aware, there is no problem being on it for long time.

If you are serious about bringing your cancer under control, you will need to organise a careful daily plan. In fact, you will need to concentrate on yourself selfishly for at least the first three months. Before I forget, a further reminder to always take any tablets or capsules with a full glass of quality water. If you take them with merely a sip, they can sit virtually dry on your stomach lining and irritate it. They will dissolve far more easily if there is plenty of liquid in your stomach.

You will need to have some idea how long the whole dental procedure will take, so that you can order enough supplies. However, I recommend you only order small supplies to begin with, to make sure they suit you. There is no way I can guarantee that these particular preparations will be suitable for absolutely everyone, as there is always someone out there who finds they cannot tolerate them. If they do upset you in any way, it is usually something simple like a little nausea. They have never done anyone any harm, in my experience.

A simple word of caution is needed here, for you to be aware of a possible adverse effect from doses of zinc. If you have ever been exposed to copper for any reason, and you have a higher body content of copper than is healthy, even if you are not aware of it, taking zinc can displace copper from where it is lodged in your body. This released copper has then to be disposed of via your liver and bile duct into your intestines, which will then cause considerable digestive problems and probably make you feel ill.

I had one such a patient for the first time recently who, when she told me how ill the selenium and zinc had made her feel, then remembered that she had had the same symptoms many years ago when she drank well water while on holiday. This water was tested and found to be high in copper. A white blood cell copper analysed at Biolab turned out to be far too high. So I then had to take time to clear out the excess copper from her body. This story illustrates the beauty of a medical detective approach to people's illnesses.

When the patient told me how ill my advice had made her, whilst I naturally apologised, I also used the information to find out what had gone wrong and what to do about it.

Over the years I have learned which particular supplements to recommend to which patients. I have also learned how long they should continue to take them after the dental work has been completed, but that is far too complicated to explain here, and it needs to be individualised. In the circumstances, I suggest that, perhaps two weeks after the dental work has been completed, you drop the selenium to 100mcg and the zinc to 30mg per day, and continue on Bio-Chelat once a day away from any other nutrients. To speed up the clearance of mercury (and other toxic substances) from your body, you could also apply the Segiun Patches, or one of the cheaper alternatives if you want to, to the soles of your feet.

With Bio-Chelat you can effectively stop selenium and zinc, although the company advises to take a small amount of zinc regularly, such as 15mg of elemental zinc last thing at night. So taking Bio-Chelat plus zinc may be more effective than the alternative, and cost less in the long run. I suggest you continue to take at least 100mcg selenium per day.

If you cannot afford to have your mercury amalgam fillings replaced, you just don't want to, you haven't been convinced of the value of doing so, or it won't happen for any reason, may I suggest you consider taking five drops of Bio-Chelat three times a day in a glass of water shortly before meals continuously, although it doesn't matter if you forget it or give yourself a break every now and again.

In principle, I am not happy that anyone should take large doses of selenium or zinc for too long, although I often recommend larger doses than I have recommended here to some patients when I am advising them and seeing them regularly myself. I am perfectly happy for you, and virtually anyone, to take Bio-Chelat and apply patches to your feet for as long as you want. However, when you have brought things under control as far as you can tell, it is perfectly reasonable to have a break, and do the Bio-Chelat and Segiun Patches treatment every so often, to keep yourself as clean as you can. There is no way any one of us can totally avoid exposure to toxins in our air, food and water.

If you can find a biologically trained dentist, by contacting IAOMT♥, ask him or her to check if your cancer is on an acupuncture meridian in relation to a particular tooth. Many is the time one of my cancer patients has found an abscess under a tooth relating to their cancer. Dr Weston Price (see the PricePottenger Foundation), an American dentist, brought this whole area of concern to our attention in the middle of the last century.

Osteopathy/Chiropractic

Many an osteopath or chiropractor will tell you that the body cannot possibly heal itself if your spinal column in particular is out of line. Many bodily problems can be improved by treatment from one of these specialities, but try to find someone locally who is recommended as being particularly helpful. Try to find someone who is considered to have healing hands. Although we all have to learn to begin with, I suggest you find someone who is getting on in years and has had many years of experience. While you should let him or her treat you in their own particular way, tell them where your cancer is, and ask them to search in particular the spinal area that corresponds to the nerves that go to the organ containing your cancer. They are usually experts in anatomy. This is similar to what I suggest you talk to a dentist about.

Reflexology

The science of Reflexology suggests that certain areas of your feet (and your hands and ears to an extent) reflect organs of your body, and, if a trained Reflexologist examines your feet, certain areas will be found to contain what is described as feeling like 'crystals'. When those areas are massaged, they can be quite painful and you can often feel a pain or some sort of sensation in the organ to which that area refers. By massaging that area it is suggested that the particular organ is being 'cleared', and, as the so-called crystals clear, the functioning of the organ is also cleared to function more effectively. I feel it is perfectly reasonable to suggest that the organ involved goes into a state of 'stasis' and cannot clear itself of toxic substances that may be damaging it. It would appear that reflexology can relieve that stasis and so help the organ start to heal itself.

I know mainstream medicine does not believe in this sort of attitude, but I am giving you my many years of experience, and passing on to you what so many of my patients have found have helped them. It doesn't mean to say that it will help you, but I hope you will try many, if not all, of these ideas, and find out which ones appeal to you, you seem to enjoy, you feel are helpful to you and you can fit into your busy programme.

Homoeopathy

Homoeopathy is considered to be an 'alternative' treatment, yet there are thousands of homoeopathically trained practitioners, many of them medically qualified. They have learned that homoeopathy can be used to treat all sorts of conditions, including cancer. The principal behind 'classical' homoeopathy is based upon an observation made by an Austrian Physician Dr. Hahnemann, around 1760, that if he took a substance when he felt well, in a sufficient dose, he would develop a series of symptoms, similar to symptoms that patients sometimes consulted him about. His first experience was a dose of cinchona bark, which gave him all the symptoms of the ague or 'flu', yet he knew that, if patients consulted him about such symptoms, an extract of cinchona bark was what he was likely to treat them with.

So he started trying out all sorts of substances, many of them known poisons, to see what they did to him, writing down his symptoms and signs in great detail. He also managed to persuade other people to go through the same process, called a 'proving'. He then compared what the other provers had observed and found that many of them developed similar symptoms to him. In this way, over the years, he developed a whole range of 'treatments' for specific symptoms. Since then, of course, the art of homoeopathy has developed into a great skill, and, although I am not an expert, I have learned a great many approaches from friends over the years.

Because many of the preparations that the provers wanted to try would not dissolve in water, and possibly only with difficulty in alcohol, they started banging solutions in glass bottles on the family bible, being a fairly thick and pliable medium. Then they discovered, possibly by serendipity, that the more they diluted a preparation, the more potent and effective it was, in complete contrast to the known fact that, to have a more potent effect, you needed to increase the dose of a medicine or give more of it or give it more often.

Then they realised that it was the banging on the family bible, or the process of 'succussion' as it became known, with each dilution, that seemed to be parting an energy to the preparation. It had to be something of the sort, because the more they diluted it, succussing it each time, the more effective it appeared to be, yet the degrees of dilution that they found continued to have an effect were such that they calculated there could not be a single molecule of the original substance left. And yet it seemed to work. And so the practice of homoeopathy gradually developed into the science and art it has become today.

Very recently a young man in his twenties consulted me about his Hodgkin's disease, having also had a Non-Hodgkin's lymphoma treated a year or two ago. One symptom that was making his life a real misery was profuse sweating at night. He was surprised when I told him that that was a typical indication of something wrong with his lungs, and was common in tuberculosis or sarcoidosis, both of which conditions involve the lungs. Nobody had explained that to him. He said he would wake at night in a pool of water, and it was a rather smelly pool. He was also concerned as he was going to sleep that night in a relative's house. As night sweats (and daytime ones as well) and other symptoms are commonly suffered by women going through the menopause, it occurred to me to try Lachesis at a 30C potency. Lachesis is a snake venom, and, if you are bitten by such a snake, you will develop symptoms similar to the menopause. It often works very well in menopausal women, though not always. He rang me the next day to say it had completely prevented him from sweating that night. In addition to helping clear such annoying symptoms, I believe that, if a homoeopathic treatment works, it may also help to heal the underlying cause of the symptom.

So please consider consulting a local homoeopath. As always, make sure you feel comfortable with the person you choose and that you gain something from the experience.

It needs to be said that we should all have a sense of responsibility about what we do. This web site is designed to teach you about things I have found to be very helpful to many of my patients, over many years. As I don't know you personally, I cannot say for certain what you should do. So, be observant, and keep checking that your body is happy with what you are doing. Keep scrupulous notes about what you take, when you take them, and what you do, and how you feel. Be your own detective, and make sure that what you choose to do is having the effect you are looking for.

Never persevere with anything if it does not seem to be helping you within a reasonable time frame. Perhaps you should grade your various signs and symptoms on a 0 to 10 scale, with 0 being bad, and the bigger the number the better you are feeling. There is no need to do this every day, but perhaps once a week. Maybe you should do a summary every Sunday evening of how things have been for the past seven days, but the detail I will leave up to you.

Before we move on, I want to stress something of importance. Mainstream medicine's approach is to fix your problem for you. You don't have to do anything apart from swallow the tablets or submit to an operation. Basically you leave it all to your doctor. Having read all that you have read in this website, you will by now realise that I am encouraging you to do things for yourself by learning all about yourself. I want you to start taking control of your own life. What you really must understand is that it has probably taken many years of doing all sorts of wrong things and having all sorts of wrong things done to you, for your cancer to develop to this stage. You therefore cannot, and must not, expect things to resolve overnight. Yes, I hope you will at least start to feel better quickly, but you cannot expect your cancer to disappear immediately. If you attend a chiropractor, let it be known at your first visit that you want a course to get you back into balance again. If you start to see a reflexologist or a homoeopath, say the same. Whatever works, stick with it. Don't stop doing it because you feel a bit better. Only stop seeing someone who is helping you when they say you don't need to be treated by them any more.

How To Compliment Orthodox Treatment

I made it quite clear at the beginning that I will not advise you not to follow your regular doctors' advice, nor to follow it. You have to make up your mind which path to follow. Plenty of people have done well with an operation, chemotherapy, radiotherapy and various drugs, even if they have felt unwell to a degree some of the time. Doctors in orthodox medicine are well aware that the current approach to cancer makes many people feel unwell, and that, in due course, better, safer and less toxic drugs will become available. Unfortunately they can only recommend what is currently available.

It is because of this that many people search the net for either a completely different approach to their cancer, or for ways to minimise the adverse effects of the approach they have chosen to follow, since they believe it will help them. I have no wish or intention to alter that situation.

An Operation

So, assuming you are to have an operation, what can you do to help yourself? All the following advice assumes you have time to do something, rather than being operated on in an emergency, in which case there may be no time. The least you should do is try to obtain some homoeopathic doses of Arnica to take before the operation and after it. Try to obtain drops that are so much easier to take. It is my belief that everyone should have a supply of Arnica at home for any bruises. For an operation the 1M dose is excellent in my experience and that of my patients. Lower potencies, such as 6C are obtainable in most Health Food Stores, usually as lactose or sugar tablets. I have just discovered that drops of Arnica 1M can be bought by the public from Ainsworths Homoeopathic Pharmacy.♥

If there is time, take a dose of Arnica 1M as follows:-

- 36, 24 and 12 hours before the operation and just before going down to the operating theatre.
- As soon after you come round from the anaesthetic as possible.
- Every hour for the rest of that day.
- Any time you happen to wake during the night.
- Every two hours the next day.
- Every three hours the day after that.
- Four times during the following days until about one week after the operation, after which you can stop if there are no further procedures to be carried out on you.

If possible, take some multivitamin/multimineral supplements to build up your nutrient stores. Try to obtain a powder form of neutral or alkaline vitamin C (not ascorbic acid which is too acidic for some people's stomach, so you could take Bio-EnRgy C), take three or four doses in water a day, starting low, and gradually increase the dose each time up to your bowel tolerance. This may be too much wind, indigestion, abdominal pain or loose stools. If any of these occur, reduce the dose of vitamin C. I have already explained this earlier on.

Consider taking at least 15mg of elemental zinc away from food, and tidy up your diet, cutting out all alcohol, caffeine, sugar, salt, red meats, animal milks and animal milk products, and all 'junk' food. Drink lots of good quality water.

You need to be aware that most doctors have not been trained in nutrition, some thinking that you should be able to obtain all the nutrients you require from a so-called balanced diet. They may even be of the opinion that taking vitamins and mineral by mouth merely produces expensive urine. They are unaware that your body takes in nutrients and excretes them in due course. It is like saying that you should not drink water until you stop passing it! If you were to follow that approach, you would soon be dead.

How To Reduce A Raised Homocysteine Level

Despite the large amount of evidence in the medical literature on the importance and harm of a raised homocysteine level, it is my opinion that either the medical profession is not interested in it, doesn't believe it is important, or is waiting for a drug company to come up with a chemical patentable product to lower it. In fact it can most effectively and safely be lowered by nutrients, vitamins B6, B12, B2, folic acid and betaine (trimethylglycine TMG for short). Occasionally zinc is needed, and possibly magnesium as well, but it is likely that you will already be on zinc supplements in any case because of your cancer or mercury amalgam fillings.

Depending on the severity of your homocysteine level, you should take between 400mcg and 2000mcg folate, 500mcg and 1500mcg B12, 50mg and 100mg B6 (half that dose if in the form of pyridoxal-5-phosphate), 15mg and 50mg B2, 10mg and 20mg zinc, and 750mg and 6g TMG per day, but as your homocysteine levels fall, you could lower your nutrient intake to keep it low. You should have your levels of blood homocysteine tested every so often.   For more information about Homocysteine, there is a marvellous book entitled 'The H Factor' by Patrick Holford and Dr. James Braly.♥

Chemotherapy

Chemotherapy drugs kill cells. Unfortunately they kill good cells as well as cancer cells. Hopefully the balance is in your favour. It is likely that your immune system will also take a bashing. These drugs also seem to alter the bowel flora, damaging or killing the desirable friendly organisms, often leaving potentially harmful organisms untouched, which can then proliferate. Whatever the general effect, there is a lot of cellular damage and cellular death, which your body then has to try to clear out.

If you are to start a course of chemotherapy, at least follow the advice I gave above in relation to having an operation, except that homoeopathic Arnica may not be relevant. I suggest you consult a trained homoeopath before you start the course of chemotherapy, as there are many preparations that can help minimise the adverse effects. Many of my patients have found that taking homoeopathic doses of the chemotherapy drug or drugs, usually in a 30C potency two or three times a day for at least a week after each dose, can significantly reduce the adverse effects, without stopping the intended effect of the chemotherapy. However, you may not be able to obtain these without the help of a homoeopath.

Chemotherapy fires free radicles at you, which is how your doctor hopes to kill off your cancer cells. For that reason it is sensible to take large doses of anti-oxidants during chemotherapy, which includes vitamins A C E and selenium, Alpha-lipoic acid, Pycnogenol, Co-enzyme Q 10, Revenol and all the anti-oxidants in fruits and vegetables, which is why special capsules of dehydrated fruits, berries and vegetables are so valuable in my experience♥.

You need to be aware that many doctors don't want you to take anti-oxidants during chemotherapy, as they assume they will 'quench' the free radicles of the chemotherapy and stop it working. Chemotherapy is so powerful that there is no possibility of this happening. At the very least, anti-oxidants will minimise any damage to your normal cells. Many studies have demonstrated this, but your doctors may not be aware of them. An 'Article on Anti-oxidants' (see the Appendix) should put your mind at rest about this. In addition, try to obtain a copy of the article "Lamson, D. and Brignall. Antioxidants in cancer therapy: Their action and interactions with oncologic remedies. Alt Med Rev 1999; 4(5): 304-329." Many of the 180 studies cited showed not only increased effectiveness of many cancer chemotherapy agents, but also a decrease in adverse effects, when given with antioxidants.

Coffee enemas are a must, if you have chemotherapy. Practice doing them before you start your course of chemotherapy, so that you can do them as often and as easily as you want to, and especially as soon as you arrive home from the hospital after each dose of chemotherapy. My patients found they significantly reduced the bad effects of chemotherapy, and made them feel so much less unwell than would otherwise have been the case. They can also often significantly reduce any pain you may be suffering from.

Radiotherapy Protection

If you have decided to have a course of radiotherapy, which tends to be more localised than chemotherapy, or are in the process of having it, there are basically six pieces of advice I can give you, although other people might offer additional pieces of advice. It also fires free radicals at your tissues, for which reason much of my advice in relation to chemotherapy is worth following.

1. The first is to obtain a supply of Aloe Vera gel and plaster it all over the irradiated area of skin every hour until you go to bed, when you get home after a dose of radiotherapy. As it tends to be a bit sticky, it is perfectly all right to wash the area before finally retiring, otherwise you are likely to be uncomfortable during the night.

Apply this every day after each dose throughout the course, but do not apply it before you go to hospital each day. So, if your appointment for radiotherapy is mid-morning, do not put any Aloe Vera gel on from going to bed the night before to attending the clinic that day. Each treatment takes only a few minutes, so, if you only live a few miles away from the hospital, and you don't have any errands to run on the way back, you could arrive home by about 1 pm. Start applying Aloe vera gel as soon as you can, and set some sort of alarm clock to remind yourself to apply some more every hour until you go to bed.

When your course of radiotherapy has been completed, continue to apply Aloe vera gel to the same area two or three times a day for at least a week, but longer if you want to. There is no real limit to how long you keep applying it, so it is up to you, and depends upon how you and your skin feel. If, after stopping applying it, your skin seems to start feeling burned again, restart applying it and continue doing so until you feel comfortable again.

The dose of radiation that you are likely to be given, or have been given, will have been a 'standard' dose, i.e. just about everybody is given the same dose, although occasionally the Oncologist may recognise that a particular person is very fair skinned and may try to make allowance for it. However, he is likely to be thinking of the deeper tissues that he is aiming at, when he calculates the dose, and, if the superficial tissues are affected in the process, he will consider that that is not of great importance in the long run.

I have seen many patients whose skin has been burned or badly affected in some way by radiotherapy before they came to see me, but many others whose skin has been protected and preserved by applying Aloe vera gel as I have described. I have even had the odd Oncologist who has been impressed by this approach and who has remarked at the difference it has made. Unfortunately, it will not protect vulnerable tissues beneath the skin.

2. The second piece of advice I can give you is to take homoeopathic Rad Brom 30C♥ at least three times a day while you are having radiotherapy, and for at least a week after it has finished. You may need to consult a trained homoeopath to obtain a supply, and this may not be a bad thing in any case, as a homoeopath could be very helpful to your overall health. Basically I would advise you and every cancer patient to have at least one 'other' adviser to help them, assuming you will at least have your General Practitioner and one or more hospital Consultants seeing you on a regular basis. This situation may be different in other countries whose system I do not know.

Avoid having anything to eat or drink for about ten minutes before or after each dose, and some homoeopaths advise that you avoid garlic, coffee and peppermint while taking homoeopathic preparations. You should, of course, have already given up all forms of coffee, if you take any notice of me, but avoiding garlic may be a bit tricky. You may need to change your toothpaste, in the circumstances.

3. The third specific piece of advice I would like to give you while you are having radiotherapy is to take plenty of anti-oxidants. Some doctors advise cancer patients not to take anti-oxidants while they are having chemotherapy or radiotherapy, because they are aware that their treatment is having its cancer cell damaging effect by producing free radicals at the cellular level. They assume that anti-oxidants will stop their treatment from working.

I can assure you, from my experience and that of my patients, and many published papers, that that is not the case. (See above under chemotherapy) In fact it is exactly the opposite. Chemotherapy and radiotherapy are so powerful that nothing I know of can stop them doing damage to susceptible cells. There is, however, a certain amount of difference between cancer cells and normal cells. One of the most important differences is that cancer cells lack certain protective enzymes, such as catalase, while they also contain other enzymes that normal cells do not, such as telomerase. This enzyme in principle helps cancer cells to become immortal, as it can manufacture telomeres, which are the tail end of the DNA. In health, every time the DNA of a cell divides, a little of its tail, the telomere, is lost. When there is no more telomere to divide, the cell dies.

By taking anti-oxidants while having chemotherapy or radiotherapy, the effect upon your cancer cells will be just the same as it would have been if you had not taken anti-oxidants. However, your good cells will be protected to a degree from the unwanted effects of all that free radical production. The less overall cellular death that can be achieved in you, the better will be the result and the less unwell you will feel.

I suggest you take large doses of the anti-oxidants I recommended a little earlier on in this chapter.

4. There is a particular herb that seems to help protect all your non-cancer cells from damage by radiotherapy called Schizandra. I could probably have placed this in the anti-oxidant paragraph, but it seems to be a preparation with specific value in radiotherapy, so I have given it its own personal mention. The dose is one tablet taken three times a day any time.

5. The fifth piece of advice is to take Wobenzym N♥ digestive enzymes in very large doses. Radiotherapy initiates a massive inflammatory response, as is perfectly clear if you look at its effects upon the skin. As it is aimed at tissues that contain the cancer, which is presumably below the skin, you can imagine how much more inflammation there is in the deeper tissues. There it is virtually on fire, both in the cancer cells it is aimed at and in the nearby healthy cells that are inadvertently exposed at the same time.

Wobenzym enzymes have been shown to have very potent anti-inflammatory activity, but, in the circumstances, very large doses of these enzymes will be needed to help quench such a massive fire. The tablets are all of one size and I advise you to work up rapidly to twelve tablets three times daily between meals. Yes, I mean thirty-six tablets a day! This means taking as soon as possible twelve tablets between two hours after breakfast and one hour before lunch, twelve tablets two hours after lunch and one hour before your evening meal, and a further twelve tablets between two hours after your evening meal and anywhere up to going to bed. The purpose of taking them at these times is to make sure that they are absorbed into the blood stream well away from food, and that they are not taken to help digest your food. If you need digestive enzymes for that purpose, you will need to take other forms with food.

On the other hand, if you are reading this piece of advice for the first time and are in the middle of a course of radiotherapy, take one tablet three times on day one to make sure your bowels can at least tolerate the smallest dose worth taking, remembering that radiotherapy can sometimes damage your bowels and render them less tolerant of anything you put into them. If you are all right by day two, try to take three tablets three times that day. If still all right the next day, take six tablets three times the next day, then nine, then twelve tablets three times a day, reaching the full dose fairly rapidly. If you can take them, you need them.

You will need to continue on the full dose for at least a month after the course of radiotherapy has ended, after which it may be possible to reduce the dose gradually to about twenty-four tablets a day for quite some time. How long will depend largely on how you progress with all the treatments you decide to follow.

There are effectively two formulations of Wobenzym, the best known being a most popular preparation readily available in Germany, known affectionately as the 'Red Dragees', because of their bright red, shiny, sugar-coated surface. I am not at all happy that you take these for that reason, although you could tediously wash off that coating from thirty-six tablets every day, if you want to. However, because of the extreme value of their active contents/ingredients, their formulation has been improved and they have been re-packaged as Wobenzym N in America, where they are available as well as in England.

6. The sixth piece of advice that I feel is worth giving you at this stage is that you carry out coffee enemas. These have been fully described earlier on, and you should start doing them so that you are comfortable with the procedure and can do one

whenever you need to.

The above are basically what you need to do, but there are two other antiinflammatory supplements worth considering adding. One is Omega-3 EFAs, and I recommend Eskimo-3 oil♥, probably at a dose of a 5ml teaspoonful twice a day or hemp seed or flax seeds if you are vegan.

The final recommendation as an anti-inflammatory is Mangosteen♥. It is rather expensive but can be very effective in this respect. The dose would be 45ml three times a day, preferably 1⁄2 hour before meals.

Chapter 5

Where to Start

Now that I have discussed a whole range of things that you can consider doing yourself, I would like to try to put this all into perspective and discuss various levels, depending upon the state of your cancer. I will therefore suggest what you do, should any of the following circumstances apply to you: You may have had an operation but have completed a course of chemotherapy and/or radiotherapy, you have recovered from it all, you are nearly back to your old self again, or soon will be at the rate you are improving, and you have been given the 'all clear'. You want to keep it that way and want to know what to do to give yourself the best chance possible.

You may have had an operation but have completed a course of chemotherapy and/or radiotherapy some time ago, but your cancer has come back again. You are considering having another course of treatment, but with a stronger drug. The first series made you feel most unwell and you don't fancy going through it all again. You are concerned that, if the first drugs didn't work, why should the second, more toxic, ones.

You have been through all the preliminaries of diagnosis, including a biopsy and scans, and you have been recommended to have some sort of operation plus follow-up drugs, chemotherapy and radiotherapy. You are trying to make up your mind whether to go ahead or not. You are considering alternatives.

You think you might have cancer, but you don't want to go to your own doctor because you know what that would entail. Alternatively, you know you have cancer, but don't want any treatment that mainstream medicine recommends.

You want advice on alternatives.

You have a strong family history of cancer and you want to give yourself the best chances of not developing it yourself.

You are going to follow the advice of the doctors you have seen in hospital and want not only to do well, but you also want to minimise possible adverse effects of the treatment.

Situation Number 1

In the first instance, ask yourself why your cancer developed at all. Go through the various explanations I gave in your consultation with me, and think which could apply to you. Were you under stress of any sort shortly before the first signs of cancer appeared? How did you cope with it? Did you 'abuse' yourself at the time by drinking a lot more coffee, tea or alcohol? What sort of diet did you have at the time? Were you too busy or sidetracked to eat properly, so you ate more convenience or fast foods at the time?

Diet

If any of these apply to you, make the appropriate corrections if you have not already done so. Read again the basic dietary recommendations that I have made, even though it is possible that it may not be absolutely right for you. Consider having the Alcat or one of the other blood tests done, which might identify idiosyncratic reactions to certain foods you could never have identified as being harmful to you by direct observation of what you eat. Then amalgamate the information from both systems, i.e. stay off the foods that I recommend such as animal milks and products and sugar, even if the blood test suggests that they are 'safe' for you. In addition, avoid any foods that the blood test suggests are not safe for you, certainly for four or five weeks to begin with. Each blood testing system has its own way of presenting

146

relevant information. Most have a grading system of severity. Be aware that, if you have been avoiding a normally regularly eaten food for a number of weeks for any reason, especially if you have been suspicious of it, your blood test might suggest you are safe to consume it. The reason for this is that, by avoiding it for a period of time, your sensitivity to it can temporarily disappear, but could soon reappear were you to put it back into your diet on a regular basis.

Observe the effect of these dietary changes on you. Do you feel generally better? If so, in what way do you feel better? Have you lost some weight that you could afford to lose? Have you possibly put on a little weight if you were previously under weight? Do you feel generally trimmer? If the answer to any of these questions is in the affirmative, you can be reasonably sure that the diet you are now following is as correct for you as you can imagine.

This now gives you an oasis of foods, which you can either stay on for as long as you want to, or, if you gradually re-introduce others, you can go back to, if you start to feel less well. Since the various blood tests test for about one hundred and fifteen items, you should be left with about eighty or so on your green list, from which you may need to remove a few more, i.e. the ones I recommend everyone with cancer should avoid in any case, irrespective of what the blood test suggests.

If you have clearly benefited from your 'new diet', and there are plenty of foods to make an adequate set of meals from, you could stay on this limited list for a very long time. The longer you do stay on a diet that is undoubtedly good for you, the more your body will cleanse and heal itself. However, it is probably not practical to remain this rigid for very long, so, at some time, you will decide to start to extend your range. I do not agree with some of the instructions that are sent with some results, especially if it is suggested that you start the programme of re-introducing foods with those that you have been advised to avoid.

I was the Medical Director of the NuTron Company many years ago, and our test was similar to the Alcat test. However, the NuTron test is no longer available. I designed the details of how a person should follow the appropriate diet, and how to proceed at the next stage. To be fair, the mechanics of the Alcat test are superior to those of the NuTron test, which basically means that it is more accurate, even though no test can guarantee to be 100% accurate in all circumstances. Despite that, I believe there are certain ways these tests should be used in practice, and my way of proceeding at the second stage, i.e. the stage of adding more foods after the initial stage, is the way I would prefer you to proceed.

Unless the recommendations have changed, the Alcat test brochure suggests that you add any food that you have been avoiding, many times and in large amounts, until you 'prove' that it is safe for you to include back into your diet, because you are not able to make yourself ill in any way by doing so. Then you do the same with the next food and the next food. I have a number of objections to doing things this way. The first is that, in life, you would never eat large amounts of any food many times a day, or you ought not to, so why do so as a challenge experiment. In any case, eating that much of any food a number of times a day might easily make you feel unwell in a way the same food probably would not, if you only ate a sensible amount once. In addition, while any food you challenge your body with from now on might not produce an obvious reaction, such as a headache or a pain somewhere, it might stimulate your cancer quietly in the background in the form of additional inflammation.

Remember, you will have had the Alcat test done to identify safe and unsafe foods from an inflammatory point of view. If a particular food has been placed in the yellow list, there is a little suspicion that it may not be suitable for you, and may possibly somehow be involved with your cancer. Nevertheless, having avoided that food for at least four weeks, and if you continue to stay off the worst offenders in the red list and the others I want you to remain off for a long time, such as sugar, alcohol, junk food, caffeine and animal milks and products, etc., your 'sensitivity' to that food could easily lessen to such an extent that it disappears altogether.

The second reason is that I want you to be able to show that eating a sensible amount of a food only once does not make you feel ill in any way that you can tell. I want you to be able to extend your diet as widely as possible and continue to feel well.

So, the way I would like you to do things is as follows. Make a list of those foods you would like to re-introduce back into your diet. Do not include in such a list any foods I have advised you to stay off because they are bad for cancer patients, such as sugar and animal milks and products, in my experience. Also, do not include any foods that you already know make you feel ill in any way, so you have always avoided them. If any of those foods are not on the list of foods tested by the Alcat system, i.e. are not anywhere on your results sheet, test them first, because you have no idea whether they would have ended up in the safe or unsafe category had they been tested. Then test foods in your yellow list. The way to test them is to add a food to any meal, or eat it on its own if you prefer, taking a normal helping and only eating it once. If you don't notice any effect you could possibly blame on that first food, make a note that, eating a sensible amount of that food only once appeared to be safe.

Don't eat that food again for now, while you test another food on the next day in exactly the same way, again selecting for your second test a food you don't consume very often anyway, also one not on your results sheet anywhere. There should be many foods not tested by the Alcat system that you could test if you are prepared to eat them, before you move on to those foods on your yellow list.

It is likely that, by the time you have tested all the foods not on your Alcat results sheet plus all those on your yellow list, you could have an additional 'safe' list of ten to twenty foods to add to your oasis of safe foods. Try not to eat any of these foods too often. Look at the list and see if two or three of them go together, and, if possible, rotate them all by not eating any one of them more often than once in four days. If there are twenty foods you have tested and feel comfortable to add to your safe list, you could eat any five of them once in every four days, or any four of them once in five days.

There is nothing perfect about this system, but it is worthwhile trying to plan what you will eat for a few days ahead, to make sure you have in stock all the ingredients you will need. While this may seem to be a bit tedious and time consuming, remember you are trying to achieve something important for yourself. You are trying to make sure your cancer does not return. If that means you have to modify your way of life to a certain extent, then so be it, as far I am concerned.

It may, in fact, become a 'way of life' for you, certainly when you are at home and in complete control of your eating habits. However, try to feel relaxed enough about what you are doing most of the time not to be worried if you break the system every so often when you are away from home. Be as strict as you can with yourself, but don't let it worry you if you need to let the system slip for a while every so often. Remember, this is only part of your whole plan, and other things you will want to do most of the time you may also let slip every so often.

Hormones

Many cancers have a hormonal involvement, especially cancers of the breast, ovaries, uterus, cervix and prostate. In my experience, dominance of oestrogen in relation to progesterone is likely to be involved in just about all of these cancers, so, if your cancer is one of these, modulating (balancing) these hormones will be of importance to you.

Many women have had years of pharmaceutical hormones in the form of the contraceptive pill, IVF treatment, or HRT, and there is increasing evidence in the published literature of the link between these preparations and cancer, especially if you have a genetic predisposition to cancer. If you had a history of any sort of pre-menstrual symptoms, that to me is further evidence of oestrogen dominance in relation to progesterone, as I explained earlier on.

So what can you do about this imbalance in your hormones? Strangely enough, getting your diet right for you will play a major part in this. When women with pre-menstrual symptoms followed the diet recommended by the Alcat test, or they asked me to guess to save them money, very often the next pre-menstrual phase was virtually symptom-free. Indeed, sometimes their next period took them by surprise! On other occasions, it took one or two cycles to bring symptoms under control. If my guess did not help, I would always suggest that my guess had not been correct.

Unfortunately, a lot of the 'oestrogen' that humans (and animals) are being exposed to nowadays comes from the environment we are creating for ourselves. Women on the contraceptive pill have to go to the toilet and pass water, so, if you drink water that has been recycled in any way, there is a chance that such water will contain residues of hormones, even if the level is extremely low. It will, however, accumulate slowly over the years.

Then there are all the xeno-oestrogens (false oestrogen-like chemicals) that we are exposed to in our daily lives, such as petrochemicals, plasticisers, fertilisers and a myriad of chemicals used in manufacturing processes, separate from any hormones that are given to animals to fatten them up before slaughter, that we may then eat. You may be trying to eat organically now, but have you possibly eaten them in the past? The effect can be cumulative from a variety of sources over the years.

One thing you can try to do is reduce your exposure to them, but this is not as easy as you might think. Even organic food is often wrapped in plastic film. The majority of bottled water is in plastic bottles, and sometimes the water actually tastes of plastic. However, you can do your best, but don't turn it into a fetish and let it become a greater stress than not doing anything about it at all.

Oestrogen Detoxification

All forms of oestrogen are broken down in the liver, so, if there is any chance that any aspect of your cancer is associated with oestrogen, good liver functioning is essential. Keeping your liver fully hydrated by drinking plenty of quality water is a good start. Various herbs can also be used, such as silymarin, to stimulate and cleanse the liver, although combinations of herbs and nutrients may be more effective. I use a liquid tincture form, Harmonik Liver Cleanse and Tonic, as half a teaspoonful in water 1/2 hour before meals three times a day. As tinctures are usually preserved in alcohol, I recommend that the dose be put into a cup, a small amount of hot water be poured onto it and left to stand for few minutes to allow the alcohol to evaporate before cool water is added for it to be drunk.

On occasions, after oestrogen has been broken down in the liver, the metabolic products may be regenerated back into oestrogen by an enzyme within the intestine, and be reabsorbed back into the blood stream. However, Calcium-D-glucarate, at a dose of 500mg three times a day with meals, can prevent this from happening. Unfortunately, I cannot tell you if you are one of those people for whom this could be a possibility. I can only suggest that, if your cancer is clearly associated with excess oestrogen, you take Calcium-D-glucarate for at least three months to begin with, while you are doing all the other things that you feel are worthwhile, and getting things under control. Remember that, if you get your diet right for your metabolism, possibly by following the advice of the Alcat Test, your hormonal balance should improve considerably.

There are many hormonal balancing preparations on the market, and soyabased ones are well known for this. However, the Alcat Test often suggests that soya is not suitable for a particular person, so something else, such as wild yam preparations, may need to be tried. Be aware, however, that wild yam cannot be converted into progesterone in the body, as some people seem to suggest. Nevertheless, there is a lot of evidence that suggests that peoples of the world who consume wild yam as part of their regular daily diet, do not suffer from hormonal problems to any degree, in contrast to so many women in the so-called West. This food contains many natural chemicals that act as hormonal modulators (balancers). If taken in supplementary form, once a hormonal problem has arisen, so in larger doses than would have been consumed as part of a person's regular diet, it can be very helpful to bring things under control.

Another way of 'antagonising' too much oestrogen is by using its natural balancer, namely progesterone. As far as I am concerned, the only effective way of obtaining adequate doses of bio-identical 'natural' progesterone is by rubbing on progesterone cream once or twice a day, using a maximum dose of 20mg in twenty-four hours. This preparation may be difficult to obtain, but, unless you are under the care of a nutritionally trained person, make sure that it is having a beneficial effect, or, more importantly, not appearing to have an adverse effect. While it should make symptoms such as breast swelling or tenderness in the pre-menstrual phase improve, very occasionally it may do the opposite, so it should be stopped immediately, although increasing the dose can sometimes do the trick. Always apply it to soft skin of any part of your body, to assist absorption, changing the site of application as often as possible. If you have breast cancer, there is no need to apply it to the affected breast.

A cheaper, and sometimes just as effective a method of balancing oestrogen and progesterone, is to improve the 'efficacy' of progesterone, using homoeopathic progesterone 200C, three times a day, either continuously if you no longer have a monthly cycle, or from mid-cycle until the onset of your period, if you do. Simply measuring the level of hormones in a blood or tissue sample can give a false impression of what is happening. The hormone can only have its effect if there are adequate numbers of 'receptors' for it to attach to. Even then, the 'activity' of receptors can vary from time to time. They can also be interfered with by toxic substances, such as mercury, 'candida', many chemicals and food intolerances, as well as be less efficient in the presence of a deficiency of certain nutrients, such as B vitamins, especially vitamin B6 (pyridoxine) and magnesium.

To obtain a supply of homoeopathic 200C progesterone, you may have to consult a homoeopath, which would probably be a good thing anyway. If you do, ask for it to be as drops to be used under your tongue, not lactoseor sugar-containing pillules, as these materials would be contra-indicated in someone with cancer.

Tamoxifen Alternative

Many patients with breast cancer are recommended to take tamoxifen or one of the alternatives. It is entirely up to you whether you take it or not. However, many of my patients have decided, for their own reasons, that they don't want to take any drugs, including not having chemotherapy. I never put any pressure at all on anyone to do, or not to do, anything. I always identify what their attitude is, and offer them any advice I can.

Most women with breast cancer are aware that the tamoxifen-like drugs have anti-oestrogen activity. If you have been recommended to take one of these drugs, whether your tumour has been shown to be oestrogen positive or not, this must surely be an acknowledgement by your Oncologist that oestrogen excess or dominance is playing a part in your cancer. You are likely, therefore, to be aware that some form of anti-oestrogen approach is worthwhile considering.

Indole-3-carbinol is just such a preparation, and has definite anti-oestrogen activity, and is considered by many doctors to be a useful natural alternative to tamoxifen and its like. Strangely enough, I have had one person with cancer, whose Alcat Test showed cabbage to be a food on her suspicious list, but this must be most unusual. Indole-3-carbinol is basically extracted from cabbage, so, instead of taking it in supplement form, regular consumption of cabbage soup might be worthwhile trying, so long as it doesn't give you wind! I have not heard of anyone complaining of wind on indole-3-carbinol yet, so I assume the ingredients that cause wind are not present in the final product. Nowadays I use indole-3-carbinol in combination with DIM as Dim Vitex♥, in a dose of one capsule three times a day.

Anti-Oxidants

Since, in general, many doctors and scientists would accept that your cancer could have been caused by 'free radicals', and, if at any time you have had a course of chemotherapy and/or radiotherapy, both of which damage cells by creating free radicals in them, it would seem to be logical to increase your levels of anti-oxidants in whatever way you can.

When a person is truly healthy, the amount of nutrients that are required on a daily basis to keep that person healthy is surprisingly small. The RDA (Recommended Daily Allowance) levels were essentially set with that in mind, but it is seldom recognised that more nutrients may be needed when the person is less than in perfect health. When a problem has developed in the body, such as cancer, it has been my experience that large doses of nutrients are needed to correct or reverse the situation, especially when it is reasonable to assume that nutritional deficiencies are involved. There is certainly plenty of published scientific evidence to suggest that, if an enzyme function is not working very well, pushing it to extremes can often make it work.

When people were finally released from World War 2 prisoner-of-war camps, usually in an emaciated condition, and suffering from diseases such as beriberi and other known nutritional deficiency syndromes, if they were given nutritional supplements many times the Recommended Daily Allowance, they recovered far more quickly than those who were merely rehabilitated by as good food as was available at the time.

You can see, therefore, why taking comparatively large doses of anti-oxidants could be advisable, if your body is in a bad state because you have cancer. But what should you take, and in what doses? The best-known anti-oxidants are vitamins A, C and E, beta-carotene and selenium, although some people might add their favourites to such a list. However, all natural fruits, vegetables, nuts, seeds and herbs contain a vast number of anti-oxidants. So, in principle, the more of such foods you can consume, the better it should be for you. Alternatively, you could eat as good a diet as you can manage, but add special capsules of dehydrated fruits, berries and vegetables♥ to your daily intake, possibly doubling the dose to begin with.

I need to add a word of caution here, and that is if you have the Alcat Test carried out and it suggests that some of these supposedly healthy foods are not good for you at present. If this is the case, you will have to make the appropriate changes, but I will have to leave that up to you.

Some people take four or five doses of vitamin C a day, ideally using a powder form such as Bio En'R-Gy C powder. Other forms in large doses can irritate your bowels. Start with a very low dose, such as the equivalent of half a mustard spoonful (if you know how small a mustard spoon is) at a time, and gradually work up to taking as much as you can tolerate. I have known some cancer patients tolerate 50g of vitamin C a day, which is a very high dose. Dr. Linus Pauling, Ph.D., the double Nobel Prize winner, recommended that everyone, especially anyone with cancer, should take 10g vitamin C a day, or 1 dose of liposomal vitamin C.

If you take too much vitamin C, it is likely to upset your bowels in some way. It may cause heartburn, wind, diarrhoea or pain, so you need to start very low and work your dose up slowly. Some people, and I am one of them, cannot take much at all, although I can take Bio En'R-Gy C powder in large doses. However, if you find you can take very large doses, you may well find that your tolerance changes with time, i.e. you gradually find you cannot tolerate as much as you could originally. This is a good sign in my experience, and suggests that your anti-oxidant needs have diminished. You should then, of course, lower your daily dose of vitamin C.

Vitamin E doses of around 400 International Units (IU), preferably as mixed tocopherols, should be taken later on in the day, such as between supper and bedtime, if you are slim or underweight, as Vitamin E tends to be anabolic, that is, helps to build up tissue, and night time is the time to rebuild your body. If you are average or overweight, it probably doesn't matter when you take it.

Beta-carotene is converted into vitamin A in the liver. Some people feel that beta-carotene has useful anti-cancer activity of its own, so to take some of it as well as vitamin A is probably worthwhile. I suggest 15mg of betacarotene and 10,000 to 15,000 IU of vitamin A in 24 hours, while some cancer patients take a lot of carrots and carrot juice. However, if you look at the palms of people who are taking a lot of carrots, they are 'discoloured' yellow. This suggests to me that they are taking too much in the way of carrots and that their liver cannot convert all that beta-carotene into vitamin A. To my mind, this is overloading the liver, which cannot be a good thing under any circumstances.

There is a mass of published evidence that demonstrates the importance of selenium in all sorts of medical problems, especially cancer. Selenium is an important anti-oxidant, which I have also found to be useful in patients who suffer from environmental allergies, i.e. they are made ill by sprays, petrol and diesel fumes, and cigarette smoke, etc. I have already mentioned that selenium is an important antagonist of heavy metals, such as mercury, so, if you have amalgam fillings in your teeth, re-visit my description of what to do about that and what dose of selenium to take. Otherwise, take at least 200mcg of selenium, preferably as 100mcg twice a day 1/2 hour before meals. There is an interesting article in the Appendix about selenium.

Revenol, by the multi-level marketing company Neways, is an excellent anti-oxidant preparation because of its range and variety of ingredients. Three of them, namely white pine bark extract, maritime pine bark extract and grape seed extract, are described as being very many times stronger in antioxidant activity than vitamin C itself. Revenol also contains reasonable levels of beta-carotene and small levels of vitamins C and E. Two tablets twice a day is the maximum dose of Revenol worth taking, if you are going to rely on it, although, once you have things under control, possibly after about three months, you could reduce the dose to one tablet twice a day. The label suggests the higher dose for only three days, but, if you have cancer, your needs are likely to be far greater. As always, you must make sure somehow that you are making appropriate progress with whatever you are doing and taking.

There are also many other anti-oxidants available, but I can't possibly describe them all. If you want to find your own, or follow the advice of someone you may be consulting, as well as reading this web site, that is fine by me. Make sure, however, that, as with all supplements, you feel they are helping you and not upsetting you in any way. In many respects, a small amount of a variety of anti-oxidants is probably the best approach, in which case a single tablet of Revenol could suffice. As your cancer is likely to be at least partially involved with free radicals, taking some level of anti-oxidants has to be worth serious consideration.

Essiac Tea
I cannot leave this section without reminding you of Essiac Tea, possibly taken as Harmonik Ojibwa Indian Tincture and Tonic.

Intravenous Infusions
When someone with cancer consulted me, especially if they knew they still had cancer, and also if they were undergoing chemotherapy and/or radiotherapy, and may be about to have an operation, intravenous infusions of vitamins and minerals were something I could offer them, which they nearly always accepted as they were usually aware that that was something on offer. In the past I have done enough blood tests on cancer patients to know that they were nearly always nutritionally deficient when I first saw them. Many people undergoing standard treatment don't feel very well. They often feel sick, have upset bowels and a poor appetite, so, at a time when they should be improving their nutritional state, exactly the opposite occurs.

If I tried to improve things by suggesting vitamins and minerals by mouth, there was a very good chance that the preparations would upset them, usually making their nausea worse, in which case they naturally stopped taking them. Giving vitamins and minerals intravenously not only helped people to feel better, it also bypassed the bowel and its poorly functioning absorption mechanisms. This whole process could help counteract the undesirable effects of their other treatment, without interfering with its intended effects, making it all the more likely that they would complete their course of chemotherapy and/or radiotherapy successfully.

I have a number of patients who are totally convinced that the intravenous infusions of vitamins and minerals, which often included doses of vitamin C up to 50g, or even higher, helped achieve what they wanted, which was to complete a course of chemotherapy, which their researches had shown to be an effective treatment for their kind of cancer. They also reported to me that their Oncologists were very impressed by how well they had done overall, and how well they had coped with the therapy's known adverse effects, while all around them other patients were feeling most unwell, some having to interrupt the course of treatment when their blood count was affected too badly to continue. I remember one patient in particular who continued to work throughout his course of chemotherapy and even won a National Championship one weekend in the middle of the course. Not surprisingly, he has done very well.

I am sorry to say that it may be very difficult for you to find anyone who will be willing to give you intravenous infusions of vitamins and minerals. In The United Kingdom, there are some doctors who do this work, but they are few and far between, and are not evenly spread throughout the country. I have to assume that many people who read this book will live in other countries than mine, so, if you want to have some infusions, you will have to find your own doctor to do this.

I have lost count of the many thousands of intravenous infusions of vitamins and minerals I have given over the years (although my records of them are intact), not only to cancer patients, but also to anyone who I thought might benefit from them. Not everyone noticed a benefit, but the vast majority did. I have never had a severe reaction, but, if there is any likelihood that doses of vitamin C will go up as high as 50g, it is very sensible to have a blood test done for a red blood cell enzyme called glucose-6-phosphate dehydrogenase. If this is absent, large doses of vitamin C intravenously, possibly over 25g, can cause haemolysis of the red blood cells, in which case the patient will suddenly pass virtually black urine and feel most unwell. Their haemoglobin will fall dramatically and they will need a blood transfusion.

I did this test on all cancer patients, on the assumption that I would most likely give them large doses of intravenous vitamin C, but, in any case, I never gave more than 5g vitamin C the first time.

In case you can find someone to give you vitamins and minerals intravenously, here are the doses I used to start with:

* Vitamin B1-100mg; Vitamin B2-25mg; Vitamin B3-25mg; Vitamin B5-250mg; Vitamin B6-100mg; Vitamin B12-1mg; Folic acid-2.5mg
* Vitamin C-5g
* Magnesium sulphate 50%-1g
* Elemental zinc 20mg
* Elemental molybdenum-100mcg
* Elemental selenium-100mcg
* Elemental chromium-100mcg
* Elemental manganese-100mcg
* Glutathione 300mg

I might also put in a small amount of sodium bicarbonate, such as 2 to 5ml of 8.4% strength and 4meq of potassium chloride. I tended to put all of this into about 300ml sterile water and gave it over 1½ to 2 hours, making sure the patient drank at least three glasses of water while it was running in. It is possible to work out the osmolarity of such a solution, to try to make it isotonic. This will make the whole procedure more comfortable.

After a few infusions, I may well have left out the folic acid or zinc, unless the patient was being given a chemotherapy drug that was known to be a folic acid antagonist.

Having clarified the patient's glucose-6-phosphate status was within the lab's reference range, I would significantly increase the dose of vitamin C the next time to 50gm, and to 75 or even 100gm, but never with brain tumours, as large doses of vitamin C intravenously can cause swelling of a brain that contains a cancerous tumour in it. Large doses of vitamin C are not anti-oxidant, but in fact produce large doses of hydrogen peroxide, so I sometimes gave 0.03% hydrogen peroxide instead, especially if there was any reasonable chance that the person's cancer involved a fungus. However, hydrogen peroxide needs to be given on its own, so, if the patient also needed nutrients, I needed to give a second infusion, meaning that the person could be with me for at least three hours of infusions.

If a patient lived near me, or they chose to rent somewhere near me, I gave a daily infusion of high doses of vitamin C, in which case I only put in other nutrients once a week.

In my opinion, giving intravenous nutrients before and after chemotherapy was very effective, as I have already said. However, the majority of Oncologists don't want anyone having chemotherapy to have anti-oxidants at the same time, presumably assuming the anti-oxidants will counteract the free radicals that the chemotherapy produces. In fact there are very many studies published in peer-reviewed medical journals that say exactly the opposite. Nutrients and anti-oxidants given at the same time as chemotherapy not only seem to make the chemotherapy work more effectively, but they also protect your normal cells from the potentially harmful effects of the chemotherapy. There are two review studies reported in the Appendix about this. So may I suggest that you do not tell your Oncologist that you are taking nutrients, or certainly do not ask his advice. He simply does not know the literature.

The frequency of the infusions depends upon a number of factors, such as the distance you live from the person who gives them to you, the severity of your condition, the quality of your veins, the effect they have upon you, and such facts as whether someone can accompany you, as a companion is a good idea, even if it is not always essential.

If travelling a long way tires you out, making the journey too often may be counter-productive. On the other hand, you may decide to have a course to begin with, in which case you may choose to stay nearby. If you have known cancer, try to have one a week, certainly to begin with.

One obvious problem is that, even if you can find a doctor willing to give you these intravenous infusions, unless he or she is doing them all the time, they are not likely to be able to obtain the individual doses very easily. If such a doctor were doing them all the time, then they are likely to have their own protocol. So this is merely a guide, which I thought was worthwhile describing in this book, because my patients by-and-large found them so valuable and effective. I would like to offer two pieces of simple advice. One is to always immerse your hands in water as hot as you can stand for a few minutes, especially if the weather is cold, to make your veins become more prominent. The second is to try to have had at least one glass of water shortly before you arrive at the clinic, as that expands your blood volume, and also makes your veins more prominent.

I always offered to inject a tiny dose of local anaesthetic into the skin before I inserted the cannula into a vein (after checking they are not allergic to it), especially if

I was going to insert it into anywhere apart from the front of the elbow, such as the wrist or back of hand, which tends to be more sensitive, and therefore a more painful area to stick a cannula into.

This attention to detail turns what might have been an unpleasant experience for some people into one that they could take in their stride. Many of my patients had had bad experiences of blood being taken, or cannulae being inserted, by inexperienced operatives. Some kindly warned me that other people had had great difficulty in finding a vein, so were surprised when I managed quickly, easily and painlessly.

Situation Number 2

Perhaps the most important decision you need to make is whether to have any more chemotherapy or not. There is no way I can answer that for you, so you would be wise to move to the Decisions chapter, where I describe a process you can go through to help you make the right decisions for yourself. No one can make them for you, even if you want someone else to do so for you. I don't know you, nor do I know how you felt when you previously had chemotherapy, nor do I know how you think.

It might be helpful to have a blood test carried out to help you. If you can co-opt help from your GP, try to have a blood test carried out for Fas-ligand, p21 gene expression and Survivin, by SureScreen Life Sciences or Neuro-Lab. Other laboratories may do similar tests.

A high level of Survivin suggests that chemotherapy would not kill cancer cells by the expected process of inducing apoptosis. Were this to be the case, and you were to have more chemotherapy, it is possible that it would not only not work, but might do far more harm than good. I assume that that is what has already happened to you, unless your Oncologist unfortunately chose the wrong chemical for you. Low levels of Survivin suggest that your cancer cells could be killed by apoptosis.

On the other hand, were the Survivin level to be within the laboratory's reference range, it might help you to decide to proceed with the recommended form of chemotherapy, so long as you have questions I suggest in the Decisions chapter answered to your satisfaction.

The Survivin test is the most important one of these three, the other two providing additional information of overall value in relation to your body's ability to deal with your cancer, if you give it a chance and the right materials.

Fas Ligand is a special protein that is sometimes produced by cancer cells and some immunological cells. It has a destructive influence. High levels may destroy immunological cells, thereby limiting the ability of the immune system to kill cancer cells, so you don't want your levels of Fas Ligand to be too high.

P21 is a gene that promotes the self-destruction of cancer cells, so high levels are desirable. Conversely low levels indicate that there may be resistance to the destruction of cancer cells. If you decide to accept your Oncologist's recommendation to have his next course of chemotherapy, move to the advice I give under Situation No. 6 below.

If you decide not to have any more chemotherapy, then go back to Situation No. 1 and follow the advice given there. However, you will need to consider doing more as the situation you now find yourself in is more advanced. This is where it would be valuable to have blood tests done by SureScreen Life Sciences or Neuro-Lab to find out the level of cancer in your body and the status of your immune system. While it is logical to assume that your immune system is in a bad way, I do not always find it to be so. In addition, sometimes one aspect is very active, but another part is very poor and needs boosting.

However, I accept that many of you may not be able to persuade your General Practitioner or Oncologist to carry out these tests on your behalf, as they have not been assessed by the National Health Service in the UK, the FDA of America, or any other medical authority, so far as I am aware. You might, however, be able to persuade them to take the blood sample for you, pay for it, have the results sent to them, and at least be willing to give you the results and discuss them with you. You can only try.

Radiotherapy Protection

If you have decided to have a course of radiotherapy, or are in the process of having it, there are basically eight pieces of advice I can give you, although other people might offer additional pieces of advice. So please refer back to page 141, where I have already given advice on how to protect yourself from the adverse effects of radiotherapy.

Situation Number 3

Here again you have decisions to make, so you will need to read the details in the Decisions chapter, and you will need to have answers that satisfy you whether to proceed with the recommended treatment or select which you are prepared to follow and which you are not prepared to follow. Before you make up your mind, I'm afraid you will need to go through the details in the History and the Treatment chapters to satisfy yourself that you feel the information gives you enough to get on with and you feel confident that it will work. This takes a lot of courage, but please don't let anyone push you into a corner. Take enough time to come to the right decision for yourself.

Situation Number 4

Perhaps the most important thing for you to do in this situation is have a blood test done by SureScreen Life Sciences or Neuro-Lab of Telomerase, Pyruvate kinase and Laevo-rotatory lactic acid, or some other laboratory's test, to see whether any of them suggests that you do have cancer somewhere in your body. The disadvantage of these tests is that the ones I am talking about are non-specific, which means that, if they are positive for cancer, you don't know whereabouts the cancer is in your body. However, if you are suspicious of a lump, you might as well assume your cancer is there.

In any case, you will need to do something about the presence of cancer in your body, so, if you do not want to consult a mainstream doctor, proceed along the lines of my History and Treatment details, assuming your cancer is where you suspect it to be. For now, you have no other alternative but to assume that is where your cancer is, even if you subsequently have evidence it is somewhere else. However, in the meantime, you should have started a process of healing your body generally.

Situation Number 5

This is a situation I was once consulted about, by a lady who had a horrendous family history of cancer, over thirty female family members having had one sort of hormonal cancer or another. She had been advised to have both of her ovaries removed, as that was where cancer could develop silently. However, five female family members had followed that advice, only to develop and die of breast cancer within two years of that operation. A nasty problem!

She had a blood test for Telomerase, Pyruvate kinase and Laevo-rotatory lactic acid, only one of which was just a fraction outside the laboratory's reference range. This helped her make up her mind not to proceed with removal of both her ovaries, but I went through her full history very carefully to be able to make life style recommendations, including diet, etc., to try to prevent cancer developing anywhere in her body. I also recommended she repeat the blood tests regularly.

Even if tests do not show any evidence of cancer at the time the blood sample is taken, if there is a strong family history of cancer, there are plenty of things you can do to try to ensure cancer never develops. Prevention is always better than attempting a cure. In any case, I am of the belief that cancer develops because people do certain wrong things. I have also shown that, if those wrong things can be identified and eliminated, your cancer can be brought under control. So, if you want to prevent cancer from developing in the first place, don't do the things that might cause cancer. That is one of the reasons why I try to take 10g vitamin C every day, among other things.

Situation Number 6

Start by tidying up your diet in the way I have already described. Read about the anti-oxidants, start taking them and any other nutrients, and reach the full dose before your hospital treatment commences. The most important ones are vitamin C, selenium and alpha lipoic acid, for just about everyone, although I have tried to indicate others for certain cancers and certain situations. Remember, most chemotherapy drugs induce nutritional deficiencies in one way or another, which can explain some of the adverse effects. Start doing coffee enemas so you are comfortable doing them wherever you are, and especially when you come home from a dose of chemotherapy.

Find a homoeopath locally and explain what you are about to start. Tell him or her about the adverse effects you have been told may occur so that, if they do, you either have the correct preparation ready to hand, or you can contact him (her) to ask for the appropriate preparation. Ask if they are able to provide you with a homoeopathic dose of the chemotherapy drug you will be given, or are able to obtain it for you. Ask for preparations as drops rather than lactose or sugar pillules.

Try to find a doctor who will give you vitamins and mineral intravenously. Ask to have a blood test for glucose-6-phosphate dehydrogenase so that high doses of vitamin C, as high as 75g if necessary, can be applied, and try to have an infusion as close before and after a dose of chemotherapy as possible. Unfortunately, chemotherapy can sometimes damage or destroy your veins, making it hard to find a suitable one for the next infusion of either nutrients or chemotherapy.

Always ask to be allowed to place your hands in hot water before a cannula or needle is inserted, which will make your veins stand out more easily. If you know where a cannula is likely to be inserted, rub local anaesthetic cream onto the area of skin 1/2 to 1 hour beforehand, but take the cream with you, which the hospital or your own GP can prescribe, in case there is any delay in their starting your treatment, in which case you can apply more.

The Chances Are You Have Cancer

Although you may be reading this website out of curiosity, it is most likely that you, or the person you are looking for information for, have cancer now. You may possibly have a lump or something wrong with you that makes you fairly sure you have cancer, you may possibly have only just been diagnosed with cancer, you may be being treated for cancer, you may have been treated for cancer in the past and given the all clear but it has come back again, or the treatment you are having or have had is clearly not working and you are deteriorating. Whatever your situation, let us simply assume you have cancer. You want a basic plan of what to do to help yourself. You want help with what supplements to take. Recognising that I don't know you or your history, I will therefore try to give you what we could call a starter pack.

Take Vitamin C. Try to work up as quickly as possible to 16g per day, ideally in four separate doses throughout the day. Most forms of Vitamin C irritate the intestines to a degree, but I have found Bio En'R-Gy C powder to be very well tolerated. An alternative is the use of liposomal vitamin C.

Take 4g of Slow Release vitamin C last thing at night. If you take these tablets, reduce your daytime powder to 12g in three separate doses so making your total daily dose 16g. It would be best, however, if you could find someone to give you 20g or more intravenously daily for at least 2 weeks to begin with. You should still take the above doses by mouth in between. Vitamin E doses of around 400 International Units (IU), preferably as mixed tocopherols, should be taken later on in the day, such as between supper and bedtime, if you are slim or underweight, as Vitamin E tends to be anabolic, that is, helps to build up tissue, and night time is the time to rebuild your body. If you are average or overweight, it probably doesn't matter when you take it.

Selenium 200mcg twice daily, preferably half-an-hour before meals.

Alpha-lipoic acid 100mg three times daily any time. Vitamin C, Vitamin E, selenium and alpha-lipoic acid work synergistically.

Vitamin D. 10,000IU daily for about 4 weeks, after which you could reduce the dose to 10,000IU on alternate days or take 5,000IU daily.

Wobenzym N digestive enzymes to break down the coating around cancer tumours to expose them to the other preparations. Rapidly build up to 12 tablets three times a day, away from food, so ideally 2 hours after one meal and 1 hour before the next. If you wake up in the night to go to the toilet or are willing to set an alarm to wake yourself between 2am and 4am, take a dose then, in which case you should take 9 tablets three times during the day and another 9 in the night. If you do wake, you could also take a night time dose of Vitamin C.

The above seven preparations are what I would strongly suggest you consider starting with. However, there is a seventh preparation that I think just about everyone should consider, including people who are well or the carers, and that is the special capsules of dehydrated fruits, vegetables and berries♥.

Seriously consider doing coffee enemas. They hardly cost you anything and can really help the process of detoxification.

Having read the rest of this site or book, you may well feel there is something else you ought to add to the above list. That is something you will have to decide for yourself, as I don't know you.

Don't forget to improve your diet and drink plenty of quality water as I have described.

Management Of Specific Cancers
Everything I have been talking about may be relevant to you, or only a few parts, but I would like to clarify certain types of cancers, what may be important to you and what to do about them.

If you have breast cancer, seriously consider taking some form of oestrogen balancing treatment, such as bio-identical progesterone and calcium-D-glucarate, as well as avoiding all animal milks and animal milk products, among other aspects of a change in your eating habits. The same probably applies to prostate cancer, although you will also need something to stop your body converting your diminishing supplies of testosterone into DHT. I recommend an herbal tea preparation called Harmonik Male Tonic♥. If you have a lymphoma, i.e. any form of cancer that involves primarily swollen lymph glands, assume your body has been overcome by some form of infection, a virus or a fungus most likely, that your immune system has not been able to deal with adequately. You will need chlorine dioxide or some similar anti-infective agent. In my opinion it would be better to take more frequent smaller doses per day than one or two big doses. In addition, you will need to improve your immune system. The preparation I've found to be really good is Biobran♥.

If you have a cancer in any part of your bowel, which includes your liver, and possibly your kidneys, assume there is something inflaming that part of your body, so you should consider what you eat or drink in particular. Be also aware that you may well have an idiosyncratic food reaction, something that can be very difficult to identify, so seriously consider having the Alcat Test done on a sample of your blood. In pancreatic cancer, assume you need extra digestive enzymes, as your pancreas has been trying to provide enough over the years for the process of digestion, and has presumably failed.

In skin cancers, try not to burn your skin at any time, although it is much more difficult once you already have skin cancer. In any form of leukaemia, assume once again, that some form of infection is involved, so consider a treatment with chlorine dioxide or similar preparation. In brain cancer, have you used mobile phones too much, or have you travelled to unusual places and driven off-piste and picked up an unusual infection? You should use chlorine dioxide if you have. If you have lung cancer and have never smoked or been exposed to cigarette smoke or asbestos, there is a possibility that you have a lactase deficiency or milk intolerance which has laid down an inflammatory layer of mucus in your lungs that has turned into cancer in due course.

Beware Of A Crisis
Many people who have started on this or a similar regime have been astonished at how well they have done quickly and how well they have started to feel. There is a good chance that this regime will start to destroy your tumour very quickly. There can then come a stage when you enter a crisis, when your lump may suddenly increase in size, making you fear it is spreading. This is likely to occur between 3 and 9 weeks after you have started the regime and could last a few weeks. It is understandable that you fear everything has gone wrong and your choice of treatment was unwise after all, as everyone had been telling you. Nevertheless you are likely to still feel well. However, persevere with the treatment, as your tumour has entered a stage of its destruction to such an extent that there is a lot of debris and dead cancer cells to be eliminated from your body.

I have heard it suggested that it might be sensible to leave off all supplements for a maximum of 5 days to allow your body to recover. However, it is my feeling that your need for these supplements is all the more important at this time of hard work for your body. The only additional recommendation I can make for you at this time is to carry out coffee enemas, possibly up to four times a day, as these will help eliminate all that debris. You could, of course, have been doing them all the time. Make sure your second morning urine pH is between 6.5 and 6.8. The elimination of dead cancer cells is likely to make you become temporarily even more acidic than before, so you may need to increase your intake of AlkaLiza.

Why Do Some Patients Still Die?

Despite apparently following all the advice I have to offer, some patients still die, even though many do incredibly well and seem to go into permanent remission. My staff and I became very fond of them all, and were very sad when someone we had seen a number of times died. I always asked myself why? I asked myself what I could possibly have missed. I considered that God may 'want' the person for some reason I was not privy to, and was never likely to be. Yet I knew that every cancer patient who consulted me had the power to heal himself or herself, and that I was merely here to point them in the right direction. The more I talk to patients and their relatives, the more I am convinced that there is one area that I may fail to resolve. That is your emotions, things and events in your past that may still be bothering you, that you may have buried deep inside you, so that you cannot even remember what they were all about. If they are still there, they continue to send 'poisonous' chemicals throughout your body, inevitably reducing the effectiveness of your immune system and its healing capacity.

So please search your soul and try to rid yourself of anything in the past that could still be affecting you, even if you are not aware of it at present. Perhaps you should consider sending a team of cleaners into your body to sweep away any rubbish they can find. Find a way of achieving an inner peace and 'clarifying' your past life. Perhaps you should use a form of visualisation, some way that appeals to you.

You don't have to dig up any past events and become aware of them and what effect they had upon you. In fact I don't want you bring them into your conscious mind at all. They have gone. They are in the past. You don't need to resurrect them. You simply need to wash them away, wash yourself clean of anything undesirable in your past. So some sort of visual therapy involving flowing water springs to mind, perhaps a river that has played its part in your past, perhaps the River Jordan.

Dr John Diamond, MD, has studied this whole area in great depth, and you might benefit by obtaining a copy of one of his books, such as 'Life Energy: Unlocking The Hidden Power of Your Emotions to Achieve Total Well-being'♥. Fine if you want to, and I offer it to you as a suggestion, but for many of you, visualising anything undesirable being washed away in a fast-flowing river may be all you need to do. You may need to do it a few times, and each time you should feel the cleansing power of the water.

Chapter 6

The Carers

People seldom realise just how important carers are when someone has cancer. Carers are usually a relative, but may be a friend or simply someone who is willing to help. Whoever they are, they should also be helped. They rush around taking the patient to hospital or GP appointments, often ignoring their own health, sometimes missing meals or having easy foods instead or simply grabbing a bar of chocolate to give themselves energy to keep going. They may drink too many cups of tea or coffee with sugar, and possibly slump into an armchair later in the day with a stiff drink to help themselves relax after rushing around all day looking after someone else. If they smoke, the number of cigarettes smoked in a day may well increase. It's not good. They seem to have abandoned themselves. They also need help.

I have always considered the carers. I have always wanted to help people to improve their life styles before they become ill, so this is often a golden opportunity, and there are usually plenty of ideas to suggest at this stage. It is always so encouraging when I next see the patient (who hopefully is feeling better) to hear that the carer is also feeling a lot better.

So what can I advise such a person to do? Let's start with food and drink. I'd rather not use the word 'diet', as it has so many connotations. I'd prefer to talk about 'healthy eating', and I am assuming the person considers they are in good health at the moment, even if they admit to the odd annoying symptom every so often. If there are more than a few silly niggles, may I suggest reading chapter 3 again, the Consultation, to see if any ideas spring to mind. After all, most people who eventually develop cancer can recognise some aspects of what I discuss, giving them an opportunity to make changes in their life style to start undoing problems that may have been going on for years.

For other people, their history may well suggest exactly the same, but they have never developed cancer nor are they likely to, because they do not have a genetic predisposition to cancer. Although I have explained this earlier, it is worth going over this again. Although there is an enormous amount of research going on into genetics at present, so far as I am aware genetic abnormalities very rarely actually cause problems in life, although a person may be born with a genetic abnormality for all to see. Nearly all of us have some genetic trait that is different to the next person, which gives us our personal characteristics. However, some of those traits can become responsible for any symptoms or illnesses we develop. The most important aspect of this is to recognise that we can switch our genetic predispositions on or off, if we can identify the switches.

Let me give you an example of this. Imagine a man who has a strong family history of migraines, with perhaps his mother, uncle, brother and sister all having suffered from migraines to a degree throughout their life. That person clearly has a genetic predisposition to migraines. By careful observation he identifies that eating cheese, chocolate and drinking red wine can produce a migraine, being intolerable if he consumes all three together. He also discovers that if he avoids the three offending items he can be migraine-free. He still has his genetic predisposition to migraines, but he no longer suffers attacks. He has turned his genetic predisposition off. Any time he wishes to demonstrate he still has his genetic predisposition, all he needs to do is consume some cheese, chocolate or red wine.

I use that example with patients saying that their cancer is equivalent to that man's migraines, adding that we need to identify what the patient's equivalent is to that man's cheese, chocolate and red wine.

So back to our 'fit' carer who should try to avoid extremes, and be aware if addictions are developing, especially to tea, coffee, sugar, alcohol or junk food. Be honest with yourself. Obviously you should try to give up smoking if you smoke, but choose the right time to stop. Perhaps obtaining a copy of my book 'Stop Smoking'♥ might help.

Eating a cooked meal isn't essential, although it can be valuable in a social sense in a family situation. If a cooked meal is temporarily impractical, make sure you have an adequate supply of fruits, vegetables and salad items at home, and possibly eggs. Preparing a healthy salad on a plate shouldn't take you long, and there is no reason not to slice up some fruit in it as well. Adding some dried fruit, nuts and seeds will make a really healthy meal. Supplies of cold oily fish are also useful.

If you do have a spare moment, or can call on the help of a friend, make a large supply of soups and keep it in the refrigerator. When you want a quick but healthy snack, measure out a quantity into a saucepan, heat it gently and drink it enjoyably. There is no reason not to have tea and coffee, in moderation, but drink as much quality water as you can. Water companies do their best to produce drinking water, but the majority of the water going into a household is used for washing oneself, clothes, dishes, cars, etc, so I recommend improving the quality of tap water by filtering it, especially getting rid of the chlorine.

You may not have time for exercise, but at least try to go for a good walk every so often. Try to do something most days that makes you a bit short of breath. There's no need to be extreme. If you are a bit overweight, now might be a good time to do something about it.

There is no way I can recommend nutritional supplements such as vitamins and minerals, as I don't know anything about you, but there is a 'supplement' of sorts that is in principle good for just about everybody. There is no argument that it is best to obtain all nutrients from food, although when someone is ill, specific supplements may be needed. The World Health Organisation and most Governments recommend we all consume at least five portions of fruits and vegetables per day, but the majority of people get nowhere near that figure. In fact the ideal is nearer ten, not five, but it is a waste of time suggesting such a level, as no one would take any notice.

This is where the special capsules of dehydrated fruits, vegetables and berries♥ come into their own. If added to a good diet, they are a wonderful support. There are at least twenty-eight published independent clinical studies to date showing how valuable these capsules are to human beings.

Chapter 7

Decisions To Be Made

This Decisions Chapter has been carefully designed to give you a quiet environment with gentle music playing to provide an opportunity to relax while you consider a number of decisions you need to make about your cancer.

Over the years patients have asked my advice about whether to do something or not. As you have started to read this chapter, I assume you have a decision to make, although I also accept you maybe reading it purely out of curiosity.

From the beginning I need to repeat that I cannot make any decisions for you, but I hope my advice will help you to make the right decision for yourself. I'm sure you have made many decisions in your lifetime, but you may not have thought at the time that it was very important which way any of your decisions went.

However, just think for a moment of some of the decisions you have made and how you made them. Perhaps the first important one was which subjects you chose to study at school. To be fair, you probably had your parents and teachers to guide you, and it may have been fairly obvious at the time because you enjoyed certain subjects. Also you may have already decided what you wanted to do when you left school. Nevertheless you probably did make a decision at that time that might have affected your whole future life. How many hours and days did you spend talking to people close to you about what to do? Or were you one of the lucky ones who knew exactly what to do, like I was, since I wanted to be a doctor from the age of seven, following in my father's footsteps?

Perhaps the next decision was whether to get married or not to a particular person. Did you have any doubts? How long did you take to make up your mind? For how many hours did you talk to your parents and friends? In the end, did you make the right decision, or did it turn out not to have been such a good decision after all, even if you thought it was absolutely right at the time. More to the point, how did you make whatever decision you did make? Did you simply let your heart decide? Were you swept off your feet, so virtually had little choice in the matter? Or did you weigh things up sensibly, trying to come to the right decision for you?

I imagine another major decision you have had to make at some time in your life is whether to buy a particular house or not. Only a few people are fortunate enough to find the perfect house, in the perfect location, at the perfect price, as soon as they start looking. For most people it is a major headache where to buy. Their ideal location in relation to their place of work is too expensive, too down market, not near enough to the best schools, or some other reason. So, once again, decisions had to be made. Can you remember how you made them, and what discussions you had about how to make them?

Then perhaps you found yourself helping your children to make decisions about their own choices of school subjects. And so the world goes round. Did you find the decisions you did make were complicated or easy? Did you actually get involved in any particular decisions about yourself, or was your life mapped out for you by others? If that is the case, is this the first important decision you have had to make in your life, one that you feel could have such an important impact on your future?

I'm sorry, but you still have to make the decision for yourself, irrespective of how much advice you can obtain from whatever source. But at least I will help you with your decisions, and I hope to help you make the right ones for yourself.

But, first, what is the decision you have to make? It is likely to be one of the following:

- Should I have a biopsy of my lump or not?

- Should I have the lump removed or not?
- Should I have chemotherapy or not?
- Should I have radiotherapy or not?
- Should I have a particular drug or not?
- Should I let a surgeon operate on me or not?

When a patient in front of me asks my advice, my first question is to ask them what their current feeling is. So, ask yourself whether, at this stage, you are inclined to have the treatment or not. On a scale of 0 to 100, with 0 being definitely not to proceed and 100 being definitely to proceed, and with 50 as the point of balance, are you at present anywhere above or below the 50-point mark? See if you can answer that question before you read any further, but don't worry if you remain resolutely at the 50-point mark.

If you were able to make a decision one side of the 50-point mark, make a note of it now and write down your decision somewhere where you can refer to it whenever you want to. It is very important that you recognise the decision you have already made. This is your status quo, your current position on the decision you need to make. From now on you need to receive fairly strong information and justification to change your status quo. Don't change your status quo without a good reason.

A patient I saw for the first time a few years ago had been diagnosed with cancer in the tail of his pancreas on a scan. He told me he did not want a biopsy to confirm the diagnosis and he did not want an operation or any orthodox treatment such as chemotherapy or radiotherapy. He wanted to follow a natural approach and asked me what could I recommend. I did what I always do, and gave him my best recommendations. Right at the end of the consultation he told me that, on the next day, he had an appointment with a new surgeon, and he was going to see what he had to suggest.

He rang me the next evening to say that he had told him that he could give him a 95% chance of curing him if he let him operate on him. He changed his mind, didn't he? He went ahead and had the operation. I watched his cancer markers come down to zero from a level before the operation that confirmed he had cancer somewhere in his body.

Another way of looking at how to make a decision is "If in doubt, don't". If you are not sure whether to marry someone or not, don't. If you are thinking of moving house, why are you considering it? "Oh! I just fancy a move!" or "It's springtime and all my friends are moving". Those are not good enough reasons, but "I can't stand the house I am living in!" or "I really love the look of that house and I would love to live in it" are good enough reasons to move, all other things being equal. So, with these thoughts in mind, let us now consider the first question "Should I have a biopsy or not?"

One of your doctors, a Specialist I assume, has recommended that he stick a needle into the lump you have found and consulted him about. Possibly your General Practitioner has felt the lump and wants to refer you to a Specialist for the biopsy. Whichever is the case, you still have to decide whether to proceed or not. The purpose of the biopsy is to make a definite diagnosis, or to confirm or reject a suspicion of cancer. Doctors in mainstream medicine feel uncomfortable if they can't make a definite diagnosis by having a sample of the lump examined under a microscope.

A further reason is that, once the diagnosis has been confidently made, it helps the doctor to decide what the most appropriate treatment is for that diagnosis. The doctor who examines the sample under a microscope will also stage the cancer, which is medical speak for how bad it is. He will also help the cancer Specialist with the prognosis, which, again, is medical speak for what your chances are in the long run. Remember, most doctors assume you will do whatever they suggest. To be fair to them, most patients do follow their advice, usually not asking any questions at all. After all "You know best, Doctor" is an easy way out of making a decision for yourself.

One cancer patient who consulted me not so long ago had to wait in the waiting room after she had seen a Consultant. After quite some time, she asked the nurse why she was having to wait so long, to which the reply was "The doctor is deciding how to treat you". The nurse was visibly shocked when the patient said, "Do you mind. I will decide what treatment I have". What doctors and staff sometimes forget, or may not even be aware of in the first instance, is that The General Medical Council, in its booklet 'Duties of a Doctor' says, "Doctors should encourage patients to be fully involved in decisions about their care".

But I have digressed a little, as I often do, so, back to the point in hand. At this stage, i.e. before the biopsy is taken, no one really knows what is going on, unless you have many lumps that have appeared and he is sure what it is, or the doctor merely wants to do the biopsy because it is what he always does. In the circumstances, there is no point in asking him what treatment he is likely to recommend, because he doesn't know himself yet. However, you could ask him what treatment options he is likely to recommend if the biopsy were to turn out as he suspects.

In the main, the treatment options for cancer are an operation, radiotherapy, chemotherapy, some other drug regime, probably hormonal in some way, or a combination of them. If you have breast cancer, you may be advised to have a lumpectomy, a wedge resection or a mastectomy, with or without subsequent reconstruction, as well as possibly various parts of your lymph system in your armpit being removed. This may be followed by local radiotherapy and a course of chemotherapy, occasionally one of them without the other, plus a drug by mouth.

If you have cancer of the prostate, be aware that a biopsy of the prostate can sometimes be a very painful experience. Biopsy of a breast lump is not usually painful, but the simple procedure of sticking a needle in it, sometimes a fairly wide bore one to obtain a reasonably large specimen, and sometimes more than once, can occasionally inflame the whole area. Some of my patients have told me that they felt the biopsy made their cancer grow faster after it had been done. To be fair to the surgeon who took the biopsy, he probably assumed he was going to proceed fairly soon to some sort of operation anyway, so that it shouldn't matter.

If the biopsy is what a doctor might consider a 'run-of-the-mill' procedure, then you need to ask yourself a simple question, and, at the same time, decide where your answer would be on the 0 to 100 scale. Would you proceed to have whatever treatment the Specialist recommends? Would you be prepared to have a local lumpectomy, a mastectomy with or without a degree of axillary clearance? Would you be prepared to have radiotherapy and/or chemotherapy?

If you would be prepared to have some of these options but not others, it is important to tell your Specialist, because it may make a difference to whether he decides to do the biopsy or not. If, however, you would not be prepared to undergo any of the treatment that might be recommended, there is no point in having the biopsy in the first place. That is why it is so important for you to consider the points I made in the previous paragraph. When I was in General Practice in the late 1970s, I tried to explain as fully as possible to all my patients what was likely to happen at a later stage in certain conditions. I am digressing for a moment here to what I explained to women when they attended my surgery in the early stages of pregnancy, especially if it was their first pregnancy, so they had not had any previous experience of what would happen over the next few months. Remember, scans that are used so frequently nowadays were not available in those days, but the principle I am on about is still the same.

I would explain the frequency of visits, what we would do at each visit, and all the blood tests that it was wise to have done. I explained that, at approximately sixteen weeks, she would be offered a blood test to see if there was the possibility that her baby had some sort of abnormality. If this were positive, it would be repeated to make sure a mistake had not been made in the laboratory. If it were still positive a more specific test would be done. If there were no doubt that the baby did have a problem, then she would be offered an abortion.

I feel it can sometimes be very difficult for people to make a decision when they are suddenly confronted with it, like you might be now. So to have to consider, as early as possible, what one might do were a particular problem to arise at a later stage, is worth thinking about. In those days, I felt that mentioning a remote possibility to a woman in the early stages of pregnancy, when her hormones were settling, gave her a chance to consider her attitude at a time when it didn't matter, and would probably never occur anyway.

You might think this was not a good idea, but I never found anyone who felt I was wrong to bring up the subject that early on. I feel the attitude I held then was right and still is. Doctors sometimes have a habit of thinking they must make 'the right decision' for the patient, so may not give all the options. As far as I am concerned, my patients are just as intelligent as I am, so, if I explain things to them properly, I am teaching them everything I can for them to decide what to do for themselves.

Having explained this to the woman (and I always insisted her husband be present or at least a close family member or friend at the time), I would then ask if she had any idea what attitude she would take. Inevitably some would say they had no idea. Others were wise to say they would have to think about it, which was exactly why I had mentioned it so early. Then there were a few who said that, no matter what the result, they wouldn't have an abortion under any circumstances. I would then suggest that, in that case, there was no point in having the blood test done in the first place.

Do you see what I am getting at? If you are not prepared to have the treatment that would be recommended as a result of a test, why have the test done in the first place? This situation entirely applies to you if you have decided not to have the treatment that your Specialist is likely to recommend. However, it changes if you might.

The next question on that list that you may need to decide upon is "Should I have the lump removed?" The same applies to "Should I have an operation at all?" The answer to this one depends upon a number of factors, but remember, you have been recommended to have an operation by a Surgeon.

Some years ago a friend asked my advice about his mother. She had been found to have an obvious breast lump (which was clearly a cancer), when she was being washed in the shower. However, she was totally unaware of it or its significance, because she also had fairly bad Alzheimer's Disease. Her son naturally took her to her General Practitioner who referred her on to the local breast cancer centre, where she was advised to have a mastectomy. When my friend asked me whether she needed to have the operation, I suggested that perhaps it wasn't necessary in the circumstances of her other health problems, especially as the whole procedure of going into hospital, having a general anaesthetic and all those bandages would likely confuse her even more.

So my friend went back to the hospital Consultant and asked him if the operation was really necessary and also asked him if he would recommend the operation if his own mother were the patient in question. He duly replied that there was no need for the operation to be done. When my friend asked him why he had made the recommendation in the first place, he said, "Because I'm a Surgeon and my job is to operate." My friend's mother died of old age a few years later, none the worse for not having the mastectomy.

I have no doubt that today's Surgeons are caring people. They know that patients are better informed than ever before. They now accept that patients are likely to ask a lot of questions, and are not always going to accept immediately any advice they are given. Gone are the days of Sir Lancelot Spratt of the 'Doctor In The House' film, when a patient was cowed, or bullied, into accepting his advice. Woe betide anyone who had the temerity to even ask him a question. To him the patient was something to operate on, but to be fair, he was also an excellent surgeon.

What I am really saying is that you need to examine your personal position. You also need to ask your Specialists a number or questions. Perhaps the first one should be "With all the experience you have had over the years, could you please try to tell me what, in your opinion, is likely to happen to me if I do not agree to an operation?" In addition you could also ask, "What is my prognosis if I do have it?" And, "Are there any alternatives?"

Clearly I do not know the state of your cancer, how minimal or how bad it is. Has anyone indicated that you only have a short time to live, or have they told you that everything should turn out well, and that you should have many more years of active life? If that last statement, does it depend upon your following what has been recommended?

In an attempt to help you answer this last question, I would like to move on to consider the next three questions, basically whether you should have chemotherapy, radiotherapy or some other drug treatment.

If you have cancer, all of these treatments are likely to be fairly toxic, although some people seem to cope with them remarkably well. In the introduction I explained why chemotherapy usually makes people feel so unwell, and, for now, you need to assume it will make you feel bad to a degree. Yes, you will be given other drugs to minimise the adverse effects, but they don't always work, and may even make things worse. The side effects of the drugs given to you to minimise the chemotherapy's side effects may themselves have other undesirable effects. How you will feel I cannot possibly tell you, as we are all different and no one has yet been able to identify who will feel bad and who will not.

Nevertheless, you must ask your Specialists what they think might happen to you. Of course they will hope their treatments will work for you, otherwise they wouldn't recommend it. They also know that part of the long-term effects of radiation and chemotherapy is to cause cancer itself. There is nothing new about this, but they are dealing with the 'here and now'.

If you suspect that your Specialists don't feel you have much of a chance, even if they treat you, you need to ask two simple questions. "What is my prognosis if I don't have any treatment?" And, "Will your treatment give me a useful extension to my life?" Perhaps you could also ask, "How do you think I will feel during what is left of my life, if I do have your treatment?" You could also challenge them by asking, "Would you have the treatment you are recommending if you were in my shoes?" If the Specialist replies, "Possibly not", you can guess what he is thinking. Remember, he feels he must try to help you if he can.

So what sort of answers to these questions might you receive? Let me first paint a possible picture that may or may not apply to you. You had breast cancer five years ago, which was treated with a mastectomy followed by a few weeks of local radiotherapy, then a six-month course of chemotherapy. Everyone was happy with the outcome and you were seen regularly for follow-up when you were examined, blood may have been taken for a few tests sometimes, and you were given the all clear. Your routine visits to the clinic were recently extended to one year.

A few weeks ago you developed a cough, which lingered on longer than usual. However, friends had had much the same, as there was a nasty bug going around at the time. So you didn't think anything of it. In due course you decided to consult your GP about it when you felt a pain in one of your ribs. Having listened to your chest and not heard anything wrong, he suggested a chest X-ray 'to be on the safe side'. When he received the report he arranged an urgent appointment for you back at the hospital. More X-rays, blood tests and extensive scans were done, for you to be told, "I'm sorry, but the cancer has come back and it has spread into your lungs and many of your bones".

You now have what is described as 'terminal cancer'. You have been given three months to live. "We could try a course of chemotherapy, if you like."

Now your questions take on a different angle. You have basically been told that there isn't much that can be done for you, but that they are prepared to try something if you would like them to. You have one or two simple questions. First, "How many weeks or months longer is your recommended treatment likely to give me?" If the answer is something like "Possibly three months", you have to decide whether those three months are important to you. Perhaps you have something personal to sort out, possibly your will or something else important, that needs a little time. After all, you may well have been advised to go home and 'put your things in order'.

You could ask that question in a slightly different way and say, "How much more useful life is your treatment likely to give me?" At the same time you also need to ask, "How am I likely to feel with your treatment?" "Is it likely to make me feel ill?" "Is it likely that the treatment you are recommending will make the remaining time I do have left hardly worth having, assuming that I am likely to have to spend some of that time in hospital?"

All of the answers you need to weigh up for yourself. You have to decide whether the time you are likely to have left would be best spent with your family. You have to decide whether the extension to your life that the recommended treatment, with its possible unpleasant effects, is worth having. To some people, any extension of their life is worth having. To others, what is on offer may not be.

What I have described so far is likely to cover the majority of people who have a decision to make. You don't need to be in as extreme a situation as I have described above. If, nevertheless, you have a problem of any sort, whether it is serious or not, the questions I have outlined are still appropriate. It's just that the answers will be different. There is one other question that you could ask, whatever your condition,

173

and that is what Oxford Don Michael Gearin-Tosh asked of his Specialist when he was diagnosed with Multiple Myeloma, a condition that is usually fatal within a year or two from diagnosis. "Can you cure me?" When he was told there was no cure for his condition, he basically said, "Then I don't want your treatment. I will find a cure for myself." You can read his story in his book entitled 'A Living Proof. A Medical Mutiny'♥, which he wrote when he was still alive eight years later! It makes fascinating reading.

Whatever your condition, however bad your situation is, unless it is an outand-out emergency, take as long as you need to come to the right decision for yourself. In my experience, the longer you take to make a decision, the more doubts you have about whether to proceed or not. That then puts you somewhere below the 50-point mark.

Talk it through with those you trust, those closest to you, after you have all the information you can obtain. If necessary, you could ask for a second opinion. After all, the answers to your questions will be given according to the experience of the doctor you ask them of. Another doctor may have a different opinion, or he may give you much the same answers. To be fair, no doctor can be sure, so he can only give you what he believes is likely to be the right answer, based on his own statistics, observations and experience. He also knows that some patients survive longer than others, but he doesn't know why that is, or who will be fortunate to survive longer than he anticipated.

Make sure you have had an answer to all the questions you need to ask. Don't ask too many people to help you in your decision-making. Keep it to a small circle of people you think you can rely on to help you decide. But, remember, some of the advice may be conflicting, so may confuse you even more. Consider why someone gave you a particular piece of advice. Have they had a similar experience before with one of their own close relatives? Did that person do well, or was it a total disaster? In many respects, if someone has had a previous experience of this sort, they may not be particularly suitable to ask, even if they are sympathetic. Their reply is likely to be influenced by their experience. They are not likely to see it from your point of view, only theirs. On the other hand, such experience could open your eyes in a particularly relevant way.

Beware of people who say, "If I were you, I would do so-and-so". They are not in your shoes, and you are not in theirs. In my opinion, the best people are those who let you do most of the talking, prompting you every so often, allowing you to come to your own conclusions.

Finally, before you leave this Decisions chapter, I want to give a hopeful message. At this stage, whether your condition is serious or not, whatever statistics or answers you have been given by your Oncologist, you do not fit into them. They do not apply to you. The reason I can say that is because you are looking for something else to help you. The very fact that you are reading this web site means that you are seeking another opinion, but this time, from a doctor who thinks in a different way to the doctors whose advice you have sought so far.

Chapter 8

Problems That Need Solving

In this chapter, I want to have a chat with you about certain problems that you are having at present that you acknowledge are causing you a certain amount of stress.

In other areas I have tried to indicate just how bad stress is, together with the physiological effects stress has on your body. As a reminder, stress not only exhausts the whole of your adrenal system, both the part that makes adrenaline and the part that makes your steroid hormones, but also makes your body become relatively more acid. That new environment makes organisms mutate so that they can survive in it, and that mutation usually turns them into a harmful organism, or a more virulent one if they were already harmful to a degree.

This whole situation also creates a need for more nutrients than usual, especially vitamins B5 and C and magnesium, and it is in times of stress that people tend to eat badly, smoke more, drink more tea, coffee and alcohol, and generally 'abuse' themselves nutritionally at a time when better nutrition than normal is required.

It is amazing how often I pick up, at the first consultation, significant areas of stress, sometimes going on for years and years. Some people seem to attract stress, almost as if they need it. Yet it is only when I point out to them the harm it is doing to them, and how it is playing its part in their cancer, that their eyes are suddenly opened.

Many people, possibly most people, and probably most people who are ill in any way, have very deep-seated problems, possibly even going back to childhood. The work of Dr. John Diamond MD is particularly interesting in this respect. In his book 'Life Energy: Unlocking The Hidden Power Of Your Emotions To Achieve Total Well-being'♥, he describes a nine-year-old child stroking her mother's Caesarean scar and crying "Mummy how could I do that to you? I am so sorry." He describes this as the patient martyring herself because she feels responsible for her mother's illness or unhappiness. While I accept that it may not be possible for some people to avoid certain stressful episodes in their lives, I am sure there is nearly always something that can be done about them. After all, a problem is only a situation that needs a resolution.

I ask the patient to describe their problem, hoping it won't take too long. Most of the time patients are only too willing to describe what is troubling them, and it helps me to understand part of their problem. Sometimes, of course, people don't want to talk about such things, as it is too upsetting or too personal. That alone tells me how important it is to their cancer. People's body language is also most enlightening when they start to describe these episodes, and I have boxes of handkerchiefs at the ready!

Sometimes I feel sure that whatever is troubling the patient is the most important thing for them to deal with, and I spend some time on this, basically feeling that they will be wasting their time and mine, and their money, until they sort it out. That doesn't mean that there aren't other things that we can start on, but it does suggest to me that it is the number one situation that needs a resolution.

When I have completed my history of each patient, I explain that there are usually a number of causes for their cancer, and, for the sake of my mathematics, I say I have identified at least five. Much of the time I don't know whether each one is twenty per cent of the problem, or one is eighty per cent and the rest twenty per cent between them. Then occasionally one part of the history is so clearly the most important that I feel obliged to point it out. Sometimes that major point is the stress or emotional problem the patient is struggling with.

There are many approaches people can follow to resolve their important deep-seated issues. One is reading a copy of 'The Journey'♥, and the other is the work of Dr. John Diamond, who I have already mentioned. Hypnotherapy may also help some people. However, the purpose of this chapter is to explain how I advise people to deal with life's situations that are currently affecting them, and sometimes people find they can then use the same approach to deal with other deeper-seated problems. Having explained to me what the problem is, I ask one or two simple questions around it, such as "Are you handling the problem well?" "Is the problem affecting you badly?" "Is the situation making you feel Ill?" "Is the problem affecting your daily life?" "Is the way you are handling the situation working?"

The answer to all of these questions tells me how the person is coping with their problem. Usually the answer to the first is "No", the second is "Yes", the third is "Yes", the fourth is "Yes" and the fifth is "No".

I then explain the harm it is doing, including all the information on the physiological effects on the body, and simply say "Then something needs to change, doesn't it? And you are the person that can start making a change. And if you change, you may be surprised how the situation changes around you. It may not matter what you do, so long as you do something."

While pointing all this out, and helping people to resolve their issues, I also start treating the physiological effects on the body, such as help to alkalinise with AlkaLiza♥, advise them to take the special capsules of dehydrated fruits, vegetables and berries♥, support their adrenal glands with AD206♥, and use whatever I consider appropriate to deal with any pathological organisms (see details in the Treatment chapter)

So, let me give some examples of my approach. Many years ago a young couple consulted me about her problems. It doesn't matter what they were. I helped in a number of ways, so she was considerably better. However, she became stuck at a certain level of improvement, and it took me some time to find out what the problem was.

She had an elder sister by two years who was absolutely queen bee in the family. Both she and her sister were married with two children by now, and they all lived fairly close to each other and their kids went to the same school. Absolutely everything had to revolve around the elder sister. Even their mother apologised that she couldn't baby-sit for my patient, as she was too busy constantly helping the elder daughter.

Things had, in fact, I eventually discovered, basically started when the elder sister got married (this all occurred some years before she first consulted me), although things had always been one-sided all their lives. The younger sister's medical problems included her feeling exhausted sometimes, and she never knew when a bout would come over her, so she asked if there could be a room available for her at the wedding reception hotel so that she could lie down if she needed to. This was duly organised.

On the wedding day, my patient needed to lie down some of the time, although she struggled on as best she could. Obviously she had worn herself out helping with the preparations. Apparently because she did not dance in attention throughout the whole reception, her sister had never forgiven her. Petty, you might think, but that was what they told me.

Since then things had gone from bad to worse, her sister demanding that their mother have nothing to do with her sister, because she had insulted her, and help her whenever she wanted. Her mother had agreed, sort of apologising some of the time.

When I first heard this extraordinary story, I discovered that the current problem was that neither of them wanted to take their children to school in the mornings and fetch them in the afternoons because they would inevitably see the elder sister who would look at them with such disgust that it upset them. They were thinking of moving house so that they didn't need to confront her, but this would result in the kids having to change schools, which they didn't want to do, as they liked the school and were doing well there.

I was truly astonished at this story, but have heard many amazing ones since then, and they all have a very bad effect upon the sufferers. My patient clearly admitted that the situation made her symptoms so much worse, which was why they were thinking of making such a major change in their lives.

I then asked them why they let the elder sister bully them so much. To me it seemed that she was trying to punish her younger sister (and the family as well) for not dancing in attendance all the time at her wedding. They accepted that the elder sister's attitude was working, making them both feel anxious and the patient feel quite unwell.

I asked them why they were letting the elder sister get away with it, and, quite honestly, they didn't know. It had simply been going on for so long. I told them that they were allowing the elder sister to get away with it, and that it was their own fault for letting it happen. I suggested that they change something simple, so that they were no longer affected badly, no longer bullied by her and no longer affected by her. I told them both to take the kids to school next day, and, when they saw the elder sister, to smile at her and give her a cheery welcoming wave. This way she was no longer in charge, no longer bullying them, no longer held the upper hand, and no longer succeeding in hurting them.

My simple approach worked wonders because they made a simple change to the way they received her attitude. They stopped letting the situation get under their skin. When they got back in the car after dropping off the kids, it even made them giggle to think what they had just done. The elder sister totally lost her hold over them, her control of them, and both my patient and her husband started to feel a lot better. The elder sister is now thinking of moving house!

The second story is about a big strong man who, as with the patient I have described above, let a family situation upset him so badly for many, many years, that it was clearly stopping him for recovering his health. He acknowledged that, when certain things happened, he immediately became worse, and just couldn't control himself. So long as the situation didn't apply he was remarkably well only to plummet when things went wrong.

What was the situation? His father had verbally bullied him most of his life, pushing him to do better. Then he started being bullied verbally in slightly different ways by his father-in-law, which his wife acknowledged. I had many long-distance phone calls from them both about how well he was doing in general, only to be told that every so often he would plummet.

Clearly it was difficult for me to undo all the hurt of the past, but I told him that, if he could solve whatever was bugging him in the present, it might, in one fell swoop, solve the problems of the past. So I asked him what particularly annoyed him about his father and father-in-law nowadays. His answer astonished me. "They keep turning up at the weekend, uninvited, for afternoon tea, just to annoy me. They seem to know what it does to me, and they seem to enjoy seeing me struggle". I asked him when he had last invited them to come over at the weekend. That almost let out a torrent of abuse, and he said there was no way he would ever do that. I asked him why not, and he said that they would be as awful as always. However, his wife saw what I was getting at. She immediately realised that, by inviting them to come over, he was taking the upper hand. He would be in charge of the situation, not they.

I had an ecstatic phone call from him shortly after that to say that, when he had invited both of them to come over for tea the next Sunday, both parents had made some sort of excuse that they were doing something else, and couldn't come over. He apparently saw how he was regaining control over his life because he invited them to come over the following week, but again found them too busy! As I expected, having now regained that life control, it had already started to wipe out all the problems of the past.

My third story is about a woman who consulted me about her oesophageal (gullet) cancer. After she had answered some of my initial questions, I asked her if she had any ideas why her cancer had appeared. Immediately her husband chipped in with, "Oh! I know why. She has drunk tea and coffee unbelievably hot all her life. I don't know how she can tolerate it. The drink is straight out of the kettle and down her throat!"

My immediate thought was that that would possibly scald or burn her throat and even possibly make it a target for cancer to attack one day, but I couldn't see it as the main cause. I then asked her about any stress that she might have been under in the years before her cancer first appeared. She told me her mother had had very severe and complicated Alzheimer's disease and that there were no local facilities to look after her, so they had had to keep her at home, which lasted for five years. She said I couldn't possibly imagine how difficult that had been, and I agreed with her.

To make matters worse, her mother had been a diabetic for many years and was severely overweight, which made looking after her even more difficult, especially as she had refused to eat what her doctor had advised. Even testing her blood sugar levels to give her the correct dose of insulin by injection had been a daily struggle.

All that had been bad enough, but she developed gangrene of both legs and her daughter had had to sign the hospital papers agreeing to amputation of both limbs. The operation was very difficult and her mother died soon after that, never coming home again. I asked her how she felt about that, which was when the tears started to flow and she said, "I still feel guilty. My action killed her. I feel responsible for her death."

With great care I tried to point out that she had probably done the right thing, and felt sure her husband and others had already said the same, plus other soothing platitudes as gently as I could, knowing perfectly well that that would not appease her or assuage her sense of guilt.

My answer was to recommend that she read the book 'The Journey'♥, a copy of which I gave her. I asked her to read it and ring me when she had read it at least twice. I felt that when she met her mother round the campfire (until you read the book you will not understand what this means), she would thank her for her loving care and attention for all those years, apologise for being so difficult, and tell her she had made the right decision about she operations and that there was nothing to feel guilty about.

I completed the history, and made some simple suggestions, but encouraged her to concentrate on this in the first place, as I was sure it was the most important feature of her personal story. Perhaps she took my advice, read Brandon Bays' book, consulted a Brandon Bays therapist, started to feel better and brought her cancer under control. Perhaps she took my advice, read Brandon Bays' book, consulted a Brandon Bays therapist and felt at peace with herself, but let her cancer take its course, eventually dying with dignity. Or may be she took no notice of me at all.

I don't know what happened to her, because I never heard from her again. Perhaps it was all too much for her. Perhaps she felt she simply couldn't face it all over again. I hope and pray that, whatever happened to her cancer, she ended her days at peace with herself and her Maker.

What I am trying to say in this chapter is that, if a situation is having a bad effect upon you, you are the person that can, and must, make a change. And, if you make a simple change, there is every chance that the situation will change around you in a simple way. You may not succeed in altering the personality of someone else, although you just might, but simply altering your response to someone else's attitude may make all the difference you are looking for.

Two out of these three stories had a happy and satisfactory ending, and, who knows, may be even the third. I am now totally convinced that dealing with such emotions is vitally important. For the majority of people it should be possible to do something, especially if you are aware of what the problem is. It is just a matter of opening your eyes to the situation.

Deep-seated problems, however, may need to be washed from your body in a river of loving, flowing water. So let me expand this idea awhile. Some people may have problems they know exist, but don't know what they are or where they have buried them. And may be it is not important to find out what they are or where they are. Perhaps it is only important to clear them out, so they are gone forever.

Try to follow this suggestion. Get yourself into a comfortable relaxed frame of mind, as though you are going to do some relaxation, visualisation or affirmation exercises. Take a few nice fairly deep breaths, each time saying to yourself "Relax, relax, relax" three times as you gently breathe out. Feel yourself in a calm, controlled frame of mind. Now conjure up an image of yourself sitting in a comfortable chair in a tranquil place, near water, possibly by a stream where you played as a child, by the River of Jordan if you like, or simply invent somewhere where there is flowing water. Fell the calm of the place. Let it flow over you.

Now watch as your spirit quietly rises from the chair and walks into the flowing water. Yet it is still you. Let the water gently lap round your ankles. Feel the wonderful peace and calming effect of the place. Lap it up for a while.

Then when you are ready, release one of your deep-seated problems into the water and let it flow away. Watch as it mixes with the current and disappears round a corner or past a smooth rock and out of sight. Feel how purified you and your spirit have become. Enjoy the feeling of freedom. It doesn't matter what the problem was or from where you have released it. You don't need to know the facts, merely that, whatever it was, it has gone. You are free of it at last. It no longer troubles you. It has gone forever.

Perhaps you have done enough for now. May be you feel there are more problems to release. Let go of another one if you want to, but it might be better to be satisfied for now and return to the stream another day. Take your time. There is no hurry. There is always another day. Simply enjoy what you have done and feel liberated.

By reading this book you should be able to obtain as much information as you want. You can spend as much time as you like reading any chapter over again. As it is your copy you can make notes at the side of certain pages that you want to read again or simply underline any passage that you think is important to highlight. I believe you will find ideas in this book that either no one else has suggested to you before. Hopefully some of them will help you to decide to do something for yourself. Whether you do or not is entirely up to you, but I doubt if you would have read this far if you are not going to start helping yourself to get better.

So, have faith in yourself. Believe that you can make a difference. Believe that you can beat all the odds. After all, it has been done many times before, and there is no reason why you should not join that special group.

Chapter 9

How To Avoid Developing Cancer

I think it is now generally accepted that some people have a genetic predisposition towards cancer, but the same applies to arthritis, asthma, migraines, in fact virtually every medical disease known to man. However, there is no need for that condition to develop in you, because you can switch your genetic predisposition on or turn it off. If you walk into a dark room and want to turn on the lights, you need to know where the switch is. It may be behind the door, next to the door, or have been placed in an unusual position, but one that is more convenient for the usual user for some unknown reason. Nevertheless, if you want to switch the light on and off later on, you need to know where that switch is.

It's exactly the same with cancer or any medical condition. It's just that the switch is probably different in different people. After all, we are not all the same, so why should we think our switches are all the same?

Let me explain that further. Imagine a man who suffers from migraines. His mother, a brother and a son also suffer from migraines, so there is no doubt that he has a genetic predisposition to migraines, which he has passed on to one of his sons. However, by direct observation he discovers that he can become free of migraines if he avoids eating cheese and chocolate and drinking red wine. By doing so, he switches off his genetic predisposition. Any time he wishes to, he can switch his predisposition back on again by eating some cheese and chocolate or drinking some red wine. It's up to him. He has the choice. It's basically that simple.

The problem is, however, not nearly so easy in life to identify your switches, but there are certain ideas I would like to suggest you follow to give yourself the best chance of not developing cancer. Remember, we all have cancer cells in our body, but our immune systems sort out the bad guys and destroy them. Even then, it is highly likely that, if a few cancer cells escape eradication in the early stages, it can still take many years for a fullblown cancerous tumour to develop. So what should you do? First I suggest you take stock of what you eat. Ideally I suggest you cut out all or nearly all animal milks and animal milk products. Such dairy items play no part in human metabolism. There is no animal on God's earth that has milk or milk products after weaning, unless we humans give it to them. I have expanded on this theme in the appendix.

Also I would advise keeping alcohol and caffeine down to an absolute minimum, remembering that there is caffeine also in tea, cola drinks and chocolate. Avoid all chemical additives where possible, especially aspartame and GM foods in my opinion, although I accept other people have a different attitude. Again I have published Dr. Mercola's attitude to GM foods in the appendix. Consume as much in the way of vegetables and fruits as is reasonable, do not eat red meat too often, and certainly do not have any added sugar if at all possible. Make all your flour-based products wholemeal. Eat oily fish twice a week, avoiding meat from large fish such as tuna, because they have eaten smaller fish, which have eaten even smaller fish and so on down the line, tuna tending to concentrate toxic substances like mercury in their tissues.

Where possible, eat only organic food, but don't make too much of a fetish about this. Remember organic foods have not been sprayed with fungicides, so will develop their natural Salvestrols, which in turn are protective against cancer.

What should you drink? Water is by far the best for you, so long as you improve the quality of your drinking water in some way by a filtering system of sorts. There are plenty of herbal teas that are positively anti-cancerous. The odd cup of tea and decaffeinated coffee won't hurt you.

Should you take supplements? This is a thorny subject, but in my opinion you should. Life is full of surprises and stresses. I would advise about 6 to 10 grammes of vitamin C per day, 5000IU vitamin D3 + 150mcg K2 (depending on where you live and the amount of sunshine you achieve), a simple multi-vitamin/mineral from a reputable provider, a handful of digestive enzymes last thing at night, and possibly 1000mg of omega-3 essential fatty acids at least three times a week. Last but not least, I strongly suggest you order a supply of capsules of dehydrated fruits, vegetables, berries♥, which may possibly be better for you than all the other suggestions I have made put together. The more nutrition you can have from fruits and vegetables the better. That's what our metabolism is based on.

Check whether you are sleeping or living in a geopathic stress area, and do something about it if you are. Never have any teeth filled with mercury amalgam, and have any teeth with root fillings extracted and the base cleaned out by a biologically-trained dentist. Avoid stress wherever possible, and if you are affected by stress, do your best to resolve it one way or another. I would suggest you try to avoid ever having antibiotics. There are plenty of natural ways of dealing with infections. My wife and I have never had an antibiotic ever in our lives. Finally, try to do something every day that makes you a bit short of breath.

Chapter 10

Planning Your Day with Breast Cancer

Now that you have read all the way through this book, I am going describe a daily plan for a woman with Breast Cancer. You must surely realise that there is so much you can do to help yourself. Having said that, it is possible that, although I wrote a chapter on 'Where to Start' you may still be unsure how to plan your day. So I will now suggest what you consider doing.

Clearly what you do and how much you do depends to a certain extent on your current situation, so I will start by describing various scenarios and provide a day's plan for each.

Scenario 1

You think you might have breast cancer, but you don't want to go to your own doctor because you know what that would entail. Alternatively, you are pretty sure you have breast cancer, but don't want any treatment that mainstream medicine recommends. You want to know what to do.

Some people would say you are stupid not to consult your doctor, while others would say you are very courageous. In any case it would be useful to have some sort of diagnosis, so you have some idea what you are dealing with. Effectively only a doctor can make a positive diagnosis by feeling any lump you may have in a breast and by arranging a biopsy and various tests, such as a mammogram, which for the sake of this discussion I assume you don't want to have.

You could consider a thermoscan, which is a non-invasive test using a camera that measures the heat coming off your breasts. Such a test cannot positively diagnose breast cancer, any more than a mammogram can, but it can identify a clear abnormality in a breast, especially when compared to your other breast. If a thermoscan is clearly suggestive of breast cancer, you could assume that you have a positive diagnosis. If you then start a suitable programme, a repeat thermoscan in due course will tell you whether you have made any progress or not.

So What Should You Do?

I have always felt it is important to know why your breast cancer developed in the first instance, so may be you should go through my history chapter, and see what you can identify.

Failing that, it is important that you look at your lifestyle and make some changes, starting with diet. Cut out all dairy products (including beef as milk comes from the cow), sugar, white refined flour products, alcohol (and tobacco of course), caffeine, all carbonated drinks and 'junk food'. Try to get as close to becoming vegan as possible, or try to make your diet at least 75% from non-animal sources, and use grains sparingly if possible. Follow my dietary advice in chapter 5, where I make suggestions for all meals and snacks. To assist your achieving as much fruit and vegetables as possible, I strongly suggest you consider taking the special capsules of dehydrated fruits, vegetables and berries♥ on a regular basis. That sorts out your eating plan.

Next look at geopathic stress. Obtain a copy of Rolf Gordon's book 'Are You Sleeping In A Safe Place?', which explains it all very well. If you have a problem with geopathic stress, Rolf can help you sort it out, but you may wish to find your own dowser to do it. I appreciate this subject is unusual, but I have found it to be very important in many people and it is usually not at all expensive to remedy.

Apply Magnascent iodine to the breast that you suspect has cancer in it, at least twice daily to begin with, so as soon as you have washed in the morning and before you dress, and when you undress in the evening before going to bed. Fortunately iodine dries very quickly. Iodine is not only anti-oestrogenic (useful if your history suggests oestrogen dominance relative to progesterone, in which case consider homoeopathic progesterone 200C twice a day fifteen minutes after breakfast and your evening meal, as I described in an earlier chapter) but also anti-fungal (also useful if your cancer is a protective mechanism against a fungus). How many courses of antibiotics have you had over your lifetime?

Incidentally, you will probably notice that the iodine has been absorbed by the time you apply some more a few hours later, indicating your need of it, which should help to improve your thyroid gland's functioning (Dr. Max Gerson gave all cancer patients whole thyroid as he was sure they were deficient). In fact you should take your underarm temperature for ten minutes before getting out of bed in the morning, so you may need to set your alarm ten minutes earlier than usual. If your cancer is in your left breast, put the thermometer in your right armpit, and vice versa. Normal in the armpit is 97.4°F or 36.5°C. Anything somewhat below that is suggestive of a deficiency of thyroid and/or adrenal glands. As you improve overall, your basal temperature should rise towards normal. If it doesn't, you may need some specific thyroid support.

There is a distinct possibility that your immune system is less efficient than it should be. While various herbs, such as Echinacea, can improve it, Biobran is the best as far as I am aware, but it is a bit expensive, at least £3.00 a sachet, and you should take at least one sachet twice daily for the first two weeks, after which you can drop the dose to one sachet a day. It doesn't matter when you take Biobran during the day.

The chances are that you should take a range of anti-oxidants, such as vitamin C, ideally in powder form, at least 10g per day, but preferably up to 16g per day, spread throughout the day into four separate doses of 4g each, Alpha-lipoic acid 100mg twice daily, selenium at least 400mcg (ideally 200mcg twice daily 1/2 hour before food), vitamin E 200IU twice daily, and vitamin D at least 5000IU per day + 150mcg K2 (can be taken any time), possibly starting with 10,000IU for about two months if you do not live in a country where you are exposed regularly to the sun, to quench excess free radicles. Alternatively you could have your vitamin D levels measured, but only accept the reference ranges I mentioned in chapter 3. You could tailor your vitamin D intake according to your results. You could take other anti-oxidants, but this should be sufficient to start with. See how you get on.

It is likely that you are too relatively acidic, so measure your second morning urine pH. By this I mean discard the sample you pass when you get up at your normal time, drink a glass of water, set about washing and dressing, and measure the next sample you pass in about half-an-hour and before you eat anything. It should ideally be between 6.5 and 6.8. If it is persistently low, take AlkaLiza as I described in chapter 5 under the heading 'Alkalinising (deacidification) drops'.

Detoxifying your body generally is a good idea, and you will start that process as soon as you improve your diet. However, you could either have a series of colonic irrigations or you could do coffee enemas, one a day to begin with.

I have rarely seen a breast cancer patient who didn't have some sort of emotional problems, usually involving a few years before the first signs of cancer appeared. It is vital that you resolve these as far as possible, but, not knowing what they are, I can't tell you exactly what to do. Maybe you should read the book 'The Journey'♥ by Brandon Bays and consult a Journey Counsellor. You should certainly start doing relaxation, visualisation and affirmation exercises, as I explained at the beginning of chapter 4, at least once a day, possibly when you have time to yourself in the evening, instead of watching pointless TV. By all means watch programmes of interest, but see if there is a half hour slot where there is nothing interesting on to do these exercises. Don't forget you can do some of them any time during the day, including when you are washing the dishes.

Look at your life and reconsider whether there is something stressful or undesirable about it that you could change. For example, is your job getting you down, or do you have to travel to and from work for far too long each day?

Would it be sensible to make some changes?

What chance do you have of some exercise each day? It doesn't have to be extreme. A brisk walk of half-an-hour any time would be useful. Try to sort something out.

The chances are that your cancer involves 'infections' of some sort. For that reason I suggest chlorine dioxide, possibly working up to 4 drops of 25% sodium chlorite plus 20 drops of 10% citric acid, best taken 1 hour after your evening meal, or later, repeated 1 to 1½ hours later. If you take chlorine dioxide later in the day, don't take any anti-oxidants for four hours before the first dose of the evening.

Finally, as cancerous tumours tend to produce a mucus/protein coating around themselves to try to hide from your immune system, take digestive enzymes, such as Wobenzym N♥, possibly four tablets three times a day, ideally two hours after one meal and one hour before the next. However, if you take your last dose just before going to bed, you don't need to eat after that dose. If you can only manage one dose of digestive enzymes a day, take as many as you can last thing at night. Taking only a few is better than none at all.

This is a daily routine if you go out to work. If you don't, you could still follow this timetable, or modify it to suit your own lifestyle.

- Set your alarm ten minutes earlier than usual to measure your armpit temperature for ten minutes before getting out of bed.
- When you get up, go to the toilet and pass water. Discard this sample (if you get up during the night to go to the toilet, discard this sample also). Drink a glass of quality water, wash and apply iodine to your breast. Prepare breakfast. Dress in due course. By the time you have completed this process, you should be able to pass water again. Measure the pH of this sample and write the result in a logbook of sorts. On alternate days, take your first dose of selenium 200mcg and see if it alters the pH of that second morning sample. If it doesn't, take selenium every morning. If that second morning urine sample is too acidic, put ten drops of AlkaLiza into a litre bottle of quality water and drink it throughout the day. Take more or less drops of AlkaLiza according to your second morning urine sample's pH.
- Eat an appropriate breakfast.
- After breakfast, swallow 1 Alpha-lipoic acid 100mg capsule, 5000IU (possibly 10,000IU to begin with for one month) vitamin D capsules + 150mcg K2, Co-Enzyme Q 10 200mg, vitamin E 400 IU and the green special capsules of dehydrated vegetables♥ with at least 4g vitamin C in a full glass of quality water. Go to work.
- Two hours after finishing breakfast, empty a sachet of Biobran into a full glass of quality water and drink it, swallowing at least 4 tablets of Wobenzym N at

the same time.

- Late morning have at least 4g vitamin C in a glass of quality water.
- At least one hour after taking Wobenzym N tablets, eat an appropriate lunch.
- After lunch, take two capsules of the purple special capsules of berries and grapes with quality water.
- Two hours after finishing lunch, take at least 4 tablets of Wobenzym N.
- Mid-afternoon take another 4g vitamin C in a full glass of quality water. · Leave work at your usual time.
- Once you have done whatever you need to do at home, go for a brisk 1 hour walk.
- Once back at home, carry out a coffee enema.
- Half-an-hour before an appropriate evening meal take a second dose of selenium 200mcg. After the meal, take two of the red special capsules of dehydrated fruits♥, 200mg Co-Enzyme Q 10, 400IU vitamin E. For the first two weeks take a second sachet of Biobran.
- About 1 hour later have a dose of Chlorine dioxide, hopefully 4 hours after your last dose of vitamin C. Repeat the dose 1 to 1½ hours later. Follow the instructions I gave you in the Appendix. If you do take chlorine dioxide, increase the amount of vitamin C you take at the three doses earlier in the day, trying to reach 16g. If you do not take chlorine dioxide, take a last dose of vitamin C as late in the evening as is practical, and try to spread out the four doses as evenly as is reasonable throughout the day.
- Some time in a gap in the evening do your relaxation, visualisation and affirmation exercises. Don't forget you can do some or all of them at any time during the day, even if you are sitting at work between telephone calls relaxing, in a bus queue on the way to or from work, or say an affirmation while washing up.
- Last thing at night have a warm leisurely bath putting Epsom Salts in one night and hydrogen peroxide the next. When you get out of the bath liberally apply magnesium lotion to soft parts of your body and let it soak in.
- Apply iodine to your affected breast.
- Have at least 8 hours in bed at night if at all possible, and the more you have in bed before midnight the better.

Continue this programme, and really concentrate on doing it properly so it almost becomes second nature to you, for the first three months at least, then possibly have a repeat thermoscan to see what progress you are making. Remember it may have taken a number of years for you to have developed these initial features suggestive of breast cancer, so you can't expect to eliminate it in a few weeks. First you have to slow it down and then you have to clear it from your body.

Make a daily chart of things you do and also chart any symptoms and how you feel generally. If you used to feel tired, suffer from headaches, have poor skin or are overweight to any extent, as examples, give each of them a score, say 1 to 10, and note how they change as the days and weeks pass by.

Please do NOT examine your breast on a very regular basis as doing so can irritate it, but it is perfectly reasonable to examine yourself once a month, of course at the same time of the month if you are still having a regular cycle.

Make a daily plan something like this.

7.00am. Set your alarm. Put thermometer in the appropriate armpit and leave it there for ten minutes. Record your temperature on a daily chart.

7.10am. Get up, pass water and discard it. Have a glass of quality water. Take a first dose of 200mcg selenium on alternate days to see if it affects the pH of your second morning urine sample. Wash yourself, but do not dress yet. Prepare breakfast, but don't eat it yet.

7.40am. Pass a sample of urine (your second morning sample) and test its pH. Record the result on your daily chart. If it is too acidic, prepare your litre bottle (glass only please) of quality water into which you have put appropriate number of drops of AlkaLiza, to drink throughout the day. Take this bottle to work with you.

7.45am. Apply iodine to your breast. Let it dry.

7.50am. Dress.

8.00am. Have an appropriate breakfast.

8.30am. Take 100mg Alpha-lipoic acid, 200mg Co Enzyme Q 10, 400IU vitamin E, 5000 to 10,000IU vitamin D and two of the green special capsules of dehydrated vegetables♥, with at least 4g vitamin C in quality water. Go to work.

11.00am. Take at least 4 tablets of Wobenzym N with quality water plus the contents of one sachet of Biobran. You can take with water from your AlkaLiza bottle.

12.30pm. Take at least 4g vitamin C in quality water.

1.00pm. Have an appropriate lunch and then take two of the purple special capsules of dehydrated berries♥.

3.30pm. Take at least 4 tablets of Wobenzym N with quality water.

4.30pm. Take at least 4g vitamin C in a full glass of quality water.

5.30pm. Leave work at your usual time. Once at home do what you need to do.

6.00pm. Take your second dose of selenium.

6.05pm. Go for a ½ hour brisk walk.

6.45pm. Do a coffee enema.

7.15pm. Have an appropriate evening meal.

7.45pm. Take 100mg Alpha-lipoic acid, at least 2000IU vitamin D, 400IU vitamin E, 200mg Co-Enzyme Q 10 and two of the red capsules of dehydrated fruits♥ with 4g vitamin C in quality water. For the first two weeks take a second sachet of Biobran.

8.30pm. If you suspect your cancer might involve any specific organisms, take an appropriate dose of Chlorine dioxide.

9.30pm. Take a second dose of the same number of drops of Chlorine dioxide.

Sometime during the evening do a full set of relaxation, visualisation and affirmation exercises.

10.00pm. Have a leisurely bath, having put Epsom Salts in one night and Hydrogen peroxide in the next night. After you get out and dry yourself, apply iodine to the whole of your affected breast and rub in magnesium lotion into other areas of soft skin. Leave both to soak in.

10.25pm. Complete your daily chart of anything worth recording, such as a change in any incidental symptoms, and, of course, how you feel generally. This may be the most important feature to make a note of.

10.30pm. Get into bed and do more visualisation and affirmation exercises. It doesn't matter if you don't complete them before you fall asleep. Doing them as you fall asleep may prolong them while you sleep.

Follow a pattern like this strictly every day of the week, doing essential chores, housework and major shopping at the weekend, assuming you don't go to work on Saturdays and Sundays. Such a plan doesn't mean you can't do incidental shopping during the week, but you need to get thoroughly organised. You may need to avoid going out to meet friends for a while, although missing part of a day's approach shouldn't matter too much, so long as you don't abuse yourself at the time. You can enjoy friends' company just as much with a glass of spring water as a glass of wine.

Scenario 2

The second scenario is likely to be if your situation is more serious. You may have already had a lumpectomy or a mastectomy after all the appropriate tests of mammogram, X-rays and scans, and are going through a course of chemotherapy and/or radiotherapy.

What I have described in the first scenario is still appropriate to you, and you should adopt it, but you may have to modify the timing of some of your nutrient intakes to fit them in with being in hospital having an infusion of chemotherapy or a course of radiotherapy. In addition, you will need to do more.

If you have an infusion of chemotherapy, as soon as you get home, carry out a coffee enema. This is virtually guaranteed to help you avoid or minimise possible adverse effects. If you do that first coffee enema of the day around lunchtime (because the chemo was given to you in the morning), do another one a few hours later, and possibly a third.

In my experience it would be a good idea to have a nutrient infusion (vitamins and minerals intravenously) shortly before and shortly after a chemotherapy session, if you can find someone to do it for you, but I am assuming that will not happen.

Because chemotherapy fires free radicals at you, you need to increase your intake of anti-oxidants significantly, especially vitamin C, so try to get up to 50g per day if you can, or consider taking liposomal vitamin C. You could double the selenium to 800mcg, but don't take more than 800 IU vitamin E. You could add Revenol at one tablet twice daily and take others such as curcumin, resveratrol, etc, but that should be enough to start with. It may be sensible not to take any chlorine dioxide at this stage, so that you can take more anti-oxidants and spread them out throughout the day. Take some if you get out of bed to go to the toilet during the night. Have supplies ready in case you wake up.

Your doctors may not be happy about your taking anti-oxidants while having chemotherapy, but I can assure you there is plenty of scientific evidence of their value, as I explained earlier in this book. If necessary, keep that information to yourself. You will need to take these bigger doses for a minimum of two weeks after the chemotherapy course has been completed.

Try to obtain a homoeopathic dose of the chemotherapy you are to have and take a dose of 30C potency twice or three times daily while having a course and continue for at least two weeks after the course has been completed.

Visualise the chemotherapy destroying the cancer cells and put up a protective barrier around your healthy cells while the drug is being given to you, and continue the visualisation for at least the next two to three days.

If you are having a course of radiotherapy, the above still applies to you, but it would be wise to add one or two other things. As chemotherapy is given intravenously, it spreads to all parts of your body, even those parts that don't want it. Radiotherapy, on the other hand, is more targeted at a particular part of your body. While it is hopefully aimed at your tumour, it inevitably passes through the skin and affects tissues around the target. Hopefully the anti-oxidants you take will help to minimise the adverse effects on your healthy cells, while the Wobenzym N tablets will exert a strong anti-inflammatory effect. For that reason, double the dose of Wobenzym N if you can.

As soon as you return home from a dose of radiotherapy, plaster Aloe Vera gel all over the area of your body that was exposed to the radiotherapy and do that literally every hour until you go to bed. If you find the effect of leaving Aloe Vera gel on your body a bit sticky, it is perfectly reasonable to wipe off or wash off the last application you apply before going to bed, but leave it on as long as possible to soak into your skin. Schizandra is an herb that seems to have a specifically beneficial effect when having radiotherapy. Take a dose morning and evening at the same time as all the others, if you can manage so many.

Scenario 3

Some time ago you were given the all clear but your breast cancer has come back again.

All I have said above still applies to you, especially if you are going to have a further course of chemotherapy, possibly with a stronger drug. Don't forget to have the questions answered to your satisfaction that I described in that particular chapter of this book.

Perhaps what is even more important now it has come back is to go back to square one and read chapter 3 of my book, when we went through your medical history, and try to understand why you developed breast cancer in the first place. You will have difficulty clearing any cancer from your body if you don't know why it developed in the first place.

Once you have established to your satisfaction what the original reason or reasons were, you will need to add the appropriate approach to your timetable or modify it in some way. In particular, think more about 'oxygen therapies', possibly considering the Oxygen Concentrator equipment, or trying to find someone to give you hydrogen peroxide infusions, or try a simpler approach of taking something like 'Oxygen Elements Max', or something similar.

Chapter 11

Planning Your Day with Prostate Cancer

Now that you have read all the way through this book, you must surely realise that there is so much you can do to help yourself. Having said that, it is possible that, although I wrote a section on 'Where to Start' towards the end of chapter 5, you may still be unsure how to plan your day. So I will now suggest what you consider doing.

Clearly what you do and how much you do depends to a certain extent on your current situation, so I will start by describing various scenarios and provide a day's plan for each.

Scenario 1

You think you might have prostate cancer, but you don't want to go to your own doctor because you know what that would entail. Alternatively, you are pretty sure you have prostate cancer, but don't want any treatment that mainstream medicine recommends. You want to know what to do.

Some people would say you are stupid not to consult your doctor, while others would say you are very courageous. In any case it would be useful to have some sort of diagnosis, so you have some idea what you are dealing with. Effectively only a doctor can make a positive diagnosis by feeling an enlarged prostate gland by doing a rectal examination, and by arranging a biopsy and various tests, which for the sake of this discussion I assume you don't want to have.

You could consider having a blood test for PSA, Prostate Specific Antigen. Such a test cannot positively diagnose prostate cancer, but if it is above, say, 10 units, that is highly suspicious of cancer, though not diagnostic. If it is that raised, you could assume that you have a positive diagnosis. If you then start a suitable programme, a repeat blood test in due course will tell you whether you have made any progress or not. If any symptoms of urination improve, that would also be an indication that you are benefiting from whatever programme you have chosen to follow.

Alternatively, you can have the telomerase test, which in some respects is much accurate than the PSA in my opinion, but you will have to pay for it.

So What Should You Do?

I have always felt it is important to know why your prostate cancer developed in the first instance, so may be you should go through my history chapter, chapter 4, and see what you can identify.

Failing that, it is important that you look at your lifestyle and make some changes, starting with diet. Cut out all dairy products (including beef as milk comes from the cow), sugar, white refined flour products, alcohol (and tobacco of course), caffeine, all carbonated drinks and 'junk food'. Try to get as close to becoming vegan as possible, or try to make your diet at least 75% from non-animal sources, and use grains sparingly if possible. Take as much asparagus in your diet as you can, even tinned variety, having first tried to check that the contents of the tins do not contain any toxins. Be aware that asparagus will make your urine smell strong. Follow my dietary advice in chapter 5, where I make suggestions for all meals and snacks. To assist your achieving as much fruit and vegetables as possible, I strongly suggest you consider taking capsules of dehydrated fruits, vegetables, berries and grapes on a regular basis. That sorts out your eating plan.

Next look at geopathic stress. Obtain a copy of Rolf Gordon's book 'Are You Sleeping In A Safe Place?'♥ which explains it all very well. If you have a problem with geopathic stress, Rolf can help you sort it out, but you may wish to find your own dowser to do it. I appreciate this subject is unusual, but I have found it to be very important in many people and it is usually not at all expensive to remedy.

Work up to taking Magnascent iodine three drops twice daily in water. Iodine is anti-oestrogenic (remember I suggested in my explanation of prostate cancer that I believe as we get older, we men convert too much of our reducing levels of testosterone into di-hydrotestosterone (DHT), which is the bad chemical as far as our prostate gland is concerned). I also recommend you apply about 20mg of natural progesterone cream to varying soft areas of your skin each day, but you must pass it with 3 weeks on and 1 week off. The simplest way to remember is to stop on the first of each month, and restart on about the seventh. Iodine is also anti-fungal (also useful if your cancer is a protective mechanism against a fungus) and generally anti-infective. How many courses of antibiotics have you had over your lifetime?

Incidentally, taking iodine by mouth should help to improve your thyroid gland's functioning (Dr. Max Gerson gave all cancer patients whole thyroid as he was sure they were deficient). In fact you should take your underarm temperature for ten minutes before getting out of bed in the morning, so you may need to set your alarm ten minutes earlier than usual. Normal in the armpit is 97.4°F or 36.5°C. Anything somewhat below that is suggestive of a deficiency of thyroid and/or adrenal glands. As you improve overall, your basal temperature should rise towards normal. If it doesn't, you may need some specific thyroid support.

There is a distinct possibility that your immune system is less efficient than it should be. While various herbs, such as Echinacea, can improve it, Biobran is the best as far as I am aware, but it is a bit expensive, at least £3.00 a sachet, and you should take at least one sachet twice daily for the first two weeks, after which you can drop the dose to one sachet a day. It doesn't matter when you take Biobran during the day.

The chances are that you should take a range of anti-oxidants, such as vitamin C, ideally in powder form, at least 10g per day, but preferably up to 16g per day, spread throughout the day into four separate doses of 4g each, Alpha-lipoic acid 100mg twice daily, 15mg Lycopene twice daily (particularly helpful for the prostate), selenium at least 400mcg (ideally 200mcg twice daily 1/2 hour before food), vitamin E 400IU twice daily, and vitamin D + 150mcg K2 at least 5000IU per day (can be taken any time), possibly starting with 10,000IU for about two months if you do not live in a country where you are exposed regularly to the sun, to quench excess free radicles. Alternatively you could have your vitamin D levels measured, but only accept the reference ranges I mentioned in chapter 3. You could tailor your vitamin D intake according to your results. You could take other anti-oxidants, but this should be sufficient to start with. See how you get on.

It is likely that you are too relatively acidic, so measure your second morning urine pH. By this I mean discard the sample you pass when you get up at your normal time, drink a glass of water, set about washing and dressing, and measure the next sample you pass in about half-an-hour and before you eat anything. It should ideally be between 6.5 and 6.8. If it is persistently low, take AlkaLiza as I described in chapter 5 under the heading 'Alkalinising (deacidification) drops'. Detoxifying your body generally is a good idea, and you will start that process as soon as you improve your diet. However, you could either have a series of colonic irrigations or you could do coffee enemas, one a day to begin with.

I have rarely seen a prostate cancer patient who didn't have some sort of emotional problems, usually involving a few years before the first signs of cancer appeared. It is vital that you resolve these as far as possible, but, not knowing what they are, I can't tell you exactly what to do. Maybe you should read the book 'The Journey'♥ by Brandon Bays and consult a Journey Counsellor. You should certainly start doing relaxation, visualisation and affirmation exercises, as I explained at the beginning of chapter 5 of this book, at least once a day, possibly when you have time to yourself in the evening, instead of watching pointless TV. By all means watch programmes of interest, but see if there is a half hour slot where there is nothing interesting on to do these exercises. Don't forget you can do some of them any time during the day, including when you are washing the dishes.

Look at your life and reconsider whether there is something stressful or undesirable about it that you could change. For example, is your job getting you down, or do you have to travel to and from work for far too long each day? Would it be sensible to make some changes?

What chance do you have of some exercise each day? It doesn't have to be extreme. A brisk walk of half-an-hour any time would be useful. Try to sort something out.

The chances are that your cancer involves 'infections' of some sort. For that reason I suggest chlorine dioxide (as well as iodine), possibly working up to 4 drops of 25% sodium chlorite plus 20 drops of 10% citric acid, best taken 1 hour after your evening meal, or later, repeated 1 to 1½ hours later. If you take chlorine dioxide later in the day, don't take any anti-oxidants for four hours before the first dose of the evening.

Finally, as cancerous tumours tend to produce a mucus/protein coating around themselves to try to hide from your immune system, take digestive enzymes, such as Wobenzym N, possibly four tablets three times a day, ideally two hours after one meal and one hour before the next. However, if you take your last dose just before going to bed, you don't need to eat after that dose. If you can only manage one dose of digestive enzymes a day, take as many as you can last thing at night. Taking only a few is better than none at all.

Daily routine if you go out to work. If you don't, you could still follow this timetable, or modify it to suit your own lifestyle.

- Set your alarm ten minutes earlier than usual to measure your armpit temperature for ten minutes before getting out of bed.
- When you get up, go to the toilet and pass water. Discard this sample (if you get up during the night to go to the toilet, discard this sample also). Drink a glass of quality water, wash and apply 10mg natural progesterone cream to any soft area of skin.
- Prepare breakfast. Dress in due course. By the time you have completed this process, you should be able to pass water again. Measure the pH of this sample and write the result in a logbook of sorts. On alternate days, take your first dose of selenium 200mcg and see if it alters the pH of that second morning sample. If it doesn't, take selenium every morning. If that second morning urine sample is too acidic, put ten drops of AlkaLiza into a litre bottle (glass only please) of quality water and drink it throughout the day. Take more or less drops of AlkaLiza according to your second morning urine sample's pH.
  · If there is a further 10 to 15 minutes available before starting breakfast, put ½ level teaspoonful of Harmonik Male hormone tincture into a cup of hot water, leave to stand for a few minutes to allow the alcohol to evaporate, cool appropriately and drink (or take an equivalent dose of saw palmetto).

- Eat an appropriate breakfast.
- After breakfast, swallow 1 Alpha-lipoic acid 100mg capsule, 15mg Lycopene, 5000IU vitamin D capsules + 150mcg K2, vitamin E 400 IU and two green top capsules of dehydrated vegetables with at least 4g vitamin C in a full glass of quality water. Put in up to three drops of Magnascent Iodine.
- Go to work.
- Two hours after finishing breakfast, empty a sachet of Biobran into a full glass of quality water and drink it, swallowing at least 4 tablets of Wobenzym N at the same time.
- Late morning have at least 4g vitamin C in a glass of quality water.
- At least one hour after taking Wobenzym N tablets, eat an appropriate lunch.
- After lunch, take two capsules of the special berry blend capsules♥ with quality water.
- Two hours after finishing lunch, take at least 4 tablets of Wobenzym N.
- Mid-afternoon take another 4g vitamin C in a full glass of quality water plus up to three drops of Magnascent Iodine.
- Leave work at your usual time.
- Once you have done whatever you need to do at home, go for a brisk ½ hour walk.
- Once back at home, carry out a coffee enema.
- Half-an-hour before an appropriate evening meal, take a second dose of selenium 200mcg with a second dose of Harmonik Male Hormone tincture (or alternative saw palmetto preparation).
- After the meal, take two capsules of the red top fruit blend, 15mg Lycopene and 400IU vitamin E. For the first two weeks take a second sachet of Biobran.
- About 1 hour later have a dose of Chlorine dioxide, hopefully 4 hours after your last dose of vitamin C. Repeat the dose 1 to 1½ hours later. Follow the instructions I give in the Appendix. If you do take chlorine dioxide, increase the amount of vitamin C you take at the three doses earlier in the day, trying to reach 16g. If you do not take chlorine dioxide (which may be unnecessary especially if you take iodine drops), take a last dose of vitamin C as late in the evening as is practical, and try to spread out the four doses as evenly as is reasonable throughout the day.
- Some time in a gap in the evening do your relaxation, visualisation and affirmation exercises. Don't forget you can do some or all of them at any time during the day, even if you are sitting at work between telephone calls relaxing, in a bus queue on the way to or from work, or say an affirmation while washing up.
- Last thing at night have a warm leisurely bath putting Epsom Salts in one night and hydrogen peroxide the next. When you get out of the bath liberally apply magnesium lotion to soft parts of your body and let it soak in.
- Apply 10mg natural progesterone cream to other soft skin areas of your body.
- Have at least 8 hours in bed at night if at all possible, and the more you have in bed before midnight the better.

Continue this programme, and really concentrate on doing it properly so it almost becomes second nature to you, for the first three months at least, then possibly have a repeat blood test to see what progress you are making. If your PSA test has gone up, but you feel a lot better and your urinary symptoms have improved, don't be alarmed, as this actually suggests that your approach is killing cancer cells which are releasing more of the protein that is measured as PSA. The same applies if you have the telomerase test done. Remember it may have taken a number of years for you to have developed the initial features suggestive of prostate cancer, so you can't expect to eliminate it in a few weeks. First you have to slow it down and then you have to clear it from your body. It is if your PSA test keeps increasing that you need to do more to bring it under control.

Make a daily chart of things you do and also chart any symptoms and how you feel generally. If you used to feel tired, suffer from headaches, have poor skin or are overweight to any extent, as examples, give each of them a score, say 1 to 10, and note how they change as the days and weeks pass by.

Make a daily plan something like this.

7.00am. Set your alarm. Put thermometer in an armpit and leave it there for ten minutes. Record your temperature on a daily chart.

7.10am. Get up, pass water and discard it. Have a glass of quality water. Take a first dose of 200mcg selenium on alternate days to see if it affects the pH of your second morning urine sample. If it doesn't, take selenium every morning. Wash yourself, but do not dress yet. Prepare breakfast, but don't eat it yet.

7.15am. Apply 10mg natural progesterone cream to any soft skin area. Ring the changes as much as possible so as not to overuse one area.

7.40am. Pass a sample of urine (your second morning sample) and test its pH. Record the result on your daily chart. If it is too acidic, prepare your litre glass bottle of quality water into which you have put appropriate number of drops of AlkaLiza, to drink throughout the day. Take this bottle to work with you.

7.50am. Dress.

8.00am. Have an appropriate breakfast.

8.30am. Take 100mg Alpha-lipoic acid, 15mg Lycopene, 400IU vitamin E, 5000IU vitamin D + 150mcg K2 and two capsules of the green top dehydrated vegetable blend, with at least 4g vitamin C in quality water, plus up to three drops of Magnascent Iodine. Go to work.

11.00am. Take at least 4 tablets of Wobenzym N with quality water plus the contents of one sachet of Biobran. You can take with water from your AlkaLiza bottle.

12.30pm. Take at least 4g vitamin C in quality water.

1.00pm. Have an appropriate lunch and then take two capsules of the dehydrated purple grape and berry blend.

3.30pm. Take at least 4 tablets of Wobenzym N with quality water.

4.30pm. Take at least 4g vitamin C in a full glass of quality water, plus up to three drops of Magnascent Iodine.

5.30pm. Leave work or at your usual time. Once at home do what you need to do.

6.00pm. Take your second dose of selenium with your second dose of Harmonik Male Hormone tincture or saw palmetto equivalent.

6.05pm. Go for a ½ hour brisk walk.

6.45pm. Do a coffee enema.

7.15pm. Have an appropriate evening meal.

7.45pm. Take 100mg Alpha-lipoic acid, 400IU vitamin E, 15mg Lycopene and two capsules of the dehydrated red top fruit blend with 4g vitamin C in quality water. For the first two weeks take a second sachet of Biobran.

8.30pm. If you suspect your cancer might involve any specific organisms, take an appropriate dose of Chlorine dioxide.

9.30pm. Take a second dose of the same number of drops of Chlorine dioxide.

Sometime during the evening do a full set of relaxation, visualisation and affirmation exercises.

10.00pm. Have a leisurely bath, having put Epsom Salts in one night and Hydrogen peroxide in the next night. After you get out and dry yourself, apply 10mg natural progesterone cream to soft skin areas and rub in magnesium lotion into other areas of soft skin. Leave both to soak in.

10.25pm. Complete your daily chart of anything worth recording, such as a change in any incidental symptoms, and, of course, how you feel generally. This may be the most important feature to make a note of.

10.30pm. Get into bed and do more visualisation and affirmation exercises. It doesn't matter if you don't complete them before you fall asleep. Doing them as you fall asleep may prolong them while you sleep.

Follow a pattern like this strictly every day of the week, doing essential chores, housework and major shopping at the weekend, assuming you don't go to work on Saturdays and Sundays. Such a plan doesn't mean you can't do incidental shopping during the week, but you need to get thoroughly organised. You may need to avoid going out to meet friends for a while, although missing part of a day's approach shouldn't matter too much, so long as you don't abuse yourself at the time. You can enjoy friends' company just as much with a glass of Spring water as a glass of wine.

Scenario 2

The second scenario is likely to be if your situation is more serious. You may have already had a prostatectomy after all the appropriate tests, such as X-rays and scans, and are going through a course of chemotherapy and/or radiotherapy.

What I have described in the first scenario is still appropriate to you, and you should adopt it, but you may have to modify the timing of some of your nutrient intakes to fit them in with being in hospital having an infusion of chemotherapy or a course of radiotherapy. In addition, you will need to do more.

If you have an infusion of chemotherapy, as soon as you get home, carry out a coffee enema. This is virtually guaranteed to help you avoid or minimise possible adverse effects. If you do that first coffee enema of the day around lunchtime (because the chemo was given to you in the morning), do another one a few hours later, and possibly a third.

In my experience it would be a good idea to have a nutrient infusion (vitamins and minerals intravenously) shortly before and shortly after a chemotherapy session, if you can find someone to do it for you, but I am assuming that will not happen.

Because chemotherapy fires free radicals at you, you need to increase your intake of anti-oxidants significantly, especially vitamin C, so try to get up to 50g per day if you can. You could double the selenium to 800mcg, but don't take more than 800 IU vitamin E. You could add Revenol at one tablet twice daily and take others such as curcumin, resveratrol, etc, but that should be enough to start with. It may be sensible not to take any chlorine dioxide at this stage, so that you can take more anti-oxidants and spread them out throughout the day. Take some if you get out of bed to go to the toilet during the night. Have supplies ready in case you wake up.

Your doctors may not be happy about your taking anti-oxidants while having chemotherapy, but I can assure you there is plenty of scientific evidence of their value, as I explained earlier in this book. You will need to take these bigger doses for a minimum of two weeks after the chemotherapy course has been completed.

Try to obtain a homoeopathic dose of the chemotherapy you are to have and take a dose of 30C potency twice or three times daily while having a course and continue for at least two weeks after the course has been completed.

Visualise the chemotherapy destroying the cancer cells and put up a protective barrier around your healthy cells while the drug is being given to you, and continue the visualisation for at least the next two to three days. If you are having a course of radiotherapy, the above still applies to you, but it would be wise to add one or two other things. As chemotherapy is given intravenously, it spreads to all parts of your body, even those parts that don't want it. Radiotherapy, on the other hand, is more targeted at a particular part of your body. While it is hopefully aimed at your tumour, it inevitably passes through the skin and affects tissues around the target. Hopefully the anti-oxidants you take will help to minimise the adverse effects on your healthy cells, while the Wobenzym N tablets will exert a strong anti-inflammatory effect. For that reason, double the dose of Wobenzym N if you can. Chemotherapy wipes out the friendly organisms in your bowel, so you will need to take probiotics at least three times a day during and for at least one week after the course has ended.

As soon as you return home from a dose of radiotherapy, plaster Aloe Vera gel all over the area of your body that was exposed to the radiotherapy and do that literally every hour until you go to bed. If you find the effect of leaving Aloe Vera gel on your body a bit sticky, it is perfectly reasonable to wipe off or wash off the last application you apply before going to bed, but leave it on as long as possible to soak into your skin. Continue to apply it for the next few days after the course has finished.

Schizandra is an herb that seems to have a specifically beneficial effect when having radiotherapy. Take a dose morning and evening at the same time as all the others, if you can manage so many.

Scenario 3

Some time ago you were given the all clear but your prostate cancer has come back again.

All I have said above still applies to you, especially if you are going to have a further course of chemotherapy, possibly with a stronger drug. Don't forget to have the questions answered to your satisfaction that I described in chapter 9 of this book.

Perhaps what is even more important now it has come back is to go back to square one and read chapter 4 of my book, when we went through your medical history, and try to understand why you developed prostate cancer in the first place. You will have difficulty clearing any cancer from your body if you don't know why it developed in the first place.

Once you have established to your satisfaction what the original reason or reasons were, you will need to add the appropriate approach to your timetable or modify it in some way. In particular, think more about 'oxygen therapies', possibly considering the Oxygen Concentrator equipment, or trying to find someone to give you hydrogen peroxide infusions, or try a simpler approach of taking something like 'Oxygen Elements Max', or something similar.

Chapter 12

Patient Examples

I'm now going to describe how I helped two patients. Because their conditions are so common, I will first describe a patient with breast cancer and then a man with prostate cancer, because these two conditions are the most common female and male cancers.

Patient Example No 1
The patient is a 43-year old married lady with two children. She had cancer in her left breast, which had been diagnosed by a mammogram and a biopsy. When she found the lump a couple of weeks ago in the shower, she was naturally shocked and alarmed. She made an urgent appointment with her General Practitioner, who examined her breast and felt the lump was sufficiently suspicious for her to be referred for an urgent appointment at the local Breast Clinic. "They are very good there and get on with things". She had an appointment within three days.

At the Clinic there were many other women of varying ages, mostly with their husbands, partners or a friend or relative. Her immediate feeling was that the place was full of anxious women, presumably all in the same boat, i.e. all had suspected breast cancer. The whole atmosphere she found daunting, gloomy and very frightening. Almost as soon as she arrived she wanted to get out of there, despite the care and understanding of the staff. She was so grateful her husband was with her, otherwise she would have left there and then. He helped to calm her down, even though she knew he couldn't reassure her that all would be all right.

The surgeon she saw was very kind, but in a way almost too efficient. She realised there was quite a queue of other women to be seen, but she felt she was on a conveyor belt. He had hardly finished examining her before he picked up a syringe to take a biopsy, and, effectively assuming she would let him get on with it, he stuck a needle into the lump. It was only afterwards that she felt she hadn't really been consulted about the biopsy, but it was too late to say anything. She was then sent for a mammogram. She found both procedures really rather painful, especially having the mammogram done just after a needle had been stuck into her breast. But then it was all over. A few days later she had a second consultation with the surgeon, who confirmed the diagnosis of cancer. He outlined the treatment plan of a lumpectomy with some armpit glands being taken out to see whether the cancer had spread, after which they would decide whether to give her a course of chemotherapy or radiotherapy or both, and probably tamoxifen.

When she arrived home, she was in a state of shock. The hospital team had all been very reassuring, but an aunt of hers, and a close friend, had both recently died of breast cancer, and she had seen how it had not worked for them and how ill they had felt some of the time, especially when they were having chemotherapy. It now occurred to her that she wasn't sure that she wanted to follow their approach, and surely there must be another way.

To be fair, it had never occurred to her, when her aunt a close friend were dying, what she would do if she ever developed breast cancer. She assumed that their doctors had done everything they could to cure them. She assumed they had had the very best, and the very latest, treatment available. Yet it hadn't stopped them from dying. In addition, the end was pretty horrendous, both being admitted to a hospice towards the end.

That weekend her daughter came home, and she told her all about it. She was amazingly supportive, simply listening to her mother to begin with. Eventually her daughter suggested that she start searching the web for some other approach, so she left early on the Sunday. She wanted to get at her computer at her flat as soon as possible.

That Sunday evening her daughter rang up full of excitement. She said she couldn't believe how much information she had uncovered. She said she was going cross-eyed trying to read as much as she could, as there was so much about all forms of cancer. Yes, there were plenty of sites describing the standard approach of mainstream medicine, what breast cancer was all about, where it might occur, what might happen over a period of time, all about the various treatments and their side effects, loads of statistics she didn't fully understand, and where it might spread to. All of this she found dry, rather boring and very frightening, but she felt she ought to read it to understand the condition better.

It was only when she had dug a bit deeper that she started to find information that was more uplifting. It started to give her hope. All the other stuff gave her no hope at all. She began to realise that there was a lot her mother could do, and that she didn't necessarily have to follow the treatment plan that had been outlined for her at the hospital. That was when she came across my name in someone's website. After a bit of a search, she found my number and rang me at 9pm on that Sunday evening, and we had a 20-minute chat. I saw her mother soon after that, accompanied by her husband and her daughter, of course. She gave me a potted history of what I have just described, after which I obtained the following history from her.

I asked her about the last few years of her life, and what they had been like. That was when her husband immediately spoke up about the stress she had been under, helping her aunt (her mother had died many years ago in a car crash and the aunt with breast cancer had been her mother's younger sister and very much like a mother to her). It had devastated her to see the effect the cancer had had on her aunt, and she had helped out as much as she could. Fortunately she hadn't lived too far away, so at least travelling to her hadn't been too much of a problem.

Her aunt had died about three months ago, and her death had really saddened her. She had wept bitterly at the funeral, almost reliving her mother's funeral. Then her best friend had died of breast cancer, although it had taken a couple of years after the secondary spread was found in her lungs and liver. Her husband was sure that the death of two loved ones so close together must have had a terrible effect upon her, to which I agreed.

I explained that stress has a devastating effect upon the hypothalamic/pituitary/adrenal axis, i.e. the body's normal response to every day stresses, effectively exhausting it. I described the work of Dr. Fryda of Germany, and felt that supporting her adrenal glands and probably her thyroid gland would be of value to try to mitigate some of the harmful effects of the stress. I therefore recommended Biocare's AD206, at one capsule three times daily with food, although I am sure there are similar preparations in other countries. I also suggested she take drops of AlkaLiza to alkalinise her body, according to what she found when she tested her second morning urine pH.

I also asked her to spend the next few days, before she started either of those preparations, taking her armpit temperature for ten minutes every morning before she first got out of bed. As she was still having periods, she was to note the time of the month on the chart. I explained that I was looking for evidence of a low morning temperature, which is clinical evidence of poor functioning of the adrenal and/or thyroid glands, irrespective of the result of any blood tests. I also explained how many patients had felt better for simply having these glands supported, and that, by doing so, it would help her whole metabolism start to heal. Once healed, she would be able to stop such supplements.

Incidentally, she told me at that stage that her periods were becoming heavier, and that she was suffering more and more from pre-menstrual symptoms, especially breast tenderness. I told her that was an important observation, and that we would come back to it shortly.

As a medically qualified doctor, I was able to prescribe whole thyroid extract, usually Armour thyroid, and I always started with a low dose as a therapeutic trial. There is a preparation called Nutri Thyroid♥ that is effectively whole thyroid extract with the hormones taken out, so doesn't need a prescription. Whole thyroid gland extract is a range of amino acids, other chemicals and minerals (especially iodine), so taking such a preparation will help to feed the gland itself and help it to function better.

If you don't have a doctor like me to help you, you won't be able to obtain thyroid hormones, so, another interesting approach is to buy some old-fashioned iodine and put a drop on the inner aspect of one of your wrists. Touch both wrists together, so that there is a yellow dot on each one, allow to dry, and see how long it takes for both spots to clear. If they are still there in 24 hours, you don't need iodine. If they both disappear within a few hours, you clearly do need iodine, so you should continue putting a drop on your wrists until they don't disappear quickly. The quicker the iodine disappears, the more iodine you need. This is an interesting test although it is not perfect. It is merely a guide (Please refer back to the description of iodine and its value earlier on).

Of all the essential minerals, iodine needs the most perfect pH environment to be absorbed and utilised properly. As she had been under such severe stress, and most likely had still not recovered from it, let alone the stress she was now going through, her body would almost inevitably have become acidic. I also explained that an acidic environment promoted cancer, or more to the point, cancer cells thrive in an acid environment. Also, comparatively harmless organisms, which I might identify elsewhere in her history, become pathological (harmful) in an acid state. Having enough available iodine helps your thyroid to use it properly.

Because she had brought up the subject about her periods, I felt it was reasonable to go back to that subject and see where it led us. She had brought along with her her latest blood tests, all of which looked ok to me. Even her haemoglobin and her thyroid function tests were comfortably within the laboratory's reference ranges, yet she was suffering a significant degree of fatigue. Yes, a good night's sleep could be very helpful, but she had always had so much energy, as she had demonstrated when helping her aunt. When I pushed her, she acknowledged that she had started to run out of steam at least a year ago.

I took a blood test for serum ferritin (iron stores), expecting it to be very low. Most laboratories give far too wide a reference range of something like 10 to 350 units, saying that there is no shortage of iron so long as you are above the 10 mark. I told her I have never accepted that, so showed her a copy of the paper published in the British Medical Journal (mentioned earlier) that agreed with what I have been saying for a very long time that around 50 units is the cut off point we should be aiming for.

Unfortunately all too many doctors in my experience take laboratory reference ranges as normal ranges. They are not normal, but are a useful guide. If the screening test of haemoglobin is ok, they tend to say there is no shortage of iron in the body. However, they have forgotten, or possibly never knew in the first place, that iron is not only needed to make haemoglobin, but also for myoglobin (muscle globin), the immune system, hair follicle growth and a number of other metabolic functions. For reasons that are not clear to me, sometimes all the iron goes to make haemoglobin, starving the other functions in the process. Many is the woman who has benefited from iron supplements (best taken last thing at night away from other supplements if at all possible with some vitamin C), when her haemoglobin was perfectly respectable, yet she was feeling tired for no other reason that could be identified. Remember, however, we don't want too much iron, as cancer cells feed upon iron. There is always a balance to consider.

I then asked her about her periods and the few days before their onset. I found it very interesting to ask what I considered to be a straightforward question, but I had to make sure the patient has understood me. Otherwise I would not receive the answer I wanted. She told me her periods had gradually become heavier over the past few years, but she had assumed that that was fairly normal, as she must be approaching the menopause. However, her husband had suggested that she see a Gynaecologist, who had found a small fibroid.

When I asked her about any pre-menstrual symptoms, she looked at her husband and asked if she was moody or not at that time, and he said she was not. I then said that I hadn't asked if she suffered from pre-menstrual tension, but any pre-menstrual symptoms. When I asked about abdominal bloating, sugar craving and breast tenderness, she said yes to all of them, saying that they had also increased over the years. When I pushed her, she agreed that these symptoms and the onset of her fatigue might have coincided.

That was when I explained to her that all of this meant that she was suffering from a dominance of oestrogen in relation to progesterone. I then described to her a 'normal' menstrual cycle and how the various hormones change during the month, and why, if a woman suffers from breast tenderness and other pre-menstrual symptoms, polycystic ovaries or fibroids, it indicates a hyper-oestrogen state. Since her breasts had been 'stimulated' for a few days every month, I felt this predisposed her to breast cancer.

If too much oestrogen were part of the reason why she now had breast cancer, I explained that part of her treatment would be to counteract that, which was why her doctor had recommended she start tamoxifen, being an anti-oestrogen drug. However, her daughter had discovered that one of the longterm effects of tamoxifen was an increased risk of uterine cancer. As she told me she didn't want to take it, I suggested the natural alternative to tamoxifen was Dim Vitex, an extract of broccoli and other cruciferous vegetables. I suggested that, as she was still having periods and what I considered were unacceptable pre-menstrual and menstrual symptoms, that she use those symptoms to see if the treatment she chose to follow made any difference to them.

Sometimes it is a good idea to block the reformation of oestrogen in the bowel, by taking Calcium-D-glucarate. Also, as she was a little overweight, I hoped the diet that I was about to recommend to her would help her to lose some weight. The reason for this is that body fat can manufacture oestrogen. I also felt that taking homoeopathic progesterone 200C three times daily from day 12 of her cycle would somehow balance her oestrogen/progesterone levels. I don't know exactly what it does, and I doubt it alters the blood levels of progesterone. I assume it 'sensitises' cellular receptors to progesterone, making what levels there are in the body more effective. Many women have found it to be extremely effective in minimising or obliterating pre-menstrual symptoms, and it is not at all expensive. I like liquid drops of homoeopathic preparations.

Sometimes I recommend that the patient rub in bio-identical or 'natural' progesterone cream once or twice a day, using soft skin anywhere on the body and changing the site as much as possible. 10 to 20mg per day should suffice, starting from about day 12 of the cycle. If a woman were post-menopausal, I would suggest daily from about 25 days per month. The easiest way to remember is not to rub any on from day 1 of each calendar month for the first 5 to 7 days, restarting on day 5 or 7. If you start using the cream halfway through the month, carry on to the end of the next month, i.e. don't have a break at the beginning of the month. However, I nearly always start with the homoeopathic drops, especially as they are cheaper.

If pre-menstrual symptoms become a little more pronounced the first month you rub in natural progesterone cream, either increase the dose to mop up the receptors more quickly, or, if it is too uncomfortable, stop using it and double your dose of Dim Vitex until things settle down, then reduce the original dose of one capsule three times a day.

I then asked her a number of basic questions, going through the form I asked all patients to complete before they came to see me the first time. It amazed many patients that I asked so many questions of them, but I hoped they had read my Patient Information Leaflet and realised that I was not only interested in their cancer but also their whole body and their whole life. Every piece of information gave me a clue I could make use of to help a patient resolve their problem. Remember, I considered myself to be a medical detective. Sometimes it was the 'other' symptoms that improved first that told me things were starting to go in the right direction. Yes, I could have spent a lot of a patient's money doing tests every week to see how their cancer was progressing, but I liked to ask the patient how they were feeling and, if necessary, do tests to confirm what we suspected was happening.

She acknowledged having been told some time in the past that she had Irritable Bowel Syndrome or IBS. I told her to listen to the name irritable bowel syndrome! I explained that IBS is a catchall name for almost any bowel symptoms, such as indigestion, pain, alternating constipation with loose stools, etc., but was probably caused by something she was consuming regularly. I told her that it would be interesting to see what effect the diet that I would be recommending had upon her bowels in due course.

When I asked her about episodes of cystitis, she said they had been the bane of her life when she and her husband had started having intercourse, necessitating many visits to her doctor for a course of antibiotics, which cleared up the cystitis, but nearly always gave her thrush. That prompted me to give her a copy of the book I wrote in 1987, entitled 'Conquering Cystitis'♥.

I noted that she had had quite a lot of teeth filled with mercury amalgams. I explained my concern about them, but also made it quite clear that the subject was controversial at present, because the majority of doctors and dentists didn't share my concerns. I asked her or her daughter to research the subject and let us discuss it at her second consultation. Because she hadn't been sleeping very well for quite a long time, I suggested that she try melatonin, starting at 1mg an hour before going to bed, and building up the dose gradually to see if it helped. It usually did at a certain dose, which was different for different people. I explained that there is an Italian professor who recommends his patients take up to 35mg if they have cancer, as he feels it is particularly healing in such patients. I hadn't gone anywhere near that dose yet, feeling that it may not work if it hadn't helped by 10mg. But I did explain that melatonin is an important detoxifying hormone, and to obtain a good night's sleep covered by melatonin was very important. Worry of any sort, stress, depression and, of course, caffeine can switch off your natural production of nocturnal melatonin, which is responsible for controlling the sleep/wake cycle. It can also help to prevent jet lag.

Having covered her 'current' symptoms, I then went back into her childhood as far as she was able, saying that obviously she couldn't ask her mother anything, since she had died tragically some time ago. Her father might be able to help if necessary. She had had measles, mumps and rubella as a child, but had not had chickenpox until she was in her 30's, having it very badly then. This came as no surprise to me and I told her that I had discovered that many women with breast cancer either had had a bad dose of chickenpox in adulthood or even shingles. I felt that somehow the chickenpox/shingles virus (herpes zoster) was involved in breast cancer in particular, and that I would treat it homoeopathically at a later date, dealing with it in the reverse order of events in her life history. I would use Malandrinum 200C twice daily for a minimum of 14 days, followed by a combination of Rhus tox 12C and Box jellyfish 12C also for a minimum of 14 days.

She could not remember anything of importance in her childhood until I asked about operations, when she remembered she had had her tonsils and adenoids removed around the age of seven, as she had suffered with them quite a lot until then, often needing a course of antibiotics. I told her that indicated a milk intolerance to me, and that she had probably had a milk intolerance all her life. She then told me she hated milk and never drank it. She always gave it away when she was at school. But she smiled when I asked her what she put on her breakfast cereal, in her tea and coffee, and if she ever ate yoghurt or cheese. She said she loved cheese, probably craving it. I explained that she had ignored her body's warnings of all those years ago, something people do very often. That was when I suggested she obtain a marvellous book entitled 'Your Life In Your Hands'♥, in which the author explains how she discovered dairy products to be the main cause of her breast cancer.

She had been quite an active teenager, becoming involved in many school sports, but she had suffered badly from glandular fever at college aged twenty, having to take off a whole term to recover. In fact she reckoned she had never been quite the same ever since. I told her how the Epstein Barr bug could have a very long-term effect upon a person, in particular adversely affecting liver detoxification mechanisms. Again I would need to treat that homoeopathically in the right order. It could be one reason why she might not be detoxifying oestrogen efficiently. I told her I would want her to take a course of liver detoxifying herbs, made rather like a herbal tea mixture, with silymarin as one of the main ingredients.

When I asked her about the house they lived in, she said it was all right, but that she had never been completely happy in it. It was a nice house, but they just couldn't put their finger on what was wrong with it, and they were thinking of moving. Her husband agreed with her. I then mentioned 'geopathic stress' to them, and suggested they obtain a copy of the book entitled 'Are You Sleeping In A Safe Place'♥.

At this stage I asked her and her family if they were happy about what they had heard so far. I told her that I would like to do a standard clinical examination of her in due course. I wanted to know what they wanted to do. I knew she had been recommended to have some treatment at the hospital, and I didn't want to influence her decisions. I was aware they had come for advice, and I told her I would support whatever decision she decided to make, and that she, and only she, had to make the right decision for herself. If she wanted to go away and think it all over, that was fine by me. So I left then awhile to have a family discussion.

When I went back into my consulting room, there were smiles all round and they said they wanted to continue and hear all I had to say. I told her she could change her mind any time she wanted to, but, with her permission, I would write to her doctors and tell them what I had found and what I was recommending. She would, of course, receive a copy of any letters I sent to anyone about her, and that I would never say anything behind her back that I wouldn't say to her face.

As she had decided at that stage to listen to my advice and follow it, I asked her how she would judge whether what approach she was going to follow was actually achieving what she wanted to achieve. I even asked her what she wanted to achieve, to which she replied that she wanted to clear her body of all evidence of cancer. I told her that, so far as I was concerned, there were three ways to identify the effectiveness of any treatment. The first was quite simply a question "How do you feel?" If the answer were that she was feeling better in any way, she was sleeping better, she had more energy and her bowels were working normally, then that was a good start.

She could examine her breast herself, or have a doctor like me examine it for her and make a note of any changes, or she could have a regular ultrasound scan. I didn't recommend that she have regular mammograms, as I would be concerned about the squashing of her breast and the possible damage that might do, as well as the radiation to which the breast would be exposed, since we know radiation causes cancer. She could have periodic MRI scans but she would probably have to pay for them herself. I did, however, suggest she have a Thermoscan of her breasts and possibly her whole body while she was about it.

I then reminded her of some blood tests that I had mentioned in my Patient Information Leaflet, feeling that, if she were prepared to pay for them, they would be of real value, first to identify the status of her cancer at present, the state her immune system, plus one or two other pieces of evidence, such as I have described in an earlier chapter. In addition, we could repeat whatever we agreed to be worthwhile every so often, to see how things were progressing. So I examined her clinically, not finding anything of great importance, except for the size, dimensions and characteristics of her breast lump. I examined both breasts and both armpits very carefully, but could not find any lumps in her other breast or either armpit. I made a careful note of my findings in her notes. I then took a blood sample for serum ferritin, a range of tumour marker tests and for glucose-6-phosphate, in case I wanted to give her very high doses of vitamin C intravenously.

I then summarised the whole consultation, explaining to her what I thought her cancer was all about. I told her that it was unlikely that her own GP or hospital Consultants would agree with this attitude, and asked her if she felt happy with it. She told me she had never had such a comprehensive explanation of anything from anybody, and was quite comfortable with my approach, as were her husband and daughter.

I summarised that her underlying causes were a life-long milk intolerance, many courses of antibiotics causing thrush and probably a deep-seated fungus, glandular fever damaging her liver's detoxification mechanisms and the chicken pox virus, possibly affecting her immune system. I added to that her oestrogen dominance in relation to progesterone, all the stress she had been under with her mother, her aunt and her best friend dying, the possible geopathic stress, plus the creation of an acidic environment that is ideal for pathogenic organisms and cancer to thrive in.

Part of her current problems would also be her poorly functioning thyroid and adrenal systems, and the inevitable nutritional paucity that the whole lot had induced, especially as, at a time when her diet and nutritional intake should improve, she probably ate on the hoof, snacking all too often, and drinking too much tea and coffee. Fortunately she didn't take sugar in either of these drinks, nor smoke.

When I had finished, she was open-mouthed, and said was there any wonder that she had developed cancer, but at least, now that the underlying causes had been identified, there were lots of things she could do to start reversing all that damage. I also told her that it was impossible to say when her cancer had started to develop, but it was likely around the time when she noticed pre-menstrual breast tenderness.

So I began advising her what I wanted her to do, starting with the diet I wanted her to follow (see the details above). I then recommended certain supplements and other things, as follows: -

1. A form of indole-3-carbinol I use called Dim Vitex, one capsule three times a day, preferably half an hour before meals, to act as an anti-oestrogen.
2. Calcium-D-glucarate 500mg three times a day, half an hour before meals and taken with the Dim Vitex, to block possible reformation of broken down oestrogen in the bowel.
3. A starting dose of Armour thyroid of 30mg in the morning any time for the first two weeks at least, possibly doubling the dose then, to support the thyroid system. For those who cannot find someone to prescribe whole thyroid, try Nutri Thyroid.
4. Biocare's AD206, one capsule three times daily with meals, to support the adrenal glands. However, I asked her not to start the Armour thyroid or the AD206 for about a week, until she had taken her morning armpit temperature and rung me with the results. I felt sure she would need both.
5. A little bottle of homoeopathic progesterone drops, to put one drop under her tongue three times a day from day 12 of her cycle until day 26 or as soon as her period started. I told her that one drop was enough and two were merely a waste but not an overdose. I advised her not to have anything to eat or drink for at least 10 minutes before or after a dose. I hoped this would modify her premenstrual symptoms, not expecting it to have much effect on her period itself very quickly.
6. Melatonin capsules 1mg. She was to take one capsule about an hour before going to bed, taking an extra capsule each night until she achieved a good night's sleep, preferably without any hangover effect in the morning. I told her not to exceed 10mg without speaking to me first. You may have difficulty obtaining these.
7. As her history of antibiotic usage, thrush and IBS suggested to me the probability of a fungal overgrowth, I recommended she take Biocare's Bioacidophilus to replenish the friendly organisms within her bowel, and I gave her a supply of chlorine dioxide.
8. A supply of AlkaLiza and some pH testing papers.
9. As I always want to look after any helpers or carers, I suggested her husband have a supply of capsules of dehydrated fruits and vegetables♥, giving him a copy of all the scientific studies that had been carried out on them. I explained that taking two of

the red top fruit capsules with breakfast, two of the purple top capsules with lunch and two of the green top vegetable capsules with supper, he would be taking the active and valuable ingredients from twenty-five fruits, berries and vegetables in a day, with all the water, salt, sugar and most of the fibre having been removed. No one could possibly consume that amount of fruit and vegetables in a day! If she and other members of her family wanted to take them as well, I encouraged them to do so.

10. We then discussed intravenous infusions of nutrients. As she had read my Patient Information Leaflet before she came to see me, she knew that I often suggested them to patients, as I believe ill people, especially those with cancer, are deficient in a number of vitamins and minerals. She therefore decided to try one, knowing that they took about 1½ hours to run in. The details are in an earlier chapter. Unfortunately most patients won't be able to avail themselves of these, but there are a few doctors in the UK, quite a number in some European countries and many in USA who give them. It is likely, however, that they will want you to have a consultation with them before they give you one.

11. I gave her three books to read, 'Are You Sleeping In A Safe Place', 'The Journey' and 'Love Medicine and Miracles'.

12. Finally I made an appointment to see her again for a second consultation in four weeks time, asking her to ring me in a few days to tell me how she felt after the infusion, inviting her to consider having one once a week, especially if it made her feel better.

Four weeks later we had our second consultation, by which time I was already getting to know her, as she had attended each week in between for a nutrient infusion. She had felt so much better after the first one, having more energy, feeling generally brighter and sleeping better, although it took a few nights of building up the dose of melatonin to 5mg before she had what she described as a really good night's sleep. By the time she came back for the second infusion, I had had the results of the glucose-6-phosphate blood test, which was within the laboratory's reference range, which meant I could safely increase the dose of vitamin C towards 50g or higher. If G-6-PD were deficient, it would have meant that she had a rare enzyme deficiency, and that large doses of vitamin C intravenously would seriously damage her red blood cells, something we clearly didn't want to do. If a person were to have this deficiency, it appears to be perfectly safe to take large doses by mouth.

As soon as she and her husband and daughter came in for the second visit, she was asked to complete two forms, one a general one about the various symptoms she was still suffering from (to compare with the same form she had filled in before her first visit), the second one to indicate whether she felt the same, better or any worse. She had indicated that she felt 60% better! She was sleeping well, she was no longer nearly as tired as before and her bowels were behaving themselves. She had lost 10lb in weight and had dug out old clothes she had always loved wearing but had not been able to fit into for quite a long time. She said she was looking forward to losing at least another 14lb, after which she was planning to buy a new wardrobe.

She then turned to her husband who said he had followed the same diet and had lost 16lb! They were clearly both delighted. Using the homoeopathic drops as I had advised, she said she couldn't believe how little she had had in the way of pre-menstrual symptoms, especially the swelling and discomfort in her breasts. This I felt was of particular importance, as it showed that her breasts were being affected less by oestrogen at that time of the month, and that I hoped such symptoms would disappear in due course. I made a note to make sure I asked her about that at subsequent visits.

She had decided not to examine her breasts, but to leave them alone for a whole month. She felt that otherwise she might become obsessive about them, and, if she were to examine them too often, doing so might aggravate them. When I eventually examined them, my opinion was that there was certainly no increase in the size of the lump, and, if anything, it was a bit smaller and not so hard. Not wishing to give her false hope, I explained that that was certainly news on the good side, but that the changes could be the result of letting it all settle down after the biopsy.

What I felt she really wanted to know was the results of the blood tests we had done on her, so I went over the laboratory tests results first. They were as follows; -

1. Telomerase. Any word ending in '..ase' signifies an enzyme that manufactures the chemical named in the first half of the word. This came back at a level of 230 units, whereas when a person does not have cancer, it should be zero. I told her that cancer cells produce the enzyme called telomerase to manufacture telomeres, the tail end of the DNA. Normal cells cannot do so, so have a finite life. The fact that cancer cells produce telomerase, effectively makes them immortal. I explained that this meant that she had some cells in her blood stream that were cancerous. Before she had time to feel alarmed that her cancer had 'spread', I explained that, although she might feel that she didn't want to have any cancer cells in her bloodstream, if she didn't, there would not be anything for her immune system to respond to. I also warned her that a subsequent test result might go sky high, possibly around 15,000, but that would indicate the release of the telomerase enzyme from dying cancer cells.

2. Pyruvate kinase. This is another enzyme and it forms pyruvate, which certain types of cancer cells produce; so another indication of the presence of cancer in her body. It came back raised at 35.2 units (the lab's reference range is up to 15).

3. Laevorotatory lactic acid. The first word means 'left-handed', rather than dextrorotatory meaning right-handed in chemical terms. This one came back somewhat raised at 5.4 units, whereas it should be effectively unmeasurable. I told her that, in my opinion, it indicated some form of 'fungus', and I reminded her of the theory that sometimes cancer is a protective mechanism against a fungus. With her history of lots of antibiotics over the years, many episodes of thrush and persistent bowel problems, I thought that some sort of fungus was likely to be involved in her condition.

I told her that these three were the tests I did at present that indicate the presence or absence of cancer in her body. I also told her that the results were no surprise to me, and simply reflected what we knew, i.e. that she did have cancer. I also explained that they were merely a picture of her at present, and that we did not know whether they were going up, staying steady or going down. Subsequent tests would tell us how her cancer was progressing.

4. Interferon Gamma. This is one of three tests that tell me the state of a person's immune system. It reflects the Natural Killer cells, a most important aspect of the fight against cancer. Her level was far too low at 550, when it should be somewhere between 5,000 and 10,000.

5. Interleukin 12. This reflects macrophages and dendritic cells, two other cells of importance in the immune system. Again her level was far too low at 230, the reference range being 3,000 to 10,000.

6. Tumour Necrosis Factor Beta. This reflects the Thymus Helper cells, also

important to the immune system. This was considerably better at 1,598, but again too low, as the lab's reference range is 5,000 to 10,000.

With all three tests of her immune system being too low, I suggested that we needed to boost her immune system, basically to wake it up. I told her that, when I see someone who has had a course of chemotherapy, all three are usually less than 50, i.e. they have virtually no effective immune system to speak of. So what chance would such a person have of bringing their cancer under control?

7. P185. This test suggests the degree of activity of any cancer. As its full name is P185 Her-2 protein, I explained it is related to the latest so-called wonder drug for breast cancer, namely herceptin. Her level was 4.4, within the lab's reference range of up to 6.8 units, basically showing that her cancer was not aggressive. That brought a smile to her face. I explained that that therefore gave us time to sort things out without feeling we needed to rush. In any case, I reminded her that she was already feeling better.

8. P53. The full name of this one is Anti p53 Antibody, which is rather like a double negative. Hers was mutated. It could also have been wild (working normally) or deleted. Hers was simply damaged, so presumably not working properly.

9. Vascular Endothelial Growth Factor (VEGF for short). This was very slightly raised at 1,600 units, when the lab's reference range is up to 1,500. It reflects new blood vessel growth. Sometimes cancer cells produce their own blood vessels to extract nutrients for their growth. I told her I wasn't worried at that level, but that I would want to repeat it fairly soon, as I thought it might have been caused by the healing process initiated by the needle biopsy. I also felt that the fact the breast lump felt softer to me was an indication that it was not growing new blood vessels.

10. Transforming Growth Factor Beta (TGF-Beta for short). This was comfortably within the lab's reference range of 1,500 units at 230 units. I explained that sometimes cancer tumours put out this chemical to suppress the immune system, rather like anti-ballistic/ballistic missiles, i.e. they are trying to protect themselves from the immune system, rather fascinating when you come to think of it.

I summarised all these tests by saying that they showed she had cancer (but she already knew that), some sort of fungus was probably involved, and we had a level of her cancer that we could retest at a later stage to see how things were progressing. Her immune system need boosting, and we needed to do something about her p53 Gene, as it was probably not sending out the message for old cells to die when they should do so by the process called 'apoptosis'. I would like to repeat the VEGF test in about one month's time, just to make sure it was dropping down not going up.

Her serum ferritin came back at 7 units, the lab's reference range being 15 to 320 units, so well below the level of 50 units that I think is important. This could explain some of the fatigue she was still feeling, even though she was feeling less tired in general. Her second morning urine samples showed she was still too acidic.

Further Treatments
1. As a result of these test results, I encouraged her to be very strict on the 'sugar' side of her diet, asking her temporarily to avoid all fruit for a while. She told me her morning candida/saliva test had been thoroughly positive, i.e. her saliva had sunk

rapidly to the bottom. I asked her to continue doing the test, but only twice a week for now, to monitor the effect of the treatment. I also made sure that she was taking at least the fruit blend of the dehydrated special capsules to compensate for the lack of fruit itself for a while.

2. To improve this situation overall, I recommended Biocare's Bioacidophilus, one capsule after each meal three times a day.

3. Because of the 'fungal' indication from her history, the saliva test, and now the raised levels of Pyruvate kinase and Laevorotatory lactic acid, I advised her to take one capsule three times a day of Salvestrol Gold for the first month, then reduce it to twice daily, preferably taking it 1/2 hour before meals. Only professionals can prescribe this product, but anyone can obtain Fruit Force capsules. The Salvestrol Gold is many times stronger than the Fruit Force capsules, so without advice from an appropriate person, most people should only take one Fruit Force capsule three times a day. The company is regularly upgrading their knowledge about salvestrols.

This product is an extract, from various fruits, of chemicals that have been named 'salvestrols' by their discoverer, the Professor of Pharmacy at Leicester (UK)'s De Montfort University, Dr Jerry Potter. His research has shown that salvestrols not only interfere with the metabolism of cancer cells, but that they are anti-fungal, so a logical choice in her case.

4. Her laboratory test results showed that her immune system was in rather a poor state. This could be because of the cancer itself, or because of the causes of her cancer. Had she had any, it could have been because of some form of treatment, but she hadn't had any chemotherapy or radiotherapy. As her 'Interferon Gamma' test was particularly low, reflecting the functioning of her Natural Killer Cells, the product I recommend her to take to stimulate these cells was called Biobran♥ (possibly called MGN3 in USA). In UK, it comes in a sachet, and is unfortunately rather expensive. The contents taste like mild Weetabix to me. I recommended that she take the contents of one sachet three times a day for twenty-eight days, then reduce it down to one sachet per day.

As her TNF-beta test was low, reflecting the functioning of her thymus, I recommended an herb called Echinacea at a dose of 1g three times daily, preferably away from food for one month only. Tablets can be easily bought from a local Health Food store. Some people feel a person should ideally take this preparation in this sort of dosage until their test results show that their immune system has responded adequately. I offered Imm-Kine as an alternative.

5. Biocare's iron, working up to three capsules last thing at night to improve her iron stores. I explained that iron preparations should be taken away from most other minerals, as there is competition for their absorption. I also felt she ought to take vitamin C as Longevity Plus' Bio-En'R-Gy C, working her total daily dose up to her bowel tolerance.

6. Finally, I suggested 400mg Co-Enzyme Q10. I wasn't aware of the interesting work of Dr. Alan Lieberman and Dr. Sherri Tenpenny at that stage.

Patient Example No 2
This patient was a seventy-two year old man with prostate cancer. His PSA (Prostate Specific Antigen) was 32.4 units when I first saw him. Anything above 4.0 is considered suspicious, but there is considerable controversy about its value. Nevertheless, it is a useful guide. Despite its name suggesting that it is specific to the male prostate, apparently women can have a very high level when they are

recovering from breast cancer!

This gentleman came to see me accompanied by his wife and middle-aged son, who said he was interested in what I had to say, in the hope that he could prevent himself from developing the problem when he was older. I said I would come back to the matter of age in due course.

His history was fairly typical of many prostate cancer patients I saw, in that he had started to complain of minor bladder problems, mainly having to get out of bed at night annoyingly too often, about five years previously. It hadn't really bothered him too much, as a number of his friends had much the same problem, and they had all said it was merely a problem of getting older. It was only when his local General Practice had sent him a letter saying that they held a Well Man clinic on a Thursday afternoon, inviting him to attend. He thought it would be a good idea, so he went along.

Having made an appointment for a couple of weeks ahead, he had been sent a questionnaire to fill in before he attended. He was surprised how few boxes he thought were relevant to him. He didn't have headaches, his eyesight seemed pretty good for his age, he was still very active, but he did accept that his bladder control had deteriorated recently. It was this part that interested the nurse who saw him initially, although she took his blood pressure, got him to blow into a machine to see how efficient his lungs were, and did an ECG, a tracing of his heart. He passed all of these tests with ease, but she felt he ought to have a quick talk to the doctor about his bladder troubles. The doctor did a basic examination, saying that he wanted to take some blood for routine blood tests as well as his PSA, after which he did a rectal examination and said he thought his prostate felt a bit large. The routine blood tests eventually came back within the lab's reference ranges, but his PSA was raised at 10.6 units. His doctor said he wanted to refer him to a Specialist Urologist at the local hospital, and that he would organise the appointment for him.

At the hospital, more blood was taken for PSA again, which eventually came back at 12.2 units. The Specialist said he wanted to arrange for him to have a biopsy of his prostate "to see what is going on". He told me it was one of the most painful experiences he had ever had, although he was assured that didn't always happen. He passed blood in his urine for two days after that. To cut a long story short, because the results were lost for a while, etc. he was eventually told that he had cancer in his prostate. The Specialist said it wasn't too bad, but it would be sensible to do an MRI scan of his pelvis and a bone scan to make sure it hadn't spread anywhere.

Both his scans had shown no spread, so his specialist team felt that the appropriate treatment was a 6 or 7-week course of localised radiotherapy and an injection about every three months to reduce his testosterone levels. The radiotherapy had irritated his rectum and bladder, and he was still affected by them a little. This had all happened about two years ago and his PSA had fallen to almost unmeasurable levels.

A couple of months ago he developed a backache, which he blamed on having been a little too enthusiastic in the garden. When it didn't clear after about a month he consulted his GP again, who arranged for an X-ray, which showed that his prostate cancer had probably spread to his spine. A bone scan showed it had also spread into his pelvis. He was very upset about this as he felt all the treatment he had received had not only made him feel quite unwell and had damaged parts of his body, it had clearly not worked. His son had done some research, which was why he had come to see me. Although I eventually took a detailed history, I started by explaining what I thought might interest him. First I asked him what the injections had done to him, to which he replied that he assumed it had cut out all production of testosterone. I told him it had effectively chemically castrated him, through an action in part of his brain called the hypothalamic/pituitary area, as it was assumed that testosterone was the cause of prostate cancer.

If that was the case, I said to him, then why didn't prostate cancer occur in twenty-year-old randy young men, rather than in older men whose testosterone levels were presumably diminishing? The answer is, I told him, that it is not testosterone but what it is converted into, namely dihydro-testosterone (DHT for short) that is the culprit, and more of it is produced from testosterone as men grow older. What causes more DHT to be formed is too much oestrogen, especially xeno-oestrogens, or false oestrogens from pesticides, petrochemicals, plasticisers, etc. that we are all being exposed to more and more these days. These gradually accumulate in the body over the years and are absorbed into fat.

I suggested that it was not unreasonable to reduce the production of testosterone, as that would therefore produce less DHT, but surely it would be more reasonable to reduce the conversion of testosterone to DHT and antagonise, or do something about, oestrogen. I said I was aware that the testosterone reducing drugs seemed either to lose their effect after about two years, or possibly started to become oestrogenic themselves. It was also accepted, however, that these drugs stopped working after a time.

He told me that he had hated the effect of the chemical castration, as his body hair had changed to a more feminine type and distribution, he had developed breasts, his voice had become higher, he had put on weight especially round his tummy and he had felt he was the wrong person in his body. All this and the treatment hadn't worked! I told him there was some research that suggested that some men were doing well on oestrogen, and I was keeping my eye on such developments.

I told him I would talk about the treatments that I recommended at the end of the consultation, but that I needed to go through his history. Apart from his prostatic symptoms and the symptoms of his treatment, he thought he was in quite good shape, and had had very little wrong with him for most of his life, yet I noticed he was on tablets to control his blood pressure. He had also had a certain amount of eczema during his lifetime, more when he was young than later in life.

This interested me, because when people shed skin as people with eczema or psoriasis do, they lose a lot of zinc, and zinc is an important mineral to maintain the local immunity of the prostate. I also told him that each ejaculate contained about 2mg zinc. The Recommended Daily Allowance (RDA) of zinc is 15mg, most people taking in less than that amount in their daily diet. So, with eczema helping to eliminate zinc, he probably had a chronic zinc deficiency.

He suffered a certain amount of fatigue, but thought it was quite reasonable in the circumstances. When I questioned him further, however, he acknowledged that he had never been tired at all before the diagnosis. At the same time his wife felt the radiotherapy or possibly the drugs he was on had caused his fatigue. He then remembered that one of the questions he had said 'no' to when he filled in the form at the Well Man Clinic was fatigue, so clearly that had started after then.

I went through other aspects of what he might have been taking from his doctor or buying from the local chemist, and noticed a regular intake of a particular antacid.

Yet he didn't indicate on his symptom chart that he had ever suffered from indigestion or too much acid. He explained to me that he didn't suffer from either of them, because the antacids controlled them well! It was only then that he realised that he was misleading me about his health, because he accepted that there had to be a reason why he needed the antacids to control such symptoms.

He then explained that quite some years ago he had started to complain of bringing up acid an hour or so after most meals, but that, early on, he had found some tablets that controlled the symptoms so well he had virtually bought a bulk supply and simply took them after every meal, which had done the trick. He had effectively forgotten about the symptoms because he never went without his tablets. He couldn't remember when he had last had a meal without following it with a tablet. Taking his tablets wherever he went was almost more important to him than remembering to take his house keys!

He had had his tonsils and adenoids out at the age of seven years old, having lots of throat infections, but antibiotics were not discovered in those days, so he never had any. They had tried to put grommets in both eardrums on a number of occasions, but they had kept falling out. He had eventually grown out of them in his early teens. I told him that that was a classical indication of a milk intolerance, and milk products were probably the cause of his acid indigestion, as well as possibly tea, coffee and alcohol.

I found it interesting that, about fifteen years ago, he went on holiday somewhere in Africa and became infected by a parasite called Giardia lamblia. He had been treated locally at the time, but he had never had a stool sample checked since then. When I asked him if there was a possible coincidence that his indigestion started around then, he acknowledged it was a possibility, but he couldn't be sure.

When I asked him about exercise, he told me he had been a cycling enthusiast, although he hadn't done much for the past five years or so, clearly doing less as he had got older. In principle I didn't feel that cycling per se could be blamed for his prostate cancer, but, if he had had some form of chronic infection in his prostate, massaging it by cycling just might have made things worse. I had asked every prostate cancer patient about cycling, as I thought it would be interesting to see if there might be a connection, but I hadn't found it to be so, and he was the only one I had met who had indulged in the sport.

While I can understand some people being sceptical about geopathic stress, I asked him how long he had lived at his present address. When he said over twenty years, I asked him if they had done any building or extensions to the house, and he said they had built a new lounge and new bedroom above it about five years ago, into which they had moved. If that new bedroom had been built over an area of geopathic stress, he might have been exposed to it every night since then, so I felt that that might possibly be involved.

I explained that I seldom find only one cause for a person's cancer. Yes, smoking and asbestos are known causes of lung cancer, but not everyone who smokes all their life or who has been exposed to asbestos develops lung cancer. It seems to need other factors to add together to end up with producing cancer. So, I usually find at least five factors that could be involved. I question if one might be 80% of the problem, with the rest making up the remaining 20%, or could they each represent 20%. Perhaps it needs at least 60% to be dealt with before the 'total load' is reduced sufficiently for the condition to start being brought under control.

Finally, I asked him if he had been under any stress in the past five years or so.

Both he and his wife then told me about their youngest son who had been involved in a horrendous motor-cycle accident six years ago, lying in hospital unconscious for nearly two years, having multiple operations to try to rebuild his body, for him only to have died in the end. Then there was the inquest followed by the trial of the driver who had fallen asleep behind the wheel, the whole business being exhausting, stressful and terribly sad. I explained some of the things such stress does to the body.

When I examined him, I noticed a number of white spots on his fingernails, which I told him were most likely a sign of a zinc deficiency. I also heard a heart murmur, but he said he didn't remember anyone ever listening to his heart. Otherwise I didn't find anything else of significance.

Because he had read my Patient Information Leaflet before he came, and had felt really happy with the approach I described, he had rung me and asked me to write a letter to a local laboratory asking them to take blood for the tests that I recommend, not only full haematology and biochemistry, serum ferritin and thyroid function tests, but the full range of laboratory tests. I therefore discussed the results of these with him.

In his 'standard' tests, I noted that his MCV (Mean Corpuscular Volume basically the average size of each red blood cell) was just outside the lab's reference range of 100 units, at 102. This suggested to me a deficiency of vitamin B12 and/or folic acid, which could explain some of his fatigue, even though there was no sign of anaemia. What was astonishing, however, was his serum ferritin at over 1000 units (lab reference range of 15 to 350). That was when I asked him what work he had done. When patients answer the question about 'employment', if no longer working they nearly always put 'retired', but never retired from what. In his case he had been a steel worker all his life, working with all sorts of metals, mainly in the ship building industry.

I told him we now had another cause of his prostate cancer, namely iron overload, even though his skin was not particularly 'tanned'. I reminded him that cancer cells feed on iron, one reason why cancer patients are often anaemic.

His test results were as follows: -

1. Telomerase 439 (reference range effectively zero)
2. Pyruvate kinase 66.5 (reference range up to 15)
3. Laevorotatory lactic acid unmeasurable.
4. P185 33.2 (reference range up to about 15).
5. P53 mutated (should be normal or 'wild').
6. Interferon Gamma less than 50! (reference range 5,000 to 10,000).
7. Interleukin 12 less than 50! (reference range 3,000 to 10,000).
8. Tumour Necrosis Factor Beta 450 (reference range 5,000 to 10,000).
9. Vascular Endothelial Factor 10,560 (reference range up to 1,500).
10. Transforming Growth Factor Beta 330 (reference range up to 1,500).

In summary, the first two of these results (the third was clear) showed him that he did have cancer markers separate from his PSA that could be used for monitoring his progress. The P185 indicated a moderate degree of activity. The mutated P53 gene suggested that the normal process of apoptosis was not functioning. Items 6, 7 and 8 showed his immune system to be in such an appalling condition that it either did not even 'know' he had cancer, or had been overwhelmed by the cancer or effectively destroyed by the treatment he had had. In the circumstances, I told him it was not surprising his cancer had spread. No 9 was a bit worrying, as it showed that some aspect of his cancer was developing or had developed its own blood supply to extract what it wanted from his body. Rather than worry him about these results, I explained that they provided me with a picture of his metabolic status and that there was plenty we could do about it all.

First I recommended that he change his diet in the way I have explained above. As he had already indicated that he wanted to stop all his drugs, as they were not only making him feel unwell but also because they clearly hadn't worked, we talked about his doing so, but I advised him to inform his doctors about this. Having accepted that his cancer may have been caused by the reasons I had given him, he said he would like to try the herbal preparation to reduce the conversion of testosterone into DHT, and apply natural progesterone cream to his skin.

We then talked about the other supplements I mentioned above, especially zinc, selenium, lycopene and vitamin C, suggesting that he start with these and see how he went on. Because I felt he was probably still suffering from the inflammatory effects of the radiotherapy he had been given, I recommended Eskimo-3 oil and Mangosteen juice. As he still had bladder-type symptoms, I suggested he consult a local homoeopath for the appropriate remedies.

As he had read about them in my patient information leaflet, he asked if he could have an intravenous infusion of vitamins and minerals, and I suggested that I take a sample of blood for three tests, namely glucose-6-phosphate dehydrogenase and vitamin B12 and folic acid once I had inserted the cannula. I also suggested that he start the diet in three days time so that he could let me know the effect of the infusion alone.

The g-6-pd was so that I could safely give him high doses of vitamin C intravenously for a while to get things started. The other two were of clinical interest as his MCV blood test was a bit high, indicating a possible deficiency of either of these two. His g-6-pd levels came back within the lab's reference range, but his B12 and folic acid levels were clearly low, one of the possible reasons for his fatigue.

I explained to him that the contraceptive pill could induce in a woman a deficiency of vitamin C and B6 and folic acid, and of zinc and magnesium, so it was logical to me that his feminising treatment with pharmaceutical drugs could have done the same.

As a result of the laboratory tests, I recommended he take one sachet of Biobran three times a day for at least a month to boost his Natural Killer cells, as indicated by the very low level of Interferon gamma. I also recommended one capsule of Imm-Kine three times a day to boost the other aspects of his immune system, and C-Statin 500mg three times a day to strangulate the new blood vessel formation, as indicated by his raised level of VEGF.

That whole experience took well over two hours to discuss, separate from the 1½ hours the infusion took to run in. I told him that I wanted to see him for a follow-up consultation in about four weeks, when we would discuss many other aspects of his history, including showing him how to do visualisations, etc. I also suggested that he consider coming back for a weekly intravenous infusion of nutrients, if he benefited from the first. In fact he rang me three days later to say that his levels of energy had improved enormously for the infusion, so he booked in for some more.

Chapter 13

What To Do About Cancer

You have now read a lot of information about cancer, and you may be somewhat confused, so I am now going to summarise what you should do. In the first case, please don't panic. Take your time. It is extremely unlikely that you HAVE to make a decision about anything now, unless you are in an emergency situation. So, as I say, take your time. Have an Indian head massage, go into a church, or take a long walk in the beautiful countryside somewhere near you, driving out of town if you live in the middle of a big city. Do something different, something that will help you to relax.

Yes, I know it is no fun having been told you have cancer, or that it has all come back after they had given you the all clear some time ago. But that is because no one has told you what to do about yourself. No one has suggested that that there is no reason why you should die from cancer, if you decide to start treating yourself. But you have to take charge of your life. You have to be prepared to do things for yourself. You have to be prepared to change a number of things in your life style.

So where do you start? Basically I am going to repeat what I said in the history chapter, towards the end. Consider the following as possible causes of your cancer; some otherwise innocent damage to the area where you now have cancer; what you consume as foods and drinks and what you miss from the right diet for you; stress in all its forms both recently and possibly hidden deep in your soul; toxic substances such as heavy metals, especially mercury, but also the myriad chemicals we are all exposed to in our daily lives; the more easily identified poisons such as cigarette smoke; root canal fillings on acupuncture meridians of your cancer; infections, especially viruses and fungi; your bowel ecology; hormonal imbalances; nutrient deficiencies including vitamin D if you live in a comparatively poor sun area; your anti-oxidant levels to quench all those free radicals; your pH and biological terrain; an inefficient immune system; the effect of any drugs you have been prescribed either before or for your cancer, especially their nutrient draining effects; and finally geopathic stress. How many of these possible causes could apply to you? Remember, cancer crept up on you because you were not doing the right things, or were doing clearly some wrong things. There's no point in blaming yourself for any misdemeanours in your past life. They are in the past. They've gone now. You're going to tidy things up and start from now.

Start with what you eat. Go back to that section and make appropriate changes. Possibly have some tests done so you know where you stand at present. If you have a hormonal cancer, such as breast, prostate, cervical, uterine or ovarian cancer, consider seriously if you have a hormonal imbalance, with dominance of oestrogen playing a major part. This is particularly likely in breast cancer. In prostate cancer, I need to raise another important aspect. Mainstream medicine effectively castrates you chemically, by blocking the effect of testosterone in your body, one way or another. However, if testosterone really is the bad guy, why have you developed cancer in your prostate when your levels of testosterone are diminishing as you have got older? Surely, if testosterone were the big bad guy of prostate cancer, wouldn't your randy twenty-year-old young man develop it? In fact testosterone itself kills prostate cancer cells, but it is the first metabolite of testosterone, namely dihydro-testosterone (DHT) that is the real culprit.

Then the next question is, what causes us to convert more of our dwindling supplies of testosterone into DHT? Once again, the answer is oestrogen, especially xeno-oestrogens, from pesticides, plasticisers and petrochemicals, etc. Our world is awash with xeno-oestrogens. So in prostate cancer, you need to antagonise oestrogen, namely with bio-identical progesterone, among other things.

If you have a lymphoma, i.e. swollen lymph glands anywhere in your body, think of infections. After all, that is what their job is, to deal with any local infection. It is just that your immune system has not coped with whatever your infection is, so apart from taking a specific anti-infective treatment, you will need to improve your immune system. In my opinion, it's all very basic and simple, but you have to be prepared to do something yourself.

If you have cancer in your mouth, oesophagus (gullet), stomach or any part of your intestines, think of what you have put into your mouth over the years. In lung cancer, it is nearly always what you have put into it, namely cigarette smoke, or asbestos, allowing for the fact that you have a genetic predisposition to lung cancer. I am now fairly sure that milk leaves an inflammatory deposit of some sort in the lung which you eventually try to cough up. In the end it turns into cancer. In brain tumours, have you used a mobile phone too much over the years, especially since you were much younger, when your brain was developing?

In cervical cancer, have you had any infections in that part of your body? Have you ever had an abnormal smear? Have you ever had thrush? In kidney cancer, what have you been passing through your kidneys? In pancreatic cancer, have you eaten many foods for a long time with virtually all the enzymes removed from them in their processing? In testicular cancer, did you have mumps some time in the past?

Do you see what I'm getting at? These explanations may not be relevant to you, but at least I am giving you some ideas of what could have caused cancer to develop in you, which then gives you something to take control of in your life.

This brings us back to the basic reasons why you have cancer. Yes, it may be as a result of the life style you have led, a poor diet, or the stresses in your life that you couldn't avoid, or the chemical exposures that weren't your fault, or you didn't know at the time were unwise. All of these have led to a number of problems that need to be resolved as soon as possible. You need to start doing something about the state that you find yourself in now.

Your body has probably become too acid and you are most likely producing too many free radicals that are not being adequately quenched and not quickly enough. Your immune system may be overloaded or poorly functioning. Your Biological Terrain is probably in a mess. You may be harbouring the cancer-forming fungus. Your diet may be loaded with sugar or contain too much iron, which cancer cells feed on. How much more do you need to begin to realise why you now have cancer?

I have attempted to open your eyes to possible mechanisms for your cancer. Any one, or all, of these may be playing a part. Many of these mechanisms have points in common.

I don't promise that it will be easy, nor can I promise that it will be successful. Also I expect you to search the World Wide Web for as much information as possible to help yourself. After all, this is my approach based on over thirty years of medical practice, and it is always possible there is another approach that I haven't heard of yet.

I hope you now have a greater understanding of yourself and your cancer. I hope you will also have lost some of your understandable fear of cancer, and begin to realise there is a lot you can do for yourself. As far as I am concerned, there is no hurry, so take your time.

Start believing in yourself. Start believing that you can make all the difference you want for yourself. Remember, I am the teacher (the word doctor comes from the

Latin word docere = to teach) and you are the pupil for now. How much do you want to learn from me? What are you prepared to do to achieve what you want to achieve? It's up to you.

So, enjoy yourself, feel enlightened, smile, be happy and radiate confidence in what you are going to do. Be positive and forget the doom and gloom merchants. If someone has given you a poor prognosis, forget it. You no longer fit into their statistics. You are going to do something for yourself. You are now in charge.

Chapter 14

Multiple Sclerosis

Multiple sclerosis is a debilitating condition of the central nervous system. The peripheral nerves are not affected directly, i.e. if nerve conduction tests are carried out, peripheral nerves are said to be intact. So, effectively, the message sent from the brain down nerves is somehow wrong or inadequate. The patient, however, is aware of the clinical symptoms not in his or her brain, where the damage is, but in the periphery, namely in the functioning of individual muscles or sensations in the skin.

Over nine thousand people diagnosed with multiple sclerosis consulted me when I was practising medicine. They tended to have been defined by a Consultant Neurologist as 'relapsing and remitting', 'primary progressive' or 'secondary progressive'. The relapsing and remitting type could progress in due course to become secondary progressive when the variations in symptoms stopped occurring and started on a general downhill direction.

I prefer to divide MS patients into groups according to their symptoms, because I found that the management tended to be different in them, although there was considerable overlap. The majority of the patients I saw had what I called the 'functional' type of MS, that is that their muscles were involved. Patients told me that when their muscles started to be affected, they somehow didn't work normally. In these circumstances they found that perhaps they might start to trip over nothing, or they might start to stagger, so were often accused of being drunk. Many found they couldn't walk normally or use their hands correctly, or their muscles were stiff and/or went into spasm all too easily.

I often helped such a patient get back into their car after a consultation, and sometimes their legs were so stiff, we literally couldn't bend them to fit them into the front seat. With patience, however, their legs would always relax eventually, but it could take a long time and was particularly difficult when it was raining. I assumed this was because the patient became anxious that we would get wet, so their muscles went into spasm due to the anxiety and effort not to be a nuisance. I picked up long ago from patients' histories that any anxiety made things worse. The harder they tried the worse things often became. Most of them, I discovered, would clench their teeth in an effort to do things and I found that advising them to relax their jaw could sometimes help. But more of this later.

Depending on the degree of severity by the time they consulted me, functional type MS patients either walked in with varying degrees of difficulty, usually with one or two sticks (they might have found a Zimmer walking frame to be more supportive) or they came in a wheel chair, again with varying degrees of ability to use their legs. Some patients were totally unable to move anything in their lower limbs. Many MS patients struggled on, resolutely refusing to take to a wheel chair as they felt that that was the beginning of the end of their independence. Little did they realise that they were not only not helping themselves but also making things more difficult for their carers. I always encouraged them to remain as independent as possible for as long as possible but to be willing to use a wheel chair to make things easier for themselves and everyone else. In any case, I encouraged them to believe they would soon start to improve, so whether they made use of a wheel chair or not was entirely up to them.

The second group was what I called the 'sensory' type of MS, namely they suffered from a variety of sensory symptoms. They could complain of pins and needles or patches of numbness anywhere on their body. Mostly, however, one or both lower limbs were involved, and could be described as a stocking-like effect.

Sometimes the whole of one side of the body was involved but the other side was completely clear. An upper limb might be affected, or they might complain of a tight band around their waist. Some patients, usually women, said they couldn't feel when they were urinating. One side of the face might be affected, or there might be a numb ring around their mouth, diagnosed in one patient by a Professor of Oro-facial Medicine and Surgery as the 'circum-oral facial syndrome', a diagnosis that didn't help the patient as he said there was nothing he could do about it!

A small number of patients complained of such a fierce degree of pain that they were on morphine when they came to see me. I was fortunately able to clear the pain with large doses of vitamin B12 intravenously. Sometimes when the numbness in the feet was bad, patients couldn't feel the soles of their feet at all, so tended to slap their feet on the ground to tell them where they were in space. We normal people walk without thinking as our nervous systems do all the thinking for us.

By-and-large, I found the sensory type of MS easiest to treat, but such patients were in the minority.

Then there were the 'mixed types', where there was a degree of functional and sensory symptoms, one or the other predominating. Many patients told me they may have started with sensory symptoms, but these had disappeared when the functional symptoms began.

Although I tended not to put them in a separate category, some patients first symptoms were a bout of optic neuritis, when their vision was disturbed in almost any sort of way, from colour distortion through blurring of vision to total blindness for a while, fortunately nearly always in only one eye. The other main feature was a degree of pain in the eyeball, especially when the eye was moved, indicating some form of inflammation. Such patients always ended up as an emergency in the Eye Department. Although optic neuritis can be the first sign of MS, Eye Specialists are loath to diagnose MS on one attack, as sometimes there may not ever be another similar attack, or, if there is, it may not occur for many years. Also more specific symptoms of MS might also not occur for many years. As current treatment for MS is so poor, and patients are all too aware that they might end up in a wheel chair (a picture of a person in a wheel chair is on the front page of the Multiple Sclerosis Society Pamphlet which tends to frighten them), Eye Specialists don't wish to cause the patient undue anxiety which might then precipitate the development of an attack of Multiple Sclerosis.

Clinical Medical History

So how does a doctor make a diagnosis of MS? How did I come to the conclusions I did about the causes of MS? After all, according to most doctors, as I have already said, no one knows what causes MS. But I have a different way of thinking. I assume there must be a cause, and that it is my job to find it. If you can find a cause, the next question is "Can you get rid of the cause?" Then perhaps the next important question is "Will the patient lose his or her symptoms or at least improve if the cause is dealt with?" So I asked a lot of questions designed to identify possible causes and made certain assumptions from the information, asking patients to try my ideas. Often it worked. If it didn't, I tried something else. To a doctor the process is called "taking a medical history".

As a medical student, I was taught to take a history for one purpose and one purpose only. That was to make a diagnosis. Once the diagnosis had been made with confidence, then a decision need simply be made on the most appropriate form of treatment for that diagnosis. Effectively that meant a prescription for a medication or a recommendation for some sort of surgical procedure. In fact learning about the treatment options was generally a much later part of the curriculum, as we concentrated on getting the diagnosis right to begin with. A reasonable theory was that the choice of treatment depended on getting the diagnosis right in the first place.

When I was a pre-clinical medical student, I remember being taught all about the anatomy and physiology of the body. While I realised that it was important to know all this, my fellow students and I longed to get into the hospital wards to start treating patients. We were sure that was where our talents lay and what we were learning to become doctors for. In other words we wanted to heal the sick.

I found the pre-clinical studies rather dry and boring at the time, and almost irrelevant. Interestingly enough, it never occurred to me that an ill person is merely someone whose normal anatomy or physiology has simply somehow gone wrong. Nor did our tutors describe this attitude to us. When I was in practice, I studied the normal, because that is what I wanted to achieve in my patients. I wanted to understand where and why the abnormal had developed, so that I could help the normal to return, mainly by undoing what caused it to go wrong in the first place.

What I am trying to get across to you is the fact that mainstream medicine as it is practised today attempts to correct the abnormal by treating the abnormal symptoms with unnatural chemicals called pharmaceutical prescription drugs. Studies have been carried out to show the possibility that the symptom has resulted from some chemical abnormality in the body, and that the prescribed drug can correct it. I could waste hours of your time refuting this argument. Nevertheless, I will repeat that the intention is that the drug is supposed to alter the abnormality that has occurred. No attempt is made to understand why that abnormality occurred in the first place.

While there is a certain value in mainstream medicine's approach, especially for acute situations such as appendicitis, a heart attack or a traffic accident, there is the missing question "Why has this occurred?" rather than "Take this medicine" or "I need to operate on you". I was certainly not taught to take a history to find out why the condition had developed. Over the years I have learned that going into a person's history in great depth can help to identify the causes that have led to the eventual presentation of their condition, whatever it is. I now want to give you all my years of experience so that you can decide for yourself what is relevant to you. I will then show you what to do about them.

Taking a history from you is quite a simple procedure. Since I wanted to find out as much as possible about you, I had to ask questions. Two questions I tried to ask early on were "What do you (the patient) want of me?" and "What do you want to achieve?" Some people with MS are so worn out, either by the condition itself or because of the treatment they have been given for it. They often told me they didn't want a cure, or didn't expect one. They merely wanted to feel better if possible, and be able to function better, not really expecting they could become symptom free.

So, what do you want? What do you hope to achieve by reading this book? The reason I ask this is because there are various ways you can help yourself. Perhaps all you want to do is as little as possible. Well, that's fine by me, and I will show you some of the simplest things you can do. Maybe, if you keep it simple to start with, you will gradually feel sufficiently improved and encouraged to try a little more. Perhaps you are searching the net for someone else, someone who you desperately want to help, but whom you think may be sceptical about, or resistant to, any natural suggestions. Their attitude may be "If it was worth trying, surely my doctor would have told me about it?" Perhaps your response should be something like "He is so busy trying to help so many sick people that he can't possibly have time to learn about everything".

Having asked you what you want, I started with the situation you had come to me about. I naturally asked about your MS, how it affected you at present, what symptoms you had, possibly any pain. What was the most important thing you wanted dealing with now? Did you currently have any symptoms of your MS, or were you in a remission stage of a relapsing and remitting type? Interestingly enough, some patients I saw had been told they had MS, possibly because of an attack of optic neuritis or other symptoms that had now cleared up, an MRI scan or a lumbar puncture, yet they didn't feel unwell. They had been told that they needed a particular form of treatment to try to prevent another attack occurring, which might make them feel unwell, so they wondered if there was anything else they could do. Each person must be treated as an individual and their own problem resolved.

How It All Started

I then went through how things started. What was the first indication of a problem in you? How did it all begin? How did you first notice something wrong? What were you doing at the time? Where were you? Were you under any particular degree of stress at the time, or had you been for some time before it all began? What did you do when you noticed the first problem? Did the first sign change in any way, for example with your monthly cycle, if you are a woman?

How soon did you consult a doctor after you first suspected something was wrong? If it was quite some time later, to what extent had things altered by then? Had any symptom become worse or changed in any way? Had any other changes occurred by then? Were you or was anyone else able to notice any changes in you?

Tell me about what happened if you went to hospital. I appreciate I occasionally saw a person who suspected he or she might have MS, possibly because a relative with MS started the same way, so had not yet consulted anyone else, but the vast number of patients I saw had already been to see their own General Practitioner and/ or someone in the local hospital in the first instance.

Did you have an MRI scan or any other tests such as a lumbar puncture? How did you cope? How long ago was all that? Did any of the tests hurt or upset you in any way? If you had a lumbar puncture, did it affect you in any way and what has happened to your symptoms since then? If you think they were affected by it, have they settled down? Have you been given a specific diagnosis? Do you understand what it means? Have you been told what is likely to happen in the long term?

The above questions applied to you mainly if you were in the early stages of your MS, and you wanted more information about what may well happen to you and what you should do. You may want help with decisions you have to make, but I cannot tell you what to do. You have to make these decisions yourself. I don't know you. I don't know how you think. I don't know just how your symptoms affect you. No one can. Only you can. I don't know your particular circumstances. In a later chapter, I have provided questions you need answering for you to make the right decisions for yourself.

If you are one of the many patients I saw who have been through a whole range of tests and been told there is little that can be done to stop you deteriorating in the long run, although a drug might minimise some of your symptoms, I need to know what treatment you have been recommended to follow, and what your attitude is to following that advice. You may still have a lot of questions to ask and decisions to make.

If you have decided you don't want any more treatment from orthodox medicine, or you want to know what you can do if you decide not to have any more, it has made you feel ill or your MS has become worse (which you believe is the result of the treatment you have been given) or you may have been told there is nothing to help you at this stage, please read on as there are many ways of helping yourself. All of this is detailed in the treatment chapter.

Although I try to remember to ask everyone what the first indication was that something was not quite right, it may not be particularly important, but sometimes it is. For example, some people become aware that something is wrong, or they first feel a burning sensation or a patch of numbness in a particular area. This suggests the possibility that the shingles virus may be involved. More about that later. Very often, however, something almost incidental may cause the first symptom or sign to appear. But, if you remember from my overall introduction, things have probably been building up in you for quite a long time, so what the final straw was that started symptoms appearing is often not particularly important. Many doctors believe that any medical condition probably started to develop in you at least five years before the first symptom was apparent.

How Good Is Your Immune System?

Sometimes the specific problem started after a period of illness, like flu', which may have somehow affected your immune system. To be fair, an infection can stimulate the immune system, but sometimes it overwhelms it, depending on the nature and duration of the infection, how often one has occurred, and possibly the state of the immune system at the time. To be honest, there is something about the immune system that I don't understand at present. In my extensive experience, MS patients do not appear to succumb to infections more than the average person. But what is a 'normal amount' of infections. Most people, let alone MS patients, have had many courses of antibiotics in their lifetime, something I will discuss at a later stage because it could have a major bearing on the development of MS in my opinion.

Where you were at the time of onset doesn't often indicate anything in particular. A patient once told me, however, that she noticed a slightly numb area on an arm in a shower in a hotel where she had stayed a number of times. The hotel, however, was associated with a number of visits on behalf of her company, the whole situation being particularly stressful. That gave me a clue to looking at levels of stress and their effect upon her body. While I may have my pet theories about the cause of MS, I am aware that there may be many causes, and probably more than one in a particular person.

What someone does when they first develop a symptom of sorts varies from person to person. This doesn't necessarily only apply to MS patients. Symptoms can affect anyone. If they are bad enough, some people go into a state of panic, some go into a state of denial, but the majority consults their General Practitioner as soon as an appointment can be made. Even that can result in an enormous range of what happens next and what the patient's reaction to it was. I like to write it all down, because sometimes it helps to clarify something about the person's personality. In any case, patients usually like to recount the story of what happened around this time, often because of a particular experience.

Pre-Menstrual Symptoms
    In a pre-menstrual woman, symptoms of any sort can change with her menstrual cycle. Breast cysts are quite common in the days leading up to a period, as is breast swelling, breast tenderness, general fluid retention and mood swings. To me, pre-menstrual problems of any sort are a strong indicator of a dominance of oestrogen relative to progesterone, and many women have told me their MS symptoms became worse in the days before the onset of their period, only to settle down when the period started.
    Let me explain this further. Once again, understanding the normal is most important for realising why things have gone wrong and, just as important, what to do about them. Clearly if you are a man, this next part will not be relevant to you, but you might find it interesting to read anyway.
    Although women's menstrual cycles vary somewhat, for the sake of simplicity I will describe a 'classical' twenty-eight day cycle, taking the start of a cycle as the first day of the period. There are two main hormones we talk about, namely oestrogen (estrogen in USA) and progesterone. In fact oestrogen is at least three chemicals, oestrone (E1), oestradiol (E2) and oestriol (E3). Oestradiol is the best known of these three chemicals as a variety of it (such as oestradiol valerate) is present in most forms of the contraceptive pill and HRT. It is also important to be aware that oestradiol and oestrone are proliferative, which means they promote cellular development, while oestriol is anti-proliferative, so calms down cellular growth. Isn't nature clever in providing balancing hormones? But things can go wrong if the balance is lost. Progesterone, on the other hand is one chemical and is calming in its effects, similar to oestriol. For about the first seven days there are low levels of progesterone and oestrogen, but at roughly day 7, Follicle Stimulating Hormone (FSH) is produced in the brain which brings to complete maturity one egg (inside a Graafian follicle), and gradually ripens many others, their turn coming another month. At roughly day 14, the time of ovulation, another hormone is released from the brain called Leuteinising Hormone (LH), which instructs the Graafian follicle to release its egg for fertilisation. The Graafian follicle now starts to manufacture progesterone.
    Under normal circumstances, the levels of oestrogen may increase, level off or may even decline somewhat, but there is still more circulating oestrogen at this stage than in the first seven days, when levels are quite low. Progesterone's main job is to prepare the lining of the uterus (womb) for pregnancy, and levels of it should gradually rise to balance oestrogen. This balance between oestrogen and progesterone is particularly important. If a pregnancy does not occur, the levels of both oestrogen and progesterone drop towards the resting state at about day 26, a period starting two days later.
    If a woman is blessed with such an ideal physiological event, her monthly cycles come and go regularly. She knows exactly when her next period will start, because she has made a note of it in her diary, and all she is aware of before the next onset is the result of minor hormonal changes. None of this causes her any problems or makes her feel ill in any way, and she takes it all in her stride. She is aware of when she ovulates, so could plan a pregnancy any time she wanted to. She may already have done things this way.
    Unfortunately, very few women have such a simple cycle nowadays. Far too many women suffer pre-menstrual symptoms, such as breast tenderness or breast swelling, a whole variety of emotional symptoms, such as irritability, depression, bouts of crying, low self-esteem, insomnia and clumsiness, weight gain, sugar and

chocolate cravings, bloated abdomen, and sometimes thrush, to name but a few. The length and severity of these symptoms can vary considerably, sometimes lasting up to fourteen days before the onset of the next period. If she also has a bad time with her period itself, she can have three weeks out of every four feeling awful! I have met many such women, and I tell you, it is not difficult to sort out, and without drugs! So where do things go wrong? It is usually at around the time of ovulation. In fact a woman may not ovulate. If she doesn't ovulate, it means she probably doesn't release an egg or produce much progesterone, if any, from the Graafian follicle. That means that oestrogen is not balanced by progesterone, so she suffers from 'hyper-oestrogenism'. If a woman does not suffer from pre-menstrual symptoms, she might produce 30 or possibly even 40mg progesterone per day towards to end of her cycle. Incidentally, in a 'brilliant' pregnancy, when the woman feels absolutely fabulous and blooming, she might produce as much as 300 or even 400mg progesterone per day. So progesterone is good for you! It is interesting that there is much more oestriol, the calming oestrogen during pregnancy, and far less of the other two oestrogens.

Oestrogen's job is to make her a woman, a natural female capable of reproducing the human species. This means that oestrogen is responsible for developing her breasts, ovaries and womb. As there are oestrogen receptors on all the cells of a woman, including brain cells, oestrogen makes her think and behave like a woman.

The problem is that, whereas a woman needs her oestrogen, too much oestrogen is not good for her, and if it is not balanced by progesterone towards the end of a cycle, the symptoms of hyper-oestrogenism, namely premenstrual symptoms, occur. If one of her female organs is particularly sensitive to the effects of too much oestrogen, then that organ will be stimulated or developed a little bit too much every month. Hence the variety of symptoms she can be aware of at the time.

Time and time again I pick up this story when taking a comprehensive history from a woman, whatever her medical condition. It can certainly apply to a woman with MS. The information is all there, although no one else has thought of considering it. Unfortunately doctors are mostly not interested in why a woman has her problems unless he specialises in them or she specifically consults him because of them.

Some post-menopausal women do not remember suffering in this way, but when I ask them about any operations, they often say they had a hysterectomy because of fibroids. This means they also had oestrogen dominance, but the effect was mainly on their womb. Others tell me of a history of polycystic ovaries, so their ovaries were the main target. Remember too much oestrogen means the balance of the three oestrogens is in favour of oestradiol and oestrone versus oestriol, and out of balance with progesterone.

Consider then what happens to a post-menopausal woman. Her monthly cycles have stopped, so she is not ovulating, she is not releasing an egg because she is not producing a Graafian follicle, so she is not making progesterone. Yet, as her monthly cycles stop, she can still manufacture oestrogen from the fat of her body and her adrenal glands. So, once again, she is potentially in an oestrogen dominant state.

You may think this is the end of the story, but it isn't, because the environment in which we all live is being polluted by xeno-oestrogens, or chemicals that have oestrogen-like activity. These come from plastics and the plasticisers they release, petrochemicals, pesticides and a whole host of chemicals in common use today. Also millions of women are taking pharmaceutical drugs of the contraceptive pill and HRT who urinate every day, which gradually reaches water tables. The water in London is said to be recycled many times, and people drink it!

What I am trying to point out is that, if I were to pick up these points in a woman's history, who also happens to have MS, it may be necessary to balance her hormones directly, usually using progesterone cream, although hormonal imbalances can often disappear with a change of eating habits. Nevertheless, helping a woman to feel much better in this respect, i.e. get rid of her annoying pre-menstrual symptoms, when no one else has bothered to do anything about them, encourages her to believe that following other recommendations of mine may well help her MS to improve. Besides, she may have said her MS symptoms become worse during her pre-menstrual build up, so it is perfectly possible her hormonal imbalances are playing a significant role in her MS.

When Do Symptoms Occur?

If you have symptoms that are not normally associated with your MS, the question about whether such symptoms are better or worse at any time of day can suggest quite a lot of ideas. If your symptoms are worse in the morning, what makes them better? Do they feel better after a cup of tea or coffee, for example? If they do, it suggests to me that you may be addicted to the tea or the coffee, or possibly the milk or sugar you may add. Over night is the longest time you are without your 'fix', so, by the morning, you are suffering from withdrawal symptoms, and they can affect you quite badly, and in a way you might not suspect. While this may be adversely affecting your MS, it may not be as directly involved as you thought. However, the fact that it is having any effect upon you is worth doing something about.

Do some of your symptoms feel better if you have breakfast? If so, you could be suffering from low blood sugar, or something in it is having the same effect I have just described for tea or coffee. If your symptoms feel worse after breakfast, you could be reacting to something you ate then, remembering that, again, you have not had that same food for a number of hours, i.e. over night. Even if you eat that food a number of times during the day, a period of overnight avoidance followed by the first 'challenge' of the day can produce symptoms from that food that might not occur when you eat it later in the day.

Be a detective on yourself. If there is anything slightly unusual about certain symptoms, see if you can analyse when they occur, what makes them better or worse or has any effect upon them in any way. Remember, there has to be a reason, even if it can sometimes be difficult to work it out. If a murder has been committed, the police detective knows someone did it, even if he has difficulty in identifying the culprit. Be aware that I am interested in the whole of you, not just what you think are problems of your MS. As I will be recommending that you change your eating habits if you have not already done so, doing some detective work on yourself may help to identify certain foods that you ought to avoid, which may also be of value in your approach to healing yourself of your MS.

It is important to remember that foods can cause symptoms and avoiding the same foods can also cause the same symptoms, so it can be very difficult to analyse any reactions. So, if you are suspicious of any food, leave it out of your diet for a couple of weeks and see if you feel any different. That is the only real way to tell if a food is not good for you or not.

I remember a man with MS many years ago telling me that the diet that I recommended to him for his MS completely cured the migraines he had been suffering from for as long as he could remember. This then had an amazing effect upon his attitude towards his MS. Without the migraines he felt he had a better chance of sorting the MS out. He found he had the energy to start to do something for himself. More to the point, since all the GPs in the practice and two Consultants he had seen had not been able to help his migraines, but I had, he felt that my simple approach towards his MS might not only be worth trying, but might actually work.

Lumbar Puncture

Having worked through these starting points, I then find out what happened. Not many patients have a lumbar puncture nowadays because of the use of MRI scans. Did you have one? A lumbar puncture helps your doctor to make, or confirm, a diagnosis of MS, although I don't think it helps him to decide on what he considers from his experience to be the most appropriate treatment. Have you undergone any treatment yet?

If you have had some treatment, how did it affect you? Did you cope with it well, or did it make you feel unwell in any way? Is there more of the same treatment to come, or is a new course of treatment being planned? Are you unsure whether to start the new course or not? Has your specialist suggested a new, possibly experimental, drug that he has been asked to try on some of his MS patients? Do you want some advice on how to make the right decision for you? If so, move to the chapter on decisions in due course.

Decisions To Be Made

If you haven't had a lumbar puncture yet and are trying to decide whether to have one or not, I suggest you also move to the chapter on Decisions, where I will try to help you decide what to do. This applies also to any decisions you have to make about whether to have an operation, or have any sort of treatment. There I will show you the questions you need to ask your specialist about the treatments he has recommended. I will also show you how to make the right decisions for yourself, in relation to your own MS and its severity. I will also ask you some simple questions about what you want in life and what you expect from your MS treatment. However, I will not tell you what to do, as it is your condition, your body and your life. You have to decide for yourself.

May I suggest you now read chapter 3, because whatever your diagnosis, I would go through your history in exactly the same way. Remember, I am assuming you have now developed MS because a series of circumstances in your life have gradually overwhelmed your body's ability to cope with them. If between us we can identify them, it is reasonable to try to do something about them and so reverse the effect they may have had on your body's metabolism. In that way, we are doing something about why you have developed MS.

What makes people feel better often includes eating regularly, lots of fruit and vegetables, drinking lots of quality water, having plenty of rest, avoiding stress, a holiday in a dry sunny area or simply the summer months. It all tells a story, so think carefully about this one. Feeling better in a dry sunny place can be because of getting away from moulds, which are so prevalent in many people's houses and gardens, or the sun may generate more vitamin D in your skin. Most people spend far too little time in the sun, partially for fear of developing skin cancer. Did you know that exposure to sunlight (and possibly therefore absorbing more vitamin D in your skin) has been shown in some studies to be protective of developing cancer. There is a Canadian MS Researcher who believes MS will one day be re-defined as a vitamin

D deficiency disease. While I listen to what he says, it is certainly not the cause of MS. I have helped many MS patients without doing anything about vitamin D.

Fatigue

Fatigue is a very common complaint of anyone who is unwell in any way, not only in MS patients. It is also one of the best indicators that the approach you are following is working or not. If my advice has been correct, your levels of energy are almost always one of the first things to improve. If they don't, I suspect I have yet to put my finger on what is of greater importance for you.

When I was a medical student, I spent some of my time learning at the 'Fatigue Clinic'. It was truly fascinating at the diagnoses that were eventually made in a wide range of people. What I really learned, however, was that fatigue could be a symptom of virtually anything. I have learned a lot more since then, and am aware that I could now teach at that clinic many things that were not even thought of at the time. What is surprising, however, is that some MS patients who have very severe symptoms do not complain of fatigue at all.

In mainstream medicine, fatigue can be caused by anaemia and low thyroid activity, but, when these are not found to be the explanation, because all tests are said to be 'normal', the symptom may be put down to stress. It is seldom considered that some prescribed drug might be the cause. In my experience, however, 'normal' blood tests often miss the point, basically because the important tests have not been done. A measurement of haemoglobin may be perfectly acceptable even to me, indicating no anaemia, but iron stores, as measured by serum ferritin, can show a different picture. Even then, doctors often accept a level of serum ferritin that I do not accept. Fortunately a paper was published in the British Medical Journal (Verdon, F. et al. Iron Supplementation for unexplained fatigue in non-anaemic women: double blind randomised placebo-controlled trial. BMJ, Volume 326, 24 May 2003, page 1124) that totally agreed with what I have been saying for years, that is that a level under 50mcg/l is not good enough. Iron supplementation helped improve the fatigue.

It is possible to enumerate all the symptoms that a deficiency of a particular vitamin or mineral might produce, but you will never find all of those features occurring in one person. This certainly applies to iron. Unfortunately most doctors believe that there is no shortage of iron if the haemoglobin is 'normal'. What they have forgotten (or may never have known in the first place), is that iron is not only required to make haemoglobin, but is also required for myoglobin (muscle globin), the immune system, normal hair follicle functioning, and a host of other minor metabolic functions.

The Thyroid

When it comes to the thyroid, most NHS laboratories will only test TSH (Thyroid Stimulating Hormone produced in the brain), assuming that, if the level is within the laboratory's reference range, there is no need to do any more testing. If everything is functioning normally, there is a nice balance between TSH and the production of hormones by the thyroid gland itself. It is rather like the thermostat in your water heater at home. If the water is hot, the thermostat turns off. If the temperature of the water falls, the water heater is turned on by the thermostat. The TSH/thyroid system is similar in this way, there being a constant feedback mechanism between the two.

One problem that this system produces is that laboratories establish their own reference ranges, assuming that the method of analysis they use is comparable to that used in other laboratories. Separate from that, there is a degree of controversy about the ideal level of TSH, and in the opinion of many doctors, most laboratories set it too high. Recently one of the American medical organisations very much involved in thyroid health dropped its upper level of TSH, and I am told this meant that overnight about two million Americans were suddenly accepted as hypothyroid, whereas the day before they were considered as hypochondriacs or merely fussing about nothing.

This, however, all to often totally misses the point as far as I am concerned. It is assumed that the thyroid gland is responding to the TSH, but, in my experience, this is often not the case. In principle, if the thyroid gland is not responding normally, the level of TSH will go up very high to try to force the thyroid to respond, which presumably it cannot do. In addition, when I have done three 'thyroid function tests' I have often found the TSH and Free T4 to be comfortably within an acceptable reference range, but the Free T4 is not being converted into Free T3, which is probably the active component. So a 'normal' TSH is missing a low Free T3, which means the patient is effectively hypothyroid. There is another fact that needs to be considered, which no amount of blood testing can reveal, which can certainly occur with perfectly respectable levels of TSH, Free T4 and Free T3 that is cellular receptors. For circulating hormones to work, they have to attach themselves to receptors on the surface of cells. In fact, all cells have countless receptors for countless chemicals, each receptor being totally specific for a certain hormone or other chemical. The 'sensitivity' of these receptors can be increased, decreased, blocked, damaged, deleted or interfered with in all sorts of ways by all sorts of situations, rendering the information purely from standard blood tests to be of little value.

What I'm really saying is that if full blood tests for thyroid function are reported as being ok, it does not necessarily mean that you will not benefit from thyroid support. Indeed, every patient who follows the very extreme Gerson Therapy for cancer is automatically put onto whole thyroid extract, (which contains the 52 or so hormones your thyroid gland normally produces), on the assumption that patients will benefit from it. If nature produces so many different chemicals, I presume there is a purpose to them all, even if we don't yet understand their importance. In addition, I also prefer the whole thyroid extract as I feel it 'feeds' the gland, because, in the end, I will want to get you off it, something that can be difficult to achieve if you are put onto the usual thyroxine that your doctor prescribes if you are found to be genuinely hypothyroid.

Again, what I am also trying to say is that some MS patients, certainly those who complain of a degree of fatigue, might benefit from a trial of thyroid support, as the nature and causes of their MS and any treatment they may have had may have suppressed the thyroid system or blocked or damaged the receptors. This in turn means that they are metabolically underactive, which in turn means that their body's ability to fight back is less efficient than it should be. It is amazing how often I saw an MS patient for the first time, who had very little energy to fight or follow my recommendations, who became a totally different person with a totally different attitude to their MS, simply for a small supporting dose of whole thyroid. To me it is important to repeat that I give patients a supporting thyroid dose. As a side thought, applying my 'common sense' rule, it always amazes me that the activity of the thyroid gland is seldom checked if a patient feels tired after having had radiotherapy applied to his neck because of cancer of his oesophagus (gullet). To me it is obvious and inevitable that the thyroid gland will be damaged by the treatment. It is impossible for it not to be; yet it is seldom considered.

Occasionally when a person is put on whole thyroid, they don't respond very well, or may even feel a little worse. This could be because they don't actually need the supplement, or possibly they are reacting to something in the tablet, such as the lactose filler. However, the most likely reason is because they have an adrenal insufficiency, and, merely supporting the thyroid system, reveals the adrenal problem. In my experience, when one hormonal system is adversely affected, all hormonal systems are likely to be affected to a degree. So, all the hormonal systems need to be considered. When I support the thyroid, I nowadays always support the adrenals.

Other Causes of Fatigue

Low blood sugar can cause fatigue, but that is not difficult to identify, usually because the patient feels less tired after eating. Fatigue generally improves if I am able to identify the correct diet for a patient to follow. Caffeine withdrawal can cause fatigue, so, if a person agrees to stop caffeine all together, I always advise them that they are likely to feel possibly more tired for a few days to begin with, after which they should bounce back up and feel a lot better than they have felt for a long time.

If your adrenal glands have become exhausted by prolonged stress, fatigue can result. Most people are aware of this, and need a period of recuperation after a significantly stressful period. Inflammation and pain can also cause fatigue. Patients suffering from rheumatoid arthritis very commonly complain of fatigue, but they are also often anaemic. The inflammation seems to cause anaemia.

Poor Sleeping Pattern

Not getting a good night's sleep can leave you tired the next day, as mums with young babies are all too well aware. Some MS patients are in pain, develop spasms at night, or their legs are so stiff or useless they can't turn over in bed to find a more comfortable position, so sleeping is very difficult, which is why they are often given something to help them sleep. This is very understandable from their doctor's point of view, but the drugs need to be metabolised by the liver, which may already be under great stress.

Pain and caffeine can switch off your production of melatonin, a chemical that is produced by the pineal gland in your brain. Some doctors prescribe large doses of melatonin to MS patients, as a good night's sleep induced by melatonin is detoxifying. A doctor in New York found that many of his MS patients were depressed, so he measured their levels of melatonin at 2.00 am and found them to be very low. When he treated them with melatonin, it helped their depression but not their MS.

But don't forget geopathic stress. When a new patient tells me they don't sleep very well, one possible explanation is geopathic stress. If that is found to be present and is dealt with, it is amazing how much better some people sleep. If you don't know what geopathic stress is, obtain a copy of Rolf Gordon's book "Are You Sleeping In A Safe Place?♥" The title says it all.

Do you remember your dreams? If you don't, or your dream recall is rather poor, you may well have a vitamin B6 deficiency, although some sleeping tablets may produce a false response to this question. I can remember dreams I had a few days ago, and can certainly recall the previous night's dream throughout the next day. Some doctors put their patients on increasing doses of vitamin B6 until their dream recall returns.

Thirst

Thirst is usually a sign of dehydration, but not always. Some people drink a lot of water, yet seem to be permanently thirsty. Certainly too much caffeine as tea, coffee, chocolate and cola drinks, as well as diuretics prescribed by your doctor, can cause dehydration. Every cup of coffee you drink will cause you to eliminate a cup and a bit of fluid. You drink the coffee because you feel thirsty, which it may well help to begin with because of the liquid. But, in the end, you lose more than you gain. I always ask MS patients to give up all forms of caffeine, as it can irritate the bladder. Some MS patients have such problems with their bladder that all car journeys have to be organised around available toilets. If easing this problem is the only thing I do, it is worthwhile for some MS patients.

I encourage all patients, whatever their named condition, to make their fluid intake to be from water as much as possible, perhaps around two litres per day. Certain herbal teas can be very valuable to improve the functioning of the liver or kidneys. Incidentally, I am not happy that you drink water direct from the tap. Water Authorities do a remarkably good job to make tap water suitable for drinking, when most water use is for other purposes such as watering your garden and plants and washing your clothes or car. I would prefer you to at least remove the chlorine, using some sort of water filter, or perhaps reverse osmosis, which is about the only way I know of totally removing fluoride and a host of undesirable chemicals, such as pesticides, hormones and lead, for example. However, it removes the valuable minerals as well, so they should be put back in.

In the meantime, while it is important to limit your intake of sodium salt, in favour of potassium, make sure you don't let your salt intake fall too low, especially if you sweat a lot for any reason, i.e. if you live in a hot and humid country. Not having enough salt in your body can make you feel tired and lethargic. Your body's salt content is approximately half way between rainwater and seawater, so you need a certain amount of salt, but not too much.

As I have already said, some people's problems, especially fatigue, are caused by adrenal exhaustion. Complete destruction of the adrenal glands was more common in the past when they were infected by tuberculosis, leading to a condition called Addison's Disease. The effect was an inability to retain salt in the body because of the lack of a certain adrenal hormone called aldosterone, although all of the adrenal steroids have some salt-retaining function. Anyone who is put onto modern steroids by their doctor because of asthma, rheumatoid arthritis or a brain tumour, knows only too well how they retain salt in many parts of their body, so showing the powerful effect adrenal steroids have on the control of salt balance in the body.

Catarrh

A history of catarrh is classical of a milk intolerance. I know tonsils and adenoids were taken out far more often in the past than they are nowadays, but antibiotics have changed that to a considerable extent. Nevertheless, I think it is unlikely that young patients were operated on for no reason at all. If you have such a history, therefore, I consider it likely you have had a milk intolerance all your life. Your body may have tolerated it to a degree, but adding that to all the other things that your history is identifying, perhaps you can see why eventually your body gave up the unequal fight.

General Aches

Aching in muscles and joints is usually caused by a food intolerance, classical rheumatoid arthritis often responding to avoiding foods of the deadly nightshade family, namely potatoes, tomatoes, aubergines (eggplants in USA) and peppers, as well as tobacco. But caffeine and animal milks and animal milk products can also be implicated. Then there can be the odd idiosyncratic reaction to a food or drink you could never suspect, nor could you ever identify it by direct observation of what you eat. It requires either a blood test (such as the Alcat TestTM) to suggest the culprit or a process of elimination and challenge, as described in my book 'Conquering Cystitis'♥.

Lower backache, however, is often a sign of a magnesium deficiency. Anything that goes into spasm could be caused by a magnesium deficiency. Calcium is required for muscles to contract, magnesium for them to relax, so there may be an imbalance between the two. A magnesium deficiency can cause other parts of the body to go into spasm, so could be the cause, or one of the causes of, asthma, constipation, cold hands and feet (Raynaud's Syndrome) and migraines. Many an MS patient has found intravenous magnesium, along with other nutrients, to eradicate muscular spasms.

An imbalance between calcium and magnesium may be caused by consuming too many milk products. I accept there are many people who do not agree with me, even if there are many who do. This is one of a number of controversial subjects that I and other like-minded colleagues have discussed over the years from our own and our patients' observations. I recognise that they are controversial issues at present, and therefore I want to make it clear that they are my opinions, but I am perfectly happy for you to disagree with me if you want to. I merely want to open your eyes to a possible alternative explanation for a whole number of things, for you to chose whether to accept them or not.

Sensory Symptoms

I have seen more patients suffering from multiple sclerosis than any other medical condition, and I am aware that many of them complain of pins and needles and other sensory symptoms in various parts of their body. In my experience, such sensory symptoms can indicate a vitamin B12 deficiency in the nervous tissue (as blood tests usually do not suggest a level below the local laboratory's reference range, many doctors refuse to try the effect of vitamin B12 injections on MS patients) or be an unusual presentation of the chicken pox/shingles virus. Cold fingers and toes can sometimes feel like pins and needles and can be a sign of a magnesium deficiency.

Palpitations

The heart is particularly sensitive to the effects of caffeine, especially in the presence of a magnesium deficiency, so any abnormal heartbeat could be explained in this way. Some dentists believe that mercury from mercury amalgam fillings can cause palpitations and other heart irregularities and abnormalities.

Abdominal Symptoms/Constipation

I could spend hours discussing the significance of abnormal bowel functioning.

Many patients tell me they open their bowels once every two weeks! I have heard of even more extreme cases than that. In my opinion, and that of most naturopaths, we should open our bowels at least three times per day, i.e. one meal in and one meal out, provided there is enough fibre overall in the diet (and possibly enough fat. Eskimos have no bowel problems, yet their diet is entirely from fish and fatty meat and no fibre), and the diet does not contain items that specifically cause constipation. In my experience, animal milks and milk products are a very common cause of constipation, goat's and sheep's milk sometimes being ok. Patients often have clues from their own experience what causes them to become constipated, but don't take them very seriously.

Naturopaths often say there is no point in doing anything until the bowels are working properly. In many ways I would agree. If you have had stubborn bowels for many years, you probably have a layer of impacted matter/faeces lining your intestines. This matter can harbour toxic chemicals, parasites and heavy metals. It can also prevent nutrients from gaining access to the body via the bowel wall, as well as inflame the bowel wall itself. Sometimes, when someone has a colonic irrigation, the equivalent of a bicycle 'inner tube' is eventually expelled, with all the bowel indentations visible. Can you imagine what that has done over the years?

Many people don't even realise they are constipated, since they have only opened their bowels two or three times a week for as long as they can remember. Even those who open their bowels once a day don't realise that that is not often enough. Can you remember what a baby does? Food going in at the top end leads to an almost immediate reaction at the other end! Unfortunately humans gradually lose this response mechanism over the years of not eating and drinking properly.

Hundreds of people have told me how much easier is has become to open their bowels when they give up such foods such as milk and milk products. For some people it can be quite difficult, as foods such as cheese have become virtually staple foods, and they can't imagine life without them. Be warned that I am likely to recommend some form of change in your diet when we get round to what I suggest you do to start helping yourself.

The importance of correctly functioning bowels cannot be overstated. There is a mass of scientific evidence that an unhealthy bowel can lead to an amazing variety of health problems. I am sure you have heard it said that "You are what you eat". However, I believe that that statement needs to be modified to "You are the result of what you absorb from what you eat". In fact this statement could possibly be modified to "You are what you fail to excrete from what you eat". Whichever is true, if you have an unhealthy bowel, you probably have the 'leaky gut syndrome'. You will absorb poorly some of the things that are good for you, and you will absorb other things that your body would prefer not to have to deal with.

As a result of a lifetime of eating the wrong things, which will vary from person to person, it is likely that most people will have developed a layer of impacted faeces in their bowels. This unwanted matter will not only partially block the absorptive layer of the mucous membrane (and damage it at the same time leading to the 'leaky gut syndrome'), but will also harbour parasites and other organisms, unwanted faecal material and a whole host of chemical residues that the body (in particular the liver) thought it had already eliminated. Some of these unwanted substances could sometimes be reabsorbed, so increasing the body's toxic load.

A Story

Many years ago, a patient told me that, before he had first come to see me, he had had a series of colonic irrigations. After the fifth, he passed a pebble that he remembered swallowing about thirty years earlier, when he was a child! Apart from his total amazement at his bowel's ability to hold onto such a thing for so long, it brought back memories of a childhood interest in pebbles, as their variety, colours and different shapes had always fascinated him. If they were dirty, he used to pop them in his mouth to clean them!

Diarrhoea and Bloating

If you suffer from loose stools, it is likely something is irritating your bowels. While this could be a parasite, it is more likely to be a food intolerance. A gluten sensitivity is high on the list of suspects, which means wheat, rye, oats and barley. However, if you have consumed a lot of sugar and white refined flour products over a lifetime, or had a certain amount (sometimes only one strong course) of antibiotics, you might be suffering from a fungal overgrowth within your bowel. While the thrush organism (candida albicans) may be primarily involved, with or without overt symptoms of thrush itself, there are many other fungal organisms that can cause these symptoms.

This whole process can be made worse by courses of steroids (including inhaled ones for asthma) and the contraceptive pill and HRT. Chemotherapy (and possibly radiotherapy) can destroy the friendly organisms within the bowel, allowing 'funguses' to proliferate, although it is rare for an MS patient also to have cancer. This situation is all the more likely if you have other fungal infections anywhere in your body, such as toe nails, athletes' foot, in your groin, between your buttocks or under your breasts, or you have been plagued by thrush, which is the bane of Gynaecologists' lives. Even dandruff can respond to an anti-fungal preparation called Nizoral shampoo, and sometimes psoriasis has a fungal origin. With a history such as this, I am likely to describe you as 'mouldy!'

Dry Skin

Dry skin often improves when patients cut out animal milks and products, but it can also indicate a zinc deficiency (which is important for your immune system, amongst other things) and a deficiency of essential fatty acids.

Mercury Amalgam Fillings/Dental Care

This is a controversial issue at present, simply because the majority of dentists and doctors haven't studied the evidence. It must be very hard to admit that how you have been treating patients all your life, i.e. filling their teeth with mercury amalgams, has, in fact, been wrong all along. Nevertheless, many dental colleagues all over the world have done just that. I used to prescribe pharmaceutical drugs when I was first qualified, as I had learned all about their value, tending to assume there was no other way, and that I would deal with any adverse effects when they occurred. I changed my mind and my practice many years ago, although I recognise that drugs have their place and value.

In terms of MS, it is clear to many of us that mercury, which is possibly the most toxic substance known to man after radioactive materials (and made about ten to one hundred times more toxic than lead, which no one considers safe is also involved), is implicated in MS. Studies by Professor Boyd Hayley in the USA have shown nerve endings literally shrivelling up in the presence of mercury. Mercury is undoubtedly a neuro-toxin. The difficulty is in convincing some doctors and dentists and some patients that the mercury amalgam fillings in their teeth are leaking sufficient mercury to get into the spinal fluid and cause their MS symptoms, especially as mercury amalgam replacement can be an expensive and tedious business. So far as I am aware, there is only one study that has shown that the spinal fluid level of MS patients has a higher level of mercury in them than a control group. This was carried out by a Swedish doctor who has MS herself, called Dr Brit Arhlrot Westerlund.

Mercury, and possibly other toxic metals, also seem to make funguses more virulent. It is very difficult to prove this point unequivocally to you as an individual. However, I want all my MS patients to have their mercury amalgam fillings replaced with a non-metallic alternative material, the work being done by a biologically trained dentist. I then need to chelate mercury from your tissues over a period of weeks or months. If you want to learn more about this, I would refer you to a number of books that have been written on the subject, some being much more forthright than others. The one I like is 'Menace in the Mouth'♥ by Dr. Jack Levenson.

In the middle of the 20th Century, Dr. Weston Price, an American dentist, travelled the world comparing the state of peoples' teeth in relation to the diet they ate. He made some amazing observations and wrote it all up in a book entitled 'Nutrition and Physical Degeneration'. In some respects the title is the wrong way round, because it seems to suggest that good nutrition leads to physical degeneration, which is exactly the opposite of what he found.

Dr. Price also made some most important additional observations, which were nearly lost to mankind, but which have been bravely resurrected by a colleague. I say bravely because he was a completely orthodox dentist who felt compelled to alert the world to the truth of Dr. Price's observations, especially as they made a mockery of all he had taught and practised for most of his life. What Dr. Price discovered was that root fillings always become infected, because it is impossible to do one in a totally sterile way. He also extracted root filled teeth from ill patients and inserted the tooth under the skin of an unfortunate experimental animal. The result was that the human patient's condition improved, while the poor animal gradually became sick, developing all the problems the human used to have! However, this situation may have a modern outcome, as some of my dental colleagues are cleaning out roots with hydrogen peroxide before inserting the root filling, and modern materials may be much better for the whole process. In the chapter on treatment for MS, I will discuss the use of Chlorine dioxide which I believe may in the long run be capable of getting round the need to have teeth extracted if they have root fillings.

Over the years, various open-minded dentists have explained to me that certain teeth are on acupuncture meridians relative to certain organs of the body. Dentists I have referred patients to have found, on a number of occasions, bad teeth, infected cavities or root fillings on acupuncture meridians related to certain areas affecting an MS patient's symptoms, such as the bladder. Presumably, as acupuncture treatment somehow works through subtle energies, the bad energies from the dental point of view add to the total load causing the symptoms. You can see, therefore, why it is important to find a dentist specially trained in such matters.

Weight Fluctuations

Many people, whatever their diagnosis, say their weight can fluctuate quite considerably. This is quite common in the pre-menstrual phase, when some women can put on 7 or 8lb (around 3.5kg) in a matter of days, losing it all as soon as the period commences. Other people are aware that their weight can change all too easily, but they don't really know why. In my experience such an observation is most likely to be caused by one or more food intolerances, so that a change in the person's diet can eliminate it. Men, by and large, however, tend to put weight on slowly as they grow older, and tend not to vary much over a short time, like many women can.

Weight fluctuations apart, it has been my experience that MS sufferers are rarely what one would normally consider to be overweight, although some may carry a little more weight than is wise. I could have counted the number of genuinely overweight MS patients on the fingers of my two hands out of over 9,000 MS patients I saw. I'm not sure of the reason for that, but there must be a reason. It could be something to do with thyroid metabolism, but somehow I think it goes far deeper than that and may be due a low-grade chronic infection that may also be part of their MS cause. I am told that the core temperature of MS patients is slightly higher than normal, but I have never had the chance to check that.

Weight fluctuations can involve both weight gain and weight loss. If weight gain is your problem, you are probably retaining fluid as your reaction to specific foods, which need to be identified and eliminated. What I have found over the years is that that fluid can be retained in virtually any organ of the body, thereby producing virtually any symptom you can think of. If it is retained in the brain, it can cause mood swings or depression. It can cause constipation if retained in the bowel wall, arthritis if in the joints, asthma if in the lungs, etc. Unfortunately there is no one method of identifying these food reactions that is perfect for everyone, but I have explained the various methods in the chapter on treatment, chapter 4.

Weight loss, or an inability to put on weight when eating a reasonable diet, usually suggests to me some form of malabsorption syndrome. The foods most likely involved are the gluten grains, namely wheat, rye, oats and barley. Only by avoiding such foods for at least four weeks will you discover whether they are the culprits or not.

Tonsillitis

One of the commonest childhood conditions that I come across is many episodes of tonsillitis, with or without ear problems. Some children suffer very badly from the whole range of problems, have grommets put in their ears and are plied with antibiotics, while others seem to get away with only minor, but annoying, periodic episodes that keep them off school for a few days. How they were treated usually depended upon the attitude of their parents and their general practitioner. What such a history suggests to me is a milk intolerance.

Many years ago I was invited to be in the audience of a television programme discussing the work of Dr. Harry Morrow-Brown, the Derby Consultant Physician who started up the Midlands Asthma and Allergy Research Association. There were many general practitioners in the audience and every one of them agreed that, if a child failed to thrive in any way, the first thing to do was take it off animal milks and animal milk products, especially from the cow. Sometimes goats' or sheep's products were subsequently found to be acceptable, but often not. We all agreed that the child was likely to do well from then on, and we had all observed it on many occasions.

If you have such a history, what I am really saying is that you have probably had a milk intolerance all your life. Can you imagine what that may have done to your body all these years, and what it may still be doing? Of course, if you have MS, it will be particularly important to avoid milk and its products in my experience. This has been thoroughly researched by Professor Jane Plant in her book 'Your Life In Your Hands'♥, but she talks about breast and prostate cancers. She explains all about the myriad chemicals and hormones that are present in these products. While organic produce may be better in this respect, I do not recommend them, especially in the first instance.

Childhood Illnesses

Having clarified the various 'other symptoms' (which, later on, may be the first signs that the approach you have decided to follow is actually working), I may go back in time and look at your history in childhood. Which childhood illnesses did you have? Chicken pox, mumps, measles, whooping cough, German measles? You might ask why these could be important, so let me explain.

I think it is generally accepted that, if you suffered from chicken pox as a child, this virus can come out as shingles later on in life, usually when some sort of stress occurs. However, most doctors have what I would call a narrow attitude to shingles, i.e. only accept that a person is suffering from shingles if there is a painful rash that follows the line of a nerve distribution, like over the eye or across a shoulder. In addition the rash should not cross the midline.

There is something else that needs to be considered about the chicken pox/ shingles story, and that is that, having had chicken pox as a child, it would appear that your immune system has not eliminated the virus from your body. It hangs around in the anterior nerve roots of your spinal cord to come out as shingles at a later stage, when you are under stress. How many other infections does your immune system fail to irradiate? In the end too many infections may overwhelm your system.

My attitude is to consider the possibility that the shingles virus may be presenting in an unusual way. If it is not 'typical' it is not considered to be relevant by most doctors. When I gave a talk about my work to a large group people in London a number of years ago I made the statement that, in my opinion, the shingles virus was somehow involved in patients with various forms of cancer and MS. During the break I was surrounded by people who asked how I had come to that conclusion. So I asked them what their experience had been, only to be told by many of them that they had had either shingles or chicken pox shortly, or a reasonable time, before the first signs of their condition appeared. So I told them that, as so many people with various conditions I had seen had told me of their experiences (because I had asked them about it), that that was how I had reached such a conclusion. I considered it possible that the virus may somehow have adversely affected the local immunity of their breast tissue with breast cancer patients.

It is interesting that many of my MS patients said that their GP had suggested the possibility of shingles, when they consulted him or her about the initial symptoms they were suffering from. As they had been complaining of a numb patch, or a sensation of pins and needles, somewhere on their body, such an idea was not at all unreasonable, and could well have been the case. However, if the symptom were on the body, it often crossed the midline, so your ordinary GP said it couldn't be shingles. But why not? Why do things have to be exactly correct for a particular diagnosis to be made?

Once the idea has occurred to me, I consider whether it might be relevant to every patient I see. Just because I don't pick up, in the history, any specific evidence of a viral or other infective involvement, it doesn't mean one isn't relevant. After all, sometimes when a patient with multiple sclerosis has an acute attack of symptoms, he or she is admitted to hospital, where a urinary tract infection is found to have been the cause, yet there were no symptoms of that infection at all. When the patient is given the appropriate antibiotics, the symptoms usually clear.

In my attempts to identify what causes any condition in anyone, I need to consider the unusual or the unexpected. In terms of cancer, it is now accepted that the Human Papilloma Virus is the cause of cancer of the cervix in many women with the condition (and probably all of them if the proof could be obtained) and they probably had had a wart or verruca somewhere on their skin at some time in their life, I see no reason why that virus might not 'surface' later on in life and partially cause the cancer. Yet the idea that the Human Papilloma Virus is implicated in female cancers is a comparatively new idea. Perhaps mainstream medicine is beginning to take an interest in causes. To be fair to my mainstream medical colleagues we haven't proved this connection, but since we can treat any of these 'infections' homoeopathically, it is not a problem for us. If the treatment is not needed, it won't matter anyway, or do any harm. Chlorine dioxide♥ might also work against any infection.

So, staying with cancer for a while to get a point across, taking this whole thinking process forward logically to every patient, if a person has or has had testicular cancer, I am interested in their history of mumps. Is it not reasonable to consider that the mumps virus may be involved in their condition, in a way similar to the chicken pox/shingles story? I think it is worth considering, and, again, the treatment is by homoeopathy. If you now have lung cancer, did you have whooping cough or possibly tuberculosis, so that your lungs have been 'weakened' and have therefore become a 'target' for something to go wrong? And, back to MS, if you now have, or have had in the past, sensory symptoms, it seems perfectly logical to me to consider the possibility that the chicken pox/shingles virus may be playing a significant part in your condition.

There is now a considerable amount of evidence that we seem to 'accumulate' a lot of infections and toxic metals in our bodies over the years and that we don't seem to clear them totally. I have therefore come to the conclusion that our immune systems do not totally eradicate many infections, but rather bring them under control so that they no longer appear to be bothering us. However, if these 'under control infections' accumulate, as I believe they do, they may somehow 'break through' and become some sort of a problem, possibly overwhelming our immune system or overloading its watching brief, especially if we also accumulate a number of toxic substances such as lead and mercury or undesirable chemicals such as pesticides and plasticisers. It is my opinion and that of many like-minded doctors and scientists that the combination of all these either makes us ill according to our genetic weaknesses or hastens old age. After all, although we are all going to die in due course, old age coming on too early could be because we have done the wrong things, or not done the right things, for that much longer. Are you beginning to see my way of thinking? Did you have warts or verrucas at any time in your life? What infections have you ever had, including vaccinations of 'live' organisms? Did you have glandular fever, or were you suspected of it? Have you had any mystery illness at any time in your life? Could these now be accumulating and overwhelming your immune system?

In terms of 'infections', glandular fever could be an important one. Many people tell me they have 'not been the same' since that illness affected them. Some of my patients had it twice, sometimes taking six months or more to get back to somewhere near normal. Glandular fever seems to strip people of B vitamins, and, if a person catches it, B vitamins given at the time may well hasten their recovery and stop it being too severe. In any case, glandular fever seems to compromise the functioning of the liver. I will always give such a person a liver tonic at some stage to boost its workings, but, unfortunately, the usual liver function blood tests that your doctor can do rarely show up any abnormality. Far more sophisticated tests need to be done. Glandular fever can also be treated homoeopathically.

Other Infections

Various laboratories do a series of screening tests for different organisms, but, as there are so very many possible pathological organisms that could be making you ill, the very one that is causing your problems may not be included in the testing panel, unless you are going to pay for a complete range. Even then, just because an organism is identified in your blood, it doesn't automatically mean it is the one causing your illness.

Anyway, have you ever suffered from any other infections, such as gastroenteritis, infections picked up in other parts of the world, malaria, etc? Might you have parasites or worms in your bowels? You worm your pets once a year (and you touch and stroke them all the time and they may lick your face and hands), but you tend not to worm yourself at all! Yet such organisms can affect your bowels' ability to absorb nutrients.

Attending to such infections is not usually the first thing I consider, but I take a note of them when I first take the person's medical history, coming back to them usually at a later stage. However, when I start asking questions from childhood onwards, this is something that is not too difficult for people to remember, and they find quite easy to discuss. It then takes me on to other things. While I am asking about childhood illnesses, it seems logical to ask about any other 'infections' at the same time. I can then go back and ask more questions.

Operations

How many operations have you had? What were they for? How many general anaesthetics have you had? How well did you recover from any of them? Did you take a long time to recover from any of them, and are you taking longer to recover each time? The answers to all these questions tell me about your liver's ability to detoxify the chemicals of the anaesthetics.

Information from any operations you may have had done can be really quite revealing, and can identify something that you had forgotten about, or didn't think could be of interest to me. I have already talked about the significance of having your tonsils and/or adenoids out, but many people think that that used to be such a routine operation that they don't consider it worth mentioning, until I explain my approach to it and what it can signify. It's all about making connections with the information each patient provides. It really is medical detective work.

Having a hysterectomy for fibroids (did you know that the word hysterectomy basically means 'removal of the centre of female hysteria?) suggests oestrogen dominance to me, in relation to progesterone. Did you have your ovaries removed at the same time ("to avoid having to go back in again and to eliminate the risk of your developing cancer in your ovaries")? How old were you at the time? Were you put onto HRT? What form was it? Was it oestrogen only, as was likely since you could no longer have periods? What effect did it have upon you? If you didn't go onto HRT, did you suffer any sort of menopausal symptoms? How did you feel after that operation? Did things seem to go wrong for you from then onwards?

I've never found anything significant about having your appendix removed, although a classical case is clearly an indication of something. When I was a junior doctor we sometimes operated on obvious cases, and sometimes we did not, usually because we were so very tired. We would naturally keep an eye on the patient and be prepared to operate if things became urgent, but often, even though the diagnosis was not in any doubt, we would wait until the morning, only to find that the patient had recovered. I suppose keyhole surgery and having a peep inside through a laparoscope has changed things considerably.

Smoking

Clearly, if you smoke, you are significantly reducing your chances of overcoming your MS. The toxic chemicals produce free radicles in abundance, which not only damage any tissue in your body, but also squander your meagre nutrients, especially anti-oxidants such as vitamin C. Interestingly enough, when I ask patients what happens when they smoke a cigarette, especially if it is the occasional cigarette, they sometimes admit it actually makes them feel unwell in some way, yet they continue to smoke having not realised what it is doing to them.

I had an MS patient who seemed to stop improving, having become at least 50% better. When I next saw her I went through my history of her and noticed she had admitted to smoking occasionally when I first met her, so I made some sort of comment about smoking, basically assuming she had stopped. However she then told me that, although she seldom smoked now, she was aware that she could walk to the local pub fairly easily, but that she couldn't walk home so well if she had a couple of cigarettes while there. From a dietary point of view, that made me suggest that she avoid certain foods that are in the same biological classification (the Deadly Nightshade Family) with tobacco, namely potatoes, tomatoes, aubergines (eggplant in USA) and peppers. This group of foods is often worth avoiding for a while if your symptoms involve stiff muscles or muscles that go into spasm all too easily. When she gave up these foods, her MS started to improve further.

I have to say I am always amazed when a new MS patient, or any patient for that matter, says he or she is still smoking. In this day and age, everyone knows that it is not sensible, yet I acknowledge that, for some people, giving up cigarettes can be harder than giving up crack cocaine. The book I wrote in 1987, entitled simply 'Stop Smoking'♥ could help anyone give up.

The rest of the questions in that section tend to be for people who are 'sensitive' or allergic to various features in their environment, but a history of asthma, for example, suggests a milk intolerance to me. What I have found over the years is that classical allergies to things like pollens and animal dander can significantly lessen, or even disappear, if I manage to identify the correct diet. That whole section can provide a lot of ideas for me to work on, and often we digress into other areas of the person's history.

Questions For Women Only

As you will already have realised, this whole series of questions produces some very interesting answers, much of which I have already alluded to. A vaginal discharge, if it is abnormal in any way, may be caused by candida/ thrush or other organisms. Painful periods and pre-menstrual symptoms of any sort indicate to me a dominance of oestrogen relative to progesterone, which I have discussed in great detail already. You may already have recognised that I feel strongly that the candida organism, or other fungi, could often be a cause of a person's MS. If the history suggesting it is present, it is my experience that it is rarely eradicated from the body, and it is therefore very likely that it has gradually spread to other parts of the body.

How long a woman was on the contraceptive pill for and how she felt on it, are all part of the story. In many women, the pill predisposes her to thrush, plus the long-term risks of cancer that are now being reported, separate from the nutritional deficiencies it causes. What is interesting here is that the studies tend only to look at the effects of the pill in the long run of those women who stayed on it for a fairly long time. In some studies that may have started with, say, one thousand women, as many as half or more may have dropped out because of adverse effects. So many women found they couldn't tolerate the pill that they stopped taking it after only a short time. The studies then reported on only those who stayed the course without any significant adverse symptoms. I wonder what the outcome would have been if all the original women had put up with the side effects for a long time, simply so as not to become pregnant.

Incidentally, I suggested elsewhere that side effects from drugs are often the result of the nutritional deficiencies they cause. The contraceptive pill, and presumably HRT, both of which are not natural substances so should be classified as 'drugs', cause a deficiency of vitamins C, B6 and B12, and zinc and magnesium. So supplementation of these nutrients needs to be considered seriously.

A Story
I have already explained that my overall approach is to assume that there is always an explanation for a person's problems, and that the most important thing to do is to identify what that problem is or those problems are. I am therefore a medical detective, but my effectiveness is based on my being able to think of what questions to ask and the accuracy and value of the answers I am given. As I have already said, there is always a cause for anyone's problems, and it is my job to help you find it, but sometimes it can be difficult to find. I can ask a question that is intended to elicit a useful answer, but for a variety of reasons it may fail. It is likely to be the comparatively unusual explanations that might be missed, because the patient fails to recognise the importance of the question, or simply dismisses it out of hand.

However, occasionally I met a patient like the one who consulted me for the first time some time before I retired, whose history identified remarkably little to explain why she had developed MS. We had virtually reached the end of my usual question and answer session, when I told her that, so far, I had not found any significant reason for her MS at all.

I suggested we complete my questioning and asked her if she had had any operations, to which she replied "Nothing of importance". Her daughter sitting quietly next to her suggested that two hip fractures and two hip replacements were possibly operations of some relevance. In a rather laid back way she explained that she had fallen off a tractor on two separate occasions. When I asked her what that was all about, she told me she had farmed with her husband in the past.

"Did you use any chemicals?" I asked her, to which she replied, "Not really".

That was when her daughter said, "Mum! We all did sheep dipping for ten years!" The chemicals used for such purposes have a strong attraction to nervous tissue, as they have a high fat content, and these chemicals dissolve more readily in fatty tissues.

Reproductive History

The earlier a woman starts having periods and the later she goes through the menopause, the more cycles she is likely to have had, which means the more oestrogen she may have been exposed to in this way during her lifetime, especially if she had some pre-menstrual symptoms, unless she was 'protected' by a number of pregnancies. I say 'protected' because the placenta (afterbirth) produces a lot of progesterone, which is a protective hormone.

Miscarriages are an unfortunate and unnecessary event, which can seriously upset a woman for a very long time. Some women never quite get over a miscarriage, equating it to the loss of a child. This can lead to a permanent degree of stress with all its implications. However, miscarriages are nearly always associated with a deficiency of a number of essential nutrients, especially folic acid and zinc, although miscarriages are the subject of another, separate book.

Difficulties conceiving suggest a number of nutrient deficiencies, and problems during a pregnancy likewise, especially of magnesium, vitamin B6 and zinc. Magnesium supplements, in my opinion, should be given to any woman who starts to develop features of PET (pre-eclamptic toxaemia), especially as magnesium by injection is now one treatment of choice if eclampsia (a fit) occurs.

Post-natal depression can often be helped considerably by the use of natural progesterone cream. After all, the mother had a lot of circulating progesterone while the placenta was still in her womb, and suddenly the levels drop. Vitamin B6, zinc and magnesium, in particular, may also help.

Failure to breast-feed is more complicated, often being influenced by the mother's attitude and desire or lack of interest in breast-feeding. Sometimes, however, it is never properly established despite the mother's and the Health Visitor's best endeavours, which may well be because of a difficult birth, a general anaesthetic, or quite simply a magnesium deficiency caused by the mother becoming stressed if breast-feeding isn't established quickly. Stress itself causes a loss of magnesium from the body, as well as other nutrients such as vitamins C and B5 (pantothenic acid).

Toxic Chemicals From Hobbies

Having clarified your current symptoms and how they affect you, how it all started and what has been done about it so far, I usually ask about any other significant episodes of your medical history that you think might be relevant. Many people have an instinct or a suspicion that something that has happened to them in the past may possibly be relevant to the MS they are now suffering from. For example, have you been exposed to potentially toxic chemicals at any time in your life, as in the story I mentioned a few paragraphs ago? Have you ever bought an old dilapidated house and done it up yourself, using a lot of chemicals on old wood, for example? Did you scrape off a lot of old paint yourself? Did you live in that environment for quite some time?

As a further thought on this subject, do you (or does any member of your household) have any particular hobbies, such as model soldiers, which you paint yourself? Are they made of lead? Have you used solder for fixing together model railway tracks? Do you do a lot of painting and lick your paintbrush? Do you make pottery and paint it? Most people have hobbies of some sort, which may possibly involve something potentially toxic. After all, these chemicals have to be detoxified by your liver, and excreted through your kidneys, either or both of which may in any case be under a lot of strain from your condition or any chemical or drug treatment you may have had, either recently or in the past.

When I asked this of an MS patient a number of years ago, she eventually remembered working in a very cramped kitchen when she was much younger. Someone found some cockroaches in some cupboards, so the management arranged for a pest control company to come in and spray a very smelly and choking chemical every month for the next two years. She had managed to contact five of the six people she had worked with, only to find that two had already died of cancer, two had multiple sclerosis, and the fifth had what would nowadays be diagnosed as chronic fatigue syndrome. She couldn't find the sixth. So think about what you have done in your life or what you might have had done to you over the years. Consider what it may have done to you in general terms or more specifically to certain organs of your body, with your nervous system as the main target.

Stress & Problems

If it hasn't already come up, it is at this point that I ask more specifically about stress. It is amazing how often a person with MS has been under a lot of stress before things came to a head, sometimes for a very long time. Many people have problems that have been with them for a long time and they just don't know how to deal with them. I can see the pain their problems have caused, which I am sure have played a major part in their having developed MS.

I am not a trained Psychologist, but I have been exposed to a lot of people's problems. I have also lived for quite a number of years, which sometimes brings with it a degree of wisdom. I have my own opinions on how to sort problems out and make decisions, and they have worked well over the years. Of course I cannot guarantee success. In any case, although we all say, "I have a problem", from time to time, in my opinion a problem is merely 'a situation that needs a resolution'. So, if you would care to read the chapter on Problem Solving starting on page 175, I will help you to solve your problems in a simple way. No, I won't solve your problems for you, because I cannot possibly feel the situation as you do. Nor can I live your life in your environment.

In that chapter I explain some simple facts of life, in a way similar to the attitude I describe in chapter on Decisions, starting on page 167. I also describe a number of examples of the advice I have given in the past, and how the person resolved their situation. Clearly I don't know what your problems might be, but I hope my advice and the examples I give will be of help to you.

One thing I can say at this stage is that, in some people, it is absolutely vital that they resolve their problems. Without such a resolution, recovery may be nigh on impossible, or certainly very difficult. A few years ago, I identified a major stress in a cancer patient's history at her first visit (which is one of the examples I give in that chapter) and told her and her husband that that was the first and most important thing she must do. I also suggested a way to deal with it. I don't know whether she is still trying, didn't like my advice, or expected me to resolve her cancer for her. In any case I felt that she would be wasting her and my time and her money if she didn't sort that out first, as it was so severe. Whatever the situation, she never came back to see me. Perhaps she simply couldn't cope with it.

All of this can take quite a long time to talk through as people often have a number of things they want to get off their chest. While telling me some of these details may not have been helpful in my quest for useful information about how best to help the patient, I may have been the first person who had bothered to listen to them. I therefore had to have a sense of understanding, but I also had to be aware that we had a limited amount of time between us. As it was, a first appointment with an MS patient lasted 1½ hours, but rambling anecdotes could use up far too much of that time.

The Dangers Of Antibiotics

This is a most important question. I always asked the patient in front of me if he or she had had any antibiotics, how many courses there had been, how long they continued and what they were given for. What's your history of antibiotic usage? The more you have had at any time in your life, the greater the chance of disturbing the balance of your intestinal flora, allowing thrush, other candida organisms or other fungal organisms to gain a foothold. The answer I was often given was "Oh! The usual amount". But I don't know what that is, since I am not aware I have ever had a course of antibiotics in my whole life.

Some people tell me they were on a daily dose for two or three years for acne when they were a teenager! They may have been given periodic courses for sore throats, flu' or cystitis. Asking about antibiotic usage also has the value that it reminds people of treatments and medical conditions they had forgotten to tell me about. Part of this memory game was helped by my asking about any health problems in the years before starting school, at junior school, senior school, late teens and early twenties when possibly at College or University, the rest of the twenties, thirties and forties, etc.

The significance of a history of tonsillitis has an additional meaning, namely the harm that may have been done to you by all the antibiotics you may have been prescribed. While most doctors will happily give anyone a prescription for an antibiotic when they consider it to be appropriate, they often don't recognise the damage such drugs can cause to the bowel flora. In some people, a single course may destroy the friendly bacteria within the bowel, leading to a whole variety of bowel symptoms, from diarrhoea to constipation, pain, wind, indigestion, mucus production and undigested food in your faeces. In other people it may take a number of courses to start a problem, and, of course, thrush is a regular result of a course of antibiotics.

What is usually not recognised is that vaginal thrush is the obvious external indication of a fungal overgrowth of some sort elsewhere in the body. As the antibiotic was taken by mouth, it is logical to suggest that the thrush organism, Candida albicans, is present within the bowel. To be fair, there are many other fungal-type organisms that can produce the same effect, but candida albicans is the best known and the most common. There are at least 250 'candida' species, and most don't cause thrush. I have discussed this problem more fully in my book 'Conquering Cystitis'♥. There is an Immunologist living on the South Coast of England who says that candida is the cause in all cases of MS, but his method of treating it is too extreme for most people. However, he may well be right to a considerable extent, so we mustn't overlook his observations and experience.

Leaky Gut Syndrome

An additional harmful effect that antibiotics can have is that they can give rise to a condition called 'the leaky gut syndrome', in which the bowel wall has been damaged and become more 'porous' than it should be. As a result, food particles that have not completed the digestive process gain access to the blood stream in a form that sets up an alarm reaction (called a kinin-inflammatory response). Such a reaction can occur in any organ of the body, possibly where you have set up a 'target', the brain of an MS patient to be precise. There is a certain amount of evidence appearing in the medical and scientific literature that MS involves inflammation.

Where You Live

I always try to ask patients about where they live. There are many aspects that need to be considered here. How happy do you feel in your home? How long after you moved to your present address did your problems begin to reveal themselves? Why did the former owners move away? What is the health like of other people living nearby? Are you aware of any overhead power lines, electricity transformers or mobile phone masts near where you live? Do you feel better when you are away from your home? Do you only feel better away from your home when you travel to a dry country such as the Mediterranean in the summer? Do you tend to feel worse in the dark days of winter?

If the answer to some of these questions is yes, you may have geopathic stress affecting your home, and a book entitled 'Are You Sleeping in a Safe Place'♥ by Rolf Gordon will help to put this more into perspective. A beneficial effect of a dry country holiday suggests that some or all of your problems are fungal in origin. Feeling worse in the darker months suggests either a condition called Seasonal Affective Disorder or that you are deficient in Vitamin D, and I have already said that there is a Canadian Ph.D. researcher who believes MS will one day be re-defined as a vitamin D deficiency disease.

Finally, please read what I say in the chapter on homocysteine, starting on page 337. It is not something that is obvious, but it can be very important to someone with multiple sclerosis. Anything that affects your blood vessels in a target organ could be relevant to you. It can be a silent killer or make you a target for its effects.

Why Does MS Develop?

As we are coming to the end of your history, I thought it would be reasonable to try to summarise your situation, and see what you have discovered about yourself. Remember, it is my opinion and my way of thinking about all forms of ill health, not only MS, that you are now ill because you have been exposing your body to things in your environment that might have 'poisoned' you gradually over the years. In addition, you may have been exposed to poisonous substances during your lifetime, unbeknown to you, all of which have gradually overloaded your system, causing it to break down in due course and produce your current condition. You may have a genetic 'weakness' in your central nervous system that has acted as a target.

It is vital that you try not to blame yourself for things that you did not know were bad for you, and, likewise, please do not feel guilty about those things that you knew were unwise, like smoking and drinking too much alcohol, because not only can we reverse any harmful effects they may have had upon your body, but also feeling guilty is a total waste of time and energy. You are now going to move forward.

If patients ask their doctors why they have developed MS, it is unlikely that they will receive a satisfactory answer, because doctors in mainstream medicine are seldom interested in such reasons as 'why?' They are likely to be told something like "It's just one of those things", or "We don't really know". In truth, most doctors are not interested in 'why?' because their whole approach is based upon dealing with the problem the patient is describing. Their job, they feel, is to treat the symptom somehow. To be fair, most patients go to their doctor and effectively say "Doctor. I have a problem. Will you please fix it for me."

So, unfortunately, mainstream medicine, with all its researchers and all its bright-minded doctors, continues to treat patients either by an operation to remove the offending structure or drug it into submission. Yet there must be a reason why MS developed in you and a number of explanations are forth coming. So, if between us we can identify some or all of the reasons, and do something about them, it should be perfectly possible to undo your MS.

It seems logical to me that, if there is something wrong with your bowel, one of the causes to be considered must be what you put into it, i.e. what you consume. Countless thousands of people over the years have lost their symptoms of wind, indigestion, acidity, tummy pain, constipation, diarrhoea, bloating, mucus, etc., all symptoms of so-called irritable bowel syndrome (IBS), by changing their diet. There are many published studies in mainstream medical journals that say this.

If you consult your doctor because of arthritis he gives you a drug that you swallow. That drug is absorbed into the blood stream and circulates round to where the inflammation is to put out the fire. So why is it not perfectly reasonable to consider that the cause of the inflammation was something else you swallowed in the first place? That approach applies just as well to any medical condition, including MS. After all, the symptoms of IBS are caused by inflammation, and MS is now being thought of as an inflammatory disease. And yet, if you ask your doctor about diet, you are likely to be told to eat and drink whatever you want, as diet has nothing to do with MS, or any medical condition for that matter.

Well, my patients and I heartily disagree. We are sure your diet is important, and, if you have not already made some changes, I will be recommending them to you. There is also considerable evidence that the environment within your bowel has something to do with it, and, if over the years you have had drugs that alter that environment, such as steroids and antibiotics, that is a further problem.

I am a believer in the possibility that a fungus can cause MS in some people, although I don't know how common it is. It may be relevant to nearly everyone, so far as I know. I know of one colleague who is adamant it applies to every MS patient. I am certainly aware that far too many people have had quite a lot drugs that predispose to it, namely antibiotics and inhaled and oral steroids (and chemotherapy and radiotherapy of course). Also a diet high in sugar and refined carbohydrates, yeasty foods and alcohol, provide the ideal environment for funguses to develop and thrive.

There is now considerable evidence that prescription drugs cause an effective loss of certain essential nutrients from the body, and that the so-called adverse effects that many of them often produce may actually be caused by those deficiencies. The mechanism varies from drug to drug, some reducing or blocking their absorption, some interfering with their utilisation and metabolism, while others increase their rate of utilisation or excretion. Whatever the mechanism, your body needs more nutrients to compensate for all this, which is why so many of my MS patients benefited from having them intravenously.

Then don't forget what I said earlier on about the acidifying nature of stress, and how that causes comparatively harmless organisms to mutate into pathogenic ones. Also that more acid (really a less alkaline) state provides an ideal environment for harmful cells to develop and thrive. A comparatively acid environment is also a poor oxygen environment, and many MS patients benefit from hyperbaric oxygen. Many MS patients have had more than their fair share of stress before the onset of their MS, which led many of them to 'abuse' themselves by drinking too many cups of tea or coffee (with milk and sugar) and alcohol and smoking more cigarettes than before, and generally not attending to their diet. All of this will have meant a poor nutrient intake and significant loss of essential nutrients at a time when an improved nutrient status was required.

How Much Of This Applies To You So Far?

There is considerable evidence that bowel cancer develops in areas of the world where the soil is low in selenium, assuming the people who live there eat food grown in that low selenium soil. To be fair to you, you may not know whether that applies to you or not, but, in any case, I will certainly want you to have high doses of selenium if you have your mercury amalgam fillings replaced. Mercury, especially from mercury amalgam fillings, squanders selenium, and one of the best antidotes to all the chemicals we are exposed to in our daily lives is the powerful antioxidant selenium. Do you have any teeth filled with mercury amalgams, or have they recently been exchanged for a non-metallic alternative material? Were you given any specific chelation treatment? If not, you will need to read the advice I give in the section on Treatment, starting on page 131.

Geopathic stress may well be affecting you. I recognise most people have never heard of it, but if you look for it and find it yourself, the whole process opens your eyes to another possible explanation for your MS. Remember, there may be five or more possible 'causes' for your MS. One may be 80%, the rest being 20% between them, or they may each be 20% of your problem. Until you start undoing some of your causes, you won't know.

Geopathic stress involves not only harmful rays coming up through the earth's crust, usually magnified by underground water, it also includes electromagnetic waves from electricity pylons, power substations and sometimes electronic and electric devices in your home, including such simple equipment as a radio-alarm clock beside your bed all night long. With brain cancer, mobile phones are thoroughly suspect in my mind, and I am particularly concerned about this risk to young people who use their mobile phones for so long, when their brains have not yet fully developed. These phones use microwaves, the same as in microwave ovens, which you are constantly being advised by the manufacturers to have checked for leakages because of the known danger from being overexposed to their radiations. To me it is always possible that mobile phone microwaves simply increase the amount of free radicals your body has to deal with.   It is interesting that the Russians banned microwave ovens in the 1970s.

I have already said that I believe stress to be a major problem in MS patients. It not only creates a more acidic environment with all that that leads to, it also wears out your adrenal system so that you lack reserves to deal with your MS. So, if you recognise it in yourself, please do something about it.

If you are a woman, to what extent might your hormones be involved? How did you answer my questions about your menstrual cycle, especially about any pre-menstrual symptoms? While most doctors would not consider hormones to be involved in MS, may be it is in some people.

What is the state of your immune system? How effective is it for dealing with your MS? An important possible cause of MS that is very difficult to identify with any confidence is 'infections', especially viruses such as the chicken pox/shingles virus and other organisms like chlamydia. The glandular fever virus, usually the Epstein Barr virus, should not be difficult to recognise as a possible cause from your history.

The Causes Of Multiple Sclerosis

If you ask your doctor or Neurologist what is causing your MS, you will probably be told no one knows, but that a lot of money is being spent on research. The research is almost entirely into treatments for MS, mainly drugs. To be fair, various ideas have been put forward over the years, but everyone seems to be looking for a single cause for MS, on the assumption that all MS patients are the same and have the same cause.

However, I considered I identified many possible precipitating factors, and, if these were cleared out of the body or somehow resolved, the patient's symptoms either improved or disappeared. I don't use the word 'cure', preferring to use 'remission'. It would appear that many patients went into permanent remission.

So what causes did I find to be playing a part in patients' MS symptoms?

1) Individual food intolerances
2) Toxic metals such as mercury and lead
3) Toxic chemicals such as pesticides and some added to foods including MSG and aspartame
4) Nutritional deficiencies, especially of vitamin B12, magnesium and vitamin D (one Canadian researcher believes that MS will one day be redefined as a vitamin D deficiency disease)
5) Infections such as the chicken pox/shingles virus, fungi such as candida species and many others including chlamydia
6) The usual forms of stress
7) Geopathic stress
8) Occasionally drugs and some supplements causing imbalances
9) Social poisons such as cigarette smoke and alcohol
10) Root canal fillings, especially old ones
11) Temporo-mandibular joint imbalances
12) Hormonal imbalances
13) A struggling immune system
14) The functioning of your bowel or leaky gut syndrome

There may be others I have missed out that you recognise could be important to you. Never assume I know it all. I learn something new every day, often from a patient, so you might be able to teach me something. So, in summary, to put it another way, consider the following as possible causes of your MS; what you consume as foods and drinks and what you miss from the right diet for you; stress in all its forms both recently and possibly hidden deep in your soul; toxic substances such as heavy metals, especially mercury, but also the myriad chemicals we are all exposed to in our daily lives; the more easily identified poisons such as cigarette smoke and alcohol; root canal fillings on specific acupuncture meridians; infections, especially viruses and fungi; your bowel ecology; hormonal imbalances; nutrient deficiencies including vitamin D if you live in a comparatively poor sun area; your anti-oxidant levels to quench all those free radicals; your body's overall pH; an inefficient or overstrained immune system; the effect of any drugs you have been prescribed or supplements you have self-medicated with, either before you developed MS or you are on for your MS, especially the nutrient draining effects of any drugs, and any nutritional imbalances you might have caused by not supplementing correctly; and finally geopathic stress.

Dealing with any one of these can at times be difficult. For example, there is no one way to identify the foods that are having an adverse effect upon a person. There are elimination diets, various blood tests and other mechanisms that suggest food intolerances, but not one of them is 100% accurate or even appropriate for a particular person. Nevertheless food intolerances need to be considered seriously.

If I was fortunate to identify the right eating pattern for a patient immediately, many symptoms could start to improve within one week, although they might suffer from withdrawal symptoms. I described this in detail in the book I published in 1987 entitled 'Conquering Cystitis'♥. Despite the title, the principle I wrote about in the book can apply to anyone whatever his or her condition.

Chapter 15

Treatment For Multiple Sclerosis

Proper Eating For MS Patients - What To Avoid

From experience, I was able to 'best guess' what dietary recommendations to make, basically what foods or drinks to avoid and what to consume. If that didn't work we could try another method, the patient even considering spending money on a blood test. To begin with I therefore suggest you consider avoiding the following: -

1) Dairy products, whole and skimmed milk from cow, goat, sheep or any other animal, all variety of cheeses (including vegetarian varieties as they contain milk acted on by a vegetable rennet), yoghurt, butter and cream (although I might allow organic butter and cream back in at a later date). You will need to read the ingredients on packages very carefully, remembering that milk ingredients can have various names such as whey, casein and lactose. The best way to avoid such mistakes is never to eat anything from a packet. Ideally you should always obtain basic ingredients and put them together as your grandmother used to.

2) Caffeine in all its forms, so coffee, tea, decaffeinated varieties (they are not totally decaffeinated), chocolate and cola drinks.

3) Alcohol in all forms.

4) Refined/white flour products as in most breads, biscuits, cakes, pasta, pies and puddings, etc. Always use whole-wheat forms.

5) Sugar, brown and white, both from sugar cane and sugar beet. Also avoid all other forms of 'sugar' such as corn syrup, maple syrup, etc.

6) All chemical additives, especially aspartame and monosodium glutamate (watch out for slightly different names for the same chemical). Many foods and drinks have a whole variety of chemicals added to them to 'improve' their taste and appearance and extend their shelf life. Avoid fizzy drinks.

7) It might be sensible to avoid anything in a packet or tin, certainly anything with a list of ingredients on it.

8) If there is any reasonable suspicion of candida being involved, it might be sensible to avoid all fruit to begin with, and to take the special capsules of dehydrated fruits, vegetables, and berries, as all the sugar has been eliminated during production♥.

The above list is where I recommend you consider starting. Some patients need to avoid all gluten grains, namely wheat, rye, oats and barley, which can be quite difficult. Some patients need to avoid 'red meat' (beef, lamb and pork) and all forms of saturated fats. Others find citrus fruits can be a bladder irritant. If you suffer from muscle spasms, it would be sensible for you to avoid the Deadly Nightshade family of foods, namely potatoes, tomatoes, aubergines (eggplant in USA) and peppers. Be aware that the fifth member of this group is tobacco, which must be avoided at all costs. This is much easier in the United Kingdom nowadays as the country has effectively become a cigarette smoke-free zone except in personal private places. Don't let anyone smoke in your house. If a family member is a smoker, ask them to smoke outside if they must, but this may be a good time to encourage them to give up smoking all together. They could consider obtaining a copy of my book entitled 'Stop Smoking'♥.

So What Should A Person With MS Consume?

1) Lots of vegetables (raw where possible or steamed) and fruit,
2) Salad items,
3) Nuts, seeds and spices,

4) Whole grains,
5) Fish, especially oily fish such as salmon, mackerel, and sardines.
6) Chicken, turkey and wild game,
7) Drink quality water (bottled in glass or filtered) or caffeine-free herbal teas,
8) Ring the changes with soya, rice, oat and nut milks, i.e. buy different preparations if you want some form of 'milk' for cereals, etc., use up one then open another kind.

Wherever possible make sure everything is organic. Be prepared to grow your own.

This approach should be alkaline which is how you should eat. It will also contain lots of phytonutrients and antioxidants to help mop up any free radicals that may be partially causing your MS. When I describe what supplements you should consider, I will be recommending the special capsules♥ containing dehydrated 26 fruits, vegetables and berries, so they should be added to the best eating plan you can identify. Many authors have written of their own experiences of what to eat and what not to eat if you have MS. I have continued to be amazed at the degree to which you are all different. What suits one MS patient may be just as good for you or may be totally irrelevant. You have to find out for yourself what is the correct pattern of eating for you. I don't like the word diet as it has been used for so many different reasons. So, unless you have a clear idea where to start, follow my advice above and see whether it makes any difference to you.

What sort of difference do I mean? Well basically any improvement. You may go through some withdrawal symptoms, such as a caffeine withdrawal headache, or you may feel more tired than before, or you may develop a lower backache, but such symptoms should not last more than a few days. If they do occur, take it as a good sign that you are going to feel better soon, although they don't always occur. Drink plenty of quality water, putting ½ teaspoonful of pure sodium bicarbonate in each glass until you feel better. Withdrawal headaches seldom respond to your favourite painkiller, because they are usually caused by your tissues releasing acidic chemicals, so the bicarbonate will neutralise the acid.

Often the first benefit you notice is not what you are hoping for, i.e. an improvement in your MS symptoms. As the damage in your central nervous system may have been there for quite a long time, you can't expect the damage to be undone quickly. So to begin with, after getting over any withdrawal symptoms, you may notice you feel less tired and you have more stamina. You may sleep better. Your bowels may work better and you may notice you are opening your bowels more easily and perhaps two or three times a day of a normal stool. Headaches you used to suffer from regularly may no longer occur. Your skin may look better and people may comment on the fact. Your face may have a healthier appearance, and you may look less 'pinched' and less pale. You may lose a little weight you have wanted to lose for a long time, although my experience is that MS patients are rarely overweight. I can only remember seeing a handful in the over 9000 MS patients who consulted me. There may be improvement in other non-MS symptoms that you had become accustomed to because they were there much of the time and you didn't take much notice of them in your overall problems.

If this happens, don't be upset. It means that your overall health will be all the better for your new eating pattern. Your MS symptoms may gradually improve, but take a bit longer before you notice the change, so be patient and stick to whatever you have done so far. It is possible that you need to make further changes to your pattern of eating if your MS symptoms don't show any improvement within three months. However, if you have definitely noticed useful improvements in your non-MS health, it most likely means that what you do or do not consume has considerable impact upon your MS, but there may still be something else that you have to work on before your MS symptoms start to improve.

I know this may be frustrating, but, as I am not seeing you myself, I cannot tell you what is important for you. I can only encourage you to stick with it, continue on the new eating pattern that has already done you so much good, and move on to the next part of the programme.

Before we move on, however, it is important to say that some patients notice an improvement in their MS symptoms shortly after they start changing their eating habits, if they are lucky enough to have immediately identified what to do and what not to do. You may notice your muscles are less stiff or don't go into spasm so easily. You may find you can simply walk better and in a straighter line. Some of your sensory symptoms may diminish. If you had such a problem, you may notice that you can feel when you are passing urine again. So stick to what you are doing and see how much better you can become, while you also move on to the next part of the programme.

It is important that I tell you everything I can so that you can benefit from all my knowledge. There is one more situation that can arise and that is that sometimes when people change their life style, some of their symptoms actually become worse. For example when someone stops coffee if they have become addicted to it, they can suffer from even more severe headaches than before, although only temporarily. When someone has rung me because that has happened, I say 'Good. You will feel so much better when this headache clears'. It always does. If someone suffers from regular migraines, they can have a really bad one when they stop consuming what has been causing their migraines all along.

So I am warning you that your MS symptoms could temporarily become worse, even if you happen to be on the correct eating pattern for you. But the problem is I cannot tell you whether to stick to what you are doing or not. I can only suggest you drink a lot of water with 1/2 teaspoonful of pure sodium bicarbonate in each glass and see if things settle down quickly enough. The other possibility is that it is nothing to do with what you have started. It might be a pure coincidence and you have picked up an infection, most likely a virus, which is causing the problem. One other possibility is that you are now consuming in much larger amounts something that you should be avoiding but are not. I hope this doesn't happen to you, but you need to be aware of its possibility. If in doubt go back to what you were doing before you made the changes and see what happens. If you don't improve then the changes you made were not the cause of the deterioration.

If, however, the changes in your eating habits produce no noticeable benefit to you at all, or if you start to lose weight you can ill afford, for example, please don't stick to a diet that doesn't appear to be right for you. There's no point in it.

I admit this is a bit hit-and-miss, but it has worked for hundreds of patients although not all of them. It also doesn't cost to try this approach. The only drawback is that, if it doesn't work, you may think you have wasted time. If so I can only apologise since I am trying to save you money in the first instance.

On a few occasions patients have finally identified that they were reacting to what everyone would say was a healthy food, perhaps cucumber or garlic, as examples. These are very difficult to track down, but you need to keep in mind the fact that you may have a personal idiosyncratic food reaction, but please don't think like this to begin with and start by making things complicated.

A study has just been published to say that patients suffering from Alzheimer's Disease have been found to have high levels of Tumour Necrosis Factor-alpha (TNF-alpha) in their brain fluid, which is a recognised indication of inflammation. I am trying to find out if the same applies to patients with MS. When some of these patients were injected with an anti-TNFalpha drug they had a remarkable improvement in their condition. Whether or not it is safe to give such people this or a similar drug generally, i.e. by mouth, is highly questionable as TNF-alpha is an essential chemical that is produced by your white blood cells as soon as you are invaded by a foreign organism. Can you imagine what would happen if you had no TNF-alpha to do its job. You would have no resistance to infection! It would appear that some people have died from an overwhelming infection as a result of taking such a drug.

What I am trying to get at is that if TNF-alpha is raised in your blood stream or your central nervous system, it is an indication of something causing inflammation. Mainstream medicine therefore decides that the appropriate form of treatment is to treat with a drug that can suppress, inactivate or somehow do something about this inflammation, which is fair enough, except that drugs tend to have many and varied adverse effects as they tend not to be targeted accurately enough. My approach is to identify what is the cause of the inflammation and remove it so that the inflammation stops, the levels of TNF-alpha fall and the symptoms subside.

Many scientific studies have shown that TNF-alpha is produced by white blood cells, especially neutrophils, in response to invasion by something undesirable. This can, however, be not only a virus or a bacterium but the most likely cause is an undigested food protein, one that has escaped the normal digestive breakdown mechanisms and entered into the blood stream in a form that the immune system considers to be 'foreign'. It could possibly also be a toxic chemical or a toxic metal like lead or mercury. The point is that if the source of the inflammation is not identified and removed, your neutrophils will continue to try to do their job and keep producing TNF-alpha, thereby maintaining an inflammatory mechanism in your body, so keeping your symptoms going.

There is a blood test that is based on incubating a sample of your blood for one hour with extracts of foods, then examining the effect on the neutrophils in an automated haematology analyser. Any change in their numbers or certain characteristics indicates that that food has 'activated' the neutrophils, suggesting that that food is likely to be in part causing your MS symptoms. If those neutrophils have been activated, they will have released TNF-alpha. Avoiding that food should result in a significant reduction in circulating levels of TNF-alpha. Incidentally, vitamin B12 reduces TNF-alpha levels through nitric oxide synthase. The blood test is called the Alcat Test♥.

Intravenous Infusions

When I was in practice, I found most of my patients really benefited from having vitamins and minerals intravenously, and sometimes the effect was really dramatic. I saw a young lady one day from overseas, who took a long time to drag herself from my waiting room into my consulting room, dragging one leg in particular laboriously with the help of two sticks. She had a mixture of sensory and functional MS.

After taking a complete history from her, I suggested she change her diet and have an intravenous infusion, which she knew about because I had sent her information about them in a letter before she came. She was very keen to try one. Incidentally, I suggested that she should not change her diet until she was back home, as she intended to fly back the next day.

The infusion had no obvious effect on her by the time she left my premises, but she rang me from home the next day to say she had walked virtually normally across the airport forecourt to where her car had been parked. She was so excited. The beneficial effect lasted three months, after which some of her symptoms started to come back. She came to see me again for a second infusion, and this time the beneficial effect lasted six months. The second infusion lasted seven months. After that I managed to find someone in her own country to give her infusions. For her the changes in her diet did help her, but nothing like the infusions.

In my experience, those patients with the sensory type of MS are the more easy to treat, primarily with intravenous infusions, replacement of their mercury amalgam teeth fillings and management of the chicken pox/shingles virus. Diet played a much smaller part in their MS than in the functional type. Even what I put into the infusion was generally different, as I concentrated on large doses of vitamin B12, going up as high as 30,000mcg occasionally, always with great success, lower doses being less effective.

In the functional type, I would concentrate on magnesium in particular, although I would still put in fairly high doses of vitamin B12, such as 5,000mcg. They always needed dietary changes as well as replacement of their mercury amalgam teeth fillings, and attendance to anything else I found, especially an anti-fungal approach, which was sometimes rather hard.

So, if you can find someone to give you intravenous infusions, may I suggest the following: -
For sensory types

- Vitamin B1 100mg
- Vitamin B2 25mg
- Vitamin B3 25mg (but not in women the first time as it often gave some of them a headache)
- Vitamin B5 250mg
- Vitamin B6 100mg
- Folic acid 5mg
- Vitamin B12 5,000 to 30,000mcg (working up the dose each time to find the most effective dose).
- Vitamin C 5,000mg
- Magnesium sulphate 1g
- Zinc 25mg
- Molybdenum 100mcg
- Selenium 100mcg
- Chromium 100mcg

To be able to have such an infusion once a week I found to be really helpful to so many patients, but it wasn't always practical for them to come so often.

For the functional types, everything virtually the same, but I tended not to go nearly so high with Vitamin B12, although I would always start at 5,000mcg. Magnesium would be increased slowly to 5g. I seldom gave any manganese, as I found it somehow upset a few patients to begin with.

The intravenous route is clearly superior to all other forms of management. I had a few patients with sensory symptoms that had already responded to previous infusions, but they had left it rather late to return for another infusion. When they walked into my premises, you could see the pain their sensory symptoms were causing them, so I gave them another infusion, usually of the same dose of vitamin B12 as previously, and their symptom cleared within half-an-hour of starting. You could see the relief on their faces.

Half-a dozen or so of these patients came back again the next week as their symptoms had returned, having let themselves get so bad before they returned for another infusion. This time I took a sample of blood to measure their levels of vitamin B12, to find they were at least 5000 units, i.e. five times above the so-called upper limit of normal by the particular laboratory I used. When their symptoms cleared once again for that infusion, I took a sample of blood from a different vein as soon as they were finished, and found the level could be as high as 25,000 units, twenty-five times the upper limit of reference.

So which is correct, the blood level or lack of symptoms? In my opinion, how the patient felt was the most important aspect, as no harm came from such high blood levels, only real benefit. Perhaps it is nervous tissue levels that are most important not blood levels, but how would it ever be possible to measure nervous tissue levels?

Temporo-Mandibular Joint

One of the most exciting things I ever did to a number of MS patients was to manipulate their jaw joint. This primarily applied to a person with what I would describe as a one-sided problem, i.e. someone mainly with a problem in their left arm and leg or right arm and leg.

If I looked in their mouth, I almost invariably found a big overlap between the top teeth and the bottom teeth, and the midline of their bottom jaw was slightly off to one side, when compared to their top jaw. I would ask them to show me how well or badly they could walk in a straight line, using a stick or any aid, if one was needed. I then put a wooden spatula somewhere near the back of their teeth, but lined up their bottom jaw as perfectly as I could with their top jaw. I then asked them to walk again.

You should have seen the effect that had on them all. They could instantly, and I mean instantly, walk much better. Some people dropped their stick and swung round in a circle, something their balance would not have let them do before, or they would have fallen. They were all truly amazed. It was all very exciting.

I would then ask them what such a demonstration meant. To be fair no one had any idea what I was getting at. I simply said that it showed they did not have permanent irreversible damage to their nervous system.

To be fair, I was never able to find a dentist who could correct the abnormality, but at least I told them not to clench their teeth when they found a particular movement difficult to do. As I was retiring, it was suggested that a cranial osteopath would probably be able to help. But I never had the chance to try that out.

This is a difficult situation, because it is hard to prove to you that you should have all your mercury amalgam fillings replaced by an alternative non-metallic material. However, there is a wealth of information suggesting that you should. Perhaps the most important is some of the work of Professor Boyd Hayley in USA, who has shown unequivocally that nervous tissue is destroyed by mercury. Look up the information in Google and you will find no end of books talking about the process.

One of the simplest is by the late Dr. Jack Levenson entitled 'Menace in the Mouth'♥

Having said that the whole idea of the danger that mercury in your teeth could be causing you is controversial at present, i.e. there are differences of opinion on the matter, many doctors and dentist saying there is no proof. Well I simply don't believe they have studied the literature if that is the case.

So let us assume that you will have your amalgam fillings replaced. Who should do the work? A biologically trained Dentist. In the UK, you will find a list at IAOMT. In other countries, you will need to find a dentist for yourself.

There are many ways you can be exposed to mercury in life, including through eating large fish, such as tuna, which are on the end of the life chain. Various vaccinations contain mercury as a preservative, which some people think is very dangerous, even if the authorities don't agree. It is also sometimes used as a preservative in contact lens solutions. There are various books that can frighten people about the dangers of mercury, but I think some of them go over the top. As I have already said the one I recommend is 'Menace In The Mouth' by the late Dr. Jack Levenson. While it is now very difficult to obtain an old-fashioned mercury thermometer in the UK, we are being encouraged to use long-life electric bulbs, which contain mercury, producing is disposal problem. If you ask your dentist if you can keep an amalgam filling if he extracts or replaces one, he will tell you he has to dispose of it as toxic waste. It is all very silly, yet mercury is clearly dangerous. Most people have a number of teeth with mercury amalgam fillings in them. Some people have a 'mouthful'. If they are examined carefully, it can often be noticed that some of them appear to be leaking or are corroded, or pieces have broken off exposing an extra surface of amalgam. A dental amalgam is a mixture of metals, which is what the word 'amalgam' means. The mixture contains 50% mercury, the remaining 50% being a mixture of more then one other metal. The final mixture is made up in the dentist's surgery just before being inserted into a hole prepared in your tooth. To be fair, it is a very easy material to handle, and the job can be completed competently and quickly. Some people think the public has been conned by calling them 'silver amalgams' not mercury amalgams.

The fact that there is more than one metal in your mouth, surrounded by an electrolyte-containing liquid, your saliva, turns that filling into a mini battery. Any physics teacher will tell you that electrons will move from one metal to another in the circumstances. This mixture tends to make the mercury in the amalgam move more than the others. Therefore mercury vaporizes constantly from your teeth, the whole process being promoted by eating hot food, drinking acidic liquids such as orange juice, and by the simple act of brushing your teeth. Yes, it is a gradual process, but it is going on slowly all the time. In fact, if you waft a piece of amalgam in the air, it can be shown under special circumstances to be leaking mercury all the time.

When I was a kid at school, somewhere between the ages of seven and thirteen, we were taught art by a wonderful, but strict, artist, whose dwelling was typical of the rose-covered cottages that Rupert Bear used to find, when he and his friends went on their adventures in the woods. This man's cottage was at the bottom of the football pitch.

He came in to teach us art once a week, but he also had a fund of knowledge about so many other things. One of those was how to make a crystal set, to listen to the BBC, using hairs from our heads, although exactly how he did it I have forgotten. What I do remember very clearly was that, if a wire was somehow attached to the amalgam fillings that some of us had in our teeth, the battery-like effect could be used to provide amplification of the sound his simple contraption produced!

Despite the fact that Dr. Mats Hansen has identified around thirteen thousand articles published in scientific journals that describe the dangers of mercury and how some of that mercury gradually leaks out (some of which Dr. Levenson discusses in his book), the idea that the mercury amalgams in your teeth are a danger to your health has not yet become the prevailing opinion of the medical and dental professions. There are, however, many dentists, scientists and doctors who honestly believe that anyone who has a significant illness should have their mercury amalgams assessed by a properly trained biological dentist, with a view to having them replaced by an appropriate alternative non-metallic material. I happen to be one of those doctors who believe it is a danger to your health, and, if you have MS, you should seriously consider having them sorted out.

In my opinion, there are many reasons why a person with MS, and possible all of us to an extent, should have their mercury amalgam fillings replaced. In the first place mercury is an established toxic substance. Secondly, mercury has no place in your body, and the simple act of eating, especially hot or acidic foods, grinding or brushing your teeth, and drinking anything even slightly acidic, will cause mercury to vaporize from your amalgam fillings. While some of that mercury will be exhaled, most of it will either be inhaled or swallowed, or will enter your tissues through the mucous membranes in your mouth. Some will also gradually migrate through the nerve roots in your teeth and enter your brain. It may take years, but, if you have had yours for years, it will already have entered your tissues.

Mercury disturbs many metabolic functions in your body. Dr. Levenson's book makes that perfectly clear. So, if you want the scientific facts, read his book. This toxic metal also wastes important nutrients, such as selenium and zinc, both of which are deficient in most people's body anyway, especially if they have MS, and both of which are important for your immune system, and your fight against MS.

If you do decide to have your mercury amalgam fillings replaced, it is essential that you take chelating minerals, starting shortly before the first dental session, and continuing throughout the time that the work is done, i.e. continue between visits to the dentist. I try to establish what is appropriate for each individual patient, but clearly I cannot tell you exactly what dose to use, although I can give you some guidelines. In principle, the more fillings you have to be replaced, the more chelating nutrients you might need to take on a daily basis and for that much longer.

As a rough guide, I suggest you take a total of 300 to 900 micrograms of elemental selenium, 3 to 6 grammes of vitamin C, and 90 to 150 milligrammes of elemental zinc per day. Ideally you should take selenium ½ hour before meals, vitamin C with meals and zinc 1 hour after meals, preferably taking each substance three times a day. So, try to take 100-300 micrograms of selenium ½ hour before breakfast, lunch and your evening meal, 1 or 2 grammes of vitamin C with those meals, and take 30-50 mg of zinc about 1 hour after breakfast, lunch and your evening meal. If you are rather a forgetful type, it is better to divide them into two separate doses than not to take them at all.

How long should you take such doses, when 900 micrograms could mean eighteen tablets a day, 6 grammes of vitamin C means six tablets and 150 milligrammes of zinc could mean ten capsules, making a possible thirty-four tablets a day? In theory, the best answer I could give is for as long as you need to clear mercury (and any other heavy metals) completely from your body. However, that is not a very practical answer.

So my recommendation is that you take whatever dose you decide to take, up to the maximum I suggest, starting at least one or two weeks before the amalgam replacements start, ideally reaching your target dose by the time the dental work begins. This is to make sure that you can tolerate such high doses. Please make sure you take all tablets and capsules with a full glass of water, especially if away from food, so that they don't sit dry on your stomach, in which case they might irritate it. In any case, you need to make sure that they suit you. There is a small possibility that one or more of them just might not agree with you, and you need to know this before the dental work commences.

I can well understand if someone tells you such high doses are, or might be, dangerous, or cause imbalances of other nutrients, i.e. copper, for example. However, many thousands of my patients have followed this approach successfully, although, to be fair, not 100% of them. So you need to know they suit you, and you will only find out by starting them and taking a few days to reach your target doses.

What I have found from experience is that, in general but not always, the more teeth you have filled with amalgam, the larger the fillings with a big total surface area (so the greater the amount of amalgam in your mouth) plus the longer they or some of them have been there, the bigger the doses of selenium, vitamin C and zinc you need, and the longer after the dental replacements have been completed you will need to be on such high doses, possibly for up to nine months or longer. Studies of body content of mercury support these observations.

What I also discovered very early on when I recognised the importance of dealing with mercury amalgam fillings was that the best way of telling a patient when they had been on those chelating agents for long enough, was that new symptoms coming out of the blue would occur. Such symptoms could be unusual or new headaches, spots anywhere on the body, boils, dry corners of the mouth, pain or aching in joints not previously a problem, or just suddenly not feeling so well as before in a variety of ways. These I surmised could be adverse effects of too much selenium in particular, i.e. selenium toxicity. I assumed that when these selenium toxic symptoms occurred, mercury had essentially been cleared from the body, so large doses of selenium were no longer required.

This seemed logical to me and justified their not taking, or needing, any more selenium. When they stopped the selenium (and the vitamin C and zinc, of course) these new symptoms cleared, but it took as long for them to clear as they had been present. Many patients restarted selenium, only to find the same symptoms returned very quickly. Over the years, hundreds of patients have told me of their experiences, so I have been able to warn the next ones what might happen. In every case I have been right.

When, many years ago, I learned how important it was to deal with mercury amalgam fillings in my patients, there were very few of us who were doing anything about it. I had been aware that selenium was the specific antidote to mercury, but it took me some time to identify a total programme for chelating mercury from the body that seemed to work.

Over the years, more and more doctors and scientists have become involved, and various other regimes have been recommended, some of which I have also tried. However, my patients and I did not find them any more effective than my original approach, allowing for the fact that I have increased the doses over the years. But to continue taking such large doses for many months is probably not practical, which is why I sometimes changed the programme about two weeks after the amalgam filling replacements have been completed, assuming that was roughly the time I next saw a patient for consultation. To be fair I don't know how long you need to continue on a chelation programme after the dental work has been completed, although you could follow the advice I have given above about selenium toxic symptoms developing. You can understand why I am unhappy about that, as I cannot keep an eye on you myself.

More and more people are aware of the dangers of mercury, because they have read about it, so it rarely came as a surprise to a patient when I brought up the subject, and were quite willing to proceed to have their amalgam fillings replaced when I recommended it. Some, however, wanted to have scientific evidence that they may have had a raised body burden of mercury or a reaction to it. I therefore offered to do two tests, one the Kelmer Test for levels of body mercury, the other a Lymphocyte Transformation Test that assesses your white blood cell 'response' to the presence of mercury in a laboratory setting.

These tests are done by Biolab in London♥, but I am sure there are labs in other countries that can do similar tests. However, Biolab requires a request to come from an appropriate practitioner, so that the results can be sent to a responsible person for correct interpretation in relation to your medical condition.

The Kelmer test can also be used to assess your body burden of other heavy metals, such as aluminium, arsenic, cadmium and lead, which you need to be aware may have accumulated in your body over the years, which may now be affecting your health. One toxic metal in your body is bad enough, but the affect of two is not additive but multiplied. If there are three, well, who knows what the effect might be?

After Amalgam Replacements

You will have noticed that I am recommending a considerable number of tablets to be taken around the actual dental work to replace mercury amalgam fillings. There is another protocol that is a far more convenient programme, using Segiun Patches♥ at night and Bio-Chelat♥ drops just before meals, starting with five drops three times a day for the first week, ten drops three times a day for the next week, then up to twenty drops three times daily for then on.

Exactly how long you should remain on the dose of twenty drops three times a day will vary from person to person, but, by and large, the more fillings you had, the larger they were, and the longer they have been in your mouth, the longer it is likely to take to chelate all mercury (and other heavy metals) from your body. Even then, we are all being exposed to toxic heavy metals that we can't avoid, so taking a few doses every so often will probably be valuable.

Perhaps the best way of answering the question 'How long should I take the Bio-Chelat?' is to say continue for about three months on the full dose (it doesn't matter if you forget or leave it off every now and then) and then take it occasionally. If you feel you have benefited from it, but you deteriorate in any way when you stop it, restart it for about a month and see what happens. So far as I am aware, there is no problem being on it for long time.

If you are serious about bringing your MS under control, you will need to organise a careful daily plan. In fact, you will need to concentrate on yourself selfishly for at least the first three months. Before I forget, a further reminder to always take any tablets or capsules with a full glass of water. If you take them with merely a sip, they can sit virtually dry on your stomach lining and irritate it. They will dissolve far more easily if there is plenty of liquid in your stomach.

You will need to have some idea how long the whole dental procedure will take, so that you can order enough supplies. However, I recommend you only order small supplies to begin with, to make sure they suit you. There is no way I can guarantee that these particular preparations will be suitable for absolutely everyone, as there is always someone out there who finds they cannot tolerate them. If they do upset you in any way, it is usually something simple like a little nausea. They have never done anyone any harm, in my experience.

A simple word of caution is needed here, for you to be aware of a possible adverse effect from doses of zinc. If you have ever been exposed to copper for any reason, and you have a higher body content of copper than is healthy, even if you are not aware of it, taking zinc can displace copper from where it is lodged in your body. This released copper has then to be disposed of via your liver and bile duct into your intestines, which will then cause considerable digestive problems and probably make you feel ill.

I had one such a patient who, when she told me how ill the selenium and zinc had made her feel, then remembered that she had had the same symptoms many years ago when she drank well water while on holiday. This water was tested and found to be high in copper. A white blood cell copper analysed at Biolab turned out to be far too high. So I then had to take time to clear out the excess copper from her body. This story illustrates the beauty of a medical detective approach to people's illnesses.

When the patient told me how ill my advice had made her, whilst I naturally apologised, I also used the information to find out what had gone wrong and what to do about it.

Over the years I have learned which particular supplements to recommend to which patients. I have also learned how long they should continue to take them after the dental work has been completed, but that is far too complicated to explain here, and it needs to be individualised. In the circumstances, I suggest that, perhaps two weeks after the dental work has been completed, you drop the selenium to 100mcg and the zinc to 30mg per day, and continue on Bio-Chelat once a day away from any other nutrients. To speed up the clearance of mercury (and other toxic substances) from your body, you could also apply the Segiun Patches, or one of the cheaper alternatives if you want to, to the soles of your feet. With Bio-Chelat you can effectively stop selenium and zinc, although the company advises to take a small amount of zinc regularly, such as 15mg of elemental zinc last thing at night. So taking Bio-Chelat plus zinc may be more effective than the alternative, and cost less in the long run. I suggest you continue to take at least 100mcg selenium per day for a long time.

If you cannot afford to have your mercury amalgam fillings replaced, you just don't want to, you haven't been convinced of the value of doing so, or it won't happen for any reason, may I suggest you consider taking five drops of Bio-Chelat three times a day in a glass of water shortly before meals continuously, although it doesn't matter if you forget it or give yourself a break every now and again.

In principle, I am not happy that anyone should take large doses of selenium or zinc for too long, although I often recommended larger doses than I have recommended here to some patients when I was advising them and seeing them regularly myself. I am perfectly happy for you, and virtually anyone, to take Bio-Chelat and apply Segiun patches to your feet for as long as you want. However, when you have brought things under control as far as you can tell, it is perfectly reasonable to have a break, and do the Bio-Chelat and Segiun Patches treatment every so often, to keep yourself as clean as you can. There is no way any one of us can totally avoid exposure to toxins in our air, food and water.

If you can find a biologically trained dentist, by contacting IAOMT, ask him or her to check if your MS is on an acupuncture meridian in relation to a particular tooth. Many is the time one of my cancer patients has found an abscess under a tooth relating to their MS. Dr Weston Price (see the PricePottenger Foundation), an American dentist, brought this whole area of concern to our attention in the middle of the last century.

Hyperhomocysteinaemia

Hyperhomocysteinaemia simply means raised levels of homocysteine, but what is homocysteine? It is an amino acid basically made from methionine, and which can be converted back into methionine, but it is an arterial poison. A study has just been completed in Oxford in the UK stating that B vitamins can reduce the symptoms of Alzheimer's disease if the initial cause was a raised level of homocysteine. I have known about this for years, but it would appear that mainstream medicine will not consider it seriously until a drug company comes up with a drug to reduce it. To be fair, most of the studies done so far have not been that successful in alleviating symptoms until now, possibly because the levels were not brought down low enough.

The treatment for a raised level of homocysteine is vitamins B6 and 12, folic acid and betaine, so nutrients, and most doctors don't seem to like nutrients. Unfortunately laboratories have far too high an acceptable level for homocysteine, because of the way they establish their reference ranges. The level should be below 6 nmol/l, whereas most laboratories accept 14 or 15. It is vital your level be brought down if it is raised, as a raised level can clearly become a brain artery irritant substance, and we need to remove anything that does that to you. If arteries in your brain are damaged, your nerve endings will also be damaged.

Never accept a statement from your doctor that your level of homocysteine is all right. Make sure you know the actual level, and do something about it if it is raised. That equally applies to vitamin D3.

Chapter 16

Supplements for MS

Are supplements necessary for MS patients? My clear answer is an unequivocal yes. My reason is because of the very beneficial effect vitamins and minerals given intravenously have had on so many MS patients. I would think that virtually all people who are ill in any way would benefit from extra supplements, and that probably applies to a degree to so-called healthy people as well.

The first and most obvious reason is because it is so difficult to obtain sufficient nutrients from our diet, even if we eat the best possible food, as food supplies have lost their nutritional status when compared to more than fifty years ago. Farming practices have seen to that. Yet many doctors still believe we can get all the vitamins and minerals we need from our diet. They simply haven't studied the facts. They tend to say that supplements only make expensive urine. Well my answer to that is that, in that case, we should stop drinking water until we stop passing urine!

The nutrients detractors seem to believe that the only way to treat illnesses is with drugs, drugs and more drugs. Yet a study was published in the New England Journal of Medicine in 1998 saying that, when drugs are given to patients in hospital for the right reason and at the right dose, on average 106,000 people die every year. That made it the fourth highest cause of death of American citizens. If you were to take into account the same analysis in General Practice, plus all the actual mistakes that were made, the chances are that drugs would be the number one cause of death of the American people.

There is now a lot of information that says that most drug adverse effects are caused by the nutritional deficiencies they cause. There is even developing evidence that many, possibly most people, who develop Alzheimer's Disease, develop it because of the drugs they were put on by their doctors. There is also an attempt to make it illegal to use herbs and nutrients of more than virtually useless doses, although there has never been a single death caused by a nutrient. You would be right to ask where all this pressure has come from. Then there is the simple fact that many people's illnesses are partially the result of nutritional deficiencies, because of the poor nutrient presence in our food. As far as I am concerned, an ill person needs help to recover. It's as simple as that.

There are various supplements I recommended to all my MS patients. The first is Vitamin D3♥. There is a Canadian MS Researcher who believes MS will one day be redefined as a Vitamin D deficiency disease. While that may possibly occur, I have improved many MS patients, and some have become symptom free, without recommending they necessarily take Vitamin D3. Having said that, just about every person with MS, and probably every healthy person who lives at the top and bottom of the world, i.e. whose sun exposure is comparatively poor, should probably take at least 5,000IU vitamin D3 + 150mcg K2 per day. To put that into perspective, the UK RDA is a mere 400IU. It may have been increased recently to 600IU. It really is not enough.

Humans developed in the Middle East, or certainly around the Equator, and probably wandered around virtually naked, so their daily vitamin D intake was high. Mankind has wandered the world, and many peoples have settled in the less sunny parts of the world. I believe our lack of vitamin D has caught up with us already, and is partially responsible for many of our diseases.

If you ask your doctor for a blood test for vitamin D, you may well be told it is normal. But what does that mean? It only means that your level of blood vitamin D is within the local laboratory's reference range, which is in fact the average in the population. How is that reference range identified? It is an analysis of all the blood samples the laboratory receives, possibly with the top and bottom five percent eliminated, plus any information from an analysis of people generally, but that would be from very few people. Where do most of those samples come from? From people who doctors think are unwell, or who are actually unwell. And that is your so-called normal range? In my opinion, blood levels for vitamin D should be based upon Californian Lifeguards!

If there is any history of your having taken more than the very occasional course of antibiotics, probiotics will be needed to replenish your bowel supply of friendly organisms that have been killed off by the antibiotics, apart from following an anti-candida diet and probably taking chlorine dioxide for a long time.

A good quality multivitamin/multimineral is probably a good idea, with adequate doses of omega-3 essential fatty acids. Some people recommend omega-6 essential fatty acids, but I like at least two:one omega-3:omega-6, to prevent the omega-6 fatty acids from being metabolised down a pro-inflammatory line. Omega-6's have a pro and an anti-inflammatory line, while Omega-3's have only an anti-inflammatory line of metabolism. On the other hand you could consider taking capsules of dehydrated fruits, vegetables, and berries♥, but there are no significant amounts of omega-3 or -6 essential fatty acids present in them. These capsules could help get round the need for a multimineral/multivitamin preparation, as there are at least twenty-eight double-blind placebo-controlled studies to date to show how valuable they are for human beings.

Vitamin B12 is also essential, because it is important for nerve tissue. I have clearly demonstrated that by giving doses of vitamin B12 intravenously. Unfortunately most of you will not be able to find, and may not be able to afford, having them that way, as there are only a handful of doctors giving nutrients intravenously in the UK. It is quite different in USA. So find the best form of Vitamin B12 you can, and take a lot of it, especially a sub-lingual variety.

If you are having your mercury amalgam teeth fillings replaced, you will, of course, need various chelating minerals. I have given the details in the previous chapter.

Some patients, mainly those with functional symptoms rather than sensory ones, are likely to benefit from magnesium. However, once a person has become magnesium deficient, it can be very hard to correct. That was why I found the intravenous infusions of magnesium so effective. While it could be because I could give a large dose, such as 5g magnesium sulphate, in the infusion, it is my belief that magnesium absorption is under the influence of an enzyme that is itself magnesium dependent. I don't know this for a fact, but whenever I had difficulty repleting a person's magnesium levels, a few intramuscular injections of magnesium (if an intravenous infusion was impractical) seemed to correct the so-called deficiency, after which tablets worked. One of the main drawbacks to large doses of magnesium by mouth (which functional MS patients need) is that it can cause diarrhoea. Recently, however, a transdermal lotion♥ has become available, which has worked very well.

If your MS has affected you so badly that you cannot exercise, or you are at risk of developing osteoporosis, vitamin K2 150mcg, strontium and boron, could be helpful. And, of course, if you have any reason to think that free radicals are playing a significant part in your condition, then a mix of anti-oxidants should be considered.

Finally, if you have any specific deficiencies, you will need to find someone to help you work out what your needs are.

Chapter 17

Diabetes and The Metabolic Syndrome

Most people all too often go to their doctor and say "Doctor! I have a problem. Would you please sort it out for me." That is the way of things at present. What they should say is "Doctor! I have a problem. What can I do to help myself?" The doctor knows it all, they think. But unfortunately he doesn't. People rely on their doctor to sort out their various medical problems, assuming that only he knows how to do so. "If there were another way, surely my doctor would have told me about it," they say. But your doctor only knows about what he was taught at medical school, what his post-graduate training teaches him, and what various drug company representatives tell him. Yes, that method does work for a lot of people. Drugs do work. There is no doubt about it. But they all miss one most important fact. They don't explain why the condition developed in the first instance.

To be fair, the real explanation for diabetes is quite complicated, but I have tried to explain it as simply as possible. Read all about it and be prepared to reread the summary parts, as started at the bottom of page 273.

The fact that drugs do work is nowhere more obvious than in diabetes. There is absolutely no doubt that insulin does work, even if it is not really true to say that insulin is a drug, because it is a natural substance. The discovery of insulin in the early part of the nineteenth century was a truly remarkable one, and has clearly saved the lives of thousands of people.

Yet there is a problem with insulin itself. Some doctors believe that it is the high doses of insulin that are injected subcutaneously that are actually responsible for the long-term effects seen in diabetics, the gangrene, the blindness, etc, and there is a simple explanation for this. Having said that, insulin will be used for a very long time to come, because if an established diabetic doesn't have his regular dose, he will surely die of hyperglycaemia.

In the normal situation, insulin is made in the pancreas, and passes into the blood stream together with digested food into the liver. The insulin and the food are mixed together and are metabolised in the liver and passed into the blood stream to be spread throughout the body, where it does its work. In the diabetic, however, insulin is injected into the skin, usually of the tummy, but it can be injected subcutaneously anywhere. Wherever it is injected, it does not mix with food, nor does it pass straight to the liver. It goes immediately to the tissues.

Okay, so I may be nitpicking a bit, because there is absolutely no doubt that injected insulin does a very good job, and for now I want to leave it there, because there are people who are trying to produce a formula whereby insulin can be applied in a depot form directly in the pancreas. That may well take a long time. At least people are thinking about it.

But I would like to come back to the problem of why. Why does diabetes develop in a particular person? Yes, there may be a genetic predisposition, but in my opinion, genetic predispositions can be switched on or off. You just need to know where the switch is. After all, most people are not born with diabetes. They develop it in life, so presumably their life style plays a part in this.

To me there are two particularly interesting pieces of information to come from research recently. One is that diabetics sometimes have an intolerance of animal milks and products. The second is that low levels of vitamin D predispose a person to diabetes. Having said that, lots of people, probably the majority of people in the UK at least, suffer from inadequate levels of bodily vitamin D. After all, the UK Governments' Recommended Daily Intake (RDI) of vitamin D is 400IU (possibly increased recently to 600 IU) one tenth or one-twentieth the dose I would recommend, something that is becoming more and more recognised by various authorities.

I would also encourage you to have a test for homocysteine in your blood, as a raised homocysteine level can impinge on just about every medical condition.

So, for all the information on the problem, please read the chapter on Hyperhomocysteinaemia, chapter 29.

So, if you ask the question of your doctor, 'what is the cause of my diabetes?' you will not receive a satisfactory answer. He is not interested in the cause, and, in any case, no one needs to know, because we can treat you so easily. That's where I disagree. To know why? is of great importance, because it gives you something to work on. Yes, it may be difficult, because you will have to change your lifestyle. You may even have to cut out certain foods, exercise, give up smokimg or alcohol. I don't know exactly what you need to do at this stage, but you will need to do something.

So let us look at diabetes. What has actually gone wrong? Basically your pancreas has difficulty producing enough insulin to cope with the sugar you convert from your diet, which you do every day when you eat. But why can your pancreas not produce enough insulin? Could it be that you have exhausted its ability to do what it should do? Certainly something has gone wrong with the normal process.

In a non-diabetic, you consume some carbohydrate, and your intestines convert it into sugar, which is absorbed into your blood stream. This produces a raised blood sugar level that stimulates your pancreas to produce insulin to deliver the sugar to your muscle cells and your brain. The whole purpose of this is to allow your muscles to work when they are needed, and of course your brain needs sugar to function. If there is too much sugar in your blood stream and your muscles are full of sugar, insulin redirects the sugar to fat cells. The more sugar you have in your blood, the more fat cells are made to accommodate this extra sugar. You therefore put on weight. It is carbohydrate, not fat that makes most people fat. I am absolutely sure of this. Many enormous Americans are on a fat-free diet, yet they are huge. Something isn't working.

So, quite simply, a diabetic is someone whose pancreas does not produce enough insulin when it is required.

Lets now turn to the pre-diabetic state that some people suffer from, namely the Metabolic Syndrome, or Syndrome X as it is sometimes called. Such a person may well have a raised level of cholesterol, raised triglycerides, raised blood pressure, increased platelet stickiness and increased fat accumulation around his midriff. To be fair the same could apply to a woman. You see many such people wandering around the country, with an obvious belly. They are suffering from the metabolic syndrome. Type I diabetes is insulin-dependent, whereas type II diabetes is what used to be called late onset diabetes, but can no longer be so called, because some teenagers are suffering from it. Some of them have even developed it to such an extent that they have had to have a limb, usually a leg, amputated! Type II diabetes is said to occur because of insulin resistance. Insulin is quite simply not doing its job properly.

There are various myths that I want to dispel, the first being that type II diabetes affects overweight older people. The older part I have just dealt with. Many type II diabetics (about 20%) are not overweight at all. The second myth I want to dispel is that the villain of the piece is not obesity, as it is said to be. Diabetes type II is not caused by being overweight. A third myth I want to dispel is that obesity (and therefore type II diabetes) is caused by eating too much and not exercising enough.

Isn't food supposed to give you energy? If that were true, why are diabetics always hungry and lacking in energy? Why do they eat so much?

Hunger is a mechanism that tells the brain that your muscle cells need more fuel. So why doesn't eating more provide that fuel? Presumably something has stopped the fuel doing its job. Perhaps something had stopped sugar from entering your muscle cells. If that is true, exercising is not only impossible, it's pointless, especially as the advice to eat less and exercise usually doesn't work.

The fourth myth in all of this is that the villain of the piece in the metabolic syndrome is a raised cholesterol level. It isn't. The theory goes something like this. When a person dies of a heart attack, cholesterol is often found to be blocking an important artery in the heart, so cholesterol was the cause of the heart attack. So a low cholesterol diet and cholesterol-lowering statin drugs are the answer. This is wrong thinking. I accept that there may well be a lot of cholesterol around at the time of the heart attack, but the rest doesn't automatically follow. Yes, if there is less cholesterol around things would be a lot better.

Unfortunately there is absolutely no proof that cholesterol is the real bad guy, because so many studies have shown a completely different approach. The book by Dr. Malcolm Kendrick entitled 'The Great Cholesterol Con. The Truth About What Really Causes Heart disease and How to Avoid it'♥ is really worth reading.

In my opinion, cholesterol is trying to heal something in your arteries, basically inflammation, and cholesterol is not the cause but the effect of arterial inflammation. If the cause of the inflammation is not identified and removed, cholesterol will continue to try to heal the inflammation, so there will inevitably be a build up of cholesterol. But whoever heard of inflammation as a cause of diabetes?

Myth number five is that the real villain in type II diabetes is insulin resistance, i.e. insulin is not being effective at the normal level, so you have to produce more insulin to do the same job and have the same effect.

I'd like to ask a simple question. What's stopping insulin from doing its normal job properly? If you have the answer to that question, you have the answer to diabetes, obesity and the metabolic syndrome in so many people.

In a non-diabetic person, dietary carbohydrate is converted into glucose. Your blood glucose (I will use the words sugar and glucose synonymously) level goes up and insulin is produced to deliver that sugar to your muscle cells to make energy. If your muscle cells are full, any extra sugar is diverted into fat cells, but if your muscle cells have used up all their sugar, fat can be converted into fatty acids as a form of spare fuel. Insulin resistance is said to make it difficult for glucose to enter muscle cells, so more insulin has to be generated to overcome this resistance. No one seems to know why this resistance occurs.

In the meantime glucose cannot, or more to the point does not, enter your muscle cells, so it is diverted into fat cells which have to expand and increase in number to accommodate this extra fat, especially round the midriff. If this extra sugar were not diverted somewhere, your blood sugar levels would rise inexorably, leading to hyperglycaemic (high blood sugar) coma and death. So you could call this diversion a brain protection mechanism.

However, if glucose is diverted into fat cells, it should only occur because the muscle cells are full. But if there is insulin resistance, the muscle cells are not full. In these circumstances, the entry of glucose into fat cells somehow erroneously signals to the brain that the muscle cells are full. This in turn stops fat cells from converting fat into fatty acids which muscle cells can normally use as an alternative fuel to glucose, reasoning that, if muscle cells are full, there is no need to produce the reserve fuel. However, as the muscle cells have not received their correct supply of sugar, you remain hungry and tired, and find it almost impossible to exercise. So you eat something sugary to give you a much-needed boost, but it not only doesn't work, it perpetuates this whole system.

After many years of trying to meet this extra demand for more and more insulin, your pancreas becomes exhausted, you fail to produce enough insulin, your blood sugar levels rise and you show signs of having become a diabetic. Anything that is over-stimulated for too long becomes exhausted in the end.

Exactly when a person becomes a diabetic is arbitrary, but all the signs are there to warn you of what is happening to your body. What is important is to recognise the gradual changes taking place in your shape, and do something about it. So, quite simply, if you are putting on weight especially round your midriff, are always hungry and feel constantly tired, beware!

The combination of calorie-controlled diet and exercise does work in some people, but fails all too often. The theory is that if more food is consumed than is expended, the extra will be stored as fat, and you will put on weight. Conversely, if less food is consumed than expended, you will raid your fat stores to make up the deficit, and you will consequently lose weight. It just doesn't seem to work like that for so many people.

Myth no 6. Since obesity is the result of too much fat in the body, a low fat or fat-free diet is the answer, but again it doesn't work all too often. Just look at all those Americans. They are all eating a fat-free diet, yet so many of them are really enormous. Yes, I accept that there are five calories in one gram of protein and one gram of carbohydrate, while there are nine calories in one gram of fat. So it is perfectly reasonable on that basis to say cut out fat and you will lose weight. But, I repeat, it doesn't work all too often. What is forgotten is that carbohydrate actually slows down your metabolism, whereas fat speeds it up. Indeed the opposite may be the answer. In 1957, Dr. Richard Mackarness wrote his first book entitled 'Eat Fat And Grow Slim'♥. Mac was basically the person whose work encouraged me to take an interest in this area of medicine. And what about the Atkins diet. I know there has been a lot of criticism of this approach to losing weight, but it certainly works for a lot of people. The trouble is that most people don't follow his overall approach, possibly not having read his book.

Unfortunately, for the pre-diabetic and the diabetic, high levels of insulin in the blood lock up your fat cells, making it impossible for them to release fat as the fatty acid alternative to glucose, so we need to understand why this happens. As an aside, there is an enzyme called Lipoprotein lipase (LPL) in the normal person, whose job is effectively three-fold. First it delivers fat to fat cells, second it delivers free fatty acids from fat cells to muscle cells, and third it helps convert triglycerides into free fatty acids. Also if you try to lose weight with high levels of circulating insulin, 90% of what you lose will be protein, i.e. muscle tissue. If you then put weight back on again, it will be mainly as fat.

To understand what goes wrong, we need to understand what happens in a normal person. You consume some carbohydrate that you convert into glucose (sugar) in the intestine, which is absorbed into the blood stream. This causes your pancreas to produce insulin to handle the sugar. When insulin arrives at the surface receptor of a muscle cell, it signals to a chemical called glucose transporter 4 (Glut 4) to come to the surface of the cell to receive the molecule of sugar. At the same time, chromium moves from the blood stream into the cell to make the whole process happen more efficiently. Sugar enters the muscle cell. Everyone is happy. The system is working normally.

Changing tack for a moment, I have already said who ever thought of inflammation being part of diabetes? Yet inflammation is an essential part of normal every day life. It is an essential function the body uses to fight off an invading organism, or a splinter, or anything that should not be there. You would die without inflammation. You would have no ability to deal with any invader, as has happened to a number of people who have been put onto a new drug that interfered with the process of inflammation.

In the process of inflammation, many powerful chemicals are produced. They all have specific tasks to perform. But once the invader has been dealt with, the inflammation is switched off. I will repeat that statement, because it is absolutely vital to this whole process. Once the invader has been dealt with, the inflammation is switched off.

One such chemical is called TNF-alpha (tumour necrosis factor-alpha). Any inflammation produces TNF-alpha. Unfortunately, TNF-alpha destroys Glut-4, so that glucose cannot be taken into the muscle cells. That means that glucose is diverted into fat cells. TNF-alpha also stimulates the production of fat cells, and fat cells produce TNF-alpha, so there is a lot of TNF-alpha floating around in an inflamed fat person.

TNF-alpha also destroys LPL, which can also be destroyed by calorie restriction and exercise. And, without LPL, fat cannot be used as an alternative form of fuel.

So with no glucose getting into your muscle cells, your muscle cells cannot even use their normal alternative supply of energy in the form of fatty acids being made from fat, yet you have plenty of stores of fat that you cannot use. And chromium is lost by heavy exercise and a diet high in sugar and refined carbohydrate and low in anti-oxidants especially vitamin C.

There is a possibility that more than 75% of Americans are prone to the metabolic syndrome. The initial common symptoms are an increase in weight, especially around the midriff, an inability to concentrate, unexplained drowsiness much of the time, decreased endurance during any form of exercise and generalised decreased levels of energy.

The metabolic syndrome is associated with nearly all forms of cardiovascular diseases, such as heart attacks, strokes and diabetes. There is also an increased risk of cancers, especially breast and colon cancers, Alzheimer's disease, polycystic ovaries, gout, inflammatory bowl disease and blood clotting conditions, among others.

Remember I said right at the beginning that the metabolic syndrome involves raised levels of cholesterol and triglycerides, raised blood pressure, increased platelet stickiness and fat accumulation around the midriff. Clearly there is some sort of relationship between obesity, diabetes type II and the metabolic syndrome.

So let me summarise what I have said so far. 80% of diabetics are overweight not 100%, therefore obesity cannot be the cause of type II diabetes. Overweight diabetics tend to be permanently tired, and don't have the energy to exercise. Low calorie diets and exercise tend not to work in the overweight diabetic. Type II diabetes can no longer be called late onset diabetes, as it is now affecting children, some of whom are even having limbs amputated!

Insulin resistance and being overweight are considered to be the causes of type II diabetes, and insulin resistance develops because at normal levels insulin does not achieve its purpose, namely to deliver sugar to muscle cells.

When insulin arrives at the insulin receptor on the surface of the muscle cell, its arrival signals to Glut 4 to move to the surface to receive the molecule of glucose, but Glut 4 is destroyed by TNF-alpha, which itself is an essential part of inflammation and is also produced by fat cells. Insulin's efficiency helper Chromium is reduced by endurance exercise and a diet high in sugar and refined carbohydrate and low in anti-oxidants, especially vitamin C. I'll explain the importance of vitamin C in a moment.

TNF-alpha also destroys LPL, so preventing fat from being mobilised and used as an alternative fuel to glucose. TNF-alpha induces the production of fat cells, which themselves produce TNF-alpha. So a vicious circle is set up with TNF-alpha at the centre.

The reason why vitamin C is so essential is because one of its main functions is to maintain the integrity of collagen, of which arterial walls are partly made up. In many diseases, especially cardiovascular ones, your arterial wall is constantly under challenge, especially where an artery divides. At such a point, there is tremendous pressure at the line between the two divisions, and that causes a lot of damage, with the inevitable breakdown of tissue and the formation of a clot, which cholesterol tries to repair, but in so doing, narrows the area. In due course, the whole area can become blocked entirely, leading to a heart attack or a stroke.

In the meantime, who loves you? Drug Companies, of course. First you will be on something for your raised blood sugar. Then you will inevitably be put on a statin drug for your cholesterol. Next will probably be one or two drugs for your raised blood pressure, possibly an anti-inflammatory, an appetite suppressant and an antibiotic if you show evidence of infection because of all that sugar oozing out of your skin.

Whose waiting in the wings? Surgeons, of course. One to remove your cataracts, another to amputate a limb. It's all rather nasty.

But has anyone prescribed vitamin C or chromium, or vitamin D? Has anyone told you what the cause of all of this is? I doubt it. The cause is inflammation, which produces so much TNF-alpha, which in turn causes so much damage.

What causes the inflammation? It could be an infection, possibly a virus of sorts, possibly a toxic chemical, possibly mercury, lead or aluminium, or may be even stress. It could also be gas from your gas cooker, petrol or diesel fumes. It could be all sorts of things. But the most likely source of the inflammation is food, what you eat or drink.

I'm sure you have heard of high glycaemic and low glycaemic foods. Every diabetic is told to avoid consuming high glycaemic foods and they are given a list. They are also told to eat a low fat diet and exercise. But why doesn't it work? The answer must be because the advice given is somehow wrong. To be fair it may be partially correct, but everyone seems to be missing something. That something is an idiosyncratic reaction to a food, something that is high glycaemic to the individual, but not to everyone.

I had a patient once who found wholemeal bread to produce a far greater increase in his blood sugar level than white bread or sugar itself. Then there was another patient who found aspartame to cause a tremendous increase in her blood sugar. I gave a lecture to a large group of people a couple of years ago, and asked them if anyone recognised what I was saying. One person said she was aware that pumpkin caused her blood sugar to surge; another said rice did the same, while a third said that potato did that. When I asked them whether they were still eating those foods, they all said they were. When I asked them why they were still eating them, they said because they liked the foods!

There is a marvellous book entitled 'Victory Over Diabetes' by William Philpot MD and Dwight K Kalita PhD♥, that goes into their approach to all diabetics. They admitted them all into their unit, fasted them for four or five days, then challenged them with individual foods and drinks, up to three a day, but taking a blood sample for blood sugar before and approximately one hour after each challenge. They found the most amazing effects. Everyone had their own idiosyncratic food reactions, some being absolutely bizarre. While it is perfectly reasonable to suggest that carbohydrate foods are the most likely culprits, they found meats, dairy products and fatty foods sometime caused far more of a rise in blood sugar than ordinary sugar. In fact sometimes sugar did not cause an abnormal rise at all.

Then they found some people had significant blood sugar rises to gas from gas cookers, car and diesel fumes and many different chemicals that most of us seem to be able to tolerate. However, I wonder!

One other thing I found fascinating in their book was the fact that sometimes the reaction was a significant and dangerous drop in blood sugar, not always a rise. Sometimes people had a change in blood sugar levels with very significant mental and physical changes, while other patients had no obvious symptom changes at all. They simply called this disordered carbohydrate metabolism.

Another of the things they talk about in the book is the fact that the pancreas is a whole organ, not divided into two parts, as we are always taught. Yes there are the insulin-producing Islets of Langerhans and the enzyme-producing part, and they do different things. However, Philpot and Kalita insisted that, if the insulin-producing cells were under strain, then the enzyme and sodium bicarbonate-producing parts were under even more strain. They reckoned that first the production of sodium bicarbonate was affected, then the enzyme-producing part, and finally the insulin-producing part. They judged that it was most important to support all parts of the pancreas at the same time, and I would agree with them. That's why I gave diabetics digestive enzymes after meals and sodium bicarbonate twenty to thirty minutes later, basically to virtually take over the responsibility of the pancreas, while working out what foods the patient should avoid, i.e. which foods were causing a big increase in blood sugar levels and occasionally a significant fall.

Because the digestive enzyme-producing part of the pancreas was not working properly, they assumed that a number of individual foods escaped the digestive process and were effectively absorbed almost whole into the blood stream, well at least the foods were sufficiently undigested to set up an alarm reaction in the blood stream, called a kinin-inflammatory reaction, rather than a classical allergic one. In fact they gave evidence that if they gave about 1600mg of digestive enzymes, a supply of basic amino acids, and half a teaspoonful of sodium bicarbonate twenty to thirty minutes later, they were able to block the rise in blood sugar that had been shown to occur on an earlier challenge.

So, what is waiting in your blood to deal with an invader? Neutrophils, white blood cells. When neutrophils are stimulated to attack something, what do they release? TNF-alpha and other chemicals, and because the foods are continually being consumed, the neutrophil response is not turned off.

Do you remember how I said earlier on something that I repeated, namely that once the inflammation has been dealt with, the reaction is turned off? Well it isn't turned off, because you are still eating a food or foods that are causing a reaction in the blood stream. To be fair, you are probably not aware of it, or you may have a suspicion, and in any case you like the food, so it never occurs to you to stop eating it.

It is certainly possible that gas from your gas cooker may be causing a problem, or lead, mercury, aluminium or cadmium, or car exhaust fumes, but the most likely cause of a reaction in you is one or more foods you eat, usually fairly regularly. Yes it is possible you have a genetic predisposition to diabetes, but, as I have said before, you can switch the predisposition on or off, if you know where the switch is.

Chapter 18

How To Identify Your Culprits

So how do you track down what food or foods you might be reacting to? There are basically two ways of doing that, so I will describe the cheapest method, although it may take quite a long time. First make a long list of foods and drinks you take in. Divide them up into food groups of meats, dairy, fish, vegetables, fruits, salad items, grains, pulses, nuts, herbs and drinks. Write down the name of a food on the left of the page. Draw about six lines down the page to the right, so that you can put a tick in any column against a food, depending on how often you consume that item, say daily, two to three times a week, once a week, once every two weeks, once a month, for example. It doesn't matter how precise you are, but look at the foods you consume most commonly first. Don't forget to make a note of cups of tea and coffee and any juices you have.

The majority of people probably eat or drink much the same almost every day. They have bread, butter or an alternative spread, eggs, bacon, potatoes, tea and coffee on a regular basis. So start with one of these. I assume you have a piece of equipment to measure your blood sugar. If not, may I suggest you buy one from the local chemist or drug store, or borrow one from a friend.

If you want to you could practice measuring your blood sugar levels, and may I suggest you test immediately before and about one hour after meals, just to see what happens. There is the possibility that this will help you identify the culprit(s). However, if you need to be more specific, select a named food, avoid it totally for five days (this makes your sensitivity more acute), then challenge with a suitable helping of that food entirely on its own for breakfast on the morning of day six, testing your blood sugar before and about one hour after eating the food. It would be best if you were to do a five-day fast on bottled-in-glass plain water, but it is extremely unlikely any of you will do that. I have described the five-day fast in a book I wrote in 1987 entitled 'Conquering Cystitis'♥. Were you to do a five-day fast, you would almost definitely be no longer diabetic on the morning of day six, so you would need to watch how much insulin you took, if you are on it. If you are not, you could stop your tablets, but you would need to watch your blood sugar levels very closely, for which reason you should be under the control of a medical expert of sorts.

To speed up this method, you could avoid for five whole days, say, wheat on Monday, egg on Tuesday, coffee on Wednesday, milk on Thursday and bacon on Friday, and challenge with wheat the next Saturday, egg on Sunday, coffee on Monday, milk on Tuesday and bacon on Wednesday. The food should be pure, i.e. do not fry an egg in oil, but eat it soft boiled, for example. You should only test if your before challenge blood sugar test is fairly low and not too high, say 4, 5 or 6, as you are looking for a significant rise in blood sugar level to well over 10. But don't forget a challenge could cause your blood sugar to fall precipitously.

If you are sure a particular food produces a significant change in blood sugar, make a note of it and leave it out of your diet for now. Do the same with any food you are not sure of. You can always test that food another day. The only disadvantage of this method is that you will be pricking fingers rather often, so they may become a bit sore. Yes, it may take rather a long time to get to the bottom of your testing, but there is no hurry. With any luck you will find a culprit early on, so see how you go simply avoiding it. However, it is likely that you are reacting to a food(s) that you eat almost every day, and there may not be many of them. Only time will tell.

If you are on insulin injections, it may be sensible to drop the dose a bit to make sure you don't go into hypoglycaemic (low blood sugar the dangerous one) shock, but always carry a lump of sugar around with you at all times, even if that is a former culprit. It would also be sensible to let your doctor know what you are doing, so he or she can keep an eye on you.

If you want a much quicker way of doing things, but one that will cost you two or three hundred pounds, The Alcat Test♥ tests the reaction between a tiny sample of your blood incubated for an hour with an extract of named foods. The test is based on the fact that, if a reaction occurs, neutrophils are activated, which can be picked up by an automated haematology analyser. I have already said that it is the neutrophil that releases TNF-alpha. Cut out the foods that the test suggests are positive and you could become free of diabetes. The test is very good but it is not 100% accurate, and I could give all sorts of explanations for that.

Chapter 19

Essential Supplements

By and large I usually recommend people try to remove the cause of their problems first, and I am perfectly happy for you to proceed along those lines. However, if Drs Philpott and Kalita are right, it may well be sensible for you to take amino acids at the beginning of each meal, digestive enzymes at the end of the meal and 1⁄2 teaspoonful of sodium bicarbonate 30 minutes after finishing the meal. This may well help to minimise any smaller reactions you failed to identify on testing. Be aware, however, that the preparations you take may contain something such as lactose that may cause a problem, so you would be wise to test your blood sugar levels before and one hour after taking the preparations.

So the first preparations would be amino acids, digestive enzymes and sodium bicarbonate. The rest can wait awhile, but don't leave things too long. Then there is the need of chromium, at 100mcg three times a day with meals, and vitamin C 1 to 2g at least, again divided ideally into three doses a day. A 50mg multi-B vitamin, especially with at least 50mg vitamin B6, as there is plenty of evidence that a low level of vitamin B6 is clearly associated with cardiovascular problems, and vitamin D3, at least 5000IU, + 150mcg K2 if not 10,000IU should be added, plus a multimineral supplement. Exactly how long you should remain on such a regime is impossible for me to say, but I would imagine at least three months in the first instance.

Chapter 20

The Four-Day Rotation Diet

Fortunately it is my belief that the majority of people in the United Kingdom suffer mainly from food and drink related diabetes. In America houses are all too often made of man-made materials, which contain fire retardant chemicals and similar substances, so that it is said that the air inside many American houses is far more chemically polluted than the air outside, which itself is bad enough.

Having said that, it is important to try to identify if a particular patient is reacting abnormally to an environmental chemical, such as car and diesel fumes, gas to heat the house and cook with, etc. I will explain how to do that later.

If you are fortunate to find only a small number of foods need to be avoided because of your reaction to them, and life is not too hard without them, simply cut them out for at least three months, after which you may be able to eat them one day in four, but it may be simpler to avoid them for ever. Chocolate gives me a migraine. I have decided to avoid chocolate for the rest of my life.

Having said that, take this opportunity to look at your life style, eat a healthier diet, cut out dairy products, caffeine and alcohol, white refined flour products and all chemicals and junk food as far as possible, and, of course, deal with any foods you reacted to on challenge appropriately. Take control of your life. That way you could easily become a non-diabetic, and certainly a more healthy person. You should certainly reduce your insulin requirements considerably, and may even be able to come off insulin altogether and certainly any anti-diabetic tablets you are already on. I will talk about exercise a bit later.

In the meantime, you may find that rather too many foods and drinks have caused an exaggerated blood sugar response on testing, so first of all place them in an order of severity, based upon the change in blood sugar level each item produced on challenge. Two lists may be enough, so list those that produced a big, severe change, and another list of those items that led to a moderate change. Avoid the moderate ones for six weeks and the severe ones for three months.

If this is the case with you, it is not sufficient to eat as often as you like those foods that are left, because you are almost bound to end up reacting to one or more of them, so you will be back to square one. So, in the meantime, rotate foods in a four-day fashion, eating members of a food family on one day only and not again for four days, i.e. eat a food on, say, a Monday and not again until the next Friday. I have given a list of foods to eat on a four-day rotation below, but don't forget to avoid completely, for a while, any food you reacted to. Remember you don't have to eat all of the foods listed: -

Day 1 Food Families
Meat: Beef, milk, cheese, butter, yoghurt
Fish: Scallops, snails, abalones, squid. Clams, mussels, oysters, mackerel, flounder, anchovies
Fruit:Strawberries, blackberries, grapes, raisins, bananas, plantains, apples, mulberries, plantains
Vegetables: Potatoes, tomatoes, eggplant (aubergines), peppers (red and green), chilli peppers, paprika, cayenne, ground cherries, onions, garlic, asparagus, chives, spinach, mushroom, brewer's yeast, okra, cottonseed
Grains:Wheat, rye, barley, oats,buckwheat, rhubarb
Nuts: Walnuts, pecans, macadamia, peanuts, nutmeg
Oils: Peanut, cottonseed
Sterculia: Chocolate, cocoa

Herbs and spices: Bay leaf, cinnamon, arrowroot, vanilla, flaxseeds
Sweetener: Beet sugar, maple sugar
Tea: Rose hips, strawberry leaf

Day 2 Food Families
Meat: Rabbit, chicken, quail, pheasant, chicken, quail and pheasant eggs
Fish: Sturgeon, herring, white fish, crabs, crayfish, lobsters
Fruit: Plum, cherries, peaches, oranges, limes, grapefruit, clementines, papaya, watermelons, pumpkins and seeds, cucumbers, acorn, squash, dates
Vegetables: Coconut, carrots, parsley, parsnips, anise, dill, fennel, cumin, coriander, watercress, Brussel sprouts, collards, endive, escarole, artichokes, romaine, safflower, tarragon
Nuts: Cashews
Oil: Olives and oil, coconut, almond
Herbs: Basil, horehound, sage, catnip, spearmint, cloves, allspice
Sweetener: Date sugar, fructose
Tea: Spearmint, papaya

Day 3 Food Families
Meat: Lamb, pork
Fish: Sea herring, cod, sea bass, sea trout, tuna, swordfish, sole
Fruit: Pears, raspberries, blueberries, cranberries, gooseberries, figs
Grains: Corn (maize), rice, millet, tapioca
Vegetables: Avocados, peas, black-eyed peas, green beans, soybeans, lentils, kidney beans, lima beans, beets, chard, garlic, leeks
Nuts: Filberts, hazelnuts, walnuts
Cruits: Black and white pepper
Oils: Soybean, avocado, corn (maize)
Sweetener: Carob, dextrose, glucose, cane sugar, molasses
Tea: Alfalfa, sassafras, raspberry leaf

Day 4 Food Families
Meat: Turkey, duck, goose, guinea fowl
Fish: Prawns, shrimps, salmon, bass, perch
Vegetables: Sweet potatoes, turnips, radishes, Chinese cabbage, broccoli, cauliflower, kale, lettuce, chicory, celery
Fruit: Lemons, grapefruit, tangerines, nectarines, melons, apricots, pine-apples, mangoes, elderberries
Nuts: Chestnuts, Brazil nuts
Spices: Oregano, savory, peppermint, thyme, marjoram, mace
Oils: Sesame, sunflower
Sweetener: Honey
Tea: Peppermint, lemon balm

Having avoided certain foods you identified caused a significant increase in your blood sugar, whether for six weeks or three months, add them in sequentially on the four-day rotation system, but make sure they do not affect your blood sugar levels adversely, even if they don't cause any symptoms. There are variations on this theme of four-day rotation, which you can obtain by reading a copy of Dr. Philpott and

Kalita's book.

Chapter 21

Arthritis

Arthritis affects millions of people the world over. Rheumatologists divide arthritics basically into two groups, those with osteo-arthritis and those with rheumatoid arthritis. The rheumatoid group are part of a collection of people who suffer from what is called an autoimmune disease, that is a group of conditions in which the person's immune system is said to be attacking their own tissues.

Personally I don't agree with that approach. I don't believe the immune system is so stupid as to do that, and I have evidence to prove that I am right, which I will explain at a later stage.

Osteo-arthritis is said to occur when the soft material between two joints has been eroded, so athletes tend to suffer from it, although not by any means always. It also tends to affect the larger joints of the body, whereas rheumatoid arthritis tends to affect the smaller joints, of the hands and feet, for example.

In both cases there is inflammation, although it is more obvious in the rheumatoid form, as joints are usually warm to the touch. In many cases of osteo-arthritis, the erosion of the soft tissue between the joints causes bone to rub on bone, so it is bound to be painful at times.

The standard treatment for all forms of arthritis is anti-inflammatory drugs in the first instance, although some doctors may choose one of the more modern drugs. For many people, aspirin or paracetamol may be sufficient in the first instance, but more potent drugs are likely to be needed in due course.

If there is inflammation as part of the underlying cause, what causes the inflammation? In my experience, it is most likely something the sufferer is eating or drinking on a regular basis. There is in fact no limit to the number of foods that an individual may be reacting to, although, by and large, most arthritics react to only a few foods. Occasionally, however, I have come across a patient reacting to gas to heat the house or cook with, perfumes or diesel and petrol fumes, or similar chemicals. Sometimes it can be very difficult to work out what a person is reacting to, but there is always a cause. And don't forget to have a blood test carried out for homocysteine, because it could be playing a part in your arthritis. For a lot of information about the problem, please read the chapter on Hyperhomocysteinaemia, chapter 29.

So once again, follow the advice I gave in the previous part, starting on page 285 to begin with, i.e. make a list of foods and drinks and how often you consume them. Do your own homework in the first instance. May I suggest that, if you want advice on a particular program to begin with, cut out from your diet all dairy products (animal milks, butter, cream, yoghurt, lactose, whey, and casein and read labels carefully), citrus fruits, the deadly nightshade group of foods (potatoes, tomatoes, aubergines (eggplant in USA) and peppers, and tobacco of course), caffeine (don't forget there is caffeine in chocolate, tea and cola drinks), sugar and all white flour products, all alcohol, all junk food and any chemicals added to foods, such as aspartame, MSG, etc. It amazes me how often there is a significant improvement within a month on such an avoidance pattern. However, it is perfectly possible that you didn't need to eliminate all of those foods, so you could reintroduce some of them in turn and see whether your arthritis returns.

A word of warning here. In my experience, symptoms of arthritis are comparatively slow to come back, and the longer you have avoided a former culprit of your symptoms, the longer it takes for them to return. So start challenging almost as soon as you are sure that avoiding a food has helped your symptoms to go. You may need to eat a sensible helping of that food more than once a day for a few days to check whether it causes a return of symptoms. But don't eat that food more often than you normally would. If eating the food only once produces no reaction and you wouldn't eat it very often anyway, don't bother to try it again until it would be normal for you to eat it.

For example, you may only eat tomatoes once a week. If your symptoms cleared when you avoided the whole of the family, but did not return when you tried tomatoes again, keep tomatoes as an occasional food. Just because you may have reacted to one food of a family of foods, doesn't automatically mean that you react to all of them. Your body is an amazingly complicated structure, and there is no accounting for your own particular reactions. So you will need to test them all if you want to be able eat them. As an alternative you could spend some money and have the Alcat blood test done on you♥. It is one of the best tests in my experience, but it is not 100% perfect. No test ever is. I'm afraid that's the way of the world. Having said that, your blood is incubated with a tiny amount of various food extracts at body temperature for one hour, and the effect on the sample of blood analysed in an automatic haematology (blood) analyser. In fact it is in particular the effect upon your neutrophils that the test relies on. If your neutrophils are activated by contact with a particular food or chemical, TNF-alpha, among many other chemicals, is released. If you read all the earlier chapters, you may remember that TNF-alpha is one of the most potent causes of inflammation. It is just that your joints have become the target for that inflammation.

As I have just said, the Alcat Test is not 100% perfect. One reason is that certain foods might need a stronger concentration of the food to cause a reaction, or may need longer that one hour of incubation to achieve the same. Having said that, it is a very good test, and is a good way of starting to modify your diet, if you are prepared to pay for it.

It may be more difficult to identify whether you are reacting to petrol or diesel fumes, heating gas or any of a myriad of environmental chemicals. A good history should help you to identify the possibility, especially if you are aware of it being possible. The unfortunate part is that you may not react immediately on exposure to a chemical, so finding the exact coincidence may be hard.

Do you feel generally worse in your kitchen, if you cook with gas? Do you feel worse in your car or lorry? Do you feel better or worse away from home, or in another country? Look at your life and search for any coincidences. For example, brush your teeth with a new toothbrush without using toothpaste. You never know, you might be reacting to something in the mixture. Become a detective on yourself. The trouble is that you may avoid three or four major culprits, but could still remain symptomatic if there is one more cause yet to be eliminated. Nevertheless, do your best. In my experience, it is not that difficult in the majority of people.

If you are fortunate enough to have identified the causes of your arthritis, avoid them all for ever if you are happy to do so and doing so is not inconvenient for you. On the other hand, once you have avoided them for, say three months, your sensitivity to them may have sufficiently settled down for you to be able to eat them again occasionally, possibly once a week, without becoming ill again, but only time and experience will tell. Avoiding a cause for about three months or so allows the inflammation in your body to disappear. You are no longer releasing TNF-alpha from your neutrophils.

This brings me on to the reason why I disagree with the diagnosis of autoimmune disease, which basically says that your immune system is attacking your tissues. In such a condition, taking a sample of the tissue demonstrates cells of the immune system amongst the normal cells of that tissue, and blood tests show antibodies against the tissue. There is also a theory that your immune system attacks the tissue by mistake, as a particular virus or other organism present nearby has similar make-up to the tissue, and your immune system is attacking the virus and your tissue at the same time.

My explanation is quite simple. It says that, yes, there is something attacking the tissue, causing inflammation, and not surprisingly your immune system is trying to deal with the situation. Because you are not aware what is actually causing the inflammation and are not avoiding it, your immune system is continually activated, continually releasing TNF-alpha, and keeping the inflammatory cascade going all the time. If you can identify the cause of the inflammation and avoid it, the production of TNF-alpha will cease and the inflammation will stop. I have done this many times with patients suffering from arthritis. So, if you can find the causes of inflammation in your body and avoid them, you will become symptom free. It really is that simple in principal, but finding the causes of inflammation in you may not be so easy.

If you have identified the food or chemical causes of your arthritis, what can you do about them, apart from avoiding them entirely if that is possible? There are three ways of managing the situation, all of which are quite complicated, but are worth talking about.

The first is homoeopathic desensitisation. I accept that many doctors don't believe homoeopathy works at all, but I assure you I have found it does, or at least it clearly helped my patients tolerate being exposed to the chemicals or eating the causative foods. In principal, you need to avoid the food or chemical for at least one week, or longer if you can manage it. During that time, you put a dose of a 30C or 200C potency of the substance under your tongue, twice a day for the 30C or once a day for the 200C potency. If you can stay off that substance for another week or even longer, the effect works even better. If you can't, repeat the treatment, staying off the substance for the week of that treatment. You also take a dose of potentiser before the very first dose of the week's treatment, but only before the first dose of that week.

In theory, you should only do one substance a week, and I have never tried to do more than one at a time, but there is the possibility that you could try to do more than one at a time. So this whole process could take quite a long time, especially if you need to repeat a treatment.

The whole process can be used for chemicals as well as foods, but it can be hard to obtain an extract of a chemical, although homoeopathic pharmacies do exist. This method can be used by the general public, without needing a consultant taking you through the process. Simply follow my instructions.

The second method requires the help of someone trained in the art of sublingual or intradermal desensitisation. Once at an appropriate clinic, a tiny dose of the substance to be tested, specially diluted and prepared, is either injected into the outer layer of the skin, usually of your upper outer arm, or a drop is placed under your tongue. There is then a ten minute wait for a reaction of some sort, which can be the development of symptoms, with or without a specific reaction in your skin, if injected.

If symptoms develop and the injected site grows in size, a second dose is injected, and possibly a third or fourth dilution, until there are no symptoms, and the skin site does not grow at all. To be fair it can be quite difficult at times to know when the end-point has been achieved, as some people's symptom responses take longer to settle than others, and symptom settling may not coincide well enough with the skin response.

The sublingual (under the tongue) approach can work well enough in some people, but using the skin injection gives not only the symptom clues but also a visual form of help to identify the correct end-point. The main advantage of this system is that it can be used to identify culprits as well as desensitise the person against them, and, in one particular session of three or four hours quite a number of culprits and treatments can be managed. You are then given either some drops to place carefully under your tongue on a daily basis for quite a long time to effectively desensitise you, or some liquid to inject a special amount under your skin, while you continue to consume the food or be exposed to the chemicals.

One of the main disadvantages is that you need to find a clinic where they carry out such a process and it can be quite expensive. The other problem is that occasionally your so-called end-points can change suddenly between visits to the clinic, so that they all have to be checked next time. However, the system works well in many patients, and I have known some people have twenty or more substances in each treatment package with continuing success.

There are many doctors practising this kind of medicine in America, all of who would likely be Members or Fellows of the American Academy of Environmental Medicine. There are very few in the UK♥.

There is a third way of desensitising, invented by an English Physician by the name of Dr. Len McEwen. It is called Enzyme Potentiated Desensitisation. It is a little difficult to explain, but basically an injection or cup is applied to usually your forearm, in which there are specially prepared preparations of so-called allergens, or substances to which you may or may not be reacting, after the skin there has been scarified to allow absorption of ingredients more effectively into your body. The cup is left there for a specified length of time and is renewed every so often. It is a specialised system, and requires proper training to carry it out. There are doctors in the UK and America who practise this approach.

Chapter 22

Asthma and Bronchitis

Asthma is a condition in which the person may only have a cough, but is more likely to involve breathing difficulties. The difference between asthma and bronchitis is largely that the asthmatic has problems exhaling, whereas the bronchitic has difficulty inhaling. A wheeze is usually heard on exhaling in an asthmatic, and a lot of noise is heard at the lungs of a bronchitic.

Asthma is virtually always caused by an allergy of sorts. I say an allergy, as it is not always of a classical nature. Unfortunately, most Allergists define an allergy in a rather narrow way. I define an allergy as a reaction to something, as simply described by von Pirquet in the 1920s. That something can certainly be something inhaled, like house dust mite, animal hairs or a pollen, so a classical allergy, but it can also be a food or drink. In fact it can be virtually anything. I have reached the stage when I say, "Absolutely anything can cause absolutely any symptom in absolutely any person". Having said that, it should not be too difficult to identify what the cause is or the causes are in most people, although occasionally it can be.

Bronchitis is more likely to be caused by an infection of some kind, but a reaction to something as well is always a distinct possibility. In either case, the cause or causes need to be identified and dealt with. It is for that reason that I have lumped the two conditions together. As far as I am concerned, they are effectively one condition. Having said that, mainstream medicine likes to divide them into two, because the treatment tends to be different for them. Bronchodilators and inhaled or oral steroids are prescribed for asthmatics, whereas antibiotics are prescribed for a bronchitic, often with benefit.

Allergists carry out a series of tests to identify a possible cause or causes, but still tend to treat patients with drugs, so I'm not clear why they do the tests. They may recommend certain ideas for trying to avoid the incriminating causes, but drugs are still the mainstay of treatment. The fact that the patient continues to need the drugs suggests to me that insufficient has been done to remove the causes, and further attempts are necessary. The tests that most Allergists carry out on a patient are skin prick tests, that is a tiny amount of a given allergen, such as various pollens, animal danders, house dust mite, etc. are pricked into the skin of the patient, usually the forearm for convenience. Unfortunately, however good such tests are, they can be misleading on the one hand, and provide false positive and false negative results on the other.

Years ago I worked in the Allergy Clinic at the Nottingham City Hospital. I was sufficiently fascinated by the variability in people's reactions that I carried out an assessment to see just how often they did or did not react to various items. So I analysed the next 100 people who attended with classical signs of an allergy, and carried out as wide a range of tests as were available at the time. I then invited 100 people from within the hospital who had absolutely no known symptoms of allergy that they were aware of, and carried out exactly the same tests.

To my surprise, about one third of the group with classical features of allergy had absolutely no response to anything tested at all, and about a third of those with no symptoms had many clear positive skin responses to skin prick allergens. As the study was not carried out double-blind, it was considered unsuitable for publication. Nevertheless, the results stand in my mind. Basically a third do react who should not, and a third do not react that should. Unfortunately many classical Allergists say you do not have an allergy if you do not react to skin prick testing. That is sheer nonsense to my mind, and, as far as I am concerned, I have proved the point.

Another aspect of reactions that I want to explain is what is called 'the total load syndrome', a phrase coined by Dr Theron Randolph in the middle of the 20th century. People may react to pollens and animal dander as well as certain foods, but, if you remove the most important ones, they often fail to react to lesser ones.

Years ago I was Medical Director of a company that had a good food intolerance test, but it is no longer available. However, we carried out one of our tests on a wealthy lawyer, because he said he suffered so terribly badly with hay fever that he couldn't take on a case during the season, as it was considered unseemly to cough and sniffle in front of a judge, apart for which the condition and the drugs he took adversely affected his powers of thinking. The test was carried out a while before his next season and came up with three foods in the main beginning with an S, namely sesame seeds, soya and salmon. When asked whether he ate them he said he most emphatically did, so he stopped them, much to his wife's annoyance, as she had just purchased a fair supply of all of them shortly before then. However, he gave them all up and forgot all about his hay fever, as he was involved in a complicated case of company law.

When he visited some friends, during his normal hay fever season, friends who also suffered like he normally did and all of who were already having severe spasms of hay fever, he realised he should have been suffering, but was not. So all he needed to do was stay off the three foods during the hay fever season to remain symptom-free, being allowed to eat the foods outside his season. By avoiding the foods, which were presumably his most potent intolerances, he was fine, although I advised him he would be better to stay off the foods all the time, otherwise he would probably start to react outside his season.

It has been my experience that people often react to one or more foods, but as the classical way of testing for allergies is often negative for foods, because they are not an allergy but another form of intolerance, patients are often told they do not have an allergy. Okay they don't have an allergy in the narrow way of defining an allergy according to most Allergists, but they clearly do react in some as yet unknown way.

A classical allergy is said to be IgE mediated. That's not the way it was first defined by von Pirquet in the early part of the 20th century, at a time when immuglobulins had not been identified. As far as he was concerned, he merely described an allergy as something to which a person reacted. That is my definition of the problem. It is not important to identify the exact mechanism.

Once again, unless the history or any blood tests suggested a particular way of moving forward, I would start an asthmatic or a bronchitic with a very simple dietary approach. Yes, they may react to pollens, animal dander, house dust mite or inhaled chemicals, or any of a number of other substances, but my experience has been that foods play a major part in both conditions, possibly animal milks and animal milk products being at the top of the list.

Why animal milks? Well quite simply because human beings are the only creature on God's Earth that consumes milk and milk products after weaning. No other creature does, unless we give it to them, like our favourite cat. Oh yes, we certainly like it, but that doesn't mean it is suitable for us to consume. Apart from which about 75% of the world's population has a lactase deficiency, so cannot digest milk products at all. We like sugar, or most of us do, but that doesn't mean to say it is good for us.

Then the pasteurising process destroys most of the so-called nutrients in the milk to such an extent that when calves were experimentally fed on pasteurised cow's milk they did not thrive and they died. As far as I am concerned, cow's milk is designed to build an animal with a small brain and big horns!

But what about all that wonderful calcium, I hear you say? Let us think for a moment where all that wonderful calcium came from, say one million years ago, when our human physiology was developing. What did we consume in those days? Mainly what we could pluck and dig up, I suppose, plus the odd animal we managed to kill every so often. But I would imagine our diet was largely vegan, and it would appear there was sufficient calcium in what we ate to help build our bones. Why on earth should a post-menopausal woman need 1500mg of calcium per day plus 400IU vitamin D to prevent osteoporosis, when an elephant only consumes 2g of calcium in its diet in a day, I was once told by a Veterinary Surgeon at the London Zoo? And where do cows get the calcium from? Why from the grass they eat.

In my opinion, we don't need nearly so much calcium as we are told we need, but we do need more magnesium, unless we eat such an appalling diet full of acidic foods, that we need extra calcium to help alkalinise our bodies, and to balance the excretion of calcium that such a diet causes.

Over the years, I saw many young couples that had had a series of unfortunate episodes with trying to start a family. In every case, one of the things I recommended was that they both, the mother-to-be in particular, give up all animal milks and products. In every case, as far as I can remember, they achieved a beautiful baby, without a single drop of animal milk or products passing her lips, and no calcium supplements. In addition, the mother usually breastfed the infant for up to two years, still without her consuming any milk or milk products. If that isn't a clear indication that the human being can thrive without milk, I don't know what is.

Then again, too much calcium can be harmful to the body. It is well recognised that certain blood pressure lowering drugs are called calcium channel blockers. Why should such a drug work if calcium is so important? The answer is surely that it is not. In fact one of the best calcium blockers is magnesium, but you cannot patent magnesium, whereas you can patent a novel drug. Why don't doctors suggest patients with high blood pressure give up dairy and see what it does? It should certainly help their blood pressure to fall. I have done it many times, plus recommending patients take a magnesium supplement.

Ok, so I have digressed a bit, but I will do so every so often to explain a particular approach I believe in. You don't have to agree with me, but it is my job to open your eyes to a possibility you may not have thought of before. Whether you follow my advice or not is entirely up to you. I accept many doctors and dieticians are likely to disagree with me on this matter, but there are many doctors and nutritionists who do agree with me. It is my belief that those who do not agree with me simply haven't looked at the facts. It has never occurred to them that there might be another approach.

On another matter, many years ago I was invited to be in the audience of a television programme discussing the work of Dr. Harry Morrow-Brown, the Derby Consultant Physician who started the Midlands Asthma and Allergy Research Association. There were many general practitioners in the audience and every one of them agreed that, if a child failed to thrive in any way, the first thing to do was to take it off animal milks and animal milk products, especially from the cow. Sometimes goats' or sheep's products were subsequently found to be acceptable, but often not. We all agreed that the child was likely to do well from then on, and we had all observed it on many occasions. There was no suggestion that calcium supplements be given in the circumstances.

A final reminder is to have a blood test for homocysteine, so please read chapter 29, the chapter on Hyperhomocysteinaemia.

One final point that I would like to make is that if a person were to have a high acid diet such as many Americans do with their regular intake of beef burgers, for example, (the beef, bread and ketchup are all acid-forming foods) it may be wise to take a calcium supplement or sodium bicarbonate on a fairly regular basis, or possibly rub on magnesium lotion, to provide the extra alkali to balance the acidity and spare the bone stores of calcium. However, it is clear that it would be wise not to be on such a diet in the first place.

So what methods are available for identifying possible food or drink causes of asthma or bronchitis? May I suggest you read page 278, where I explain the various methods that are open to you. Not one of them is perfect, but it really is worthwhile trying to identify your causes. By doing so and eliminating them, you could become totally symptom-free and off all drugs. To me that is something worthwhile trying to achieve.

A story is particularly relevant here, because it illustrates what asthma can be all about. I saw a young lady many years ago, who had just joined my panel of patients, having moved to live in my area with her husband. She came in asking for a repeat of her drugs. I was perfectly happy to prescribe them for her, but I asked her if she had any idea what caused her attacks of asthma. She told me there was no obvious cause as far as her specialist was concerned, having done a number of tests that had been inconclusive. So I explained my overall approach and simply asked her if she would like to try to find her cause or causes. She said she would.

It took us quite a long time to identify her causes, which turned out to be dairy products, caffeine and corn/maize. By staying off those three foods and drinks, she became totally symptom-free with one month, but off all drugs within two weeks. She was absolutely delighted.

It was interesting when I asked her about her worst attack. Her husband had been told he could take a few days of holiday at short notice, so they went to the Isle of Wight. They settled in to their hotel late in the first evening, but found it was pouring with rain when they got up the next morning, so they had a leisurely breakfast and played cards. The rain stopped later in the afternoon and the sun came out, so they walked into town and decided to go to the cinema, stopping in a restaurant for a cup of tea and some cakes.

That night she was admitted to hospital in a fearful state. The emergency crew could hardly control her asthma, but in the end she improved sufficiently for them to put her in the ambulance. She was in hospital for three days.

I asked her what she had done that evening to cause such a severe attack. I asked for details, absolutely anything she could think of. In the end I had to prompt her. They had gone into the cinema and had bought a huge container of popcorn and a large bottle of cola drink, and had eaten and drunk till they were bursting. The popcorn was made of corn/maize and the cola drink contained caffeine. When I was only halfway through obtaining the details from her, her eyes suddenly lit up with recognition. "Of course!" She exclaimed. "Two of my three causes in one go, and a big helping of them to boot." It was so obvious to me, but then I had seen things like that so often. To me it is the little things that are so important. That's why a good detailed history can be so informative. Yes, we are trained to take a history in Medical School, but not in that sort of detail. I have had to learn from experience.

But the story doesn't end there. She became pregnant about five years later and delivered a healthy baby boy. Her asthma started to come back gradually, so she came to see me again. I asked her many questions and in the end decided it had to be something to do with her new baby, so she described exactly what she did every morning. She got her husband off to work then filled a bath with lovely warm water, taking the baby in with her and playing with him and washing him. She then placed him carefully on the floor beside the bath on a layer of soft towels while she rinsed herself off. She dried herself and the baby then scattered baby powder all over the baby. "Stop!" I cried. "That's your problem! The baby powder is pure cornstarch! You're inhaling it every morning!" She had been avoiding corn/maize for the past five years, so it had taken some weeks of daily inhalation for her reaction to it to be resurrected.

Should you take any supplements? I'm sure you should, certainly to begin with. Asthma itself, and any drugs you may have been put on by a doctor, most likely caused a deficiency of a number of nutrients. The main ones are magnesium and vitamins B6, C and D. So I suggest you take a good multivitamin/multimineral supplement, extra magnesium, say up to 500mg, vitamin C at least 10g and vitamin D 10,000IU + 150mcg K2 each day, certainly for the first 2 to 3 months, after which time you can reduce the doses if you are now symptom-free. The one supplement that you probably need but might not be absorbed by mouth is magnesium. I have a feeling that magnesium absorption is under the influence of an enzyme that is itself magnesium dependent. Alternatively you may be suffering from a deficiency of stomach acid, without which, again, magnesium will be poorly absorbed. So a transdermal magnesium lotion is a suitable alternative♥.

How should you deal with the infective side of bronchitis? Until recently, I would have recommended chlorine dioxide, which I found to be so useful at the right dose, but unfortunately the FDA and European Authorities have decided it is not suitable for human use as they say it is merely a concentrated bleach and there are no human studies on it. Well, I found it really worked. As it happens, the United States Department of Health and Sciences (the parent organisation OVER the FDA) has done a human study, as many people want to use it in swimming pools, and people swallow pool water! They have declared it safe for humans to take by mouth suitably diluted. So it is up to you.

An alternative is to use a daily dose of colloidal silver, preferably three times a day to begin with and also an immune stimulant such as Biobran (MGN3 in USA)♥, at a sachet of 1g three times a day for a week then one sachet per day until the infection has gone. Unfortunately it is rather expensive. A cheaper alternative is Echinacea, but you must use a high dose of 3 to 4g three times a day for a while, then cut down and stop it altogether. And of course, most of the supplements I recommended for asthma.

Chapter 23

Cardiovascular Diseases

The subject of cardiovascular diseases is almost as big as cancer, except that there are not nearly so many different areas involved. It is, however, one of the biggest, if not the biggest, area of medical morbidity in the world. No one needs to suffer from cardiovascular disease, but far too many people still eat and drink whatever they want without any care for possible consequences.

To be fair, there is another problem that most doctors are not aware of that can cause cardiovascular disease, including many Cardiovascular Physicians. It is a raised level of Homocysteine, which is far more of an arterial poison than cholesterol has ever been. A friend of mine was an active tennis player, who suddenly started to feel ill. She ended up having a heart bypass graft, and, to be fair, she is back playing tennis actively. I asked her what her level of homocysteine is and she told me her doctor said it was normal. When I asked her for the actual level, she eventually told me it was 15. It should be less than 6.

The trouble with homocysteine is that, once again, so-called normal levels are not normal. They are reference ranges, pure and simple. But where do those levels come from? Who worked them out? Basically they come from an analysis of samples received, roughly the top and bottom 5% taken out, and statistical analysis played with the rest. But where do those samples come from? They come from people who doctors think might be unwell or are unwell. So how can that possibly suggest a normal range?

Yes, I am being critical of mainstream medicine, mainly because so many doctors don't think. They simply react in the way they have been taught. It never seems to occur to them that their way of doing things may be wrong, or that there is a simpler, safer way of doing things.

Every laboratory reference range, as I say, is identified the way I have just described; that is except for cholesterol. The apparent so-called normal range for cholesterol, worked out from samples received, is no longer acceptable. Drug companies have caused studies to be done to say that a much lower level of cholesterol is to be achieved for everyone's health, and to take a statin drug.

The trouble is that statins cause a deficiency of Co-Enzyme Q10, which even the drug companies know about. Co-Enzyme Q10♥ is the heart's most important energy chemical. It is also required by the body for a whole variety of other important functions. Without it, people will suffer from heart failure amongst other conditions, which have already started to happen, surely one of the things statin drugs are supposed to prevent.

Another reason why doctors are not treating a raised homocysteine level, that is those that even recognise the danger of a raised level, is because they are waiting for a drug company to come up with an effective drug that will bring it down. Yet it can be managed perfectly well with adequate doses of vitamins B6 and 12, folic acid and betaine, and possibly one or two other nutrients such zinc and manganese. What, use nutrients to clear a medical problem? Oh dear me no. Can't possibly use such dangerous things!

But back to the cholesterol con. Yes it is a con, according to Dr. Malcolm Kendrick, who has written a book entitled "The Great Cholesterol Con. The Truth about what really causes Heart Disease and How To Avoid It"♥. Having said that, I think he has missed a particularly important point. Why is cholesterol raised in the first instance? In my opinion it is because something is causing inflammation in your arteries, and cholesterol is trying to protect you from that inflammation. And what is causing the inflammation? That is something you need to find out. To be fair, if your levels of cholesterol are reduced, there will be less protection from the inflammation, so it is perfectly reasonable that there will be fewer problems from blocked arteries.

The trouble is that virtually all drugs have their adverse effects and those adverse effects are nearly always caused by nutritional deficiencies. But no one thinks about that. You are given another drug to counteract the effects of the first adverse reaction, then another one to counteract the adverse effects from that one, and so it goes on drug after drug, nearly all of them unnecessary if only the doctor would think logically and look for the cause or causes.

So what should you do if you already have a cardiovascular condition or want to prevent such from happening to you? Yes, you may have a genetic abnormality. It may run in your family. But you can turn your genes on and off. You merely need to know where the switch is.

Start by looking at yourself. What is your weight? Are you too fat or too thin? Are you putting weight on round your midriff? How well are you? Do you suffer from certain symptoms? Do you suffer from headaches? Are you tired most of the time? Go through my patient questionnaire as detailed on page 56, and see how many problems you may have that need to be sorted out.

What changes can you make in your life style? Do you smoke? How much alcohol do you drink, if any? How many glasses of quality water do you drink in a day? How much junk food do you eat? Do you drink liquids containing aspartame, so-called diet drinks, that do so much harm to so many people? How much sugar do you add to foods or cups of tea and coffee? How many cups of tea and coffee do you drink in a day? Do you eat a lot of chocolate? Do you eat mainly whole flour products, and lots of them? Do you eat too much anyway? Do you exercise at all? Are you under stress? How happy are you? Can you change any undesirable aspect of your life? Does any aspect of your life involve inhaling undesirable chemicals, or contact with them in any way? Do you have mercury fillings in any of your teeth? Are you happy with where you live, or is there any possibility that you could be affected by geopathic stress♥? There are so many ways to look at yourself, so many things that may be worth changing in your life style, so many ways of changing something. Start somewhere.

Ask your doctor to do a series of blood tests. Be prepared to pay for any that you want but which he says you don't need. Ask him or her to test you for routine haematology and biochemistry, including cholesterol and triglycerides, and early morning fasting blood sugar. Also you might as well have TSH, T4 and T3 for your thyroid, although a so-called normal level can be very misleading, especially if he only does a screening test of TSH (thyroid stimulating hormone) to save money.

You would be well advised to have a blood level for vitamin D, but most certainly do not accept your local laboratory's so-called reference range. Who gets in the sun in the UK, and if the sun does come out, you are either in clothes or inside a building? In my opinion blood levels should be based upon Californian lifeguards! You should be between 65 and 85 ng/ml (160-210 nmol/litre) for health. Anything less than that is inadequate for you.

Please have your homocysteine tested. Again do not accept the local laboratory's reference level. You should be below 6 micromoles/litre for good health. Incidentally, what is homocysteine? It is an undesirable amino acid found in your blood, with a high incidence of cardiovascular diseases occurring in those with high levels. It is an ordinary metabolite on the way to cysteine, and on into methionine, but those who consume low levels of folic acid and vitamin B12 in their diet and may have a genetic problem of handling folic acid in particular, are at risk of developing a raised level, with all its consequences. Finally have a test for IGF-1. If it is raised it indicates you are at risk of diabetes, heart problems or cancer.

You would be wise to test your armpit early morning temperature, as a means of seeing whether you might be hypothyroid or not, irrespective of your thyroid blood tests. Obtain an old-fashioned thermometer, shake it down before you retire to bed the night before, and, as soon as you wake in the morning, tuck the thermometer into your armpit and snuggle down under the bedclothes. Take the thermometer out of your armpit ten minutes later. You don't need to read it immediately as the kink in it will leave the level where it was when it came out of your armpit. Do this for a few days to obtain a regular reading.

Normal for the body is 98.4°F or 37.0°C, but for your armpit normal should be 1°F or 1/2°C less, so 97.4°F or 36.5°C. Anything reasonably lower than these figures strongly suggests you are hypothyroid, and would benefit from iodine in the first instance. You cannot function properly with a poorly functioning thyroid system. Also it has been my experience that a hypofunctioning thyroid probably means that your adrenal glands are also not working properly. I always supported both glands in the first instance.

If you are developing weight around your midriff, have raised levels of triglycerides and cholesterol, raised blood pressure, increased platelet stickiness and are mostly feeling more tired than you think you should be feeling, please read the chapter on diabetes, because the problem is that you will become diabetic if you are not already so, and you probably are at least suffering from the Metabolic Syndrome, a precursor to diabetes, which leads to all sorts of medical problems, including cardiovascular morbidity.

Should a cardiac patient take nutritional supplements? Most certainly he or she should. The chances are that your condition has partly developed because of poor nutritional intake and poor choices of foods, and, of course, possibly a raised homocysteine that you didn't know anything about. You may already have been put on some drug or other which will certainly make things worse. Yes, drugs can help, but it is most important to start cleaning up your life style and taking appropriate nutrients to allow your condition to improve. You don't need drugs, or very few people do, although they may be needed for a while. Start to do the things I have mentioned, and it should be perfectly possible for you to come off all drugs altogether.

The nutrients you are most likely to need are magnesium, about 500 to 600 mg, Co-Enzyme Q 10 300 mg, vitamin D 10,000 IU + 150mcg K2, a B vitamin complex, a multimineral complex and vitamin C at least 5g per day, certainly to begin with, say, or the first three months, after which you can tailor some of them down a bit, depending on how you feel. If you are feeling a lot better, but not yet out of trouble, stay on those doses until you are.

If you feel you are pre-diabetic, follow the advice I gave in the chapter on diabetes, so there will be other nutrients to add, such as chromium, amino acids, digestive enzymes and sodium bicarbonate. Yes, you may be taking a considerable number of nutrients for a time, but they will help to repair your body, but, at the same time, you must improve your eating and drinking habits, especially avoiding caffeine and animal milks and products.

One thing that so many people are not aware of is the total amount of food they eat. When my wife and I order food at a restaurant, we merely order a meal for one person, and divide it between us. We simply cannot manage to eat all that is put in front of us most of the time. In the USA, companies have decided that if they double the amount of food they provide for people, it doesn't cost them double the amount of money to provide. The result is that peoples' stomachs have enlarged, so, each time they eat, they need more food to fill themselves. Although you should ideally only follow this next piece of advice under the care of a physician trained in the art, a period of five days on water only will shrink your stomach down so much that next time you eat, you will only be able to swallow a much smaller amount than before. I have described this fully in a book entitled "Conquering Cystitis" that I wrote in 1987♥.

Then there is exercise. Start gently and gradually work up to whatever you want to achieve. If necessary, go for a good strong walk, although don't do too much too soon. It also depends on your weight, your age and how fit you are in the first instance. But please start to do something if possible.

Chapter 24

Weight Loss

Why are people overweight? It doesn't matter whether you are only slightly overweight or morbidly obese. It is time you did something about it. Put quite simply, normal weight people live longer and more healthily, overweight people do not. Being overweight is clearly associated with a whole host of medically morbid conditions, including cancer because of the extra oestrogen fat produces, and cardiovascular diseases, including diabetes.

What are possible causes of being overweight? Yes, you might eat too much, and the chances are that you do. If there are no other causes, there are certain easy facts to assimilate. Put quite simply, if you eat more food in the form of calories than the amount of energy you expend in a day, you are likely to put on weight. To lose weight, you need to eat less in the way of calories than the amount of energy you expend. For many people there is a simple balance food in, exercise out.

A number of television programs have recently compared overweight people with severely underweight people. They showed just how little the underweight people ate in a day, as low as under one thousand calories for an active woman, but more importantly they showed just how much the overweight people ate, around seven thousand calories! That is enough for three average people! Can you imagine that? There is no surprise that they were overweight, so the first thing to do is look and see if you are simply eating too much.

Many people say 'it's my glands'. What could that mean? It is certainly possible that their thyroid is not working properly, and possibly their adrenal glands. Hypothyroidism is a definite cause of being overweight, but not grossly overweight, in my opinion. If a person is morbidly obese, they are clearly eating too much, and too much of the wrong things.

What do I mean when I say 'the wrong things'? Many doctors and dieticians believe that fat is the bad guy. In my experience, and that of many of my patients, carbohydrate is the bad guy, not fat. The reason why fat got the bad nod is because it has been established that every gram of fat provides nine calories, whereas one gram of protein and one gram of carbohydrate provide five calories of energy. Therefore, fat is the bad guy. It's obvious. Actually it's not.

The trouble is that fat speeds up your metabolism whereas carbohydrate slows it down. So many very overweight Americans are on a fat-free diet, but it doesn't seem to have occurred to them that it is not working. "Yes, I'm overweight, but I'm on a fat-free diet." I repeat it's not working. Rethink your ideas.

In 1957, Dr. Richard Mackarness, the doctor who basically encouraged me to start practising Nutritional and Environmental Medicine, wrote a book entitled "Eat Fat and Grow Slim"♥, an interesting title. The Atkins Diet has always achieved the best results when it has been fairly compared. Unfortunately it has been criticised because people have not read the changes he suggested after a short amount of time on the original fat, vegetable and protein diet but no carbohydrate, which it is accepted will not do you much good if you stick to it for too long.

So I advise you to consider reducing your carbohydrate intake down considerably, but not to zero, and make it all complex carbohydrate not white refined flour. Refined flour acts like sugar. It causes a rise in your blood sugar that you don't really want. Complex carbohydrate allows your blood sugar to rise more gently.

But above all, reduce the total amount you eat at any one time. I may be wrong, but the chances are that you eat too much at most meals. Learn to eat less. You may feel unsatisfied and hungry after meals to begin with, but your stomach will gradually shrink down and not want to be filled so much in due course. Ok, so you may feel hungry for a while. Put up with it. It is only a feeling. Do something to take your mind off your stomach.

Another way to eat is small and often, but you must make sure you don't eat a bigger total that way. Put out what you intend to consume in a day, work out its calorific value, and divide it all up into six or more snacks. Never sit down and stuff yourself. It doesn't work. Back to your thyroid. Are you more than just a bit tired? Does your body not function as well as you think it should? Could you have a low functioning thyroid gland? Have all the tests your doctor has done come back normal? If so, don't believe them. Despite what your doctor says, blood tests are not perfect. They can be within the laboratory's reference range (not normal range), but you could still have effective hypothyroidism.

The trouble is that blood tests only show what's circulating in your blood. They don't show the 'activity' of your cells. Every cell in your body has thousands of receptors that respond to a specific chemical. One of those chemicals is the thyroid hormone. Actually your thyroid gland produces about fifty-two chemicals, each one having a balancing effect on the whole process. The receptors can be damaged, diminished in number, blocked, become less efficient, become more efficient, or changed in a number of ways that blood tests don't identify.

So how can you identify if that is true? Simple. Buy or obtain an old-fashioned thermometer, shake it down well before you go to bed and put it by your bedside. When you wake up in the morning, tuck the thermometer into an armpit, making sure it is thoroughly touching as much skin as possible, and snuggle down under the bedclothes for a good ten minutes. Take it out and put it on your bedside table, waiting to be read when you are fully awake. Don't worry; the reading will stay where it is, because of the special kink in the glass.

Normal for under the tongue is 98.4°F or 37.0°C, but the armpit is a bit lower, 1°F or 1/2°C. Anything somewhat below 97.4°F or 36.5°C is a sign of hypothyroidism, and you are likely to need support for your thyroid system. I used to prescribe whole thyroid extract, as your thyroid gland normally secretes at least 52 hormones of which two, thyroxine and tri-iodothyronine (T4 and T3 respectively) are considered the only important ones by mainstream medicine. A simple question. Why does the thyroid gland secrete so many hormones if they are of no use? Answer, of course they are of value. They probably balance things more effectively than the main ones. I found many of my patients felt whole thyroid supplements really helped, and, in any case, whole thyroid feeds the thyroid gland, so it is usually possible to get people off the supplement once things have settled down. Not so with thyroxine. Once you are on it, you are effectively on it for the rest of your life, because the single hormone suppresses the reflex system of thyroid stimulating hormone/thyroid hormone output.

What I found most of the time was that, if a person's thyroid system needed help, their adrenal glands also needed help, so I supported both at the same time, using a preparation called Biocare's AD206♥, plus a small dose of magnasent iodine♥, as iodine is required for all hormonal outputs, not just the thyroid gland. If your thyroid gland is underfunctioning, the chances are that you are deficient in iodine, something that applies to many people all over the world.

It is unlikely, however, that you will be able to obtain whole thyroid without a prescription from a doctor. In that case obtain a supply of Nutri thyroid♥ and start with one tablet a day for two weeks, adding an extra tablet every two weeks until you either feel better or your morning armpit temperature comes up to normal. The alternative is Biocare's TH207♥. You should also support your adrenal glands and take iodine, as above.

Ok, so all of that is normal and none of it is relevant to your weight problems. What do you do? The chances are that you are eating or drinking something your body does not like, even if you like it. It could be chocolate. It could be aspartame in diet drinks. It could be alcohol. But it could be a so-called healthy food, one you are totally unaware could be causing your overweight. Let me tell you a story.

Many years ago I was consulted by two women, at least a year apart. Their stories are remarkably similar so I tell them as one. Both were considerably overweight, one at 18½ stone (260lb or 118kg), the other 19½ stone (295lb or 137kg). They were both diabetic, arthritic, depressed and insomniacs. They were tired all the time and had regular headaches. They hated themselves. They had tried to exercise, but that had been impossible. They had both tried just about every diet anyone could suggest. They had even tried a 500 calorie diet and had put on weight. Yes, they put on weight on a 500 calorie diet. They were told that was impossible, but I told them it was not impossible as I had a shrewd idea what the cause of their overweight was. I even wrote it down on a piece of paper, sealed it and gave it to them for safekeeping. I told them there was one thing no one had observed during all that time, which I would explain later on.

I told each of them that there was one way of undoing all their problems, but it was a hard way. However it was virtually guaranteed to help them lose weight. I suggested they consider doing a five-day fast, on bottled water only for five days - nothing to eat at all. I explained that they would feel absolutely lousy to begin with, especially on day three, which was likely to be the worst. I explained that, if they already suffered from headaches, they would really suffer very badly on day three. They would also complain of severe backache and everything would hurt more than ever before, but they would start to feel better on the morning of day four, and even better on day 5, probably becoming symptom-free, or very nearly so, on the morning of day six.

I was able to advise them to stop all their drugs, which they said didn't really work anyway, and, if they stopped eating totally, their blood sugar levels would normalise. I explained that the awful increase in symptoms was caused by withdrawal from former incriminating foods, and the more severe the withdrawal symptoms, the more likely it was that they would eventually clear totally.

I advised them that they should not plan to do anything important, or work machinery of any sort. They were not to take any drugs to relieve the pain, but they could take old-fashioned sodium bicarbonate as often as they wanted to, as the withdrawal symptoms created an acidic environment that would be neutralised by the sodium bicarbonate. A hot or cold water bottle could be used or a cold flannel round the head. They were advised to be prepared to go to bed and try to sleep off any symptoms. I described this whole process in a book I wrote in 1987, entitled 'Conquering Cystitis'♥.

Both women followed the five-day fast. They both suffered badly, especially the third day as I told them they would, but their husbands looked after them, calling me for advice every so often as I had told them to. But the morning of the sixth day saw changes in both women that were truly extraordinary. The 18½ stone lady had lost 18lb (8.5kg) and was totally symptom-free, while the other lady, who had been slightly heavier than her had lost 21lb (9.5kg), and was also effectively symptom-free. They were both free of diabetes at the time, with perfectly normal blood sugar levels.

Both women said they didn't want to eat ever again, as they felt so well. I found it amazing that neither of them felt at all hungry, although they had had hunger pangs to begin with. They knew, however, that they would have to start eating eventually and couldn't fast for the rest of their lives, so they accepted a programme of reintroducing foods one at a time, three a day, from a list I had already prepared for them, and given to their husbands, so that they could obtain adequate supplies. I had chosen a list of foods that I hoped were not former culprits of their weight problems, but, to be honest, I did not know, although I had an idea.

So it came as no real surprise to me when the lighter of the two put on 7lb (3.4kg) overnight yes overnight and all her previous symptoms returned, when she challenged with carrots. The other lady put on a staggering 10lb (4.6kg) also overnight, with the return of all her symptoms, including the return of high blood sugar, also when she challenged with carrots. Both of them reacted in the same way, though less dramatically, one with cabbage, the other with cauliflower. That explained why they actually put on weight on a 500-calorie diet, because they ate more vegetables.

The important thing to notice is that, when they fasted, they hardly drank any water at all, because allergic fluid was effectively coming out of their tissues into the blood stream, to be excreted the next time they passed water. When they reacted to carrots, cabbage or cauliflower, they drank copious amounts of fluid, all of which they retained in their tissues.

This story basically explains why many people are overweight. They simply retain a lot of allergic fluid in various tissues, and the tissues that retain that fluid are the ones that don't work properly. Ok, so may be it is not truly allergic fluid, but it is a bit difficult to call it intolerogenic fluid. The word is not acceptable. The point I'm trying to make is that so-called innocent foods may not be innocent to a particular person. Each person needs to identify his or her own food or drink intolerances. In the circumstances, you need to find a method of identifying your food intolerances. Unfortunately there is no perfect way. It simply does not exist. Yes, a five-day fast would suit someone who is overweight, which you presumably are, but not someone who is underweight, for example, as it can produce all sorts of problems. However, it is not at all easy to carry out, and it can take a long time, and you need to be able to concentrate on yourself for at least one month, if not longer, but, as I have already said, I have described it in detail in the book I wrote in 1987 entitled 'Conquering Cystitis'♥.

If you are overweight, it is likely you either are diabetic, even if you are not aware of it, or are pre-diabetic. In that case, may I suggest you read chapter 17, beginning at page 275, the chapter on diabetes. Food intolerant reactions cause inflammation, and the tissues that produce symptoms are the ones affected. So you could take an Alcat blood test♥.

I have helped a lot of people lose weight with this method. Not all carried out a five-day fast, but those that did found it really worked for them, and, by avoiding what they identified as being foods they were intolerant of, their weight stabilised.

One thing to say to you is that, by avoiding a former incriminated food for, say, three months, it is likely that your intolerance of it could have disappeared, or at least become sufficiently limited that you could possibly eat that food once a week or once a fortnight. Alternatively you could try a system of homoeopathic desensitisation.

While remaining off the food, take either a 30C preparation twice a day or a 200C preparation once a day for seven days, preceded by a single dose of potentiser before the very first dose only of that food. So, if you want to try to desensitise yourself to carrot, for example, take a single dose of potentiser immediately before the first dose only of a 30C potency of carrot, obtained from a homoeopathic pharmacy♥, and take a second dose later in the day. Do this for seven days, but do not repeat the potentiser.

In my experience, this system can work well for most foods, but it may require a second or third attempt with milk or gluten products, both of which seem quite hard to desensitise to.

Chapter 25

Irritable Bowel Syndrome

Do you suffer from irritable bowel syndrome? Have you listened to the words? Irritable, bowel and syndrome. Three words. They are merely descriptive of symptoms you are complaining of. Your bowels are irritated. But by what? Answer, something within them. It is most likely to be something you keep putting into them or don't, in the way of food or drink, but it could be something that has developed in your bowels in the form of a fungus or a parasite, again as a result of what you have consumed, or taken in your mouth, at some time in the past.

So, when did you start complaining of bowel symptoms? How long ago was it? What happened at the time? Did it start after you were ill in some way or had an infection? Did you take a course of antibiotics? How much sugar have you tended to take in a day? Do you eat only white bread and junk food, and drink chemical drinks containing aspartame, the so-called diet drinks, or high fructose corn syrup?

Do you eat a lot of cheese or other foods containing a high level of yeast? Have you actually thought of what you consume? Have you analysed your daily diet? Do you tend to eat and drink from a very limited number of foods, because life is more convenient that way?

It doesn't matter what your symptoms are. Something is irritating them. Something is inflaming them. Yes, drugs can help, sometimes extremely well, but, as always, you need to work out what the causes are of your symptoms. First you need to know what is causing the problem, and that is where a detailed history comes in, because there is limited value in changing your diet if you have a parasite or fungus within you. You may be suffering from a nutritional deficiency of sorts, but that was most likely caused by what you have been eating or not eating, the parasite or fungus, or possibly by one of the drugs your doctor prescribed.

May I suggest you read chapter 3, in the cancer section, starting on page 49. I gave all patients this questionnaire to complete before they came to see me. As much as anything else it helped to orientate them to my way of thinking. Ok. So what have you found from this history of you? Could you possibly have a parasite within your bowel? This is likely if you travelled to a foreign country where there are more parasites in the environment, like India or Pakistan or Africa? A parasite is also a distinct possibility if your overall eating habits have not been too good over the years. Do you have a dog that licks your face? You worm your pets once a year, but do you worm yourself? Of course not. But why not? It seems a perfectly sensible thing to consider doing every so often, but there is no need to use hard drugs unless you want to. Yes, they may work well enough, but can be very harsh and cause other problems.

There are two preparations I would suggest, one being called Paracleanse♥, the other Diatomaceous Earth♥. They work very well against all undesirable organisms within the bowel, without causing any significant problems in my experience. In any case, it probably would do you good to clean out your bowels every so often, even if you don't have an obvious parasite in them.

Have you had any antibiotics at any time in your life? Please don't say "Oh! The usual amount" because I don't know what that is. My wife and I have never had an antibiotic ever in our lives. I saw a new patient shortly before I retired in October 2006 and asked her that question. When I told her I had never had an antibiotic ever, she said, "What! Not even when you were a child?" to which I responded "They weren't invented that long ago!" That shows how old I have become!

Is there a coincidence that your bowel symptoms began after a course of an antibiotic? Have you had just one strong course, or a course more than once for an ear infection, acne or cystitis, or something similar? If so, the chances are that your bowel is harbouring a fungus, probably the thrush fungus, Candida albicans. Do you suffer from episodes of thrush? Thrush is the bane of Gynaecologists' life. They see many cases of it and their drugs don't resolve the problem. I wrote about this fungus in 1987 in a book entitled 'Conquering Cystitis'♥.

If there is a good chance you have a fungus, you probably also suffer from the leaky gut syndrome, in which the fungus has invaded the wall of your intestine and effectively made it porous, allowing through into the blood stream certain partially unbroken down food particles and blocking the passage of certain nutrients. Under normal circumstances you have more of the friendly organisms within your bowel than unfriendly one, which, in any case, are in a single-celled harmless form. Antibiotics kill off the friendly ones but don't damage the unfriendly ones, which then proliferate unopposed and change their formation, developing branch-like threads called mycelia that spread and penetrate the bowel wall.

Under normal circumstances, there are far more of the friendly organisms that prevent the unfriendly ones from attaching themselves to the bowel wall. It's rather like a form of crowd control, but, if the friendly ones are killed off, which they can easily be with a strong single course or a number of courses of antibiotics for any reason, that crowd control effect is lost. The result can be varied, the symptoms of irritable bowel syndrome being one. This is not surprising, as the normal bowel flora has changed considerably. The friendly organisms manufacture a number of essential chemicals, which help control the single-celled fungi, as well as B vitamins.

Mainstream medicine insists that you can make up any damage caused by antibiotics yourself, but I don't agree. To be fair, it may not be obvious the degree of damage a single course of antibiotics has caused, let alone a continuous course of a year or longer for acne. Then think of all the antibiotics in the food chain, mainly in animals. We are awash with them, and effectively have little or no idea what they are doing to us. That is one reason why I recommend people eat only organic food, as antibiotics have not been fed to them at all.

To deal with fungi in your bowel, you need to follow what I call an anti-candida diet, which means no sugar, white refined flour products, yeasty foods of any sort (so no ordinary bread, etc with its yeast in it, Bovril, Marmite and similar foods such as most gravy mixes), and possibly fruit to begin with, which is why I recommend you take what I call the special capsules of dehydrated fruit, vegetables, and berries♥. You are also advised to take a probiotic, probably three times a day to begin with, such as Biocare's Bioacidophilus♥, and L-glutamine 500mg three times a day 1/2 hour before meals to help heal your likely leaky gut. You would also be advised to take one or more preparation to kill off the fungus within your bowel, such as Oregano oil, Candastatin or colloidal silver, although Diatomaceous Earth should do the same thing. If you were to consult a nutritionist, he or she is likely to have a favourite anti-candida preparation to recommend to you. Some work, while others do not. You will need to find one that does.

There is a distinct probability that the environment within your bowels is far from right. The simple fact that there is inflammation within them strongly suggests to me that the flora has been disturbed. Having said that, it may be perfectly possible to sort your bowels out with a simple dietary change of some sort. The trouble is, what dietary changes should you make?

If there is no obvious infection involved, I would start with avoiding my main possible culprits. This has worked well in many patients. Stop all animal milks and products, caffeine (including cola drinks, tea and chocolate), alcohol and added sugar. Mainstream medicine advises you to increase your fibre intake, which may be sensible advice and may well work, as some people's IBS is caused by an inadequate intake of appropriate fibre. However, that sometimes increases the IBS symptoms, suggesting that the source of the fibre may actually be causing the problem in the first place, so avoiding wheat or gluten grains is worthwhile considering for a while.

To be fair, almost any food or drink could be causing your problems. There is no food I can think of that has not been implicated in someone's IBS in the past. It can certainly be caused by chemical additives in drink, especially aspartame, or monosodium glutamate added to enhance the flavour of foods. So you may need to become a medical detective on yourself to try to find your causes.

Another way of identifying your causes is to eat for at least one week from a small list of foods you don't usually eat, such as a fish, lamb or turkey, carrots, sweet potato, an unusual fruit, coconut, pumpkin, possibly rice, tapioca or semolina and soya milk. There must be plenty of foods you hardly ever eat that you could put into such a list. Drink only filtered water. Whatever you do, try something. The only problem is that you may find you have to stay off a particular food for the rest of your life. A long time ago I discovered that my migraines were caused by chocolate. I am now off chocolate for the rest of my life by choice. Having said that, it may be possible to desensitise you to most foods by homoeopathic desensitisation, as I described in the last chapter, beginning on page 313. But, having said that, the system doesn't work with every food. My chocolate reaction is possibly caused by an enzyme deficiency of sorts. The system didn't work with me.

Finally, please have a blood test for homocysteine and read chapter 29, the chapter on Hyperhomocysteinaemia.

Chapter 26

Pre-Menstrual Syndrome

The degree to which a woman may suffer with pre-menstrual syndrome varies enormously. For some it may only be an awareness of a little breast enlargement for a few days before the onset of the next period, while, at the other end of the scale, in others it can be an absolute nightmare, with two weeks of complete hell. In these cases the woman truly fears the onset of her next pre-menstrual phase, but, to be fair, she may also suffer with her period for at least one week, having only one week in every four reasonably well, and that may not be too good either.

When very badly affected, a woman's breasts may enlarge two bra sizes and be exquisitely sensitive to being touched, so comforting her is impossible. Even wearing a bra can hurt, although it is better to wear one than not wear one. She may feel sick much of the time and may even vomit. She can feel extremely tired and complain of a headache and her moods may be dreadful, snapping at everyone and everything. Life can be awful for her.

When I asked women in the past about pre-menstrual syndrome, they sometimes said they didn't suffer, yet when I enquired further, they admitted to breast tenderness and swelling. They assumed that I was only interested in any mental symptoms. Again, some women did not appear to suffer symptoms, yet had had a hysterectomy for fibroids, which had developed slowly over the years, possibly mainly in the pre-menstrual phase when her levels of oestrogen were too high relative to progesterone.

So what's this all about? If you read the cancer chapter, you will have read about this, but, as it is perfectly possible you did not, I am going to repeat what I said there. First of all, I am going to describe a perfectly normal menstrual cycle. Then I will explain what can go wrong so easily and why, and this should give you all the things you can think of to help your symptoms improve, depending on where your problems lie.

Although women's menstrual cycles vary somewhat, for the sake of simplicity I will describe a 'classical' twenty-eight day cycle, taking the start of a cycle as the first day of the period. There are two main hormones we talk about, namely oestrogen (estrogen in USA) and progesterone. In fact oestrogen is at least three chemicals, oestriol (E1), oestradiol (E2) and oestrone (E3). Oestradiol is the best known of these three chemicals as a variety of it (such as oestradiol valerate) is present in most forms of the contraceptive pill and HRT. It is also important to be aware that oestradiol and oestrone are proliferative, which means they promote cellular development, while oestriol is anti-proliferative, so calms down cellular growth. Isn't nature clever in providing balancing hormones? But things can go wrong if the balance is lost. Progesterone, on the other hand is one chemical, and has a calming influence.

For about the first seven days there are low levels of progesterone and oestrogen, but at roughly day 7, Follicle Stimulating Hormone (FSH) is produced in the brain which brings to complete maturity one egg (inside a Graafian follicle), and gradually ripens many others, their turn coming another month. At roughly day14, the time of ovulation, another hormone is released from the brain called Luteinizing Hormone (LH), which instructs the Graafian follicle to release its egg for fertilisation. The Graafian follicle now starts to manufacture progesterone.

Under normal circumstances, the levels of oestrogen may increase, level off or may even decline somewhat, but there is still more circulating oestrogen at this stage than in the first seven days, when levels are quite low. Progesterone's main job is to prepare the lining of the uterus (womb) for pregnancy, and levels of it should gradually rise to balance oestrogen. This balance between oestrogen and progesterone is particularly important. If a pregnancy does not occur, the levels of both oestrogen and progesterone drop towards the resting state at about day 26, a period starting two days later.

If a woman is blessed with such an ideal physiological event, her monthly cycles come and go regularly. She knows exactly when her next period will start, because she has made a note of it in her diary, and all she is aware of before the next onset is the result of minor hormonal changes. None of this causes her any problems or makes her feel ill in any way, and she takes it all in her stride. She is aware of when she ovulates, so could plan a pregnancy any time she wanted to. She may already have done things this way. Unfortunately, very few women have such a simple cycle nowadays. Far too many women suffer pre-menstrual symptoms, such as breast tenderness or breast swelling, a whole variety of emotional symptoms, such as irritability, depression, bouts of crying, low self-esteem, insomnia and clumsiness, weight gain, sugar and chocolate cravings, bloated abdomen, and sometimes thrush, to name but a few. The length and severity of these symptoms can vary considerably, sometimes lasting up to fourteen days before the onset of the next period. If she also has a bad time with her period itself, she can have three weeks out of every four feeling awful! I have met many such women, and I tell you, it is not difficult to sort out, and without drugs!

So where do things go wrong? It is usually at around the time of ovulation. In fact a woman may not ovulate. If she doesn't ovulate, it means she probably doesn't release an egg or produce much progesterone, if any, from the Graafian follicle. That means that oestrogen is not balanced by progesterone, so she suffers from hyper-oestrogenism. If a woman does not suffer from premenstrual symptoms, she might produce 30mg or possibly even 40mg progesterone per day towards the end of her cycle. So progesterone is good for you!

Oestrogen's job is to make you a woman, a natural female capable of reproducing the human species. This means that oestrogen is responsible for developing your breasts, ovaries and womb. As there are oestrogen receptors on all the cells of a woman, including brain cells, oestrogen makes you think and behave like a woman.

The problem is that, whereas a woman needs her oestrogen, too much oestrogen is not good for her, and if it is not balanced by progesterone towards the end of a cycle, the symptoms of hyper-oestrogenism, namely premenstrual symptoms, occur. If one of your female organs is particularly sensitive to the effects of too much oestrogen, then that organ will be stimulated or developed a little bit too much every month. If that organ is your breasts, the stage after pre-menstrual breast tenderness or swellings is breast cysts, and eventually breast cancer. Time and time again I pick up this story when taking a comprehensive history from a woman with breast cancer. The information is all there, although no one else has thought of considering it. Unfortunately doctors are mostly not interested in why a woman has her problems.

When I took a history from a woman with breast cancer, pre-menstrual breast tenderness, breast swelling or breast cysts was a common finding. Some post-menopausal women do not remember suffering in this way, but when I asked them about any operations, they often said they had a hysterectomy because of fibroids. This means they also had oestrogen dominance, but the effect was mainly on their womb. Others told me of a history of polycystic ovaries, so her ovaries were the main target. Remember too much oestrogen means the balance of the three oestrogens is in favour of oestradiol and oestrone versus oestriol, and out of balance with progesterone.

Consider then what happens to a post-menopausal woman. Her monthly cycles have stopped, so she is not ovulating, she is not releasing an egg because she is not producing a Graafian follicle, so she is not making progesterone. Yet, as her monthly cycles stop, she can still manufacture oestrogen from the fat of her body and her adrenal glands. So, once again, she is potentially in an oestrogen dominant state.

You may think this is the end of the story, but it isn't, because the environment in which we all live is being polluted by xeno-oestrogens, or chemicals that have oestrogen-like activity. These come from plastics and the plasticisers they release, petrochemicals, pesticides and a whole host of chemicals in common use today. Also millions of women are taking pharmaceutical drugs of the contraceptive pill and HRT who urinate every day, which gradually reaches water tables. The water in London is said to be recycled many times, and people drink it!

So, is there any wonder that you and so many other women are exposed to too much oestrogen, some of it false, leading to oestrogen dominant effects on your body? And remember, that oestrogen is proliferative, so is effectively encouraging your breast and uterus cells to divide.

Ok. So that's the lesson. Now we come to what to do about your pre-menstrual symptoms. First of all, change your eating and drinking habits. Give up all caffeine (remember there is caffeine in cola drinks, tea and chocolate), alcohol, all animal milks and products, all sugar and white refined flour products. Such changes alone can radically improve your symptoms sometimes. Professor Jane Plant would advise you to turn to soya milk in her book 'Your life in Your Hands'♥, but that is not always necessary in my experience, especially as I am a bit suspicious of soya milk at present.

You will be well advised to try the effect of homoeopathic progesterone at a potency of 200C, a dose twice daily from about day 12 to day 26 if your cycle is of 28 days, adjusted appropriately if it is not.

If that does not work well enough, obtain some bio-identical cream of progesterone and apply 20mg once a day on roughly the same days as with the homoeopathic doses.

At any time you should take a multivitamin/multimineral supplement, 500mg magnesium in at least two separate doses with food, extra vitamin B6 50mg if your multivitamin/multimineral does not give you at least that much, and 10,000IU vitamin D + 150mcg K2, especially if you do not get into the sun all that often, for the first three months to begin with, then halve the dose. Any other essential nutrients you may need to take should be controlled by a nutritionist at least, or someone you can trust to advise you correctly.

Oh and don't forget to have you blood homocysteine measured and read chapter 29, the chapter on Hyperhomocysteinaemia.

Chapter 27

Post-Menopausal Problems and Osteoporosis

Postmenopausal osteoporosis occurs only in women, of course, but osteoporosis can occur in men, although it is not at all common. It is likely therefore that the condition somehow involves hormones. By and large the medical profession prescribes HRT, plus calcium and vitamin D, but they don't seem to work in my experience, apart from which HRT has long term adverse effects of possibly creating cancer of the uterus among other problems.

Postmenopausal symptoms and osteoporosis are clearly connected but the symptoms are likely to occur far sooner that any osteoporosis. A woman may simply feel more tired than she ought to feel, and she may well put on weight, especially round her hips and midriff. But her breasts may start to sag, she may start to lose her hair, and she may feel moody, lashing out at anybody and anything for sometimes no reason at all. In the postmenopausal phase, life can be quite hard for some women, who may go off sex all together, so her marriage may break up at a time when she needs understanding.

Yes, various drugs can work. Some women are put on tranquilisers, as well as HRT, calcium and vitamin D, and they can help, but they don't explain the reasons for the symptoms. As a blood test may suggest a raised cholesterol level, she may be put onto a statin drug. Her blood pressure may be raised, so she is likely to be put onto one or two drugs to bring it down. She could be started on something for her bowels if she is constipated. So, within next to no time, she could be on seven or eight different drugs, each having different effects on her body, plus different adverse effects, each most likely causing additional nutritional deficiencies, above and beyond what she started with.

Osteoporosis takes time to develop, tending to start in the mid-forties, when anovulatory menstrual cycles often occur, so there is no progesterone production. It can gradually creep up on you, with you losing the odd inch every so often. Road signs warning drivers of old people crossing the road show two people bent at the shoulders with walking sticks. It is assumed that people, women in particular, become fragile and bent as they get older. But it doesn't need to be like that. There is so much you can do to prevent it all from occurring or reverse some of it if it has already developed. The trouble is that you have to be prepared to do something. You need to look at the causes of your problems, reverse some of them, change your life style somewhat, and take some nutrients. For some women, it is all too much. They have passed the stage when they can be bothered to do anything about themselves.

So, for those who do want to do something, what is the cause of their problems? Let's start with hormones. It might be sensible to read the normal menstrual cycle I mentioned in the last chapter, starting at page 134 to save me repeating it here, because it is totally relevant. At the time of ovulation, progesterone is produced by the Graafian follicle, which continues to rise towards the end of the cycle, falling back again if a pregnancy does not occur. In a woman suffering from premenstrual symptoms, she has too much oestrogen relative to progesterone.

When a woman stops having periods all together, she stops ovulating, so does not produce any progesterone at all, as she does not produce a Graafian follicle. Having said that, anovulatory cycles often begin in the mid-forties, when osteoporosis may begin. She also does not produce as much oestrogen either to be fair, which is one reason why doctors put her onto HRT, mainly in the form of an unnatural oestrogen, although the tablet may contain a progestogen, a chemical with some progesterone activity, but some quite unpleasant side effects, such as mood swings, raised blood pressure and blood clots, sometimes causing the death of the woman.

If a premenopausal woman has had a hysterectomy for, say, fibroids, the surgeon often takes away her ovaries at the same time "to save having to go back in again should cancer of your ovaries ever happen". She is then put onto HRT without any progestogen, on the assumption she doesn't need any progesterone. In my opinion, this is wrong thinking, although I would have preferred to have treated the fibroids rather than remove her uterus in the first instance. Always keep as much of your body as you can. Once a part has gone, you can't have it back. Presumably God put it there for a specific reason, and woe betide anyone who interferes with that principle.

That reminds me of something I said in the introduction to the chapter on cancer about my training. I realised how important it was to learn physiology and anatomy, but, once I was in the hospital wards among patients, the normal seemed to have been forgotten. We were then taught how to remove an offending part of the body in the operating theatre or drug it into submission. We were not taught to even consider trying to help the body return to normal. I find that an interesting fact, and have spent the last twenty-five years at least trying to do just that.

Back to our postmenopausal woman. She is not producing much if any progesterone at all, and even her levels of oestrogen may have diminished but not stopped completely, as she is able to produce oestrogen from her adrenal glands and any fat of her body, which may be increasing as she feels less well and eats more of the wrong food to comfort herself. In addition there is an increasing imbalance between oestrogen and progesterone, in favour of oestrogen dominance. But her reproductive cycle has stopped so all that oestrogen is of no value to her.

As she has got older, she has absorbed more xeno-oestrogens, the false oestrogen in our environment from plastics, pesticides, various chemicals, petrol and diesel fumes and the food and drink we take into our bodies. We are awash with them. They are in our daily lives. They are hard to avoid, and hard to ignore. They add to the total amount of oestrogen in a woman's body, and a man's as well, of course, upsetting his prostate as I have already explained in the chapter on cancer.

How do we set about improving the lot of our post-menopausal woman? Yes, we need to balance her hormones, but, once again, we need to improve her eating habits. She needs to come off all animal milks and products, all alcohol and caffeine (remembering that there is caffeine in tea, cola drinks and chocolate), all chemical additives and sugar to start with. She may need to avoid other foods, but that is a start for now. I can't tell you exactly which other foods to avoid, because I don't know you or your history. Suffice it to say, some women may be reacting to other apparently safe foods, which may need to be identified. There is a good chance that you will feel considerably better by following the advice I have just given about your eating habits.

There are two ways to balance your hormones. The cheapest to try first is to take a dose of homoeopathic progesterone 200C twice a day continuously for about 23 days out of every month. I'm not sure what it does. I'm sure it does not increase your levels of progesterone, so I presume it somehow makes your progesterone receptors more sensitive. In any case, whatever it does, it works in some women, and is cheap, which is why it is the first approach I recommend.

If that does not do the trick within, say, a month, then obtain some bio-identical progesterone cream and rub onto your skin 20mg each day for the same 23 days each month. The best way to remember is to stop on the first of the month for about five to seven days and restart on the 6th or 8th of each month, or thereabouts. If you obtain a supply in the middle of the month, keep rubbing it in for 1½ months. It's not all that important, but it is fairly important to give your progesterone receptors a rest every so often.   Please be aware that extra progesterone often improves your oestrogen receptors, so it may be sensible to reduce your dose of oestrogen if you have been put on it by your doctor.

Should you take supplements? In my opinion, you most certainly should. You are bound to be nutritionally deficient. As far as I am concerned, everyone who is unwell in any way is at least deficient in any number of nutrients. It is one of the reasons why you are not feeling well in the first instance. You should take a multivitamin/multimineral, extra magnesium as 250mg twice a day with food, extra B6, 50mg, if your other supplement doesn't provide that much, Vitamin D 10,000IU + 150mcg K2 for at least the first three months after which you can halve the dose, and vitamin C at least 4000 or 5000mg, spread throughout the day as well as you can manage. Vitamin K2 is very important to help Calcium be placed where it should be placed I.e. In your bones. Without K2, Calcium will be deposited in any inflammation and in your arterial walls. I also liked my patients to take special capsules of fruit, vegetables, berries and grapes, because that gave them the valuable ingredients from 26 food items, with all the sugar, salt, water and fibre extracted during preparation♥.

Just following that advice may be sufficient for many of you, but it is always possible you need silicon and boron. A number of companies have produced supplements that contain what they believe to be essential for you to take to treat or prevent osteoporosis. You could try one of those, but make sure you obtain one that is well absorbed. One of the best ways of telling is if your urine turns yellow from the vitamin B2. Also check your stools to make sure tablets do not pass through you still as tablets.

There are other nutrients you might benefit from, but I can't tell you what they are. You need someone to advise you on that. It would be best if you could have some intravenous infusions of nutrients, like the ones I used to give my patients once a week, with great benefit, but it is unlikely you will manage to find anyone to do that for you. There is one problem, and that is with magnesium. I feel that magnesium absorption by mouth may be under the influence of an enzyme that is itself magnesium sensitive. That means that it may be difficult for you to absorb magnesium by mouth if your levels of magnesium are already low. That was why I found it so helpful to give magnesium as part of the nutrient infusion I gave to my patients. Once the levels had improved, magnesium was easily absorbed by mouth. It is also possible that your stomach acid production may be low, which will also inhibit absorption of magnesium by mouth. One way round that is to have transdermal magnesium lotion♥, which has really benefited some of my patients.

Finally, exercise. If you can still get around, do some exercise of a weight-bearing type, so walking is the best form. Buy a dog by all means, but you take the dog for a good brisk walk, not the dog taking you, i.e. keep walking and don't let the dog keep stopping to have a sniff at something, which he or she will prefer to do if given half a chance. If you want to try to run, that is fine by me, but walking briskly is probably the best exercise you can get, and do it at least three times a week, and more often if you can manage. It's the pounding on solid ground that does your hips, legs and spine so much good. Incidentally, exercise has been shown to be just as good as tranquilisers if you are worried or depressed. So lift your head up, stick your chest out and almost march. The best way of achieving a good posture is to lift your

330

diaphragm.

Once again, don't forget to have your blood homocysteine level measured and read chapter 29, the chapter on Hyperhomocysteinaemia.

Chapter 28

High Blood Pressure

High blood pressure is an extremely common problem in the general population, but it is not difficult to treat by natural means. But, once again, you have to do something for yourself. Ask yourself a simple question. Do you know or have a good idea what has caused your blood pressure to go up? Are you under unreasonable pressure at work? Is something in particular worrying you? Are you having a row with a family friend, or your spouse? Are bills or life in general getting you down? Come on. Think about your life. What's wrong with it? There must be something not right. What is it?

Can you resolve the problem? Can you patch up an argument? Can you change your interpretation of the problem? Have a look at the section on Decisions in chapter 7 on cancer, starting on page 167. It is full of good advice.

Whatever you do, learn relaxation exercises, visualisation and do some affirmations, again as I described at the beginning of the treatment chapter on cancer, starting on page 83. They have helped so many people, and they don't need to cost you a penny.

Do some exercise, not high-powered ones, but simple exercises. Walking briskly is one of the very best, ideally at least three times a week, more often if you can manage it. If you have a dog, take it for a walk. Don't let it stop every so often.

Stress of some sort is nearly always a major cause of raised blood pressure. Stress affects your adrenal system so badly, which has a knock-on effect onto other systems, especially your immune system, so let's look at what it does to you.

Your adrenal glands are effectively divided into two separate parts, the adrenal medulla in the centre of the gland which produces adrenaline (epinephrine in USA), the adrenal cortex round the outside producing cortico-steroids.

Adrenaline is produced as part of your body's immediate response mechanism to any 'shock'. When someone 'makes you jump' it is the fast production of adrenaline that makes you feel the way you do. The system was developed millions of years ago as the 'fright, fight or flight' response. What it does is to increase the blood flow to those parts of the body that are needed immediately, such as the heart and limb muscles. It also makes the heart pump harder and faster, and dilates your breathing tubes to allow you to take in more oxygen and blow off more carbon dioxide. Adrenaline also causes sugar to be manufactured quickly from stores of glycogen, to be readily available for your muscles to use.

At the same time, the blood flow to your skin and digestion is significantly reduced, which is why you have been told never to go out swimming when you have just had a big meal. There simply isn't enough blood to go round to serve all parts of your body at the same time. You might then develop cramp in your muscles if your digestion blood vessels win the battle for the limited amount of blood in your body.

When this system was originally developed millions of years ago, the result was nearly always a fight, a chase after an animal to kill it, or to run away from a marauding animal. Whatever the reason for the system to be brought into play, the effect was nearly always some form of exercise.

In this modern day and age, there are many times in a day when the system is 'alerted'; someone annoying you while driving; the kids making you late for work in the morning; receiving a bill you can't afford to pay; a letter from a solicitor; an argument with your boss at work. You name it. There are many such little or major episodes in most people's lives nowadays, all stimulating your adrenaline response mechanisms.

But where's the exercise? That game of squash on Friday evening is far too late. So what happens to all that sugar you keep pumping into your blood in the expectation of using it? Where does it all go, since it won't be used up in any form of exercise, except possibly by storming back to your own office? Also some of your blood vessels, the ones that were partially closed down as they were not of immediate use to the emergency, might stay that way or partially so, if the system is stimulated too often.

Whenever the levels of sugar rise above a certain amount in your blood, insulin is produced to pump it into your muscle cells. Clearly this is important if you need it to fight or run away, when that sugar will be used up. However, even in the dim and distant past, exercise did not always follow the adrenaline response, so insulin would still lower blood sugar back to acceptable resting levels, by pumping it into cells. Unfortunately in this modern day and age, the insulin mechanism is used far too many times every day when the 'alarm' system is stimulated. In addition, insulin is produced to bring down the levels of raised blood sugar as a result of most people's diet of sugar itself and white refined flour products. What this does is to keep pumping sugar into the body's cells, which gradually poisons them, turning them more and more acidic.

So the insulin mechanism and the adrenal medulla are intimately related. It is usually not recognised that the adrenal cortex also works hard under the circumstances, producing an anti-inflammatory outburst of steroids to cope with the effort of all the exercise you are likely to undergo, but in fact don't. Although the adrenal gland is divided into the two parts, they actually work very much in harmony with each other.

It is well recognised by mainstream medicine the harm that too high a level of steroids can do. After all, steroids are now available on prescription for allergies, asthma, inflammation of joints or brain tumours. But they are well known for their adverse effects, especially on the immune system. If you are under stress of any sort too often or for too long, you can see why your immune system may be affected. In addition, raised levels of steroids can directly cause a rise in blood pressure by causing water and salt to be retained, and can lower your levels of magnesium, vitamin C and B vitamins in particular, as well as use up minerals too much. The result is that you suffer from high blood pressure, and that is what this chapter is all about.

One fact that is not generally known is that the human being, most rodents and the South African fruit-eating bat have lost the ability to manufacture vitamin C from sugar, which could be why it is common practice to give someone a sweet cup of tea if they have had a shock. If you stress a goat in any way, and multiply its weight up to the weight of an average human being, it will manufacture up to 45g vitamin C immediately. This is one of the reasons why so many drugs turn out to have adverse effects when they are taken by man, having not shown the problem in many animal species in the testing phase, when they were given high doses of the drug. The animal produces a lot of vitamin C to counteract the effects of the stress of having the drug forced into them at high doses. The adrenal glands have a high need of B vitamins, vitamin C and magnesium in particular. If you drink too many cups of strong coffee, for example, because of the stress, you leach out these nutrients into your urine. Under stress, you tend to eat junk food for its ease, or microwave it which virtually kills off all the nutrients, drink too many cups of tea and coffee with extra sugar in them, drink extra alcohol as a form of relaxation, and generally let your nutrient intake slip even further down the line at a time when you should be improving it.

One of the well-known blood pressure lowering drugs is what is known as a calcium channel blocking agent. Why would anyone want to block the absorption or utilisation of calcium if it is supposed to be so good for you? And where does all your calcium come from in your diet, or at least where is the main supply? The answer is animal milks and products. So stop consuming them and see what happens, but also stop all forms of caffeine (including tea, cola drinks and chocolate), which cause calcium and magnesium to be lost in your urine. You would be wise to give up all added sugar and white refined flour products while you are about it. Make a clean sweep. Change the habits of a lifetime. Do yourself some good. Drink eight glasses of quality water each day, instead of tea and coffee.

Incidentally, one of the best ways to block the absorption of calcium is to take magnesium, but magnesium is not patentable. Magnesium and calcium compete for absorption, using the same sites in your intestine. So 250mg magnesium twice a day with food could help to bring your blood pressure down. Having said that there can be a problem with magnesium absorption in some people, which is why I found it so helpful to give a few doses by injection to begin with, after which they could absorb it well enough by mouth. It is almost as though the absorption of magnesium is under the influence of an enzyme that is itself dependent upon magnesium. If your levels of magnesium are low, you may not be able to absorb it until your levels are improved. For that reason, if you can't obtain injections, transdermal magnesium lotion♥ is a wonderful way round the problem. Many of my patients have found it made all the difference to them.

Stress also makes your body more acidic, or more to the point, less alkaline, and your body cannot work properly in an environment than does not have the correct pH level of 7.36. For that reason I advise you to eat as much in the way of fruits and vegetables as possible, in fact be as close to vegan as you can, ideally avoiding red meat unless you are a parasympathetic type of person, as such food is mainly alkaline. That is why I recommend special capsules of fruit, vegetable, and berries.♥

So in summary, look at your life and sort out any stress, change your eating habits, improve your nutritional status in regard to the stress you are under, get some sensible exercise and take specific nutrients such as magnesium, B vitamins and vitamin C. And, once again, please have your blood homocysteine level measured, and read the next chapter, the chapter on Hyperhomocysteinaemia.

Chapter 29

Hyperhomocysteinemia

This may well be a short chapter, but it is an important chapter, because it brings up the important influence of raised levels of homocysteine. If you want more information about the facts of the case against homocysteine, read the excellent book by Patrick Holford and Dr James Braly, entitled 'The H Factor'♥.

I may have touched upon the controversy as to whether raised cholesterol is important or not (see the book by Dr. Malcolm Kendrick entitled 'The Cholesterol Con How to Avoid Heart Problems'♥), but there is no doubt that raised homocysteine really is a bad guy and its reduction is very simple, which could genuinely save your life.

I know many people who have taken everyone by surprise by having a heart attack, or suddenly needing a heart bypass graft, having previously been in good health as far as anyone could tell. One of my friends was a regular tennis player, running all over the court all the time. Suddenly she started to become short of breath and was admitted to hospital as an emergency, where she was found to have three narrowed arteries in her heart and underwent an operation to open them up. She is back on the tennis court playing as though she never had a problem.

I mentioned raised homocysteine to her and, of course, she had never heard of it, but she sensibly had a test and told me her doctor said it was normal, but she couldn't tell me the exact figure, so I asked her to let me know what it was.

I am fascinated by co-called normal results. Who worked out what is normal and what is not? All laboratories do an analysis of results they achieve from blood samples sent to the laboratory, knock roughly the bottom and top 5% off and play statistics with the rest. But those samples came from people who either were genuinely ill or who their doctors thought might be ill. That, however, gives you their reference ranges for absolutely everything except one – cholesterol. Although labs call them reference ranges, doctors take them as normal ranges, again except for cholesterol. Drug companies and some doctors between them have decided that what is found and used to be called within the reference range is no longer acceptable. It should be lower, much lower. So their reference ranges are considered normal with the one exception, that is for cholesterol.

So should one be suspicious of the reference ranges for other substances? Just how far out of normal are these reference ranges? In my opinion they are merely a guide, but should be taken with a pinch of salt. So many of them are wildly inaccurate as a measure of normality.

My friend came back with a figure of 15 (that's micromols/litre). Even in the laboratory I used in the UK that is not normal, although 14 was, as a measure of all the samples they analysed. In my opinion it should be below 6! Her raised level of homocysteine explained her previous heart artery problems, and I encouraged her to do something about it.

Why is a raised homocysteine level so dangerous? What harm does it do to you? What organ does it do so much damage to? The answer is that it is an arterial poison, seeming to attack the arteries of your heart and brain in the main. Once your arteries have been damaged, cholesterol does its best to smooth over the rough bits, but in the end narrows the artery causing damage to any part of the body beyond the damage, hence a heart attack or a stroke. People with raised levels of homocysteine are also at risk of breaking bones.

Homocysteine is not obtained from the diet, but is biosynthesised from methionine and can be converted back into methionine. However, it is usually converted into SAMe and trimethylglycine (TMG for short) through various stages. If you have what is called a methylation problem, which is not all that uncommon, you cannot effectively break down homocysteine. Quite simply put, homocysteine is corrosive on long-living proteins, such as collagen and elastin or life-long proteins such as fibrilin, which is why it damages artery walls in particular.

The homocysteine problem has been described as the most important medical discovery of the century. So why is it still ignored by so many doctors? Raised homocysteine has now been shown to cause (or certainly be associated with) all sorts of medical problems, in fact just about any medical problem in the dictionary. It is undoubtedly a major cause of cardiovascular diseases, diabetes, cancers, arthritis and Alzheimer's disease, to name a few. In fact it is a clear indicator of how long a person is likely to live. The lower the level of homocysteine in the blood the longer a person is likely to live, and the higher it is the shorter a life the person is likely to have. It is probably one of the most important tests to have done, especially as a preventative, as its treatment is so easy, so safe and the results are so quick.

The treatment for raised homocysteine is folic acid, vitamins B6, B2 and B12, betaine (trimethylglycine) and zinc, and possibly magnesium. Unfortunately many of the studies reducing the level of homocysteine have not improved the long term health of the recipients, but, in my opinion, the levels were not brought down low enough as patients were not given adequate doses of nutrients and the treatments were not continued for long enough.

Having said that a study by Oxford University in England has recently shown that giving B vitamins to a group of people can significantly reduce their risk of developing Alzheimer's disease, as the condition has been shown to occur in people with raised homocysteine levels, something I have known about for years.

In my opinion the medical profession is sitting on its hands over what to do about homocysteine. In fact it is hardly bothering to measure it at all. It is almost as though they are waiting for a drug company to produce a drug that can effectively reduce the levels, and send a representative round to promote the drug, instead of using the known reducing agents of folic acid and vitamins B6, B2 and 12 in adequate doses, plus TMG, zinc and magnesium. What? Use nutrients? You must be joking. They are poisonous aren't they? And in any case you can get all the nutrients you need from a balanced diet! Apart from that I can't prescribe them on the NHS!

In my opinion, having your homocysteine level measured is one of the most important basic tests to have done as a preventative, especially if you are well at present. If you have started to develop any symptoms, it is still important to know what your level is and bring it down below 6μmol/l, but you need to take adequate doses of the relevant nutrients, such as 2mg folic acid and 50mg vitamin B6 per day, or possibly more to achieve what you want. Vitamin B12 is a problem, especially in the elderly, who tend not to absorb it very well, as the levels of intrinsic factor in their stomach may have diminished too low for their B12 absorbing capacity to work properly. In that case it is best given by injection of 500 or 1000mcg on a monthly basis. Old-fashioned GPs went round giving older people regular B12 injections, and it did them a lot of good, even if they didn't know why, but the modern doctor says 'Oh dear me no! Can't possible do things like that! In any case your blood levels are normal'. Those wretched normal blood levels again!

'The H Factor♥' book gives a concise story of the importance of homocysteine and lists the levels of nutrients that it is wise to take on a daily basis to bring your level down, depending on the level you find it at, so you can lower the doses once your level is low. A healthy level is below 6μmol/litre.

While you are having an 'unusual blood test' carried out on your blood, may I suggest you also have vitamin D and IGF-1. I have described the importance of a good level of vitamin D earlier on. IGF-1 is a good indicator of whether you are likely to develop cardiovascular disease, diabetes or cancer. Lower levels are desirable.

Chapter 30

Depression and Mental Diseases

Depression is a complicated story to talk about because there are so many causes for it. One person may have a genuine reason for being depressed, such as the loss of a dear friend or close family member, in which case it is perfectly reasonable to be depressed for a while.

But I'm talking about those people who do not have an obvious reason at all, yet can be very depressed, even suicidal. I had a colleague in one of the London Teaching hospitals, a PhD psychologist, years ago, who was also part of our group. She said about 95% of the patients who were referred to her said they were depressed at times, but for no obvious reason. "If only they could find the cause in me" people kept saying to her. "There must be a reason".

Well there is a reason as far as I am concerned, and, once again, it comes from your diet, a rather awkward one actually. The doctor who basically introduced me to this whole area, Dr. Richard Mackarness, was an Assistant Psychiatrist at Park Prewett Hospital in Basingstoke, England, although I had already been thinking along these lines before then. I sat in with him on a number of occasions, and was fascinated by the way he really helped people become symptom-free and get off their drugs, which were hardly helping anyway, by changing their diet. He even did challenge experiments on some of those patients to demonstrate cause and effect.

The most common food that people reacted to was wheat, and sometimes gluten, so also rye, oats and barley. Unfortunately such grains are the most difficult food items to have to avoid, but avoiding them can make a huge difference.

I would always recommend such a person also temporarily avoid all animal milks and products, all alcohol and caffeine, not forgetting there is caffeine in tea, cola drinks and chocolate as well as in coffee, and all forms of added sugar, and added chemicals. This still leaves a huge number of foods such as all salad items and vegetables, fruit, maize, rice, tapioca, meat, fish and eggs, nuts and seeds. It just tends to be rather awkward when eating away from home, but it can be done.

To be fair there are times when a depressed person is reacting to an unusual food, one you would think is a healthy food, so it can be virtually anything. However, start with the advice I have given above first and see how you go.

Studies have shown that exercise can be just as effective in depression as drugs. The best form of exercise is a good walk, not merely a stroll round the park, but a measured mile at least, and preferably on a reasonably firm surface like a path. Lift your head up and look forward. In fact lift your diaphragm up. That is the best way to gain a good posture. Look people in the eye as you pass them and smile. Force yourself to smile. Don't look down at your feet. Say 'Good morning' or 'Good afternoon' to people as you pass them. Force yourself to be communicative. If you have a dog, don't let it take you for a walk. You take it for a walk and make sure it doesn't keep stopping to smell something, as dogs are wont to do if given half a chance.

The chances are that your food intolerances have caused you to become nutritionally deficient, so you should take at least a multivitamin/multimineral supplement. In my opinion you should try to have a series of vitamin B12 injections, certainly 1000mcg once a week for at least four weeks, and longer depending on the effect they have upon you. You may have a special need of other nutrients, but I can't tell you what they might be. You need someone to help you with that.

Manic depression is no different from simple depression, in my experience, except that it is never caused by any reason to be sad. It always has a genuine physical reason. In this case, however, the depression is nearly always caused by consuming wheat or gluten, while the mania is caused by something else, a chemical such as aspartame, or any number of food additives, so these need to be avoided scrupulously.

Mental diseases of any sort can be caused by heavy metals, especially mercury, from your teeth, and occasionally lead, cadmium, arsenic, and aluminium. There is now adequate evidence in the scientific literature that mercury from mercury amalgam fillings can cause mental diseases, but I'm afraid most members of the medical profession are totally unaware of this being a problem or are actively dismissive of it. I have written extensively on this subject, and how to deal with it, in the chapter on cancer, beginning on page 131.

As I said at the beginning of this chapter, depression is a complicated problem, so I can't cover all the possible reasons why you may be depressed. I will, however, mention one other possible cause that is easy to do something about, namely geopathic stress.

Geopathic stress is rather difficult to explain, but it is a situation where the place you sleep could be over an area where an underground stress fracture allows energy to pass up through the earth, often being magnified by underground water. You may have heard of Radon gas or feng shui. It is in this area. To read all about it there is a wonderful book entitled 'Are You Sleeping In A Safe Place?' By Rolf Gordon♥. It is worth obtaining a copy.

What about other mental diseases such as schizophrenia? Years ago I saw one case and demonstrated to him how much better he could be if he were to stop consuming wheat, which he did for a while with great benefit. Unfortunately he then had some wheat that sent him badly schizophrenic, so badly that he was admitted to his local psychiatric hospital, where they thought my demonstration all a load of nonsense. I decided not to see schizophrenics ever again, unless they had total cooperation from their GP and hospital Consultant.

One last thing, if you haven't already done so, please read the previous chapter on Hyperhomocysteinaemia and have your level measured.

Chapter 31

Parkinsonism

Parkinsonism is a condition that tends to come on slowly, leading to increased disability by the sufferer. Symptoms vary considerably from person to person, but most people end up with shuffling gait, stiff facial muscles, a hunched back and a haunted look about the eyes. However, they tend to be able to think clearly, even if it can be hard for them to say what they want to say fast enough.

Parkinsonism is not all that uncommon, and it is one of the diseases of the central nervous system that have similar causes, even though mainstream medicine has no idea what causes it, and, to be fair, is not that interested in such reasons. In my opinion, all medical problems that affect the central nervous system tend to be caused by the same things. It is just that the causes have attacked a particular part of the brain, rather than another. Having said that, in my opinion, Parkinsonism is caused by certain environmental toxins that may not be so involved in other conditions, so, yes, you could say there are more specific problems in Parkinsonism, as indeed there are in most medical conditions.

Once again, inflammation plays a part in this condition, but the inflammation is caused by foods, toxic metals and environmental agents, together with nutritional deficiencies. Yes, I would always advise a new Parkinson patient to avoid all the usual foods and drinks, namely milk and all milk products, caffeine (including tea, cola drinks and chocolate), alcohol, chemical additives in foods, added sugar and white refined flour products as a start. There may well be other foods to be avoided that need some system to identify them.

So, if avoiding those I have mentioned don't start the process of healing, consider one of the methods of food identification that I mentioned on page 285. Perhaps having an Alcat blood test♥ will help, but it is up to you which method of identification you chose. However, whatever method you chose, you must give it time to have its effect, so stay on the appropriate diet for at least four weeks, as it can take that long if not longer to start benefiting you. As with most forms of ill health, you need to consider your whole body, not just your brain. Despite what most doctors may say, ill health is a whole body condition, and it is a particular part of the body that is causing most of the trouble. When I have taken a detailed history from many patients, it is surprising how many other symptoms they used to acknowledge. Fatigue, headaches, bowel upsets of indigestion, etc. inability to sleep properly, poor failing eyesight are some of the many symptoms patient admit to when pushed. It is just that their Parkinsonism, or whatever they have consulted me about, is their main problem, and the other symptoms are less important to them.

To be fair, most patients see a Specialist in a particular area, so a Gastroenterologist for their bowels, a Chest Physician for their asthma or an Orthopaedic Consultant for joint problems. They aren't expecting to see someone who is interested in the whole of them. It's not the way things are in mainstream medicine. In any case, if you see such a specialist, you will be treated with appropriate drugs. If you see someone like me, we will take a detailed history and try to solve all your problems, not just the main ones you think are important.

Mercury in mercury amalgam fillings plays an important part in Parkinsonism, especially if you have such fillings in your upper teeth, as there is only a thin plate between your teeth and your brain. For details of how to deal with mercury amalgam, please read the appropriate section in the chapter on cancer, starting on page 131.

Then there are all the chemicals in your environment, any you may have used at any time in the past, such as when doing up an old house, when you used all those nasty chemicals. Did you wear a mask? How effective was it, or did you simply put up with it, thinking you will get away with it? Did you ever work on a farm, perhaps doing sheep dipping? Have you ever worked with a lot of chemicals? Have you ever worked with plastics? Have you drunk a lot of water from plastic bottles or drunk contaminated municipal water? Do you live in a polluted city and have to breathe in its air? How contaminated is the house in which you live? Does it have plasterboard walls, or be made of other chemically manufactured materials? Have you eaten a lot of food with added chemicals in it? Have you had a lot of drugs for one reason or another, as they cause nutritional deficiencies?

What hobbies do you have? Have you played with toy soldiers as a child, possibly made of lead, or have you stripped old wallpaper off walls, not being aware they may have contained lead? Have you used toxic glues or paints? What about household chemicals? Do you use a lot of them, especially if you have a methylation problem, that is have difficulty breaking down chemicals in your liver? About ten percent of the population does have this problem. Could you be one of them?

So what should you do? First, follow the diet I recommended earlier on and see what that does. If you have mercury amalgam fillings in your teeth, consult a biologically trained dentist♥ and consider having them changed to an inert non-metallic material, and follow the chelation advice I gave in the chapter on cancer, starting on page 131. Assuming you have a number of environmental chemicals in your brain, you will need to find a way of clearing them. Strangely enough, coffee enemas are a good way plus Far Infra-Red saunas♥. Put a few drops of organic olive oil under your tongue and leave it there for a couple of minutes if you can, then rinse your mouth out, as many times in a day as you can manage. All these chemicals are fat soluble, so will be attracted to the oil, just as they are attracted to your brain. It will take a long time to do things this way, but it will help gradually to clear chemicals from your body. Have baths with Epsom Salts in the water. That can be very relaxing and helpful.

If possible, find a doctor who is willing to give you glutathione by infusion, as it is not well absorbed by mouth. Ask him to start at 200mg or thereabouts and gradually work up to 800mg three times a week. Glutathione is your body's most effective detoxifier. You will also benefit from regular infusions of nutrients, say once a week, of the sort I mention in the chapter on cancer, starting on page 153. If you cannot find anyone to give you infusions, or cannot afford them, try Lypo-Spheric GSH 450mg plus 1000mg essential phospholipids, and take at least three every day♥.

If you can't find anyone to give you nutrients by injection, you will definitely need magnesium, so best by transdermal lotion♥, and selenium, probably 800mcg per day, possibly even more if you have mercury amalgam fillings in your teeth. You will need vitamin C and zinc, of course. Selenium is very effective at clearing toxic chemicals from your body. Read the warning I gave about selenium in the chapter on cancer, starting on page 131. Alternatively, coffee enemas increase your production of glutathione, so consider doing one a day if practical. Again I gave details of how to do a coffee enema in the chapter on cancer, starting on page 117, item 5.

Consider taking special capsules of fruits, vegetables, berries and grapes, with all the sugar, water, salt and fibre eliminated during preparation. They significantly improve your overall nutritional intake of alkalinising foods, apart from which there are at least twenty-eight double-blind placebo-controlled clinical studies to date on the capsules to say how good they are for human beings.

How much have you had over your whole life in the way of antibiotics? Have you had any specific infections of any sort, such as glandular fever? Did you fully recover, or did it take a really long time for you to recover? Might you still have the virus somewhere in your system? Again, turn to the chapter on cancer, where I discuss the ways to deal with infections, starting on page 126.

If you have had quite a lot of antibiotics over the years, consider going on an anti-fungal approach, which basically means no sugar and yeasty foods, various anti-fungal preparations and replacement of the good organisms into your bowel, such as Biocare's Bioacidophilus♥.

This means much stricter attention to detail in your diet. So all in all there is a lot you can do to not only stop becoming any worse, but also to reverse your condition and become completely well again, not something that your own doctor is likely to tell you.

Oh and don't forget to have your blood tested for homocysteine. If it is raised, bringing it down the way I explained in chapter 29. It could make all the difference to your health.

Chapter 32

Hyperactivity

Hyperactivity is a problem mainly in children, but I sometimes wonder what happens to such kids as they grow up. Are they some of the awkward ones, the ones that go off the rails, the ones that steal or murder, or do all sorts of so-called uncivilised things? I don't know, as I haven't done any research on the matter. But I leave the thought there.

Then again, what is hyperactivity? Presumably what one person may call hyperactive another person says is merely high spirits. One person may feel capable of controlling an unruly child, whereas another person can not, possibly because there are other children to look after, or possibly because they just don't have the personality to try.

Truly hyperactive children tend to be blond, blue-eyed males. Not always, but the majority are in my fairly extensive experience. Certainly boys considerably outweigh girls as far as numbers are concerned. In fact I don't remember ever seeing a hyperactive young lady.

Whenever I knew I was due to see a hyperactive young man, I would look round my premises and put away as much as possible, occasionally leaving things out I knew he would go for. I always asked his parents to bring someone with them who could look after him in my garden or in their car, so that we could have an uninterrupted consultation. It never lasted. In due course, I would hear a loud bang as the surgery door was slammed shut, followed by the stamping of running feet along the corridor to my consulting room. It happened every time.

There are many variations on the degree of hyperactivity in a particular child, but at their extreme they are impossible to control. Smacking them doesn't work as they often seem to enjoy pain, which is one of the reasons they would soon find my blood pressure machine, wrap it round their arm and blow it up hard, almost as if they were trying to elicit something to hurt themselves.

The history I invariably obtained from the parents was of a child that never stopped crying for the first few months or a couple of years anyway. It would rocks it crib all the time, which was often assumed to be attention seeking. It exhausted its parents, often causing both of them to lose their tempers, because they were so tired, one of them getting up to look after the baby on alternate nights. Even that seldom settled the baby. If I saw the parents with the child at such an early stage, I warned them that they could wake up in alarm the first night they were allowed to sleep throughout the night, afraid that they had a cot death on their hands. Instead they would find a happy gurgling baby lying contentedly in its cot, playing with its feet or some toy.

As the child grew up a bit and started walking, he would have very short attention span for anything, and would rush around from one thing to another, often throwing things away if they didn't work quickly enough for him, or he simply got bored with it. He would walk all over his toys, often cutting his naked feet. If he fell and hurt himself, he would get up with a smile of sorts all over his face, but certainly not cry. It he was picked up, he would wriggle to get free, not to do anything in particular, but just so he could be free to do something, anything.

He would never look you straight in the eye. If you managed to look in his eyes for any length of time, there would be something strange about them, as if he couldn't see you, you were not there, almost as if his eyes were somehow not connected to his brain. I used to call that his 'zombie' mood. Yet at other times, he could be loveable and such a joy to cuddle, but that sensation didn't last for long. If it did happen, his parents would know there was a normal, loving child in there somewhere, but where?

As the child grew up, he would become stronger and stronger, so become more difficult to control, rushing all over the place, with no particular aim in mind. He would leave his toys strewn all over the place, with not a care in the world. He would be very disruptive at school, being virtually impossible to control, keep quiet or find anything suitable for him to do. At least his schooling, or whatever you want to call it, would give his poor parents a break of sorts. But then would come the meetings with his teachers or the head of the school, trying to decide what was the best for his education. An Educational Psychologist would be called in and his parents would possibly be blamed for not having exerted enough control over him in his younger years, despite their best endeavours.

And yet it is all so simple. His brain is being irritated by something, and he is suffering from a nutritional deficiency of one kind or another, especially of zinc. All you have to do is change his diet. I say 'all you have to do is change his diet' because it is not that easy. The earlier on you make the changes the better, while he is still young enough for him to be controlled by an average adult. As he grows bigger, he can be really hard to control.

What does he eat and drink? Probably absolute rubbish. No doubt he insists on cola type drinks, or bright yellow juices, which he drinks gallons of every day, because he is so thirsty. He may of course be addicted to drinking milk, by the gallon. Perhaps he only eats burgers and chips and refuses to eat anything else. Well you have to be strong and insist that he start eating and drinking properly. You have to make up your mind, plan everything in an order, and do it. Yes, please explain to him what you are doing and why, knowing full well that he won't take it in. You may need help from male members of your family, as ladies are softer and sometimes give in. That would be disastrous.

To be fair, the chances are that his brain is being irritated by chemicals in the drinks he consumes, but it could also be some of the foods he seems to be addicted to. So stop the lot. I mean it. Stop the lot, and only let him have so-called healthy foods and water.

On any named day, start the process. He is only to eat and drink whatever you provide for him and nothing else. If necessary, clear the house of everything you don't want him to eat or drink so he can't be tempted. Eat the same foods yourself. It could do you a lot of good anyway. Prepare small items of fruit and vegetables, so slices of apple, pear, pineapple, grapes of both colours without pips in them, banana, mango, plus sticks of many coloured vegetables, such as broccoli, Brussel sprouts, carrots, cauliflower, all together on a pretty plate in the middle of the table, plus a dip of sorts, oh, and plenty of water. No dairy or caffeine, so no chocolate, and no added sugar, but hard-boiled eggs are fine to begin with. They make a very attractive mixture all prepared on a single plate in the middle of the dining room table. Invite him to join you to eat from the mixture, to pick out what he wants, while you do the same. It is likely he will refuse to eat anything and demand burger and chips. But remain firm and say that is all that's available for him to eat.

Ok, so he goes hungry. It won't do him any harm. There is no problem of him not eating anything for a day of two, especially not eating foods that are probably harming him in any case, and especially if he is already overweight. Don't forget, you are doing him a favour. You are taking control of his life, as he can no longer control it himself.

The reason for having help at hand, especially from men, is to control him. You need to run a rota of, say, an hour or two, when one person takes complete charge of him, takes him out, plays with him, watches TV with him, reads to him, anything to keep him occupied. Then someone else takes over. Every so often he is taken to the food and drink on the dining room table and offered something from the table already prepared. He is not allowed to eat anything else. Even though it probably still won't get through to him, he is to be offered an explanation why you are doing this to him. Keep explaining it all to him.

Eventually he is likely to start feeling sleepy at some time in the evening. If he wants to sleep at any time during the day, let him sleep. When he wakes up, offer food and water from the table. If he refuses anything, tell him that is all there is. Yes he is likely to complain and may cry, but do not give in.

He should go to bed in the end, probably still hungry, but someone must sleep on a mattress at his door, or possibly in the same room with him. He must not be allowed to creep downstairs to find something he would like to eat. In any case, you should have cleared the house completely of everything else. If he does go downstairs, go with him and offer him food from the dining room table, and a glass of water.

Yes, it can be hard, especially if he cries in hunger, but that is likely to be withdrawal symptoms. The younger the child is when you start this process, the quicker he will respond and come out the other side, as a loving, normal, smiling and delightful child. You may have to suffer with him a second day, but again, it won't do him any harm. In fact it will do him so much good in the end. You simply have to keep up the rota of adults to read and play with him for a while. By the morning of the third day it should be all over. Your loving child should wake up and happily eat bits and pieces from the plate you offer him and drink a glass of water for the first time ever, possibly two.

The next thing to do is replenish his stores of nutrients. The poor choices he has consumed have not only lacked any nutrition of value, they have actually caused a specific loss of nutrients from his body. In particular zinc is important. If you manage to collect all a normal child's urine he passes in 24 hours and analyse how much zinc there is in it, and compare it with a hyperactive child's single urine passing after a reaction, that is if you can catch him, you will find there is more zinc excreted in his urine after a reaction than normally in 24 hours. So part of his problems is a zinc deficiency, and a zinc deficiency affects the brain. He is likely to need at least 5mg as a child in the first instance, but you can work out how much based on comparing his weight with an adult of 70lb or 11kg, who would need in the order of 45mg zinc to begin with.

He should also be given 2000IU vitamin D3, especially if he doesn't get into the sun, certainly for the first month or so, plus a child's dose of multivitamins and minerals.

I have done this many times with children. It is hard, and I always let family and friends ring me at any time of the day or night when they went through this process, as to give then assurance they were doing the right thing was important. It always worked.

Once the child is clear of hyperactivity, keep him eating and drinking the same safe foods for at least a week. That is why it is important to choose when to start, as it is silly to start five days or so before a party, which would be bound to include all sorts of awful sugar-coated, colourful items that so many kids eat and drink nowadays.

After the initial clearance, it is important to start challenging him with various food items, to identify what he might react to or not. Try to avoid all sugar, dairy products and chemical colourings and additives to begin with, and try to get him onto as wide and nutritious a diet as possible, placing emphasis on vegetables and fruits, nuts and seeds, i.e. foods that can be eaten raw if possible, and, of course, organic where possible. But it is important to test non-organic foods, as he is bound to come across them sooner or later.

This will apply to the majority of young people, but there is always one who reacts to petrol and diesel fumes or cooking gas or any number of environmental chemicals. This can be very hard to identify, but remember the adage I came up with years ago, namely 'absolutely anything can cause absolutely any symptom in absolutely any person'. If you start with that approach, sooner or later you will resolve the problem.

It could be useful to video his behaviour during this period of his life and show it to him when he is better. It can be very helpful, and he probably won't believe it is him.

That's why this is called 'Nutritional and Environmental Medicine'.

Finally have his homocysteine blood level measured. It could make all the difference to him, and, of course, read chapter 29 where I explain all about a raised homocysteine level.

Chapter 33

Anorexia Nervosa

Anorexia nervosa is so-called because the condition is considered to be caused by a nervous system problem, basically the brain. It tends to occur in teen-age girls close to puberty, so that alone should alert the authorities to one of the main problems. Most of the young ladies are also avid readers of celebrity magazines and have a tendency to want to copy certain women as far as their size, shape and style of dress are concerned. They become thin as a rake, but still maintain they are fat. They pinch the skin of their abdomen and show how fat they are. They are not. There is absolutely no fat on them at all. Their weight problem is all in their mind, and, because of that, they are taken into a psychiatric ward and force-fed. It doesn't work.

Why doesn't it work? Presumably because the basic premise is wrong. Yes, they do have a mental problem of sorts, but it is caused by a specific deficiency, namely of zinc. The average human being needs at least fifteen milligrams of zinc every day, but analyses have shown that the average intake is between ten and thirteen milligrams. But at puberty it goes up to twenty milligrams and in pregnancy it goes up to about twenty-five milligrams per day. When young people in particular are short of zinc, it seems to affect their brains. Hyperactive children, usually blond, blue-eyed males, are particularly affected by a zinc deficiency and they become hyperactive, on top of a reaction to one or more foods and food chemicals, such as bright orange orange squash containing E102 tartrazine.

Young girls around the age of puberty need a lot more zinc, and their intake will be compounded if they choose to become vegetarian or, even worse, vegan, which they commonly do. Having talked to friends, they are easily convinced that it is wrong to eat animal meat or fish. Don't get me wrong. I'm not against veganism. It's just that most vegans are not aware that they will eventually become deficient in iron, zinc and vitamin B12, as those three elements come almost entirely from animal meat. Such people need supplements of those elements. So patients suffering from anorexia nervosa need zinc in particular. They may also need vitamin B12 and iron if they are vegans, but it is the zinc that is most important to them. The deficiency affects their brain in a strange way, making them think they are fat when they are not.

A zinc deficiency is never thought of by mainstream medicine, because it has never heard of such a problem. Blood tests are never carried out for zinc, but, if they are, a white blood cell zinc measurement is probably the best cell to measure. On the other hand, there is a much simpler way of telling whether someone has a deficiency of zinc or not. There is a form of zinc that can be made up as a liquid and given to the person under investigation. If she cannot taste anything in it, i.e. it tastes like water, she is zinc deficient. All you have to do is keep giving her a dose of the liquid daily until she says it tastes horrible. She is then replete with zinc.

This whole subject has been written about in a book by Professor Derek Bryce-Smith, entitled 'The Zinc Solution'. Despite his eminence, no one has taken any notice of him or his works, possibly as he is not a medical doctor. It would appear that only medically qualified people have the right to make such suggestions, according to the medical profession. Or is it that the answer is too simple? They took no notice of Professor Linus Pauling, the double Nobel Prize winner for Medicine, who advocated large doses of vitamin C to treat and prevent cancer. He also was not medically qualified.

Having said that, Professor John Soothill was the professor of Immunology at Great Ormond Street Hospital in London.   He carried out a magnificent study of children with migraine and demonstrated the number of foods they reacted to.   He also did part of the study double-blind. I met him after he had retired and he was still incensed that the medical profession had taken no notice of the study that he published in The Lancet.   He was at the top of his tree and he was medically qualified. So what is it about the medical profession?

Because young girls suffering from anorexia nervosa refuse to eat because they think they are fat, they are also deficient in a number of other nutrients, both vitamins and minerals. I found the best way to improve their nutrient status was to give vitamins and minerals intravenously, which worked every time and remarkably quickly. Once they were thinking straight, eating stopped being a problem and they soon put on weight.

It is unlikely that you will be able to find anyone to give your daughter vitamins and minerals intravenously, so try to get her to take a range by mouth, starting with a multivitamin/multimineral supplement plus extra zinc, best taken one hour after food, if she eats any. Start with a total of thirty milligrams elemental zinc per day, split up into at least two separate doses. You could try the special capsules of fruits, vegetables and berries that I have mentioned so many times before♥. And don't forget to have her blood tested for homocysteine. It could be so important. Also please read chapter 29, the chapter on homocysteine. With any luck you will see an improvement in about two weeks. It's that simple.

Chapter 34

Alcoholism and Other Addictions

It has never failed to amaze me that alcoholics in a special unit are allowed free access to equally addictive substances as coffee, cigarettes and sugar. There is no way they will succeed to dry out if they do not give up the other addictions. Put quite simply they are addictive and nutritionally deficient, whatever they are addicted to. They have to give up all possibly addictive substances.

As far as I am concerned, they also desperately need vitamins and minerals intravenously, and that is the first thing I would do to a patient, every day for three or four days, with good levels of chromium, magnesium, B vitamins and vitamin C in particular, although I would also put in other elements such as zinc, selenium, molybdenum and manganese. I would start with at least 5000mcg vitamin B12 and 5mg folic acid.

If the person were prepared to give up the addictive substances immediately, I would add sodium bicarbonate, and give sodium bicarbonate on its own in saline at another time of the day, as withdrawal symptoms could be fairly harsh, if all addictive substances were given up all together. Giving up addictive substances seems to create an acidic status, and withdrawal symptoms that can be partially negated by sodium bicarbonate. I would also give sodium bicarbonate by mouth thirty minutes after meals.

Yes the person needs psychological help, mainly because of the reason why they became an alcoholic in the first instance. If it was merely a bad habit, it should not be difficult to give up, but the chances are that the person does have a reason why they started to drink so much alcohol in the first instance.

If you or someone you know is going to try to give up alcohol completely, and the other addictive substances, and does not have the benefit of someone to give vitamins and minerals intravenously, I suggest you take a multivitamin/ multimineral three times a day with food. There is a possibility that you need more of certain elements, but taking such a preparation three times a day for a while should improve your nutritional status efficiently enough, and make you feel generally better.

I also suggest you take a level teaspoonful of sodium bicarbonate every two hours to begin with and cut the dose down to thirty minutes after food after about three or four days on the more frequent dose.

There is an interesting theory that addictive substances contain alkaloids, and certainly cigarettes, alcohol and cocaine do contain alkaloids. It is suggested that the pegs that keep your DNA fairly firm are normally xeronine, and that an alkaloid can replace the xeronine in your DNA. That makes your DNA become rather like the toy 'slinky' that turns over and over down your stairs.

It is suggested that your addictive alkaloid has replaced the xeronine by simply displacing it with a higher amount in a form of competitive inhibition. All you have to do is displace the alkaloid where it currently is with more xeronine by a reversal of the competitive inhibitory system.

Xeronine comes from a precursor proxeronine that you obtain from your diet, which I believe is fairly high in pineapple amongst other foods of a natural sort. So a good diet with lots of fruits and vegetables should help, which is why I recommend the special capsules of fruits, vegetables and berries which gives you the valuable ingredients from twenty-six foods.♥

There is another aspect worth thinking about. That is are you eating on a regular basis a food related to your addictive substance? For example, if you need to give up cigarettes, consider giving up potatoes, tomatoes, aubergines (eggplant in USA) and peppers, as they are all part of the Deadly Nightshade family.

If you are addicted to a particular form of alcohol, what is the alcohol distilled from? If it is wine, give up all grapes, raisins and sultanas. If it is vodka, is it distilled from potatoes or grain? You need to find out. Whichever it is, you are taking that foods in a jet-propelled vehicle, the alcohol, so your food reaction may be very fast, as alcohol is absorbed in the stomach. This approach is worth thinking about. One last thing, test for homocysteine and read chapter 29. It is almost bound to be raised because of what you are addicted to. Whether it is a cause of your addiction I can't answer, but bringing it down to a healthy level will benefit you in many ways.

Chapter 35

Thrush Candida Albicans

Women are only too aware that thrush can occur all too easily. It can follow a single strong course of an antibiotic, or one or two courses of a weaker variety. Thrush is the bane of life for most Gynaecologists. You only have to talk to them. They will tell you all about it.

The trouble is they haven't thought it through properly. Yes, they may well be aware that thrush followed a course of antibiotics, but they haven't understood the basics of it. The patient took a dose of antibiotics by mouth, but the effect was a dose of thrush in her vagina. What's the connection? There has to be one.

If you study the female anatomy, you will notice there is a close connection between the anus and the vagina, so, if there is a relationship between the two, why has she been affected by something coming from the bowel? Answer. The whole length of the bowel is infected by Candida albicans, the organism that causes thrush, and it simply migrates.

A simple but basic suggestion that I need to put in here is how women wipe themselves after going to the toilet. Do they wipe from the front backwards, or from the back forwards? It should be from the front backwards, so as to minimise contamination of the vagina from the anus.

Mainstream medicine seems unaware that a single course of a strong antibiotic can kill all the friendly organisms within the bowel, leaving fungi notably Candida albicans to flourish unopposed. I have attended many talks when the speaker has said that our bowels soon recover after a course of antibiotics. That may occasionally be true, but it is not the case in the majority of women in my experience. Perhaps I only saw women who had suffered as a result of an antibiotic, while the rest recovered well enough. If that is the case, mainstream medicine should look after the few who are affected.

In the patients I saw, their whole body was affected by the fungus, and it produced a whole range of symptoms, including bowels problems, joint problems, mood swings, insomnia, brain fag, and other mental changes. Some of the time the fungus was so entrenched that it was very difficult to eliminate. The organism was really strongly embedded into their tissues, and any attempt to dislodge it was met with violent resistance in the form of severe withdrawal symptoms, sometimes almost too much for the patient.

Being a fungus, Candida albicans feeds on sugar, so a sugar-free diet is a must. But it can be more than that. It can mean avoiding for a time anything that the organism can use as food, so all fruit, all potatoes cooked at high temperature that converts its starch more into sugar than usual, and all grains may need to be avoided for a while. It can be very hard. But there is no other way. Yes, antifungal antibiotics can help, but most doctors will not prescribe more than a week's course, and, in any case, they can damage the liver amongst other problems in some patients.

Unfortunately I found that the more entrenched the case, the harder it was to clear the fungus if the patient still had mercury amalgam fillings in her teeth. There is a certain amount of information in the literature that the presence of mercury makes eradication of the fungus very difficult. I don't know exactly what it does. It may confer an extra degree of resistance to the candida organism, or it may simply somehow get in the way. Whatever the reason, it can make fungal eradication very hard.

Unfortunately it means that severely affected patients may need to have their mercury amalgam fillings removed and replaced by a non-metallic alternative. That can be quite expensive, but must be done by a biologically trained dentist, and they are few and far between♥. Please refer to what I said about amalgam fillings in the cancer section, beginning on page 131.

In addition, severely affected patients, and others less severely affected, can suffer badly from the leaky gut syndrome. This means that partially broken down food items may gain access to the blood stream and set up a kinin-inflammatory reaction in a susceptible part of the body, and small molecular weight nutrients may be refused entry to the blood. All in all, the leaky gut syndrome does no favours at all. It allows entry to the blood stream of unwanted elements and rejects entry of things that the patient needs.

There is no doubt in my experience that the candida organism can affect many organs of the body, and certainly leads to a degree of low thyroid effect, even if the blood tests are within the lab's reference ranges. Unfortunately blood tests only pick up what is in the blood. They cannot pick up whether the thyroid receptors are functioning well and normally or not, or they have been interfered with or damaged. So low thyroid, and probably low adrenals, are very likely to play a part in a patient with thrush and generalised candida. They are certainly often tired, but all the doctor's tests have failed to reveal an explanation.

So how did I treat a person with deep-seated candida? I explained the nature of their condition and tried to gain their confidence that I knew what I was doing. I certainly changed their diet, by asking them to avoid all animal milks and products, all caffeine (including tea, cola drinks and chocolate), all sugar and fruit, all white refined flour products, potatoes cooked at a high temperature so in an oven, and all junk food and food containing additives. Because of the lack of fruit, I advised they take the special capsules of dehydrated fruits, vegetables, and berries.♥

They also needed something to start the process of killing off the candida organism, and I used chlorine dioxide at a lowish dose, say 4 drops of sodium chlorite plus 20 drops of citric acid after supper, repeated between one and two hours later, possibly for many months. They also needed glutamine 500mg three times a day 1/2 hour before meals to start healing the leaky gut syndrome. If they were overweight, I may have encouraged them to follow a five-day fast to cut out all food for five days to starve the fungus, but explained how ill they might feel for a few days. I have explained all this in the book I wrote in 1987, entitled 'Conquering Cystitis'♥.

I also prescribed whole thyroid extract and Biocare's AD206♥ to improve their adrenal glands, as well as put them on a few drops of Magnascent iodine♥. Your alternative could be Nutri-thyroid♥, as it doesn't need a prescription. I was fortunate that I could give patients intravenous infusions of vitamins and minerals, as there was no doubt they were nutritionally deficient, most likely because of the effect of the leaky gut syndrome. There may not be any point in prescribing vitamins and minerals in the first instance, as they will most likely not absorb them. In the severely affected patient I may well have recommended they consult a biologically trained dentist. I knew of a number at the time.

They certainly needed the friendly organisms being replenished within their bowel, and I used Biocare's Bioacidophilus♥, at least one capsule three times a day after meals. If they wanted to try an anti-fungal antibiotic their doctor could prescribe, I was perfectly happy with that, but the course was likely to be rather short.

As they were likely to be failing to break down foods completely, I often put them on digestive enzymes after meals, and recommended 1/2 teaspoonful of pure sodium bicarbonate twenty minutes later, largely to take over the digestive processes for a while to ensure that their food was metabolised completely after eating.

There are many other preparations that individual patients sometimes took for themselves or on the advice of another practitioner they were consulting, or they had read about, but I can't advise on them all. I may not have had experience of some of them. It would certainly be sensible to seek the advice of someone trained in the arts of natural medicine. You will need support and advice, as it can sometimes be very hard to know which way to turn.

This is the last time I will say this. Please have your homocysteine level measured and read chapter 29. It could be one of the most important things you ever do, as a healthy level could help you to live a long life.

Appendix 1

In the text, various laboratories, technical supplies and nutritional supplements have been mentioned, which I recommended to my patients. I have put the asterisk ♥ against each item in the main text. How to obtain some of them is explained here. Some of the companies have agreed to give a discount, but not all. Where a discount will apply, usually the company likes you to telephone them to place an order so that you can mention the discount offered when you mention the relevant code. However, it has not been possible to make special arrangements for all items, so you will have to obtain what you want from wherever you can. We apologise for this and will amend this information as soon as we can.

Laboratories

Biolab
Both the Kelmer test and the Lymphocyte transformation test are performed by Biolab laboratory, located in Central London. Their phone number is 0207-636-5959 in UK, or International (44)-207-636-5959. It is unlikely that they will do blood samples for you direct as they need a practitioner to send the results to. If your own doctor cannot help, Biolab may be able to provide you with the name of a practitioner near you who you can visit. This basically applies to the UK, but samples can often be sent from outside the UK. However you will need to check with Biolab to make sure of the practicalities.

- Kelmer test
- Lymphocyte transformation test

SureScreen Life Sciences & Neuro-Lab (Neuro-Lab became The Galkina Laboratory Ltd on 31May 2011)
A whole range of tests are available from these laboratories that are fully described in the text. The tests are of value to identify the state of cancer in your body ideally early on, to use as a means to check that whatever approach you have chosen to follow is actually making a useful difference when the tests are repeated in a few months time.

SureScreen Life Sciences, Morley Retreat, Church Lane, Morley, Ilkeston, Derbyshire DE7 6DE, UK
Telephone: +44 (0) 1332 830990
Website: www.surescreen.com

Neuro-Lab (The Galkina Laboratory), 681 Wimborne Road, Bournemouth, Dorset BH9 2AT, UK
Telephone: +44 (0) 1202 510910
Website: www.neuro-lab.com

As with most laboratories it is unlikely that they will do blood samples for you direct, as they need a doctor to send the results to. If your own doctor cannot help, these laboratories may be able to provide you with the name of a doctor near you who you can visit. This basically applies to the UK, but samples can easily be sent from outside the UK. However you will need to check with them to make sure of the practicalities.

Alcat Test
The Alcat Test tests for food intolerances. The company does let the public have the blood test done without the guide of a practitioner as they provide support material. I have explained a lot in the text so you should be able to use both their and my explanations about what to do. The company will tell you where to have a blood sample taken so that it can be done correctly and sent to them in the proper way. You can book an Alcat Test direct by logging onto www.alcat.com or telephoning the company directly on 001-954-426-2304 in the North American Continent and the Caribbean. If you give the reference CC100, you will receive 5% discount on the cost of the test. Also for Europe please log onto www.regeneruslabs.com. Or Tel: 0333 9000 979. Email info@regeneruslabs.com and mention my name for 5% off the cost of the test.

Genova Diagnostics
Genova Diagnostics is a large international company, based in London. The UK telephone number is 0208-336-7750 or International (44)-208-336-7750. While it is possible for individuals to have tests done direct, results will not be interpreted, for which reason it is best to consult a practitioner the company recommends. If you telephone them, they will give you the details of a practitioner in your area. Their website is www.gdx.uk.net. There is a drop down area for other countries. See also below.

Genova Diagnostics has two main laboratories, one in UK as above and one in USA, having taken over Great Smokies Laboratory. In USA the number is 1-800-522-4762, or 001-828-253-0621. Their website is www.gdx.uk.net with a drop down area for other countries.

Thermoscan In The UK
Contact Carol Brough on 0207-580-7537 or on 0207-224-4622 to arrange to have a Thermoscan. Mention ref. RR100 to be given a 5% discount off the current price. You will have to find someone to do this for you in other countries.

Books
All books can be obtained from www.amazon.com. Unfortunately some of them may be out of print or simply not available.

- Are You Sleeping In A Safe Place? by Rolf Gordon ISBN 0-95140170-X. It is best to buy this book directly by ringing (44)-208-670-5883 or contact www.dulwichhealth.co.uk
- The Journey by Brandon Bays ISBN 0-7225-3839-1
- Love Medicine and Miracles by Bernie Segal MD ISBN 0-09-963270-5
- Peace Love and Healing by Bernie Segal MD ISBN 0-7126-7051-3
- Energy Juices by Natalie Savona ISBN 1844831396
- Cooking Without by Barbara Cousins ISBN 9-780722-540220
- Eat Right 4 Your Type by Dr Peter D'Adamo ISBN 0-399-14255-X
- Your Life In Your Hands by Professor Jane Plant ISBN 1-85227-809-9
- Menace In The Mouth by Dr Jack Levenson ISBN 0-9534734-23-0
- Natural Progesterone. The Multiple Roles of a Remarkable Hormone by John R Lee MD ISBN 1-897766-19-X

- What Your Doctor May Not Tell You About Breast Cancer by John R Lee MD ISBN 0-446-52686-X
- Hypothyroidism. The Unsuspected Illness by Broda O Barnes MD ISBN 0-690-01029-X
- Life Energy: Unlocking The Hidden Power Of Your Emotions To Achieve Total Well-being by Dr John Diamond, Paragon House, New York,1985
- Rebounding For Health by Margaret Hawkins ISBN 0-9520780-1-5
- Stop Aging or Slow The Process. Exercise With Oxygen Therapy (EWOT) Can Help by William Campbell Douglas II MD. ISBN 9962-636-37-X
- Living Proof. A Medical Mutiny by Michael Gearin-Tosh ISBN 0-7432-0677-0
- A Cure For All Cancers by Dr. Hulda Clarke ISBN 1-890035-01-7
- Cancer Is A Fungus by Dr Tullio Simoncini
- Knockout by Suzanne Somers ISBN 978-0-307-58746-6
- Conquering Cystitis by Dr Patrick Kingsley ISBN 0-85223-576-3. To order a copy of this book please order through drpatrickkingsley@gmail.com, giving your name and address. The book costs £7.95 plus postage.
- Stop Smoking by Dr Patrick Kingsley ISBN 0-356-20125-2. To order a copy of this book please order through drpatrickkingsley@gmail.com, giving your name and address. The book costs £7.95 plus postage.
- The Medical Detective – Memoirs of a Most Unusual Doctor by Dr Patrick Kingsley on all kindle-type book readers and website of www.thenewmedicine.info or from drpatrickkingsley@gmail.com, giving your name and address. The book costs £12.95 plus p&p.
- The H Factor by Patrick Holford and Dr James Braly ISBN 978-0-7499-2419-5

Technical

Coffee Enemas & Enema buckets.
Contact e-enema.co.uk. Health (44-1235-838551) for supplies of coffee enema kits and appropriate coffee. They are also very switched on to people's problems.

Colonic Irrigations.
www.colonic-association.org

Segiun patches
Please quote ID no 013221 after logging onto www.segiun.com. You can then join the system and you will be assigned your own number.

Matthew Manning is an extraordinary healer. He has courses and two specific CDs. www.matthewmanning.com

Dr Nicholas Gonzales
www.dr-gonzales.com. For more information about his treatment approaches, especially for pancreatic cancer, look up his web site.

Rebounder
It is important that you use a Rebounder properly, by reading the book entitled 'Rebounding for Health' by Margaret Hawkins ISBN number 0-9520780-1-5. See details in the book section.

Liquidisers
Can be bought from your local store, or you should be able to obtain one on the net.

Juice Extractors
Can be bought from your local store, or you should be able to obtain one on the net.

Far Infrared Saunas
Contact Mark Givert on 0208-445-5412 or mobile 07859-904142, quoting reference FITT23 to obtain a 5% discount on the retail cost of the product.

Patch Adams
Video available from www.amazon.com

Quality Water
There are many companies that market water filters and you may wish to search the web for one that suits you. There are simple jug filters that can stand on your kitchen worktop or ones that need to be plumbed into your water system and have their own separate tap. They may be more expensive to buy in the first instance, but you have to replace cartridges regularly with the jug types so the costs may be much the same in the long run. The under sink ones are more convenient as all you have to do is turn on the special tap. Their cartridges also need to be replaced every so often, but not nearly as often as the jug types.

Oxygen Concentrator
Information can be obtained from:

SureScreen Life Sciences, Morley Retreat, Church Lane, Morley, Ilkeston, Derbyshire DE7 6DE, UK
Telephone: +44 (0) 1332 830990
Website: www.surescreen.com

IAOMT An International Organisation Of Biologically-Trained Dentists
www.iaomt.org. The replacement of mercury amalgam fillings is a specialist subject and not one to be taken lightly. The dangers of dental mercury amalgams remains a controversial issue at present, i.e. the so-called Authorities are dragging their feet, possibly for financial and legal reasons. The FDA in America is beginning to take the matter more seriously than previously, so this issue will develop. There is therefore a difference of opinion between various groups of doctors and dentists as to the dangers of the material, mainly because dentists have been inserting mercury amalgams into peoples' teeth for such a long time and it is difficult for them to consider acknowledging they may have been wrong all along. Also they might say that there is insufficient evidence from appropriate studies to justify a change in dental practices. To be fair it is very difficult to 'prove' that dental mercury amalgam fillings cause all the health problems that some of us suggest might be the case in an individual person, especially as the cost of their replacement with a suitable alternative non-metallic material can be high and the chelation approach to clearing all mercury from the body can be quite complex. Some people believe the Dental Profession has conned the public by calling mercury amalgam fillings 'silver amalgams'. Had the public known all along that the mixture contained 50% mercury,

they might have been far less willing to have such a metal inserted into their teeth. If you ask a dentist if you may have the mercury amalgam fillings he has just replaced, he will tell you he has to get rid of them as toxic waste. That says it all in my opinion.

Supplements

Wellbeing Research
Order from wellbeingorders@gmail.com

- Harmonik Ojibwa Indian Herbal Tincture
- Vitamin D 10,000IU + 150mcg K2

Sublingual tablets of vitamin D3 are readily available. There is a huge amount of scientific information coming out about the importance of vitamin D and the consequences of a deficiency of it. Cancers in particular are being seriously considered caused by a vitamin D deficiency. It is probably wise to take one tablet of 10,000IU a day for at least two weeks, then one capsule on alternate days or Monday, Wednesday and Friday for convenience. Because many people forget to take supplements, it is now being suggested that people have an injection of about 300,000IU twice a year. If you have a blood sample taken for vitamin D levels, as 25(OH)D - cholecalciferol, do not accept your local laboratory's reference range, which is far too low according to the experts. Levels for health should be between 160-210 nmol/litre (65-85 ng/ml).

- Selenium
- Multiminerals
- Harmonik liver cleanse and tonic
- Hemp or flax seeds. It is probably best for you to obtain these fresh from your local Health Food shop.
- Spirulina tablets
- Natural progesterone cream
- Serrapeptase
- Transdermal magnesium lotion
- Co-enzyme Q10 cream
- Magnascent iodine
- AlkaLiza
- Paracleanse
- Salvestrol Platinum
- Stevia
- Vitamin B12 as 1000mcg sublingual tablets.
- Diatomaceous Earth
- Alpha-lipoic acid as 200mg plus 200 mg L-carnitine

Professor Bruce Ames
He has shown that adding L-carnitine to alpha-lipoic acid considerably enhances its effects, as well as conferring other advantages. I suggest you take one tablet twice daily of this combination product. All of the above supplements have been adequately described in the main text. You need to decide whether any of them are appropriate for you. May I suggest you start with a sensible number of supplements

and see how you progress. Don't order too much to begin with. Consider the costs. We have negotiated a reduction in the price through our web site for as many of them as possible.

The two products below have been fully explained in the main text. Supplies can be sent to anywhere in the world from the UK by ordering online at www.antiaging-systems.com with a code 'dpk10' or calling 0208-123-2106 in the UK or international (44)-208-123-2106, or 1-866-800-4677 in USA and Canada only, to obtain a 10% discount off the retail price for the first order.

- Bio En'R-Gy C powder
- Wobenzym N tablets

Liposomal Vitamin C / Lypo-Spheric Vitamin C Sachets
It is maintained that a 1g dose of this form of vitamin C is equivalent to 10g intravenously, so you could take 3, 4 or 5 doses per day instead of having vitamin C intravenously.

Abundance & Health +44 (0) 2032 394907

SureScreen Life Sciences, Morley Retreat, Church Lane, Morley, Ilkeston, Derbyshire DE7 6DE, UK
Telephone: +44 (0) 1332 830990
Website: www.surescreen.com

Mention my name when ordering with either of these companies to obtain a percentage off the retail price.

Biobran
The Really Healthy Company (44)-208-480-1000. When you order, mention reference PK100 to obtain a 10% reduction in the price.

Good Morning Protein Plus
G & G Food Supplies Ltd 01342-312811 or order from www.gandgvitamins.com

Time-release Vitamin C tablets 1g
Lamberts (44)-1892-552120.

LL's Magnetic Clay
See the web.

Chlorine dioxide
Please order from www.parasitekill@gmail.com, mentioning code WR100 for a 5% discount off the retail price.

Nutri-Link
08704-054002. This company is not willing to let people order their products without the order coming from a practitioner registered with them who knows all about their products. The alternative for E-Lyte is to buy a sugar-free electrolyte replacement

from your local Health food store.

- E-Lyte
- Artemisinin

Dim Vitex
Bio Response Nutrients 1-877-312-5777 in USA

Nutri
0800-212742.   If you order on the phone, please mention code 100116, or alternatively enter the following link, where you will be able order online the appropriate items. Retail prices are given. www.nutri.co.uk/epdos/100116

- Eskimo-3 oil
- Nutri thyroid

The Special Capsules Of Fruits Vegetables & Berries
I have mentioned these special capsules several times throughout the main text.   If you wish to know what they are please email me at drkingsley@btinternet.com.

- Arnica 1M or 30C potency
- Rad brom 30C.
- Homoeopathic progesterone 200C.
- Malandrinum 200C.
- Rhus tox 12C & Box jellyfish 12C.
- Papilloma 200C
- Helicobacter pylori 30C

Ainsworth's Homoeopathic Pharmacy
0207-935-5330 or www.ainsworths.com. Most of my recommendations can be obtained direct from Ainsworth's Homoeopathic Pharmacy, although I recommend you consult a trained homoeopath if at all possible, as there will be many other remedies such a person would recommend for your condition. Ainsworths are prepared to send preparations all over the world, although you could look for a local supplier of homoeopathic preparations. Ainsworths have a special kit for people going through the rigours of cancer itself and cancer treatments, many of the preparations being of great benefit to people according to what my patients have told me. Preferably order liquid drops.

Co-Enzyme Q10
Pharma Nord 0800-591756.

Co-Enzyme Q10 Cream
Healthpro Labs 001-(800)-791-5722.

Bio-Chelat
www.evenbetternow.com

Aloe Vera Gel
Most forms of Aloe vera gel you can buy from your local pharmacy which should do the trick well enough.

Calcium-D-glucarate 500mg
Thorne in USA & Health Interlink in UK 01664-810011.

Revenol
By Neways. As I have already explained, Neways is a network marketing company and supplies of Revenol can be obtained on their website.

Schizandra
I don't have a specific recommendation here as my original supplier no longer stocks it, so you will have to find a supply for yourself if you decide to try it.

Boswellia
Solgar – see the web.

Lycopene
You should be able to obtain supplies from your local Health Food Store.

Imm-Kine
Aidan Products 1-(800)-529-0169 www.aidanproducts.com

Pycnogenol
Obtain locally.

Resveratrol
Obtain locally.

Curcumin
Obtain locally.

Echinacea
Obtain locally.

Quinton Marine Plasma
We are working on ways of obtaining this.

Mangosteen Juice. Mangosteen is another network marketing company. As with Revenol, you can obtain supplies by registering with the company so that supplies can be sent directly to you.

Vitamin B12
Wellbeing Research (see above) 1000mcg sublingual tablets if you cannot find anyone to give you doses intravenously.

Indole-3-carbinol
Obtain locally or buy Dim Vitex from Bio Response Nutrients (See above).

Biocare
For all Biocare products, you can order from www.biocare.co.uk or telephone
0121-433-3727 in UK or International (44)-121-433-3727. Mention code 5894 for a
5% discount off the retail price.

- Broad-spectrum amino acids
- Multivitamin/multimineral
- A, C, E & Selenium combination preparation.
- Iron
- Bioacidophilus and Bifido bacteria
- AD206
- TH207
- Selenium complex
- Zinc citrate
- Pyridoxal-5-phosphate 50mg
- Vitamins and minerals for children
- Zinc drops for children
- Iron drops for children

Appendix 2

Articles Referred To In The Main Text

An Article On Anti-Oxidants

This is an e-mail that was sent to me and other like-minded doctors by Dr. Garry Gordon. It is a bit complicated in parts, but I thought it was worth repeating it in full, rather than trying to select out the relevant parts.

This is vital information! We must empower our patients to overcome the ignorance of Oncologists who truly do not have any idea why taking our antioxidants actually enhances all of their treatment. We do not neutralize their oxidation treatments and Dr Simone has all the knowledge to make this understandable, as he did at the last ACAM conference, and the credentials to make the uninformed oncologists who tell every patient to never take an antioxidant sit up and take notice that they are badly out of date on passing on this misinformation to patients.

Garry F. Gordon MD,DO,MD(H)
President, Gordon Research Institute
www.gordonresearch.com
Antioxidants and Chemotherapy and Radiation Therapy
Hi Gary - Below is the email I sent to my email list. Maybe you could forward it to your group. Hopefully we can educate the public about this important topic.

Thanks for your help,
Chuck
Charles B. Simone, M.D.

Charles B. Simone, M.D. is an Internist (Cleveland Clinic 1975-77), Medical Oncologist (National Cancer Institute 1977-82), Tumor Immunologist (NCI 1977-82), and Radiation Oncologist (University of Pennsylvania 1982-85), and is the Founder of the Simone Protective Cancer Institute (1980). He wrote:

- Cancer and Nutrition (1981, third revision 2005),
- The Truth About Breast Health - Breast Cancer (2002),
- The Truth About Prostate Health - Prostate Cancer (2005),
- How To Save Yourself From A Terrorist Attack (2001),
- Nutritional Hydration, Medical Strategy for Military and Athlete Warriors (2008),

In addition he helped to:

- Organise the Office of Alternative Medicine, NIH (1992),
- Write the Dietary Supplement, Health and Education Act of 1994,
- Win landmark cases against the FDA by showing they violated the First and Fifth Amendment rights of Americans,
- Introduce the Health Freedom Protection Act of 2005 (H.R. 2117),

He was bestowed the first Bulwark of Liberty Award in 2001 by the American Preventive Association and the James Lind Scientific Achievement Award in 2004, continues bench research with the NCI showing that proteomic patterns can diagnose specific cancers at earlier stages than we are currently able to do (Lancet Feb 2002, JNCI Nov 2002), as well as clinical research that shows in 61 human studies Antioxidants and Other Nutrients Do Not Interfere with Chemotherapy or Radiation, and Can Increase Kill, Decrease Side Effects, and Increase Survival (Altern Ther Health Med. 2007. 13(1):22-28; and 13(2):40-46).

In 1980 Dr. Simone founded the KidStart Prevention Program, the first of its kind. Since 1980 he has worked with inner city churches to teach prevention, detection, and treatment. He is a consultant for heads of state of the US and other countries, celebrities, and advises many governments regarding health care. He testifies for the Senate and House on matters concerning health, cancer, disease prevention, children's health programs, FDA reform, and alternative medicine. He appears on 60 MINUTES, Prime Time Live, Fox News Channel, and others.

Simone Protective Cancer Center

123 Franklin Corner Road, Lawrenceville, NJ 08648
609-896-2646
http://www.DrSimone.com
http://www.PrincetonInstitute.com   http://www.NutritionalHydration.com
http://www.StopFDACensorship.org

Dear Friends,
One of every two men and one of every three women in America will develop cancer - about 1.5 million cases per year. In addition, since 1930, despite the use of radiation therapy, chemotherapy, immunotherapy, and improved surgical and diagnostic techniques, there has been limited improvement in cancer survival rates for most adult cancers. Chemotherapy and radiation therapy, however, continue to have a large role in cancer treatment but produce great morbidity. About 900,000 cancer patients per year receive radiation therapy and about 750,000 cancer patients per year receive chemotherapy. So we need to decrease side effects and also increase survival.

The Journal of the National Cancer Institute just published our Correspondence entitled, "Re: Should Supplemental Antioxidant Administration Be Avoided During Chemotherapy and Radiation Therapy?" (Nov 5, 2008 - attached in pdf format or you can read it below). This work further supports our previous publications showing that people should take supplemental antioxidants during chemotherapy and radiation therapy.

Our findings are important because cancer patients have been told not to take supplemental antioxidants during treatment because a single interview in The New York Times in 1997 that was not based on published scientific work and a single research paper involving mouse cells, along with a press release by its author in 1999, led to the erroneous notion that vitamin C interferes with chemotherapy and radiation in humans. This notion soon applied to all antioxidants as physicians, patients, the media, the American Cancer Society, and scores of websites took the same position without reviewing the scientific evidence.

Our findings are clear and consistent over decades: Since the 1970s, 280 peer-reviewed in vitro and in vivo studies, including 50 human studies involving 8,521 patients, 5,081 of whom were given nutrients, have consistently shown that non-prescription antioxidants and other nutrients do not interfere with therapeutic modalities for cancer. Furthermore, they enhance the killing of therapeutic modalities for cancer, decrease their side effects, and protect normal tissue. In 15 human studies, 3,738 patients who took non-prescription antioxidants and other nutrients actually had increased survival.

Charles B. Simone II, MD; Nicole L. Simone, MD; Victoria Simone, RN; Charles B. Simone, MD. ANTIOXIDANTS AND OTHER NUTRIENTS DO NOT INTERFERE WITH CHEMOTHERAPY OR RADIATION THERAPY AND CAN INCREASE KILL AND INCREASE SURVIVAL, PART 1 and 2. Altern Ther Health Med. Jan-Feb, and Mar-Apr, 2007;13(1):22-28; 13(2): 40-7.)
Simone CB, Simone NL, Simone CB II. Oncology Care Augmented with Nutritional and Lifestyle Modification. J Ortho Mol Med. 1997; 12(4): 197-206.
Simone CB. Cancer and Nutrition, A Ten Point Plan for Prevention and Cancer Life Extension. Princeton Institute. 2006.
JNCI: Journal of the National Cancer Institute. Should Supplemental Antioxidant Administration Be Avoided During Chemotherapy and Radiation Therapy? Charles B. Simone, Charles B. Simone, II

Affiliation of authors: Simone Protective Cancer Institute, Lawrenceville, NJ
Correspondence to: Charles B. Simone, MD, Simone Protective Cancer Institute, 123 Franklin Corner Road, Lawrenceville, NJ 08648 (e-mail: mail@drsimone.com).
Lawenda et al. (1) expressed concerns about our review (2) of antioxidant and nutrient use during chemotherapy or radiation. The authors stated that we reviewed 52 human trials when in fact we discussed only 50. They dismissed the 36 observational studies we reviewed on the basis of study design. Unlike Lawenda et al., however, we included all pertinent peer-reviewed publications, regardless of randomization or sample size, to avoid bias and because observational studies provide valid information and virtually equivalent results as randomized trials, do not overestimate the magnitude of treatment effects, and are less costly than randomized trials (3,4).

Lawenda et al. further discounted 10 randomized trials that we cited because of small sample size. However, only five of nine trials with concurrent radiation and five of 16 trials with chemotherapy that they cited had a sample size more than 66 patients, and five chemotherapeutic trials had a sample size of 20 or fewer patients. Although Lawenda et al. concluded that "high-dose antioxidant supplementation during radiotherapy decreases local tumor control and shortens the survival of cancer patients," the very trials they cited do not substantiate these claims. Lawenda et al. also did not mention the survival benefit demonstrated in a 100-patient study by Lissoni et al., thus biasing their commentary.

Although most of the trials they cited demonstrated a decrease in side effects and several also showed an increase in treatment response and overall survival, one (5) reported an increase in disease recurrence and second primaries among smokers who received supplements. Although Lawenda et al. stated that "this study is the most important randomized clinical trial, to date, on the use of supplemental antioxidant and radiation therapy," the conclusion drawn by the authors of that study was seriously flawed because they used retrospective capsule counts by patients to assess supplement compliance and never verified compliance by measuring antioxidant serum levels.

Lawenda et al. further stated that "anticancer therapies may lower plasma antioxidant concentrations by altering dietary intakes." Although this is true, we reported that plasma antioxidants are decreased mainly by chemotherapy and radiation due to lipid peroxidation.

Lawenda et al. speculated that "antioxidants can exert their effects on all tissues to some degree, thereby protecting tumor cells as well as healthy ones." However, the four in vitro studies they cited showed that more antioxidants accumulate in cancer cells than normal cells, which we reported (2). Accumulation of excessive antioxidants and nutrients in cancer cells can shut down oxidative reactions necessary for generating energy. Antioxidants also produce biologic effects on cancer cells unrelated to oxidative damage: they increase cancer cell differentiation, apoptosis, and growth inhibition, and they inhibit or enhance gene expression and/or activity of numerous proteins. Antioxidants selectively inhibit repair of radiation damage of cancer cells but protect normal cells when antioxidants are used before, during, and after radiation, and there are no published studies showing that antioxidants protect cancer cells against radiation (6,7).

Lawenda et al. begin their commentary with the maxim "first, do no harm." Studies involving thousands of patients have demonstrated that antioxidants and other nutrients do not interfere with chemotherapy or radiation, but instead decrease toxicity and may improve response rates and overall survival. Perhaps, then, should the first step in doing no harm be to have a discussion with cancer patients about the utility of concurrent antioxidant administration?

REFERENCES
1.   Lawenda BD, Kelly KM, Ladas EJ, et al. Should supplemental antioxidant administration be avoided during chemotherapy and radiation therapy? J Natl Cancer Inst (2008) 100(11): 773?783.[Abstract/Free Full Text]
2.   Simone CB II, Simone NL, Simone V, et al. Antioxidants and other nutrients do not interfere with chemotherapy or radiation therapy and can increase kill and increase survival, part 1. Altern Ther Health Med. 2007; 13(1):22?28; Part 2. Altern Ther Health Med. 2007;13(2):40?47.
3.   Benson K, Hartz AJ. A comparison of observational studies and randomized, controlled trials. N Engl J Med (2000) 342(25):1878?1886.[Abstract/Free Full Text]
4.   Concato J, Shah N, Horwitz RI. Randomized, controlled trials, observational studies, and the hierarchy of research designs. N Engl J Med (2000) 342(25):1887?1892.[Abstract/Free Full Text]
5.   Bairati I, Meyer F, Jobin E, et al. Antioxidant vitamins supplementation and mortality: a randomized trial in head and neck cancer patients. Int J Cancer (2006) 119(9):2221?2224. [CrossRef][ISI][Medline]
6.   Prasad KN, Cole WC, Kumar B, et al. Scientific rationale for using high-dose multiple micronutrients as an adjunct to standard and experimental cancer therapies. J Am Coll Nutr (2001) 20(5 suppl):450S?463S.[Abstract/Free Full Text]
7.   Prasad KN, Cole WC, Kumar B, et al. Pros and cons of antioxidant use during radiation therapy. Cancer Treat Rev. (2002) 28(2):79?91.[CrossRef][ISI][Medline]

Selenium: Good News In Cancer Treatment, Nexus Magazine
This unusual story of a West Australian farmer was told to me by one of the farmer's friends who live in Melbourne. It is full of happy endings, almost too good to be true.

This farmer was diagnosed with bowel cancer. His doctor-surgeon arranged a date for him to check into hospital to have the cancer removed. In due course on the date set, after he was checked into hospital, the doctor-surgeon visited him in his room to tell him that after reviewing all the tests and X-rays, all concerned agreed that his cancer was inoperable and that all tests indicated his heart was not strong enough to survive such major surgery.

The farmer said, "Doctor, you're telling me there is nothing you can do for me?" "Yes," the doctor said, and then apologized for such a late change of decision. The farmer then requested his wife to go and check him out of hospital and for his son to pack his bag and take it to the car. He said that he would have to go home and treat himself.

For many years this farmer had treated his cattle and sheep for prevention and cure of various ailments. One drench had proved especially effective and that was Selenium Drench Concentrate. He decided to formulate a daily dose for himself based on his own body-weight, as he had so often done for his farm animals.

Over the following few months, he took this dosage on an empty stomach every morning. After several months his wife said, "I think you are getting better! You look good and don't seem to be sick at all. I think you had better visit the doctor and have him check you over!" Which he did. The doctor said that as far as he could examine him externally, the cancer was gone. He told the farmer to go home and enjoy life!

One day shortly after, a well dressed lady driving an expensive car arrived at the farm. She said, "Your doctor is my doctor and he tells me you cured yourself of bowel cancer. I have bowel cancer and I've come to ask you to share the treatment."

The farmer said, "Woman, it would be worth more than my farm for me to start acting like a doctor! But I know how desperate you are. I'll put the ingredients out and will show you what I mixed up, but I can't give it to you. My wife and I have to do the evening chores—feed the fowls and milk the cows and so on. While we're gone, you can steal the ingredient if you like but I can't give it to you!" That is exactly what the lady did and she treated herself as instructed. Several months later, she returned with bouquets and presents. She told her farmer friends she was cured and given a clearance by their mutual doctor.

Soon after, another well-dressed lady arrived by car at the farmer's house. She had been sent by the first lady. She stated she had bowel cancer and requested the farmer share his treatment with her. He said he would treat her exactly the same as he had treated her friend—which he did with the same excellent results.

Several months later and almost amusingly, the farmer's own doctor arrived at the farm, stating that he had come for more than a social visit because he, too, now had bowel cancer and wanted the farmer to share the treatment with him. Which the farmer did in the same way as for the two ladies, and with the same excellent results.

The friend who conveyed this story to me was a suspected prostate cancer victim having a very high PSA [prostate-specific antigen] count. He immediately went onto the treatment and very quickly his PSA was down to normal. Another of my friends was diagnosed positively as having prostate cancer and was planning surgery. He has been on the selenium treatment, and recently was given a medical all-clear. Friends who have gone on the treatment as a precaution—believing as I do that what will cure will prevent—have found that minor skin cancers on their hands have cleared up.

The treatment as worked out by the farmer is with Selenium Drench Concentrate, which anyone can purchase from veterinary product suppliers. It is liquid selenium. For years, the sale of selenium for human consumption has been prohibited. The active constituent is 10 mg of selenium per mL as sodium selenite. The dosage is one tea-spoonful to two litres of water, of which mixture you drink 226 ml or two-thirds of a 400 ml breakfast cup each morning on an empty stomach.

I've been taking it for several years and it certainly does not appear to produce any ill effects.

(Source: Email from Keith, dated February 26, 2004, sent to NEXUS Magazine in mid-2005)

The Incredible Story of Essiac by James Percival

Rene Caisse was a nurse in Canada. In 1923 she observed that one of her doctor's patients, a woman with terminal cancer, made a complete recovery. Enquiring into the matter, Rene found that the woman had cured herself with an herbal remedy which was given to her by an Ojibwa Indian herbalist. Rene visited the medicine man, and he freely presented her with his tribe's formula. The formula consisted of four common herbs. They were blended and cooked in a fashion that caused the concoction apparently to have greater medicinal potency than any of the four herbs themselves. The four herbs were Sheep Sorrel, Burdock Root, Slippery Elm Bark, and Rhubarb Root.

With her doctor's permission, Rene began to administer the herbal remedy to other terminal cancer patients, who had been given up by the medical profession as incurable. Most recovered. Rene then began to collect the herbs herself, prepare the remedy in her own kitchen, and treat hundreds of cancer cases. She found that Essiac, as she named the herbal remedy (her own name backwards), could not undo the effects of severe damage to the life support organs. In such cases however, the pain of the illness was alleviated and the life of the patient often extended longer than predicted. In other cases, where the life support organs had not been severely damaged, cure was complete, and the patients sometimes lived another 35 or 40 years. Some are still alive today.

Rene selflessly dedicated herself to helping these patients. She continued to treat hundreds of patients from her home. She did not charge for her services. Donations were her only income. They barely kept her above the poverty line. Over the years, word of her work began to spread. The Canadian medical establishment did not take kindly to this nurse administering this remedy directly to anyone with cancer who requested her help. Thus began many years of harassment and persecution by the Canadian Ministry of Health and Welfare. Word of this struggle was carried throughout Canada by newspapers.

The newspaper coverage of Rene's work began to make her famous throughout Canada. Word was also spread by the families of those healed by Essiac. Eventually the Royal Cancer Commission became interested in her work. They undertook to study Essiac. In 1937 the Royal Cancer Commission conducted hearings on Essiac. Much testimony was furnished that Essiac was a cure for cancer.

Eventually the Canadian Parliament, prodded by newspaper coverage and the widespread support generated by Rene by former patients and grateful families, voted in 1938 on legislation to legalise the use of Essiac.   Fifty-five thousand signatures were collected on a petition presented to the parliament.   The vote was close, but Essiac failed by three votes to be approved as an officially sanctioned treatment for cancer.

The complete story of Rene Caisse's life and struggles is told in a book written by Dr. Gary L. Glum, entitled The Calling of an Angel.   It tells of the documented recoveries of thousands of cancer patients who had been certified in writing by their doctors as incurable.   Rene continued her work for 40 years until her death in 1978. Rene had entrusted her formula to several friends, one of whom passed the formula along to Dr. Glum.

An Article Explaining Chlorine Dioxide (sometimes known as MMS)

Chlorine Dioxide Protocol

The MMS protocol was developed by Jim Humble, a gold miner and metallurgist, on an expedition into the jungles of Central America, looking for gold. It was a response to a need to help a member of his expedition who came down with malaria, more than two days away, through heavy jungle, from the next mine. After many years of experience, Humble always carried stabilized oxygen with him on such expeditions, to make local water safe to drink. Facing the possibility of a quick loss of life, he gave it to the stricken man. To everyone's amazement, he was well within a few hours. That seemed like a miracle, but Humble wanted to better understand what had just happened.

Over the course of several years, Jim Humble figured out that what made stabilized oxygen so effective in some malaria cases, was not the oxygen at all, but the trace amounts of chlorine dioxide it contained. Further research led him to come up with a way to produce hundreds, if not thousands more units of chlorine dioxide than what is found in stabilized oxygen. This is through using a higher concentration of sodium chlorite (28% vs. 3% for stabilized oxygen), in conjunction with an activator. The proof of the efficacy of this simple protocol was in successfully helping over 75,000 people in several African nations – including Uganda and Malawi – rid themselves, primarily of malaria, but also hepatitis, cancer, and AIDS.

Anyone can be overloaded with toxins. Most people probably are but won't admit it or, more likely, don't know it. Others would prefer to think they're not. If your health is not perfect, you're habitually low on energy, have trouble keeping your weight down or your blood pressure in the normal range, or are constantly dealing with inflammation or pain, or indeed have any medical condition that is adversely affecting your health, then there's likely to be a toxin, heavy metal, virus, bacteria, fungus, or parasite playing a part. Mainstream medicine will typically respond by loading you up with additional pollutants, many of which indiscriminately kill healthy tissue while going after "the bad guys" to deal with the symptoms.   Not so with chlorine dioxide. It only acts on anything harmful. Miracle or not, the effects can be amazing!

Over the next few pages, the MMS protocol will be described. When followed, it will produce and distribute chlorine dioxide to your red blood cells, which are the most effective and intelligent pathogen killers known to Nature, although your white blood cells are assumed to do all the work.

But first, a little background on the chemistry. Chlorine dioxide and chlorine are not the same.   Chlorine is a chemical element. In ionic form, chlorine is part of common salt and other compounds, and is necessary to most forms of life, including human. A powerful oxidizing agent, it is the most abundant dissolved ion in ocean water, and readily combines with nearly every other element, including sodium to form salt crystals, and magnesium, as magnesium chloride. Chlorine dioxide is a chemical compound that consists of one chlorine ion bound to two ions of oxygen. Oxidizing agents are chemical compounds that readily accept electrons from "electron donors." They gain electrons via chemical reaction. This is important because relative to chlorine dioxide, all pathogens are electron donors.

Chlorine dioxide is extremely volatile. You might call it "hot tempered," but in a very beneficial way. This volatility is a key factor in chlorine dioxide's effectiveness as a pathogen destroyer. The compound is literally explosive, so explosive, it's not safe to transport in any quantity. Therefore, it is common practice to generate chlorine dioxide "on site" at the point of use. Most chlorine dioxide production is done on a scale that would prove deadly for individuals, for example, in municipal water treatment systems, where it is beginning to replace chlorine because it produces no carcinogenic by-products. Chlorine dioxide is approved by the Environmental Protection Agency in safely removing pathogens and contaminates like anthrax. So you know it must be effective. However, the concentrations used in such applications can vary from 500 to over 6,000 parts per million (ppm), which would clearly be deadly to an individual. Using the MMS protocol you will produce chlorine dioxide around 1 ppm. You will use the MMS solution, which is safe to transport, to make nature's harmless pathogen destroyer.

The MMS solution is 25% sodium chlorite in distilled water. You can produce chlorine dioxide with a single drop, when an "activator" of vinegar, lemon juice, or a 10% solution of citric acid is added. Citric acid is recommended because of its simplicity. The natural pH of sodium chlorite is 13. Adding vinegar, lemon juice, or citric acid creates about 3 mg of unstable but still harmless chlorine dioxide.

The Process

Let's talk a bit more about how and why chlorine dioxide works by giving the immune system a new lease of life. Volatility is what makes chlorine dioxide so effective when it contacts pathogens. As we've already mentioned, chlorine dioxide is a safe and effective disinfectant in many municipal water delivery systems, hospitals, and even in bio-terrorism response. It stands to reason that chlorine dioxide would be just as effective working in the waters of the human body at the appropriate dose.

Chlorine dioxide's extreme volatility prevents pathogens from developing a resistance, mainly because when they "clash," the pathogens no longer exist. Yet, healthy cells and beneficial bacteria remain unaffected. While normal levels of oxygen in the blood cannot destroy all of the pathogens present under disease conditions, delivery of chlorine dioxide changes everything. "Halt! Surrender Your Electrons, Now!" When a chlorine dioxide ion contacts a harmful pathogen, it instantly rips up to five electrons from the pathogen, in what can be likened to a microscopic explosion... harmless to us, but terminal for pathogens. The pathogen – an electron donor – is rendered harmless due to the involuntary surrendering of its electrons to the chlorine dioxide – an electron acceptor – and the resulting release of energy. Oxidized by the chlorine ion, the former pathogen becomes a harmless salt.

This process benefits a body that has become toxic. Throughout the body, anywhere chlorine dioxide ions – transported via red blood cells – come into contact with pathogens, the pathogens give up their electrons and cease to exist. The chlorine dioxide-armed cells only "detonate" on contact with pathogens, which include harmful bacteria, viruses, funguses, toxins, heavy metals, and parasites. All of these will have pH values that are out of the body's range of good health. They will also have a positive ionic charge. The chlorine dioxide equipped cells do not oxidize beneficial bacteria, or healthy cells, as their pH levels are 7 or above, and hold a negative ionic charge. Chlorine dioxide ions will oxidize – meaning vaporize – diseased cells... anything that is acidic, with a positive ionic charge. If the chlorine dioxide ions encounter no pathogens or other poisons, they deteriorate into table salt and in some instances, hypochlorous acid, which the body can also use.

A Pathogen Terminator
Research has proven chlorine dioxide to be much safer than chlorine, as it is selective for pathogens when used in water. Furthermore, it does not create harmful compounds from other constituents in the water as chlorine does. Numerous scientific studies have demonstrated that chlorine – part of the halogen family of elements – creates as least three carcinogenic compounds when it enters the body, principally trihalomethanes (THMs). There has been no such evidence of harmful compounds being produced from chlorine dioxide. This is why, in 1999, the American Society of Analytical Chemists proclaimed chlorine dioxide to be the most powerful pathogen killer known to man. It has even been used to clean up after anthrax attacks.

A Journey Into Chemical Alchemy
Once it is introduced into the bloodstream, chlorine dioxide performs a highly energetic acceptance of up to five electrons when it comes across any cell that is below a pH value of 7. This means that diseased cells are essentially vaporized (i.e. "oxidized") while healthy cells are unaffected.

This Is How It Happens
Red blood cells that are normal carriers of oxygen throughout the body do not differentiate between chlorine dioxide and oxygen. Therefore, after you have swallowed the MMS/chlorine dioxide-rich solution, red blood cells pick up chlorine dioxide ions as they pass through the stomach wall. When the red blood cells, armed with chlorine dioxide, encounter parasites, fungi, diseased cells or anything that has a pH below 7 and a positive ionic charge, the "aliens" are destroyed along with the chlorine dioxide ion.

If the chlorine dioxide doesn't hit anything that can set it off, it will eventually deteriorate, by losing an electron or two. This will allow it to be converted into hypochlorous acid. This compound kills pathogens and even cancerous cells. Hypochlorous acid is so important that its diminished presence in the body is described medically by the term 'myeloperoxidase deficiency'. Many people are afflicted by this condition. The immune system needs a great deal more hypochlorous acid when disease is present. Facilitated by the MMS solution, chlorine dioxide delivers it in quantity.

The most salient point to know is that chlorine dioxide has 100 times more energy to do what oxygen normally does, and yet, will not harm healthy cells. By the way, if you are totally healthy and have nothing in your body that is at an acidic level below 7, there are no ill effects from taking chlorine dioxide at the appropriate dose. However, your stores of hypochlorous acid will be increased.

MMS works best to destroy pathogens that may be present in the body, when 2 or 3 mg of free chlorine dioxide are in the solution at the time it is swallowed. However, the body is supplied with chlorine dioxide in a "timed release" manner lasting about 12 hours. Be aware that, before you feel better, it is likely you will feel ill in one way or another.

Nausea

The nauseating feeling that you may possibly experience, especially if you take too big a dose, is the result of chlorine dioxide encountering and destroying a large number of pathogens. We are generally oblivious to the pathogens that are present in our bodies, but there is an increasing awareness in the medical and scientific literature of their importance to our health, or more to the point our ill health. Since they build up over time in various organs of the body, they generally affect our health slowly and cumulatively. If chlorine dioxide takes them out too suddenly, the result will be a dramatic reaction. However, the time it takes to clear the pathogens and toxins is much less than it took for them to accumulate. It has probably taken many years, possibly almost a lifetime, for some of them to accumulate.

As a person always feels unwell when they contract a case of, say, acute hepatitis, dengue fever or Lyme disease, they may continue to feel unwell for a while, in which case it will be difficult to tell whether it is the condition or the chlorine dioxide that is causing the unwell feeling. However, if the condition is treated with chlorine dioxide in its early stages, the pathogens will be killed off quickly as they are still in the blood stream and therefore available to be attacked easily by the circulating chlorine dioxide-rich red blood cells. Under these circumstances, the symptoms should be over very quickly.

In chronic conditions, especially Lyme disease and dengue fever, nearly every organ of the body can be affected to a greater or lesser extent, which is why the symptoms can be so variable, and the person can feel so ill. This variability is almost diagnostic of such conditions, especially as there are no satisfactory blood tests to prove the diagnosis. The reason for this is that there may be a number of different organisms involved, each having a different life cycle. In these cases it will take a little longer to achieve a resolution of the condition, as each organism is destroyed in its own time.

Years of "leeching" from dental amalgams can "innocently" deposit enough mercury in one's system to steal innocence, rob vitality, and erase precious memories. Lead can accumulate over the years from atmospheric exposure. Dislodging and vaporizing either or both of them may feel uncomfortable for a short time compared to the time it took for them to accumulate.

If there is nothing for chlorine dioxide to encounter, it deteriorates into constituents that are totally non-toxic. Nothing poisonous is left behind to build up, as is the case with many medical protocols. Medical treatments currently provide you no way of removing the poisons when they don't work. Chlorine dioxide, on the other hand, lasts long enough to do its job, and then the amount that does not furnish the immune system with needed ions becomes nothing more than micro amounts of salt and water. The chlorine dioxide has just a few minutes to do its job, and then it no longer exists, leaving nothing behind that can build up, or do additional harm.

The Procedure

So the procedure is simple. All you need is your bottle of MMS (25% sodium chlorite), a clean, empty, dry glass, an eyedropper and the activator citric acid 10%. Note: When following the instructions below, keep this paragraph in mind. Always activate the MMS drops with one of the food acids, either lemon juice drops, or limejuice drops, or citric acid solution drops, the citric acid drops being the simplest. Always add 5 drops of 10% citric acid to each 1 drop of MMS (25% sodium chlorite), mix in an empty dry glass and wait at least 3 minutes, then add 1/3 to 2/3 glass of water (or as much water as you like) and drink it. (You can expand the 3 minutes to 10 before drinking it.) Repeat this dose in between one and two hours, ideally doing all of this after your evening meal, possibly starting about ¾ hour after you have eaten, as it can sometimes make some people sleepy, apart from which your body does most of its detoxifying during the night.

Start modestly with as little as 1 drop of MMS plus 5 drops of citric acid on your first day (never forget to wait at least 3 minutes for the mixture to react to create chlorine dioxide, which will turn yellow and smell of chlorine, and repeat the dose in one to two hours). Take your time and do not rush. You could stay on this low dose for a few days, and then increase the number (2 and 10, 3 and 15, etc) on subsequent days, but I repeat – TAKE YOUR TIME.
There is no point in going higher than 15 and 75 respectively, but it is rare for anyone to reach this level.

Your body will tell you when you've reached the optimum dosage for you, and, if in doubt, drop the next dose. Clearing may be a bit uncomfortable, but it need not be intolerable. You may feel like you've been through a battle, and, in a sense, you have. However I suggest that, if you develop any symptoms of any sort, assume you have taken too high a dose, so put up with the effect, take the antidote, and drop the next dose, possibly even not taking any for a day. Before you can be healthy again, you need to destroy toxins, pathogens, parasites and anything harmful to you. In order to do so, they have to be uprooted and released from their "strongholds" in your body tissue. You have no idea what they are or where they are. Remember they may be buried deep in your organs.

You don't have to reach your maximum tolerated dose. Whatever dose you use will have its value, but the higher you can comfortably reach the better. It is just that the whole process will take that much longer.

This gentle approach applies to any chronic condition, and especially if you want to clean up your body. However, if you develop an acute medical condition such as dengue fever or malaria, for example, start straight in at at least 5 drops of MMS to 25 drops of citric acid, although you could possibly start at 8 drops of MMS to 40 drops of citric acid, and don't forget to repeat the dose in between one and two hours. With any luck you will feel remarkably better by the next day. If you are not quite symptom free, repeat the same the next day, increasing the dose by about one third. In an acute situation, you can take three doses a day, each one repeated one to two hours later.

Antidote
If you develop any symptoms you don't like, assume it is the chlorine dioxide working too hard within you. To clear these symptoms, either take a few doses of ½ teaspoonful of sodium bicarbonate in a glass of water or a few grammes of vitamin C in water. Don't take both. Then either don't take a dose of MMS for 24 hours or drop the next dose and gradually work back up again.

IMPORTANT

Please be aware that, as I have already said, chlorine dioxide is a very potent chemical and literally destroys anything potentially harmful it comes across. Whatever dose you take, it will do its job. It is understandable that you want to reach as high a dose as possible as soon as possible, but I would encourage you not to think like that. As most of us have accumulated a lot of undesirable things within our bodies over the years, some of which may now be causing a major illness, it is not unreasonable to suggest that it may take some time to get rid of it all, possibly six months or more.

A number of people have reported to me that they did not feel any nausea, nor did they vomit, but started to feel generally unwell, or some of their old symptoms started to come back a bit, when they had reached a certain dose of chlorine dioxide. Fortunately they rang me. My advice was that they should go back to a lower dose, possible even not taking any chlorine dioxide for 24 hours before restarting at the lower dose. This approach has worked in every case. Unlike an antibiotic, nothing can develop a resistance to chlorine dioxide, as has already been said.

So what I am really trying to say is that, if you have ANY undesirable effects, even if you become a bit more tired than before, ASSUME that the chlorine dioxide is being too active for your body's current ability to eliminate the toxins. Take a lower dose next time, and be prepared to stay low for a while. Please don't overdose. It will only make you feel unnecessarily ill.

Overall you may feel the effects, but this is a good thing. You will also feel healthy again. Any sick feeling will be TEMPORARY, a small price to pay for the longer-term possibility of lasting restored health, no matter what stage of life you happen to be currently experiencing. When the clearing is done, you won't need to take the maximum dose. You can go on a maintenance application (1 or 2 drops of MMS) to keep your insides pathogen free and your immune system strong or take a dose every so often.

I hope you have found this information helpful. In summary, when sodium chlorite is combined with citric acid, it produces chlorine dioxide, which, at the appropriate dose is a safe and effective way to boost your immune system and eliminate a full range of harmful organisms, toxic metals and chemicals that may well be making you ill.

Chlorine Dioxide In Cancer

It is well known that cancer can be caused by certain viruses, chemicals and radiation, and that a poor diet and genes can predispose a person to cancer. Mainstream medicine's approach to cancer is to cut it out if possible and/or to try to destroy it with chemotherapy and/or radiotherapy. It would appear that this approach does seem to work sometimes, but fails all too often and is extremely harsh on the patient, possibly actually being the cause of death of many cancer patients because of its damaging effect on the immune system.

Various doctors and scientists over the years have put forward other explanations as to why cancer develops in a person, and stress is certainly one of them as suggested by Dr. Fryda, in which she maintained that stress exhausts your steroid and adrenalin mechanisms, which in turn lowers the effectiveness of your immune system. It is probably accepted that cancer tends to develop in someone whose immune system is depressed.

One theory of cancer that has been around for a very long time, but which has not sat well with mainstream medicine, is that cancer is a protective mechanism, albeit a rather bizarre one, against a fungus, most likely candida.   When cancer tumours are examined under a microscope, the specimen is usually looked at using plenty of bright light.   However, if dark field microscopy is used, which tends to produce shadows, fungal spores and mycelia can often be seen.

Since most doctors have never heard of dark field microscopy, they will not be aware of this possibility.   Anyone who is aware of what candida means and how it occurs and develops will understand why it is perfectly possible that the astonishing rise in the incidence of nearly all types of cancer could possibly be because of the frequent use of antibiotics together with people's high dietary intakes of sugar and refined carbohydrates.

I gave hydrogen peroxide intravenously to many patients for many different reasons, and there is no doubt that it was a very effective treatment for any form of fungal infection and for many cancers. The problem with it was that it ideally needed to be given more often than was practical. There were also cost and travelling implications.   Thousands of people have swallowed hydrogen peroxide over the years and claimed it has 'cured' all sorts of conditions, but it can irritate the intestines so I haven't recommended it.   I always hoped that one day it would be possible to give a similar preparation by mouth. I am hopeful that we have at last found such a preparation in chlorine dioxide.

The book I have a copy of by Jim Humble is not well written, but it gives a lot of information about how it works and in which medical conditions it has already been tried. He has wandered round Africa and treated over 75,000 people with malaria, returning them to normal within a few hours! It clearly works this quickly because malaria is a condition within the blood. He also talks about treating Aids although he does not know what it does to HIV status, as they didn't have money to pay for the tests.   So far as I can understand, there are no adverse effects of any significance, except for the development of nausea and vomiting if too high a dose is used, but there is a suitable antidote for that. The nausea and possible vomiting is not a side effect of chlorine dioxide but caused by the immune system being activated too quickly and throwing too much debris too quickly into the blood stream.

Some of you may have heard of Dr. Tullio Simoncini, an Italian Doctor of Oncology, who has recently got into trouble for criticising his medical colleagues for achieving less than 10% success rate with their cancer patients whereas he gets over 90% success. He has claimed that cancer is caused by a fungus and that the fungus produces so much acid locally in the tumour that it is impossible to neutralise that acid, and hence get rid of the fungus, and of course the cancer, by trying natural methods to alkalinise the body, without harming healthy cells. He has simply injected sodium bicarbonate into the tumour with the expected success.

Clearly such injections are not going to be available, not even from Doctor Simoncini who has apparently been struck off the Italian medical register! However, the information is now in the public domain, so it is also most likely that various practitioners will take it up in the near future.   However, it might be impractical if cancer has spread to many parts of the body.

Anyway, for now I am assuming that many people's cancer may have been caused by a fungus, possibly also associated with something else undesirable, such as a virus, a parasite, a toxic chemical or a toxic metal like lead or mercury. A most important feature here is that anything, such as the above, that is harmful to the body is positively charged and has a pH below 7, while normal cells are negatively charged and have a pH above 7. This difference is of vital importance. Cancer cells are positively charged and have an acidic pH.

There may of course also be a degree of stress that is not helping. Hopefully, by now, diet is not a major consideration. Fortunately, this new preparation can deal with all of these, including the free radicals produced by the stress.

There is nothing new about chlorine dioxide. It has been used to sterilise medical equipment for decades and food preparation areas, and it would appear that no germ of any sort, be it a virus, a bacterium, a parasite or a fungus, can tolerate its devastating effects. Because its effects are so rapid, no germ has ever had time or been able to develop a resistance to it. It is like a human being trying to develop a resistance to a hand grenade. It just isn't possible.

In the human body it acts in two ways. First it improves the immune system by increasing the levels of myeloperoxidase in white blood cells, making them do their job as efficiently as they are supposed to do (in cancer and other conditions, levels of white blood cell myeloperoxidase are depleted). In the second instance red blood cells happily absorb it as well as oxygen and hence carry it all round the body. Its very powerful oxidant effects rip up to five electrons from any harmful positively charged organism, but doesn't seem to harm negatively charged good organisms or normal healthy cells. Grabbing this many electrons totally inactivates what it has taken them from. At a molecular level it is actually an explosion. In addition, it oxidises any molecule of a heavy metal, and presumably a toxic chemical, effectively inactivating it.

Putting it in a nutshell, I am hoping that the chlorine dioxide will get rid of the fungus or whatever is the cause, making cancer quite simply no longer necessary. I am suggesting here that cancer is a protective mechanism, albeit a rather bizarre one, against whatever the cause is. However, although chlorine dioxide should destroy cancer cells because they are positively charged and acidic, and Jim Humble claims it does do so, only time will tell whether this is correct.

Chlorine dioxide has to be made fresh. You are provided with two bottles, bottle A containing 25% sodium chlorite (chlorite not chloride), bottle B containing 10% citric acid. Please put one drop only from bottle A into a clean dry glass (wash the pipette thoroughly in clean water before drawing up drops from bottle B) plus 5 drops from bottle B (using the dropper provided, but again please wash the dropper in water and dry it after using it each time). WAIT 3 MINUTES then add about a third to a half a glass of filtered water (or more if you want to) and drink it. Repeat this whole procedure in somewhere between one and two hours.

It may be best to do this after your evening meal to begin with, as it sometimes makes people feel a bit sleepy. In addition the body does most of its detoxifying during the night. So day 1's dose is one drop from bottle A plus five drops from bottle B repeated in one to two hours.

On day 2, use 2 drops from bottle A plus 10 drops from bottle B (always use a 1 to 5 mixture and always wait 3 minutes before adding the water), and repeat the dose one to two hours later. Keep increasing the dose (to 3 and 15, 4 and 20, etc.) every day until you reach your tolerance level, i.e. you start to feel a bit nauseous or somehow not so well. If you are not sure, stay on a particular dose for a few days before trying the effect of a further increase. Your maximum dose is to be 15 drops from bottle A to 75 drops from bottle B twice a day, which very few people should take, but there is no harm in not taking your maximum tolerated dose. It will simply take longer to achieve its desired effect, but with less unpleasantness.

On the other hand, if you feel any particular dose is doing a lot of good, simply stick to that dose until you think a further increase is worth trying. Remember, if you take too much, it will merely make you feel nauseous or make you vomit. If that happens drink plenty of water and take 1000 (one thousand) mg vitamin C. If you don't have any vitamin C available put a teaspoonful of sodium bicarbonate in a glass of water and drink it, but don't take both at the same time.

IMPORTANT

Please be aware that, as I have already said, chlorine dioxide is a very potent chemical and literally destroys anything potentially harmful it comes across. Whatever dose you take, it will do its job. It is understandable that you want to reach as high a dose as possible as soon as possible, but I would encourage you not to think like that. As most of us have accumulated a lot of undesirable things within our bodies over the years, some of which may now be causing a major illness, it is not unreasonable to suggest that it may take some time to get rid of it all, possibly six months or more.

A number of people have reported to me that they did not feel any nausea, nor did they vomit, but started to feel generally unwell, or some of their old symptoms started to come back a bit, when they had reached a certain dose of chlorine dioxide. Fortunately they rang me. My advice was that they should go back to a lower dose, possible even not taking any chlorine dioxide for 24 hours before restarting at the lower dose. This approach has worked in every case. Unlike an antibiotic, nothing can develop a resistance to chlorine dioxide, as has already been said.

So what I am really trying to say is that, if you have ANY undesirable effects, even if you become a bit more tired than before, ASSUME that the chlorine dioxide is being too active for your body's current ability to eliminate the toxins. Take a lower dose next time, and be prepared to stay low for a while. Please don't overdose. It will only make you feel unnecessarily ill.

Incidentally, as chlorine dioxide is a very powerful oxidant, it may be best if you were NOT to take any vitamin C and other specific antioxidants such as vitamin E within at least four hours of a dose of chlorine dioxide, and possibly longer. So, if you take your first dose of chlorine dioxide around 8.00pm, take all the vitamin C you want to take by at least 4.00pm or possibly earlier, and no more that night. It doesn't matter if you fail to take your doses on a particular day. When you restart, continue at the dose you had already reached.

At this stage I do not know how long you will need to be taking chlorine dioxide. In principle, the longer you have had your condition and the deeper it is in your body, the longer you may need to take it, so at least for six months for some people to achieve the desired effect, although during that time you should have plenty of indications that things are improving in your body.

May I also suggest you drink at least eight glasses of quality water, by which I mean filtered water or bottled in glass bottles. I would also suggest you take Essiac Tea (or our Ojibwa Tonic) as this will help your body to rid itself of the toxins.

There is a caveat that needs to be added to this treatise on chlorine dioxide, for you to decide whether to take it yourself or not. As of late 2010, the FDA of America and the European Health Authorities came out against humans taking chlorine dioxide by mouth as they said there are no clinical trials on it and, in any case, it is merely a concentrated bleach. It so happens that the United States Department of

Health and Science, the organisation OVER the FDA, has carried out a study and declared it safe for humans to take by mouth. The reason was that many people wanted to use it in their swimming pools instead of chlorine, and people swallow swimming pool water!

Recently there have been some changes to the protocol for using chlorine dioxide. In the first instance a 50% solution of citric acid has now become available, so the mixture of the citric acid and sodium chlorite will be one drop of each, instead of one plus five drops of the 10% citric acid solution. Capsules have also been produced, although I am not sure how to use them, as I have not read enough about such a preparation.

The inventor of MMS, Jim Humble, has added an improvement to his dosing protocol, preferring people to try to manage one drop of the combined preparation taken every hour for eight doses (so over eight hours), although it is best to start with a quarter of the dose for a few days. This actually makes a lot of sense to me and could well improve the efficacy of MMS.

Apparently, if all the day's preparation of MMS is made in the morning and stored in an airtight screw-topped container, and an appropriate amount taken out on an hourly basis, the combination remains active all day long. In the circumstances, you are advised to take doses this often if possible for as long as possible, or until your condition improves. It is not important to be exact and take a dose every hour on the dot, but do your best. In this case, you should not take any specific anti-oxidants in the day, but you could take anti-oxidants one day and chlorine dioxide the next day.

An Article On Food Grade Diatomaceous Earth (DE)

The more you hear about this incredible product, the more you will be convinced that you need to make it a part of your daily routine. Everyday brings evidence that the more people turn to nature and natural diets and homeopathic remedies for what ails them, the healthier and happier they are. Clearly, all that we need for our wellbeing is provided to us by nature. This is certainly true for Diatomaceous Earth.

There are several uses for Diatomaceous Earth, but remarkably, now, humans too can benefit from the cleansing, filtering agents of Diatomaceous Earth. It is apparent from the research and anecdotal evidence, that food grade Diatomaceous Earth provides multiple health advantages for humans and animals as well. Used as a daily treatment, Diatomaceous Earth can alleviate the potentially deadly risks of high cholesterol, high blood pressure, and obesity, ameliorate annoying and stressful issues stemming from intestinal bacteria and parasites, bronchial inflammation, kidney and urinary infections, irregular bowels, as well as assist with vertigo, headaches, tinnitus, insomnia, and acts as an anti-inflammatory agent. Diatomaceous Earth is hands down the best remedy for parasites in our bodies. Studies show Diatomaceous Earth can help those suffering with diabetes and with arterial disease, joint pain, and may prevent or alleviate Alzheimer disease by preventing the absorption of aluminium. Diatomaceous Earth is Mother Nature's product with no harm to the environment, pets or people. A small amount of Diatomaceous Earth gets absorbed into the blood stream as silica. One of the benefits of silica is that it helps to destroy bad fats.

Diatomaceous Earth is the ground up shells of diatoms from ancient sub-aquatic material. These microscopic sponges can absorb and trap particles to 3 microns. This miraculous filter system works in our bodies to trap and eliminate toxins and clean our internal systems for improved health as these harmful elements are passed through the body - without chemicals! Once our diets naturally included sufficient silica, but with depleted soils, hybrid crops, and over processing of foodstuffs, only about 1/3 of the required silica is consumed. Diatomaceous Earth is over 60% silica and when taken, makes up this deficiency. This natural substance has similar benefits for pets and animals too. Additionally, it is a natural insect killer - killing by physical action instead of chemical. It gets on the insect and scratches their waxy coating off causing dehydration and death.

Diatomaceous Earth (DE) For People

In many countries Diatomaceous Earth is sold as a natural product for better hair, nails, skin, bones, etc. There are 2 basic types of DE: the one of marine origin, and the one derived from fresh waterbeds. The fresh water DE is the one classified as food grade diatomite due to its exceptional purity, with Peruvian DE being the purest.

The FDA (USA) has classified DE as GRAS (Generally Recognised as Safe).

When mined, diatomite is heat treated to over 600 degrees Celsius, making it completely sterile and safe from the point of view of infection. It is also pH neutral and completely non-toxic. DE contains numerous micro and macro-elements that may contribute to natural body remineralisation. Food grade DE is being used as an extremely effective natural remedy against parasites in humans. Many people have pets. Even if pets are not part of the household, worm infestation is very common. DE expels worms swiftly and effectively, without the need for chemical remedies. It is also a safe and effective preventative measure against parasites.

Several studies have shown DE to be effective in reducing cholesterol in the blood. As a powerful sorbent, natural detoxifying substance, DE can eliminate toxins from the body acting as a natural detoxifying remedy.

DE has been found to stimulate the immune system in both animals and humans. It is extremely rich in minerals, so making it a great mineral food supplement. DE collects numerous toxins and debris when it passes through the colon. While eliminating parasites, it also picks up other unwanted substances and takes them out of the body swiftly and efficiently. In cases of inactive stool movements, it is one of the natural aids for quick elimination.

DE is very rich in silicon, a chemical element that has multiple functions in the body, such as the production of bone, cartilage, hair and nails, as well as strengthening cellular membranes and blood vessels. It participates in the production of thyroxine and other hormones.

Scientific studies have shown that silicon (Si) plays an important role, cross-linking mucopolysaccharides and proteins to increase the strength and reduce the permeability of the extracellular matrix in connective tissues including the aorta and other arteries, trachea, tendon, bone, teeth and skin. It also has a catalytic role in the mineralisation of new bone. Silicon therefore aids the healing process and also helps to build the immune system.

In many ways, Diatomaceous Earth can be compared to the edible clays and zeolite (clinoptilolite), due to its powerful detoxifying, re-mineralising, immune-boosting, cholesterol-reducing properties. What sets it apart from the other two is its strong insecticide and anti-parasite properties. However, as mentioned in this article, DE is not limited to it, and serves as the most natural aid to many other body functions.

Note: All this information is purely information and should not be treated as medical advice. Please do not resort to self-treatment. Consult a doctor if feeling unwell. We do not diagnose or prescribe any treatments.

If you are advised to try DE, start with a low dose such as half a level teaspoonful for a few days and see what happens. You can always increase the dose, but gradually. A little loosening of your stools is not a bad sign, and may well be a good sign that your bowel is being cleared out.

An Article On MILK – Why It May Not Be Suitable For Human Beings.

Calcium - Its Importance And Significance.

It is perfectly understandable if some people feel they ought to be taking a calcium supplement if they have been advised to cut out milk products for any reason. The answer is in fact very simple, and there are many points that are worth mentioning.

A.   Despite the 'value' of milk from a culinary point of view, it is probably not a suitable food for humans to consume. Humans are the only creatures on God's earth who have milk products after weaning, unless we give it to them, like our favourite cat. In fact seventy percent of the world's population have no milk products because they have a lactase deficiency, which means they cannot digest milk. If they do take it, they develop diarrhoea in particular.   None of these people suffers from osteoporosis, unless they adopt western dietary lifestyles.

B.   Despite the undoubtedly high levels of calcium in animal milks and animal milk products, the form of calcium may not be easily absorbed.   The process of pasteurisation may in fact make this situation worse, apart from the fact that the process may destroy all the enzymes in milk. When calves were given pasteurised cow's milk, they died.

C.   Some of the world's largest animals are vegans, which means they do not eat any animal products. Such animals are elephants, giraffes, horses, cows themselves and gorillas, etc. None of these shows signs of osteoporosis. Despite the fact that their metabolism is different from ours and they eat an awful lot more for their weight than we do, there is clearly enough calcium in what they do eat to build up their large, strong bony skeletons. Remember, cows develop all that calcium in milk from eating only grass. Women at risk of developing osteoporosis are advised to take 1600 mg calcium per day (plus 400 IU vitamin D), yet studies are showing that this approach is not working.   Mainstream medicine's attitude is that they should take even more calcium. I suspect there is something wrong with that theory. I was told by a vet at London Zoo that elephants only take in 2000 mg calcium in their diet per day, and they don't show any signs of osteoporosis

D.   What humans ate before we became 'civilized' consisted mainly of what we could dig up, grab or pluck, with the occasional animal meat thrown in for good measure if we could catch or snare something. There was certainly nothing in that that had a high calcium content. So it is perfectly possible that human metabolism developed in a low calcium, high magnesium dietary intake. There were at least two units of magnesium to one of calcium in such a diet, whereas, with our high intake of milk and dairy products, it is significantly the other way round, i.e. more calcium and less magnesium.

E.   Over the years I have seen many couples who have either been unable to start a family, who have suffered from multiple miscarriages, or gave me some similar sad reproductive story. One of the pieces of advice I always gave the woman was to stop consuming all animal milks and animal milk products, and not to have any calcium supplements.   Nearly all of these women conceived, had a lovely pregnancy, gave birth to a perfectly formed baby and breast-fed for anything up to four years, without any adverse health or metabolic consequences occurring.   Indeed they were usually healthier than ever before.   That is surely an indication that the human species does not need a high calcium intake, and may also suggest that the former high calcium intake, among other things, was actually hindering the reproductive process.
F.   Women have for years been following the advice of the medical profession, nutritionists and women's magazines to have a high calcium intake in their diet.   So why is the incidence of post-menopausal osteoporosis increasing?   Two answers come to mind.   The first is that there is something that we have been missing all along, such as the hole in the ozone layer, the massive use of pesticides and similar chemicals in our environment, or something like the contraceptive pill that at present we are unaware may be responsible.   However, I believe that the real answer, or at least a main one, is that we may have been giving women the wrong advice all along.
G.   A final point to be aware of is that a lot of what humans eat nowadays leaves an acid residue.   Such foods are the high protein foods (such as all animal meats and products, fish and eggs, but also wheat and sugar).   The more alkaline the diet the better it is for our health.   Alkaline foods are all the vegetables and fruits, salad items, pulses, nuts and seeds, etc., i.e. a typically vegan intake, which some people would recommend for us all, although most people would not be happy to follow such a diet. The body needs to be slightly on the alkaline side for perfect health, i.e. have a pH of around 7.35.   If what we eat has a tendency to be on the acidic side, we excrete a more acid urine.   At the same time our bodies have to give up alkali to balance this acidity in the blood stream, and, although we have some available in the plasma proteins and sodium naturally present in our food, the most abundant and available source is the large pool of calcium in our bones.   Thus extra blood calcium will be excreted in the urine over the course of time, which predisposes us to osteoporosis.

Thus it can be seen that probably the main reason why humans lose calcium is because they have too acid a diet, not because there is not enough calcium in it. Indeed women who suffer from post-menopausal osteoporosis often have hardening of their arteries and/or arthritis (which involves deposits of calcium), so there is no shortage of calcium in the body. It would appear that they are simply not putting it in the correct place, because of a deficiency of vitamin K2.

Many years ago I was invited to be in the audience of a television programme discussing the work of Dr. Harry Morrow-Brown, the Derby Consultant Physician who started the Midlands Asthma and Allergy Research Association.   There were many general practitioners in the audience and every one of them agreed that, if a child failed to thrive in any way, the first thing to do was to take it off animal milks and animal milk products, especially from the cow. Sometimes goats' or sheep's products were subsequently found to be acceptable, but often not.   We all agreed that the child was likely to do well from then on, and we had all observed it on many occasions.   There was no suggestion that calcium supplements be given in the circumstances.

One final point that I would like to make is that if a person were to have a high acid diet such as many Americans do with their regular intake of beef burgers, for example, (the beef, bread and ketchup are all acid foods) it may be wise to take a calcium supplement or sodium bicarbonate on a fairly regular basis, or possibly rub on magnesium lotion, to provide the extra alkali to balance the acidity and spare the bone stores of calcium.   However, it is clear that it would be wise not to be on such a diet in the first place.

Remember cow's milk was designed to produce animals with a small brain and big horns!